# MacArthur's Japanese Constitution

# MacArthur's Japanese Constitution

## A Linguistic and Cultural Study of Its Making

### Kyoko Inoue

THE UNIVERSITY OF CHICAGO PRESS
*Chicago & London*

Kyoko Inoue is associate professor of linguistics at the University of Illinois at Chicago.

The University of Chicago Press, Chicago 60637
The University of Chicago Press, Ltd., London
© 1991 by The University of Chicago
All rights reserved. Published 1991
Printed in the United States of America
99 98 97 96 95 94 93 92 91   5 4 3 2 1


Library of Congress Cataloging in Publication Data

Inoue, Kyoko.
    MacArthur's Japanese Constitution : a linguistic and cultural
study of its making / Kyoko Inoue.
        p.      cm.
    Includes bibliographical references and index.
    ISBN 0-226-38391-1
    1. Japan—Constitutional law—Interpretation and construction.
2. Japan—Constitutional history.   3. Japan—Constitutional law—
Cultural aspects.   4. Japan—Constitutional law—Translating.
I. Title.
LAW
342.52'02—dc20                                          90-39356
[345.2022]                                                CIP

*To Richard*

# CONTENTS

# PREFACE AND ACKNOWLEDGMENTS

I first became interested in this project in 1980, quite by accident, when investigating the syntax and semantics of conditional sentences in Japanese. In searching for illustrative examples, I looked at some sentences from the Japanese Constitution in both the Japanese text and its English translation. My curiosity was stirred when I noticed discrepancies in meaning between the Japanese and English sentences, so I began to study the final English and Japanese texts, together with earlier drafts of the Constitution, to determine whether translations of key words and phrases from English into Japanese might have changed the sense of the Constitution. As my research progressed, however, I realized that to understand why the Americans used particular English words and phrases, and why the Japanese chose certain "translations" of those words and phrases, I needed to go beyond the language of the document to understand the historical, social, cultural, and legal background of both the Americans and Japanese. I began to read in these various areas, and soon realized that this project would give me opportunities to draw ideas from my own cross-cultural experience in the United States and Japan in ways that no other research had.

I first came to the United States in 1956 as a junior in college; I went back to Japan after three years with a degree in library science. For the next nine years, however, I taught English in a school where most of my colleagues were Americans. As time passed, I became increasingly comfortable speaking English and, at the same time, began to question my identity as a Japanese. I began to wonder how language affected one's sense of identity.

In 1968, I returned to the United States to study linguistics. When I finished my doctorate, I decided to remain in this country. The past thirty years of my life as a student of language have also been a personal journey in search of my own identity between the languages and cultures of the two countries. As this study progressed, I came to understand both my native culture and my adopted American culture far more thoroughly. I now have a deeper appreciation of my own cross-cultural and cross-linguistic experiences. Writing this book has contributed greatly to my personal growth in living in and between two cultures.

I owe many debts to friends who have been generous with their support during my academic career. Alton L. Becker, one of my thesis advisors, first introduced me to the works of scholars interested in language and culture. He encouraged me to pursue my own cross-linguistic and cross-cultural interests during my graduate studies, and has consistently supported me in my later academic career. I also thank Richard Buchanan and James Bennett for giving me stimulating intellectual companionship for many years, and encouraging me when my spirits were down. I thank Kuroda Shigeyuki for generously writing letters of support on my behalf for many years, including several for this project. Thanks are due also to Dan F. Henderson for his comments on my earlier work and the letters of support he wrote on my behalf.

Through this research, I have met many individuals in other fields, who generously helped me develop the project with their knowledge and friendship. Okuizumi Eizaburō, the Japanese Librarian of the University of Chicago, directed me to valuable sources on the making of the Japanese Constitution, generously shared his own expertise on the American occupation of Japan, and gave me invaluable moral support and friendship. Okuizumi Eizaburō is a shining example of professionalism in the modern field of library and information science. His arrival at the University of Chicago Library in the midst of my research was an unexpected bit of exceptionally good fortune.

My special thanks go to Charles L. Kades, the principal drafter of the initial version of the Constitution at MacArthur's headquarters. I first met Charles Kades in June 1987, when he and his wife kindly invited me for a visit at their home in Massachusetts. In the course of that visit, he spoke with me at length about the events surrounding the making of the Constitution. Since then he has candidly shared with me his recollections and interpretations of the events of that period, and was kind enough to read the first draft of my manuscript. I am deeply grateful for his friendship.

Koseki Shōichi, of Wakō University, taught me about Japanese constitutional law, directed me to the essential sources on the making of the Japanese Constitution, on which he himself has recently published a prize-winning book, and sent me several important documents from Japan. I also thank Milton B. Singer, of the University of Chicago, for directing me to some important books on American culture, and for taking the time to read the first draft of my manuscript, as well as some of my earlier papers. Thanks are due to Hoshi Ken'ichi, of the National Diet Library in Tokyo, and Saitō Masaei, formerly of the University of Michigan Library, for their professional assistance, and to Kimijima Akihiko, of Gumma University, for giving me valuable insight into Japanese law. I thank the two anonymous readers of my manuscript, whose criticisms and suggestions greatly helped me improve this work.

Various institutions have given me financial support over the years. The National Endowment for the Humanities awarded me a 1987–88 fellowship, which released me from teaching and made it possible for me to devote a year to completing the first draft of the manuscript. The American Philosophical Society, in 1987, supported my trip to the National Diet Library in Tokyo, now the central depository of the materials related to the American occupation of Japan. That trip enabled me to obtain numerous documents that are not available elsewhere. The Research Board of my own university, the University of Illinois at Chicago, provided funds for travel to Massachussetts to interview Charles Kades. The Center for East Asian Studies of the University of Chicago has given me associate membership and a library card for many years. I have depended very heavily on the Japanese collection of the University of Chicago Library for this research. Finally, the Center for Japanese Studies at the University of Michigan supported my visit to its Japanese collection in 1983.

In all the years that I have been away from Japan, my parents and brothers and sisters have supported me with their love and encouragement. They were in my thoughts constantly throughout this study, particularly because one of the provisions of the new Constitution that I studied has had some lasting effects on the life of my family. My niece, Yuki, contributed by arranging for the printing of the Japanese text of the appendixes and providing editorial assistance. Both she and my father also helped by obtaining valuable materials from the National Diet Library for me when I could not travel there myself.

Finally, the greatest debt of all goes to my husband, Richard B. Muller. No words can adequately express my thanks for all his contributions—for teaching me about American thought, politics, and law; spending countless hours with me, discussing and comparing notes about the American and Japanese societies; going over numerous versions of my manuscript; and encouraging me to keep on working. I would not have been able to complete this book without his collegial participation and assistance. I dedicate this book to Richard.

Portions of this book appeared in an earlier form in the following publications: "The Making of a Japanese Constitution: A Linguist's perspective," *Language Problems and Language Planning* 6, no. 3 (Fall 1982): 271–85, published by the University of Texas Press (chapter 1); "The Constitution of Japan and Its English Translation," pp. 199–212 in *Languages in the International Perspective*, ed. Nancy Schweda-Nicholson (Ablex Publishing Corp., 1986) (chapters 1, 3); "Democracy in the Ambiguities of Two Languages and Cultures," *Linguistics* 25, no. 3 (1987): 595–606 (chapters 1, 5); and "Japanese: A Story of Language and People," pp. 241–300 in *Languages and Their Speakers*, ed. Timothy Shopen (University of Pennsylvania Press, 1987) (chapters 5, 6).

# INTRODUCTION

When the Americans occupied Japan in 1945, their chief goal was to transform Japan into a responsible, democratic nation that would never again wage war. They believed Japan had been ruled by a despotic government that had deprived its citizens of their rights and liberties. Although Japan had been governed under a constitution, the so-called Meiji Constitution, the Americans considered it "little more than window dressing," which had done little to protect the Japanese people from the excesses of the prewar government.[1] Initially, however, they left it to the Japanese to draft a new constitution.

Japanese government officials saw no need for major changes in the Constitution. They interpreted the Potsdam Proclamation to mean that the Japanese people would have the freedom to decide what kind of government they would adopt, which need not be an American-style democracy. In fact, they believed very strongly that the fundamental character of the Japanese political system should not be changed, and that the Emperor should be retained.

In the beginning of February 1946, a series of events led the Supreme Commander for the Allied Powers, General Douglas MacArthur, to take matters into his own hands, and instruct his staff at general headquarters to prepare a new constitution for Japan. In ten days, they produced a draft in English, and presented it to the Japanese government for adoption. Government officials had little choice but to accept the American draft as the basis for further discussion. After eight months of intense negotiations, during which they were able to make a few changes, the Japanese officials presented the Japanese text to the people as their own creation. It is a democratic constitution, embodying to a considerable extent the individualistic political ideas of the Americans.

---

1. Supreme Commander for the Allied Powers, Government Section (hereafter SCAP) 1968, 1:87.

In this study, I have not tried to present a complete history and analysis of the Constitution. Nor have I investigated public opinion and the press in either country, or the activities of groups and individuals peripherally involved in the drafting, negotiating, and debating of the Constitution. Rather, I have focused on several key articles that seem to me to involve important cultural differences, and significant differences in the mode of expression in the English and Japanese versions of the document. I try to show in what ways the Constitution reads differently in Japanese, and to explain why the Japanese version is more compatible with Japanese social and political values than the English version. I will also show how the American and Japanese participants misunderstood each other, and how the ambiguities involved in cross-linguistic, cross-cultural negotiations facilitated acceptance of the final English and Japanese texts.

Chapter 1 provides a chronicle of events from the end of the war to the creation of the Constitution, focusing on the problems of language and translation between English and Japanese. This is followed by a chapter discussing the Meiji Restoration, when Japan opened its doors to the Western world after more than 200 years of isolation, and launched on a program of rapid modernization and industrialization. Although the Restoration marked a radical break with the past, it retained some important continuities with the Tokugawa era, which influenced the making of the Meiji Constitution and the conception of rights held by some of the leading intellectuals of the Meiji period. Some of these attitudes and values carry over into the new Constitution. Chapter 3 compares the language of the U.S. Constitution and the English version of the Japanese Constitution of 1946 on the one hand, and the language of both the Meiji Constitution and the Japanese text of the new Constitution on the other, looking at the ways in which these documents speak to their respective audiences. The U.S. Constitution and, to a significant degree, the English version of the new Japanese Constitution, express the people's commitment to a democratic government and their command to that government not to infringe on their individual rights and liberties. In contrast, the Meiji Constitution asserts the authority and responsibility of the government to determine and act in the best interests of the nation and the people as a whole. The new Constitution affirms a joint commitment by the people and the government to establish and maintain a democratic society and political system, but still conveys the idea, though not directly expressed, that the government has the authority and responsibility to rule in the best interests of the nation. Thus, while the Japanese have adopted a democratic governmental system through this Constitution, much of its language continues to express traditional Japanese social and political values.

Chapters 4 through 6 deal with the major themes of freedom of religion and the separation of religion and state, the Emperor, and individual dignity and the equality of the sexes in marriage and family, and describe how the Japanese and Americans negotiated these issues. These three issues are significant because they introduced new principles into Japanese political life, and incorporated significant challenges to traditional Japanese values. The Japanese had difficulty in coming to terms with American democratic ideas, and tried with varying degrees of success to assimilate the new practices to traditional Japanese values. What emerges most clearly, though, is that in many instances, neither side really understood the ideas and concerns of the other. Ironically, these misunderstandings and the language of the Japanese text may have contributed to the ultimate success of the negotiations and the acceptance of the new Constitution.

For the Americans, religious freedom was a critical issue. They thought that one of the primary sources of the oppression of the Japanese people was the establishment of Shintoism as a state religion. Thus they saw the separation of religion and state, including the prohibition of state-mandated religious education and rejection of the idea of the divinity of the Emperor, as central to guaranteeing individual freedom. But these views show how the Americans misunderstood Japanese religious tradition. Shintoism is not an institutionalized religion in the Western sense, nor does it have a theology or a set of doctrines. The Meiji government had made the Emperor the formal head of state, and had then emphasized his role as high priest of Japan by virtue of his descent from the founding deities of the Japanese nation, in order to gather support for its policies. But this did not involve imposing Shinto doctrines on the people. In fact, once Emperor Hirohito renounced his divinity, Shintoism and the state were effectively separated, although the Americans did not realize it.

The Japanese, for their part, paid little attention to the principles of freedom of conscience and separation of church and state, because nothing in their history gave them reason to appreciate the significance of these ideas. They focused their attention on the status of the shrines, since this was the one remaining instance of government support of religion. The Japanese did seriously debate the meaning of religious education, and were quite concerned when they thought that the state would not be allowed to conduct education about religions, as distinguished from religious education. The Americans were apparently not worried about this, since the distinction between religious education and education about religions was a familiar idea. They might have been more concerned had they realized that the two ideas were not at all distinct to the Japanese.

The Americans also misunderstood the Emperor's political position, failing to realize that his role was largely symbolic, and limited to ratifying decisions agreed on by the political, military, and bureaucratic leaders of the country. Since the Emperor had very little actual power, formal legal checks on his power were not nearly as essential as the Americans believed. The Japanese understood this quite well, and did not realize why the Americans insisted on legal limits to the Emperor's sovereignty. For them, vesting apparent sovereignty in the Emperor was all-important, and they did their best to persuade themselves that some vestiges of sovereignty remained in the imperial institution.

Finally, the Americans wanted to institute substantial changes in the Japanese household. Traditionally, the househead ruled the family, but also had the duty and responsibility of caring for its members in the present, honoring the ancestors, and preserving the continuity of the family into the future. The Americans believed that this system curtailed individual rights and severely discriminated against women. They sought to eliminate these perceived inequalities by insisting that marriage and the family reflect American ideals of individual dignity and equality of the sexes. This aroused intense concern among the Japanese, who realized that the changes demanded by the Americans would severely restrict both the legal position of the househead and the right of succession to that position. Yet they had no alternative but to accept the American changes.

Some were able to persuade themselves that although the legal position of the family would change, social customs would remain to support the traditional structure of the family. Once again, however, the Japanese had difficulty in understanding the principles behind the changes the Americans were promoting. They eventually arrived at a conception of individual dignity that was more akin to the notion of honor in aristocratic society than to the American idea of individualism. As such, it was compatible with the Japanese preference for hierarchical and unequal social arrangements, and also with the Japanese idea of equality between men and women, much different from that of Americans.

At the core of my study is the issue of linguistic and cultural difference. The principal negotiators on the American side did not know Japanese and were almost totally dependent on the interpreters and translators used by both sides. With little knowledge of Japanese history and culture, they were decisively handicapped in grasping the precise nature of the debates and discussions on the Japanese side. Neither did the Americans explain the reasons behind their draft constitution, assuming that its basic principles were transparent. The Japanese participants had all studied English in prewar days, and had at least a limited working competency. Some also had extensive knowledge of American and European history and the corresponding legal traditions, and a few could draw on diplomatic experiences as well. Nevertheless, they, too, were often in the dark, because they did not have first-hand experience with Americans and American culture, and they did not understand the American idea of individualism. Like the Americans, they were unaware of their lack of understanding. Thus, they often did not see the point of American demands, or the reasons behind particular constitutional provisions. Paradoxically, these mutual misunderstandings probably made it possible for the two sides to "agree" on a final version of the Constitution.

## Methodological Note

Translation has been an integral part of this work, and for me the most troublesome methodological problem. Accuracy in translation from Japanese to English is an extremely complex and formidable problem. The constitutional debates at the National Diet proved particularly difficult, partly because some of the discussions were hard to comprehend even in Japanese. Some interpellators rambled on without coherent argument, and government officials sometimes purposely evaded issues by making incomprehensible statements. Even when statements were understandable in Japanese, I was often faced with a choice between two almost irreconcilable tasks: (1) making the content of the Japanese speech meaningful to English readers by translating it so that it would read naturally in English, and (2) retaining the flavor of the Japanese speech, including its vagueness, thereby creating "unnatural" English. I feared that the former would not only skew the content, but also destroy the rhetorical strategy being used by the speaker, while the latter would make the debates awkward and very difficult reading. I have tried to render as faithfully as possible the content and intent of the speaker, sometimes at the cost of using awkward English phraseology. I hope that awkward passages will caution the reader to read carefully, to get the sense of the context in which those deliberations were made. I also hope that the cultural and historical discussions will help the reader grasp the content and intent of the speeches.

# One

# A CHRONICLE OF EVENTS

### The End of the War and the Issue of Language

On August 14, 1945, the Japanese government unconditionally surrendered to the Allied powers. In the ensuing interactions between the
American occupation forces and the Japanese, linguistic differences
gave rise to many misunderstandings, some of which turned out to have
positive consequences. Even before the war ended, however, language,
and in particular, ambiguities in translation, played an important role
in Japanese-American relations.

Throughout the negotiations for Japan's surrender, the most difficult
issue was the status of the Emperor of Japan. Among high-level officials
of the American government, as well as the Allied powers, there was
serious disagreement on the proper policy toward the Emperor. The
Japanese Imperial Army commanders were staunchly against any surrender that would entail subordination of the Emperor to the Supreme
Commander for the Allied Powers (SCAP), let alone any threat to the
imperial institution itself. Prime Minister Suzuki knew that the Emperor was anxious to end the war, and had been carefully working toward that goal. The Japanese knew that the Allies disagreed on how to
deal with the Emperor. On both sides, those who were eager to bring
the war to an end appear to have decided that the best strategy was not
to stress this issue, but to leave it ambiguous.[1]

---

1. In his memorandum of July 2, 1945, outlining to President Truman the American government's postsurrender program for Japan, Secretary of War Henry L. Stimson proposed a list of
warnings to the Japanese, including the following statement on this issue:

> The withdrawal from their country as soon as the above objectives of the Allies are
> accomplished, and as soon as there has been established a peacefully inclined gov-
> ernment, of a character representative of the masses of the Japanese people. *I per-*
> *sonally think that if in saying this we should add that we do not exclude a constitutional*
> *monarchy under her present dynasty, it would substantially add to the chances of accep-*
> *tance.* (U.S. Department of State 1960, vol. 1, p. 892; emphasis added)

Furthermore, the following item was included in the "Proclamation by the Heads of State," which
served as the basis of the Potsdam Proclamation:

When the final American peace proposal reached the Ministry of Foreign Affairs shortly after midnight of August 12, Japan time, Japanese officials were particularly concerned about two phrases in the document.[2] It appears that the Foreign Ministry "inaccurately" translated two key phrases to prevent further opposition by the extremist military commanders, and then defended its translations by insisting that it had the prerogative of providing the official interpretation of all diplomatic documents. The first phrase occurred in the third paragraph, which specified the status of the emperor and the Japanese government:

> From the moment of surrender the authority of the Emperor and the Japanese Government to rule the state shall be sub-ject to the Supreme Commander of the Allied Powers who will take such steps as he deems proper to effectuate the sur-render terms.

The English phrase "shall be subject to," which clearly implies subordination, was translated *seigen-no moto-ni okaruru-mono-to su* (Gaimu-shō 1952, p. 642). This phrase, which literally means something like "will be placed under the restraint of," does not carry the

---

(12) The occupying forces of the Allies shall be withdrawn from Japan as soon as our objectives are accomplished and there has been established beyond doubt a peacefully inclined, responsible government of a character representative of the Japanese people. *This may include a constitutional monarchy under the present dynasty if it be shown to the complete satisfaction of the world that such a government will never again aspire to aggression* (ibid., p. 894; emphasis added).

But item 12 in the Potsdam Proclamation itself simply read, "The occupying forces of the Allies shall be withdrawn from Japan as soon as these objectives have been accomplished and there has been established in accordance with the freely expressed will of the Japanese people a peacefully inclined and responsible government."

Joseph C. Grew, former ambassador to Japan and undersecretary of state from December 1944 until August 16, 1945, was another leading advocate of leaving the matter of retention of the Emperor to the Japanese, and not making it a condition for their surrender. Grew made the following statement at the Senate Foreign Relations Committee's hearing on December 12, 1944:

My point is, therefore, that the Japanese do not need to have an emperor to be militaristic and aggressive, nor is it the existence of an emperor that makes them militaristic and aggressive. There are conditions more deeply rooted in their social structure and concepts growing out of that social structure which have to be exor-cised in one way or another. It will be one of our fundamental objectives to remove those conditions. As I have said, no one today can predict what effect the impact of the cataclysm of defeat will have on the Japanese mind. There might be a com-plete revulsion from all the archaic concepts of the past. The Emperor institution might on the other hand be the only political element capable of exercising a stabilizing influence. . . . That is why I have never advocated either the retention or the elimination of the Japanese Emperor after the war. I want to wait and see. I believe this to be plain common sense. (Grew 1952, 2:1418–19)

2. "Reply by Secretary of State to Japanese Qualified Acceptance," by Max Grassli, chargé d'affaires ad interim of Switzerland, dated August 11, 1945 (SCAP 1968, 2:415, appendix A:5).

same implication of direct subordination.[3] Shigemitsu Mamoru (1952,
2:288–89), the representative of the Japanese government who signed
the surrender document on the USS *Missouri*, says in his memoir that,
although all the Japanese officials understood the implications of the
English phrase, the minister of foreign affairs, Tōgō Shigenori, stood by
the ministry's translation, and that the Lord Keeper of the Privy Seal,
Kido Kōichi, insisted on the ministry's prerogative in providing the official translation of all diplomatic documents. This "translation" thus
made it possible for the military to save face, while enabling the Japanese government to accept the substance of the Allies' terms.[4]

The second phrase, "the ultimate form of government," appeared in
the sixth paragraph, which demanded that Japan establish a democratic
government.

> The ultimate form of government of Japan shall in accor-
> dance with the Potsdam Declaration be established by the
> freely expressed will of the Japanese people.

Foreign Minister Tōgō, and the staff of the ministry, were even more
nervous about this phrase than the first. The three copies of this document included in *Shūsen Shiroku* (A Historical Record of the War's End)
vary. The first one spells the word "government" with a lowercase g,
while the other two were with a capital letter (see Gaimu-shō 1952,
pp. 639, 641, and 644, respectively). The officials were gravely concerned about the correct interpretation of the difference between *government* and *Government*. Some said that "Government" referred to the
Cabinet only, while "government" referred to the Japanese state as a
whole. After much debate, they finally translated the phrase as *Nihonkoku seifu-no kakutei-teki keitai*, "the definitive form of the Japanese government," hoping to avoid the implication that sovereignty would be
transferred from the Emperor to the people of Japan (Gaimu-shō 1952,
pp. 630–47).[5]

3. In an interview with Etō Jun, Sone Eki, then a member of the Bureau of Treaties of the
Ministry of Foreign Affairs, said that it was Sone and Shimoda Takezō of the bureau who actually
suggested this particular Japanese translation (Etō 1978, p. 144). However, in the accounts of the
problem of translating the American peace proposal collected in *Shūsen Shiroku*, an official record
of the Ministry of Foreign Affairs, Shibusawa Shin'ichi, the chief of the Bureau of Treaties, says
that he decided on this translation, with the help of Section Chief Shimoda (Gaimu-shō 1952,
pp. 630–31, 633–35).

4. None of the accounts of this incident explain precisely what effect the mistranslation had.
See, for example, Ōmori 1975–76, 2:166–82; Sakomizu 1964, pp. 269–80; and Shigemitsu
1952, pp. 280–89. This is therefore my own interpretation.

5. In his autobiography, *Chinabound* (1982, pp. 293–94), John K. Fairbank mentions that in
early summer 1945, the Office of War Information sent messages to the Japanese which implied
that the imperial institution would be respected. To quote:

## Constitutional Reform on the American Agenda

From the earliest stages of their planning for postwar administration of Japan, the Americans had two clear goals: to establish a peaceful, responsible government, and to democratize Japan. Although the initial postsurrender policies did not mandate a constitutional revision, the American determination to establish a democratic government implied that the Japanese would have to revise the Meiji Constitution. Yet the Department of State, which began planning postwar policy concerning the occupation of Japan as early as 1943, and the State-War-Navy Coordinating Committee (SWNCC), established in the fall of 1944 to deal with the complex issues of occupation, never formulated a consistent policy on rewriting the Japanese constitution. It was General MacArthur who took the initiative.

On October 4, 1945, when Prince Konoe Fumimaro, a member of the cabinet of Prince Higashikuni Naruhiko, met with him to discuss various issues of the postwar administration of Japan, MacArthur apparently encouraged him to work on a revision of the Constitution. The Higashikuni cabinet resigned on October 5, and, on October 9, Baron Shidehara Kijūrō, a 74-year-old former minister of foreign affairs, who had been out of politics for fourteen years because of his moderate views, formed a new cabinet. Meeting with MacArthur for the first time two days later, he was also advised to begin constitutional reform. On the same day, Prince Konoe, in his conversation with the Emperor, seems to have suggested that MacArthur had asked him personally to investigate the need for constitutional reform, and the Emperor apparently approved this idea (H. Tanaka 1979, p. 5). On October 13, the Shidehara cabinet decided to appoint Matsumoto Jōji, minister of state and former law professor at Tokyo Imperial Univer-

---

Our policy debate over how to treat the Japanese Emperor hinged on the question how far he was an essential prop to militarism. In general the Japan specialists felt he was essential to keep Japanese society in order and secure acceptance of the peace terms. Non-Japan specialists wanted him under some kind of constitutional control, not above it, i.e., no longer divine and sacred.

In early summer 1945 OWI beamed to Japan half a dozen commentaries by Admiral Ellis Zacharias, who had many acquaintances in Japanese Navy circles. They implied that the imperial institution would be respected in a peace settlement, something that could not be said officially under the "unconditional surrender" formula. This was a highly classified operation at the Washington end. Zacharias recorded his texts in Japanese and they were flown to Saipan for broadcasting.

It may be that the Japanese Navy commanders were aware of this possibility but could not convince the Army commanders. If so, the mistranslation may have been an important "official" resolution of the deadlock. I have no other evidence that supports either Fairbank's remark or my conjecture.

sity, to conduct the government's study of constitutional revision (Satō 1962–64, 1:148).

The Japanese government thus had officials of two different agencies—the Cabinet and the Imperial Household Agency—initiating constitutional reform. The confusion over which agency should properly be undertaking this task developed into a public feud between two constitutional scholars, Sasaki Sōichi, who was participating in Konoe's study, and Miyazawa Toshiyoshi, an advisor to Matsumoto's committee. On November 1, MacArthur put an end to the uncertainty by stating that he had made his suggestion to Konoe in his capacity as deputy prime minister of the Higashikuni cabinet, and not personally.[6]

On October 25, the Japanese government announced the creation of the Constitutional Problem Investigation Committee (Kempō Mondai Chōsa Iinkai, henceforth Matsumoto committee), to study possible revisions of the Meiji Constitution. The Japanese government, however, was not eager for either a major revision of, or immediate action on the Meiji Constitution. For one thing, it had been deluged by administrative directives for reforms issued by MacArthur's general headquarters (GHQ). It also had its hands full, trying to save the Japanese people from starvation, and dealing with chaotic conditions in the war-torn country. Two million Japanese, nearly a third of them civilians, had perished in the war, and more than 15 million were homeless (James 1985, 3:5). Repatriation of over six million disarmed soldiers and civilians scattered throughout Asia and the Pacific region began in the middle of September 1945, and, at its peak in mid-1946, nearly 200,000 people were coming home every week (U.S. Army 1966, p. 149). The government knew that a task as important as constitutional revision required more time than they could give. Moreover, the leaders of postwar Japan were not anxious for reform. Most of them were bureaucrats who had been in office before the war, and were not inclined toward radical changes. Although they were prepared to modify some clauses in the Meiji Constitution invalidated by the surrender, they were trying their best to preserve what was left of the old order.[7] On December 8, 1945, Matsumoto presented four basic principles of his version at the House of Representatives, giving ample evidence of his conservative approach.[8] Yoshida Shigeru, under whose premier-

6. For further details on Konoe's role, see Takagi 1969.

7. The officials of the Cabinet Bureau of Legislation did begin studying revisions in September 1945. Their proposals for revision are in Satō Tatsuo Kankei Bunsho 1.

8. The four principles are as follows: (1) No change will be made in the grand principle of the Emperor's right of sovereignty; (2) The Emperor will exercise his right of sovereignty on fewer matters of state, and the Diet will make decisions on a greater number of matters; (3) The minis-

ship the new Constitution was created, writes in his memoir (1962, pp. 131–32), "it was the desire of the Government to satisfy the clause in the Potsdam Declaration dealing with the democratization of Japan without altering the fundamental principles of national government laid down in the Meiji Constitution."

George Atcheson, MacArthur's political advisor from the Department of State, was rightly concerned about the lack of GHQ guidance to the Japanese as to what the Americans would consider acceptable constitutional reform. On October 4, the day MacArthur suggested that Konoe study constitutional revision, Atcheson radioed the Secretary of State for advice. Twelve days later, the Secretary of State sent Atcheson the first of a number of statements enumerating specific provisions to be included in the new constitution. These guidelines were sent to MacArthur as well, but he apparently did not relay any message to the Japanese.[9] Atcheson continued to believe that, without some American input, the Japanese government would not make revisions acceptable to the Americans. In response to his concern, the Department of State, on December 13 sent him the preliminary versions of "Reform of the Japanese Government," which became the basis for the definitive United States policy statement on governmental and constitutional reform in Japan, known as SWNCC-228. Atcheson promptly informed MacArthur of the contents of this document, and stated his concerns in no uncertain terms. As Robert E. Ward puts it (1987, p. 27),

> Atcheson thought there was a real danger that the Japanese government, in the absence of American guidance, might publicly proclaim an unacceptable draft and thereby oblige SCAP formally to reject it and order the government to make extensive changes. To avoid so difficult and mutually embarrassing a situation, Atcheson strongly recommended that the contents of SFE-142/1 be informally communicated to Dr. Matsumoto, possibly by SCAP's Government Section.

The final text of SWCNN-228 was sent to MacArthur on January 11, 1946. But MacArthur ignored Atcheson's warning, and did not inform the Japanese of its contents (ibid., pp. 27–31).

---

ters of state will advise the Emperor on all matters of state and will be responsible to the Diet for their advice; (4) Guarantees of the rights and liberties of the people will be strengthened, and ample redress will be given for all cases of violation (Satō 1955b, p. 22; my translation).

9. MacArthur is known to have received the secretary's reply, "since all telegraphic communications with Japan were routed through the Pentagon, the Joint Chiefs and General MacArthur as well" (Ward and Sakamoto 1987, p. 25).

Meanwhile, the Matsumoto committee was at work. By the beginning of 1946, the committee had prepared two texts, a very conservative version prepared by Matsumoto himself, and another, more liberal one prepared by the younger members. They worked in complete secrecy, without ever consulting GHQ, despite the urging of some Japanese who saw the danger of this procedure (Satō 1955b, pp. 21–23; 1962–64, 2:485–588). By mid-January, many Japanese were showing a great deal of interest in constitutional reform. Newspapers had published a number of different suggestions, and both the Liberal and the Communist parties made public their ideas for a new democratic constitution. Three private groups, the Constitutional Research Group (Kempō Kenkyū-kai), the Constitution Discussion Group (Kempō Kondan-kai) and the Japanese Federation of Lawyers (Dai-Nihon Bengoshi-kai Rengō-kai), had also prepared versions. Five private individuals had even drafted proposals, one of which espoused the American presidential system of government. GHQ paid careful attention to these private documents, particularly the one by the Constitutional Research Group, while waiting for the Japanese government to produce its own version (SCAP 1968, 1:94–98; Takayanagi et al. 1972,[10] 1:26–39). The Matsumoto committee continued to work behind closed doors, giving no hint of its progress, until a dramatic incident changed the course of events.

On February 1, 1946, *Mainichi Shimbun*, a leading Japanese newspaper, published on page one what it claimed to be the near final version of the Matsumoto constitution. It was clearly a constitution of imperial governance. Not only did it take thirty-nine of its seventy-six articles directly from the Meiji Constitution, but it also proclaimed Japan a monarchy, with the Emperor as sovereign.[11] The published draft was a far cry from the democratic constitution embodying popular sovereignty envisioned by the Americans.[12]

The Japanese government immediately issued a statement declaring

10. The original documents in this book came from Milo E. Rowell, who had collected them while serving as judicial affairs officer at the Public Administration Division, Government Section, GHQ, between December 1945 and the end of February 1946.

11. A translation of this document is included in SCAP 1968, 2:611–16.

12. It became known shortly after the incident that a young Mainichi political correspondent, Nishiyama Ryūzō, was responsible for the scoop. For the next twenty-seven years, however, he refused to say how he obtained the document. Finally, in an interview on February 9, 1973, Nishiyama disclosed that he simply walked into the unattended office of the Matsumoto committee, "borrowed" a draft of the constitution from one of the desks, took it back to his office, copied it with the help of others, and then returned the original to the committee office (H. Tanaka, 1979, pp. 45–47).

that this draft had no connection with the versions being prepared by the committee, and subsequently submitted the so-called Matsumoto version, approved by the Cabinet, to GHQ on February 8.[13] But it came too late, as MacArthur had already decided to act.

## MacArthur and the Far Eastern Commission

Although Japan had fought a war against the Allied powers, the Americans had decided by the end of the Potsdam Conference to exercise as much control over the postwar administration of Japan as possible. While mostly concerned about the Russians, they did not want the other Allies to interfere too much either. President Truman wrote in his memoir (1955, 1:412),

> As I reflected on the situation during my trip home [from the Potsdam Conference], I made up my mind that General MacArthur would be given complete command and control after victory in Japan. We were not going to be disturbed by Russian tactics in the Pacific.

At the end of October 1945, Secretary of State Byrnes succeeded in organizing the Far Eastern Advisory Commission to allow the other Allies to participate in the occupation. Great Britain, China, Australia, Canada, France, the Netherlands, New Zealand, India, and the Philippines all joined, but the Soviet Union refused. During its early

---

13. The Japanese text of this version, along with a general explanation, is included in Shimizu 1962–63, 4:313–19. Satō says, quoting Matsumoto, that the government might have sent GHQ only its English translation (Satō 1962–64, 2:686). The complete English text, undated, is in SCAP 1968, 2:617–21.

In his memoir on MacArthur, Courtney Whitney (1968, p. 248), chief of the Government Section, says that the Japanese had sent unofficial documents to GHQ by the end of January:

> There evidently was a schism in the [Matsumoto] committee between the advocates of a conservative and those of a more liberalized constitution, but the committee in general was dominated by the wishes of Dr. Matsumoto, who was an extreme conservative. Finally, by the end of January, the committee unofficially presented SCAP headquarters with two documents, one entitled "Gist of the Revision of the Constitution" and the other "General Explanation of the Constitutional Revision drafted by the Government"; no formal submission of recommendations was ever made.

Satō Tatsuo, however, notes the presentation of two documents appearing to coincide with those mentioned by Whitney as occurring after February 1, not before (*Jurisuto*, May 1, 1955, p. 6; see p. 35 n. 44. See also the document in Satō Tatsuo Kankei Bunsho 25, dated February 1946). Matsumoto himself (1958, p. 7) says that he presented the outline of the government's draft in English on February 8, 1946. Finally, Charles L. Kades confirmed this in his letter to me of September 20, 1988. He says, "The Matsumoto Committee did not submit unofficial drafts before the end of January, as Whitney wrote." Thus, contrary to Whitney's statement, I believe there is sufficient evidence that GHQ did not see the Japanese draft until after February 1, 1946.

November meetings, however, the Commission's strictly consultative nature became strikingly apparent. The member nations, particularly Australia, vociferously requested more than an advisory role in dealing with MacArthur. In response, Byrnes called for another conference of the "Big Three" foreign ministers in Moscow (James 1985, 3:28). There, on December 27, 1945, they announced an agreement that two new Allied bodies would be formed to supervise the occupation. One, the Far Eastern Commission (FEC), would have its headquarters in Washington, D.C., and would have limited policy-making authority. The other, the Allied Council for Japan, was to be an advisory body with a representative each from Britain, Russia, China, and the United States, and would have offices in Tokyo.

The members of the Far Eastern Advisory Commission were keenly interested in GHQ's position on constitutional reform. On January 17, when its delegation met with the Government Section staff, Senator Confessor of the Philippines asked Charles L. Kades, who later became the principal drafter of the MacArthur Constitution, what actions GHQ had been taking. Kades replied that GHQ had done nothing.

> Q. SENATOR CONFESSOR: We were given to understand by a headquarters spokesman that your section was studying the Constitution. Is that wrong?
> A. KADES: There must have been some misunderstanding. Government Section advises the Supreme Commander on policies pertaining to the internal structure of civil government. . . . It has not considered the Constitution as part of this work. It has been thought that the Constitution was within the terms of reference of your Commission.
> Q. SENATOR CONFESSOR: Isn't it so that the changes being effected in the Japanese way of life by the Supreme Commander will have to be embodied in the Japanese Constitution, thereby requiring the Constitution to be revised?
> A. KADES: Whether the written Constitution requires amendment to make the changes permanent is a question I am not prepared to answer since we have not studied the Japanese Constitution from the standpoint of making such revision.
> Q. SENATOR CONFESSOR: Does the present Constitution embody the democratic changes made by the Supreme Commander?
> A. KADES: The written Constitution does not embody these changes.
> Q. SENATOR CONFESSOR: I do not understand why constitutional revision is not a part of your work.

A. KADES: Because formal revision . . . would constitute a fundamental change in the Japanese constitutional structure, and as such be within the Commission's jurisdiction. (Williams 1979, p. 102)

Kades insisted that, while the Meiji Constitution was not acceptable, GHQ did not intend to amend it. MacArthur himself confirmed the GHQ position in a January 30 interview with the members of the Commission, stating that the matter had been taken out of his hands by the Moscow Agreement, but that he had made suggestions to the Japanese, who had begun to work on them.[14]

MacArthur might not have intended that GHQ take on the task of constitutional revision, but he was greatly concerned about the influence of the Allied powers on the occupation of Japan, and on constitutional reform. He realized that once the Far Eastern Commission and the Allied Council for Japan began functioning he would have to share control over occupation policy. According to D. Clayton James (1985, 3:34):

> He was determined to have his administration under complete control and in full operation and to implement as many reforms in Japan as possible before either of the new Allied bodies began functioning. He intended to present the "foreigners" with a fait accompli in Japan when the FEC held its first meeting in late February 1946 and the ACJ six weeks later.

When he saw the alleged draft of the Japanese constitution on February 1, he seems to have decided that it was time to act. He directed Courtney Whitney, chief of the Government Section, to determine whether he had the power to proceed with constitutional reform. In a detailed memorandum, Whitney assured MacArthur that since there was no FEC policy on constitutional reform, he had "the unrestricted authority to take any action he deemed proper." The final paragraph summarized his advice:

> 6. To recapitulate, I am of the opinion (a) that you now have the unrestricted authority to take any action you deem

---

14. The record of the interview states, "4. With reference to the question of constitutional reform, the Supreme Commander stated that this matter had been taken out of his hands by the Moscow Agreement, and he did not know now just how that was going to be worked out. He pointed out that when he started out in Japan his original directive gave him jurisdiction in the matter, and stated that he had made certain suggestions and the Japanese had begun to work on these suggestions" (U.S. Department of State 1971, vol. 8, pp. 124–25).

proper in effecting changes in the Japanese constitutional
structure—the only possible restriction being upon action
taken by you toward removal of the Emperor, in which case
you are required to consult with the Joint Chiefs of Staff;
(b) should the F.E.C. issue a policy directive dealing with
the matter of constitutional reform, then and in such event
the issuance of any constitutional reform *directive* (order)
upon the Japanese government would be subject to objection
by any member of the Allied Council for Japan and your
decision would not be controlling. (SCAP 1968, 2:623)

The first meeting of the Far Eastern Commission was scheduled for February 26, 1946, in Washington.

## The American Draft of the Japanese Constitution

On the morning of Sunday, February 3, acting on Whitney's advice,
MacArthur instructed him to prepare a draft constitution incorporating
three principles: limited monarchy, renunciation of war, and abolition
of feudalism. That same evening, three lawyers on Whitney's staff, Colonel Charles L. Kades, Lieutenant Colonel Milo E. Rowell, and Commander Alfred R. Hussey, met to sketch an outline of the constitution.
In a staff meeting the next morning, Whitney announced the formation
of a steering committee composed of these three men, with Kades as its
chairman. Members of the Government Section were assigned to eight
subcommittees to work on different chapters of the document, and
the drafting began. A week later, they had completed the initial version, in ninety-two articles, of what was to become the new Japanese
Constitution.[15]

At 10:00 A.M., February 13, Whitney and the three members of the
steering committee arrived at the official residence of the foreign minister of Japan. The Japanese officials present were Foreign Minister
Yoshida Shigeru, Matsumoto Jōji, Shirasu Jirō, assistant to the foreign

15. Although MacArthur did not respond to SWNCC-228, he apparently instructed the staff
of the Government Section to draft a constitution consistent with the principles expressed in that
document. In his interview with Takemae Eiji on August 24, 1984, Kades said,

It wasn't a directive at that time. It was just a SWNCC paper. It didn't come from
the Joint Chiefs of Staff. It wasn't like 1380. We were given it so that we would
know what their thinking was in SWNCC but it wasn't an order like JCS. JCS was
an order from the Joint Chiefs of Staff but SWNCC was just for our information.
But, I thought, it must be consistent to SWNCC because this is before the Far
Eastern Commission adopted SWNCC. If they adopted it and they were inconsistent then we will have a problem. I remember saying it is the responsibility of each
committee to compare his draft with SWNCC-228 to be sure there is no inconsistency or contradiction (Kades and Takemae 1986, p. 275).

minister, and Hasegawa Motokichi of the Foreign Office, who interpreted. Whitney presented the draft of the new constitution to the Japanese with the following statement:

> The draft of the constitutional revision, which you submitted to us the other day, is wholly unacceptable to the Supreme Commander as a document of freedom and democracy. The Supreme Commander, however, being fully conscious of the desperate need of the people of Japan for a liberal and enlightened Constitution that will defend them from the injustices of the arbitrary control of the past, has approved this document and directed that I present it to you as one embodying the principles which in his opinion the situation in Japan demands. In order that you gentlemen may understand fully the contents of the document to which I will hereafter further allude, my officers and I will withdraw to permit you freely to examine and discuss the same. (Takayanagi et al. 1972, 1:322)

The Americans then left the room and went out into the garden. The Japanese were stunned, for they thought this would be the first meeting to discuss the version they had submitted to GHQ on February 8 (H. Tanaka 1987, p. 120; Kojima 1972, pp. 290–92).

At 10:40, the Japanese officials notified the Americans that they were ready. The record of this meeting, written immediately afterward by the steering committee, captures vividly the reactions of the Japanese officials:

> The face of the Foreign Minister was dark and grim, and his expression did not change during the balance of the conference while General Whitney talked. The face of the interpreter remained a complete blank during the entire proceedings. However, it was observed that he was having physical difficulty in speaking and constantly wet his lips. Dr. Matsumoto listened to everything which was said by General Whitney with the utmost concentration but he kept looking at the other members of our group and never directly at General Whitney. Mr. Yoshida gazed intently at General Whitney with an occasional side glance that swung until it would reach the eyes of one of the undersigned, when it would immediately shift back. (Takayanagi et al. 1972, 1:324, 326)

Whitney proceeded to explain the spirit and considerations that prompted MacArthur to submit this document to the Japanese. He said that MacArthur was protecting the Emperor from being subjected to investigation as a war criminal, and that this constitution would make his position unassailable. He also indicated that MacArthur intended that the Japanese government present this constitution to the people, but with his full backing. He then went beyond MacArthur's instructions and stated that the Supreme Commander was willing to put the document to the people of Japan himself if the government did not do so. Finally, he said that only by accepting it could the conservative group survive. In short, MacArthur was willing to support the existing government, which he considered to be reactionary, if it accepted this constitution (ibid., 1:326, 328).

The Japanese delegates took the American draft back to the Prime Minister. On February 18, in a final effort to prevent a drastic reform of the Japanese Constitution, Matsumoto sent a supplementary explanation of the Japanese version, emphasizing that in spirit it was in agreement with the GHQ draft, but that in outward form the two were necessarily different because of the difference in the respective historical and cultural backgrounds (ibid., 1:352–65). By that time, Whitney had told MacArthur of his threat that the Supreme Commander would take the constitution directly to the people. MacArthur had replied, "Court, don't you know that I have never repudiated any action taken for me by a member of my staff? Right or wrong, whether I like it or not, I accept the situation as it stands and determine my next move from there" (Whitney 1968, pp. 251–52).[16]

Prime Minister Shidehara and Minister Matsumoto were greatly distressed, and apparently sat on the American draft nearly a week before informing other members of the cabinet or calling an emergency cabinet meeting (Satō 1955b, p. 20). The first conference on the "MacArthur Constitution," with no text yet available, was held at the regular cabinet meeting on the morning of February 19. The minister of welfare, Ashida Hitoshi, recorded in his diary the debate at this meeting and two subsequent meetings.[17] A pale-faced Matsumoto asked to speak, and said that an urgent matter had come up. He disclosed the details of the February 13 meeting between the four Japanese delegates and GHQ staff, his subsequent note referring to the Matsumoto version, and

16. In my interview with him on June 24, 1987, Charles Kades (1987, tape 3) said that when Whitney told MacArthur what he had said and that MacArthur could repudiate it, MacArthur said to Whitney, "That was a wonderful idea. I wish I had thought of it myself."

17. See Ashida 1986. Ashida's diary, which he kept from 1905 until one month before his death in 1959, is an extraordinary record of his life amid Japan's turbulent political history, first as a career diplomat, and later as a politician, after joining the Shidehara cabinet in 1945.

Whitney's reply of the previous day.[18] As soon as Matsumoto finished, the minister of home affairs, Mitsuchi Chūzō, and the minister of justice, Iwata Chūzō, concurred with the Prime Minister, saying that they could not accept this document. Ashida spoke up, pointing out that if the American version was made public, the Japanese press would get on the bandwagon and approve. If the present Cabinet resigned at that point, saying that it could not take responsibility, others would sponsor the American version. That would have serious consequences in the up-coming general election, scheduled for April 10. Matsumoto and the minister of agriculture, Soejima Sempachi, agreed. The minister of education, Abe Yoshishige, then pointed out that if the Cabinet were to oppose the American version, they would have to unite behind their own version. Since the Matsumoto version was not definitive, other members should be given the opportunity to express their opinions. The Prime Minister said that he would meet with MacArthur as soon as possible (Ashida 1986, 1:75–78).

At the next meeting, on February 22, Shidehara reported on his meeting with MacArthur of the previous day. He told the Cabinet that he felt MacArthur showed much compassion in trying to persuade the Japanese to accept the American draft, and that MacArthur said that he was doing his best for Japan. He had heard that the discussions among the members of the Far Eastern Commission on the fate of the Emperor were far worse than the Japanese could ever imagine. He did not know how long he would remain in the position of supreme commander, and was concerned about what would happen to the Emperor after he left. He believed that the difference between the American and Japanese versions could be overcome, for the American version stated that the Emperor was to proclaim the constitution, and would remain on his throne. The American version eliminated all the provisions for the military because, he believed, Japan should refrain from raising suspicions among other nations that it would rebuild its armed forces. If Japan did not accept the American version, it would lose an

---

18. Whitney informed Shirasu Jirō, who delivered Matsumoto's note to GHQ,

> This memorandum by Dr. Matsumoto is a repetitious defense of his draft of constitution which, as I have previously stated, has been rejected by the Supreme Commander as an instrument affording the opportunity to the people of Japan for the freedom and democracy to which they are entitled. The Supreme Commander has approved the proposed constitution which I presented to Dr. Matsumoto and Mr. Yoshida last week, and he is determined that the principles embodied in the proposed constitution shall be brought before the people and that the people shall have an opportunity for a full and free explanation thereon. (Takayanagi et al. 1972, 1:368)

ideal opportunity to regain the confidence of other nations and maintain its national security. Shidehara told MacArthur that the Matsumoto version was tentative, and that he was open to suggestions. He
asked MacArthur to listen to Matsumoto. MacArthur in turn said that,
while Whitney looked like a "cold-blooded lawyer," he had no mali-
cious intent. After hearing this report, Matsumoto, obviously agitated,
said that he wanted to confirm the opinions of Whitney and others with
whom he had to work. Other ministers, however, agreed that there was
room for negotiation (Ashida 1986, 1:78–80).

That afternoon, nine days after their first meeting, the Japanese and
Americans met again to go over the entire document in English. The
final portion of the minutes of that meeting shows how the Americans
tried to rush the matter, while the Japanese tried their best to emphasize
the need to put the document into the proper form and, presumably, to
gain time.

> MATSUMOTO: If we base the new Constitution on your draft,
> we must have your draft rewritten in Japanese. It will take a
> great deal of time to put it into classical Japanese as used by
> the Emperor. It will be difficult, people are very particular
> about form in Japanese and will argue for weeks about one
> phrase. The beginning of the Preamble will be especially dif-
> ficult to translate. The Diet argued for weeks about the
> phrase, "the will of the people," used by the Foreign Minister
> some years ago in concluding an antiwar treaty.
> GENERAL WHITNEY: As General MacArthur explained to the
> Prime Minister yesterday, we do not press you for time in
> order to orient your opinion in one way or another, but Gen-
> eral MacArthur believes that in putting this Constitution
> through speed is essential. General MacArthur feels that
> since he is in complete charge of the situation he can put a
> document such as this through; he wishes this for the express
> purpose that he explained to your Prime Minister yesterday.
> We are now in agreement as to the principles, and I and my
> staff will assist you in every way possible. I cannot impress
> upon you too much how important the time element is.
> MATSUMOTO: It is not a difficulty of spirit between us but a
> question of words and phraseology.
> GENERAL WHITNEY: We are fortunate in having so able a man
> as you, Dr. Matsumoto, to carry this work through, but speed
> is essential. I know that you must carefully work over this
> document, section by section, and I can understand that this
> may take a day or two, but it must not be spread over a
> number of days.

YOSHIDA: We will not delay unnecessarily.

GENERAL WHITNEY: You propose, then, merely to put this new Constitution in proper language and phraseology acceptable to the Japanese people, but without working any essential change in the basic principles set forth? How long will this take?

MATSUMOTO: I cannot say. I will have to have the approval of the Cabinet before I can say definitely. I must explain this afternoon's conversation to the Cabinet, but I will begin the work of putting this document into the proper language at the same time.

GENERAL WHITNEY: This afternoon's conversation added nothing new to what the Prime Minister was told yesterday by General MacArthur. I understand that the Prime Minister gave the substance of that conversation to the Cabinet this morning.

MATSUMOTO: The Prime Minister explained merely the general principles to the Cabinet, but the basic form was not discussed. After this conversation with you I will give full details to the Cabinet.

GENERAL WHITNEY: If you wish some of my officers to sit beside you as you put this Constitution into the proper form in order to determine whether the basic principles are violated by the changes in form, I will be happy to make officers available to you.

COLONEL KADES: Hasn't our draft been translated already?

SHIRASU: Yes, but it has not been put into the form in which our Constitution could be presented to the people.

YOSHIDA: We will have a Cabinet meeting on Tuesday. After that meeting we will be able to tell you how many days the work of translation and form will take. We trust that you will preserve perfect secrecy on these discussions.

GENERAL WHITNEY: Complete security will be maintained, of course. I will report to General MacArthur that you, Dr. Matsumoto, will have this work of translation completed well before the end of next week. You have the satisfaction of knowing that your fee for this work will be the highest possible—the welfare of the Japanese people.

COLONEL KADES: Would you like us to go over the English with you again, so that you are sure that you understand the principles embodied in the articles?

SHIRASU: That will not be necessary. We understand.

GENERAL WHITNEY: Good. Everything is now clear. The only problem remaining is to put this document into good form.
(Takayanagi et al. 1972, 1:396, 398, 400)

Three days later, on February 25, the Prime Minister called a special Cabinet meeting, and for the first time showed the cabinet members a tentative translation of the first two chapters of the MacArthur Constitution, prepared by the Ministry of Foreign Affairs. Minister Matsumoto gave a detailed report on the development of the negotiations with GHQ since their first meeting. The cabinet eventually reached the conclusion that the Japanese government had no choice but to rewrite its draft so that it would be closely in line with that of the Americans. They also decided that they would complete the new version by March 11. The following day, cabinet members received the Japanese translation of the entire MacArthur Constitution (Miyazawa and Satō 1954, appendix).[19] By Saturday, March 2, Matsumoto and Satō Tatsuo, of the Cabinet Bureau of Legislation, had completed a draft to be presented to the Cabinet. GHQ, however, was in a hurry. It ordered that the Japanese deliver that version on Monday morning (Satō Tatsuo Kankei Bunsho 598).

On March 4, 1946, at 10:00 A.M., Matsumoto, accompanied by four government officials, delivered to GHQ the Japanese government's draft based on the MacArthur Constitution.[20] It was still in Japanese, untranslated, and had not been approved by the Cabinet. The Americans told them that the final version had to be prepared then and there. So, the Japanese officials and the staff of the Government Section began to work, locked up in a room guarded by the military police.[21] The two sides first translated the Japanese draft into English. They made extensive use of the Japanese-English dictionaries that the Americans had brought into the room, and engaged in heated discussions about the choice of words and phrases in Japanese and English.[22] The Ameri-

19. Satō Tatsuo (1955b, pp. 19–20) says that when Matsumoto first showed him the MacArthur version on February 26, and asked him to work with him, he accusingly asked Matsumoto why nothing had been done about it for nearly a week. Matsumoto said simply that it had been kept in storage. Satō regretted accusing Matsumoto when he learned later that Shidehara and Matsumoto had been deeply troubled at that time.

20. The complete text of this version, often called the March 2 version, along with explanatory comments, is included in Shimizu 1962–63, 4:340–51.

21. Kades (1987, tape 5) told me that the session was held in a large room, which he understood to be a ballroom of the Daiichi Seimei Insurance Company, where GHQ was located. Kades asked the MPs to lock the room and guard the door so that no outsiders could get in or out.

22. In his autobiography, Edwin O. Reischauer (1986, pp. 90–91) says that in response to a sudden great demand for Japanese-English dictionaries after the outbreak of the Pacific War, the dictionaries at the Harvard Yencheng Institute were photocopied, then "innocuously labeled 'American Edition.' They sold like hotcakes, producing big profits, which became a revolving fund for the publication of books that is still in use by the Institute." Okuizumi Eizaburō (1985, pp. 4–6) gives a short but interesting account of the "pirated" editions of the Japanese dictionaries produced during World War II. The Japanese officials were astonished to see so many photocopies

cans so strongly opposed the Japanese translation of Chapter 1, on the Emperor, and Chapter 3, on the people's rights and duties, that the two sides had to discard the Japanese version and rewrite them using the MacArthur draft.[23] At 2:30 that afternoon, Matsumoto, frustrated and exhausted, excused himself and left. This left Satō Tatsuo as the only Japanese participant with a legal background. Satō, who had been working closely with Matsumoto behind the scenes until then, was un-wittingly and reluctantly drawn onto the main stage of the negotiations until the end of the entire process.

At 6:00 P.M., Whitney informed the Japanese that MacArthur had issued an ultimatum for completion of the final version, both in English and Japanese, by midnight, or at the latest by 6:00 A.M. the next morn-ing, March 5. Starting at 9:00 P.M., March 4, the two sides began negotiating, article by article, to create a final text in both languages.[24] The final version was delivered in bits and pieces throughout the night to Japanese government officials, who copied it in preparation for the Cabinet meeting the next morning (Shimizu 1962–63, 4:110).

On the afternoon of March 5, the Japanese believed that they had once again been put in a tight spot. They believed that not only did the Americans want them to publish the American version before the day was over, but also that the Americans had threatened to publish it themselves if the Japanese were not willing to do so. The evidence for these beliefs is found in two Japanese sources. In his diary on March 5, Ashida wrote (1986, 1:89; my translation):

> At 2:15 P.M., Mr. Shirasu brought ten copies of the Ameri-can version (in English) along with a "covering note" (Ashi-da's phrase) from the American side, and reported that the Americans wanted a reply as to whether we would accept this before the day was over; [otherwise they] would publish the text this evening. It appears that, in view of the atmo-sphere back home, the Americans feel that they must move without a moment's delay.
>
> If the Americans publish it, we cannot help but publish

of Japanese dictionaries at GHQ, for they were having a great deal of difficulty finding reference materials, including dictionaries (Satō 1955a, 171:29).

23. Satō says that the Americans told him that their version of Chapter 1 was final, and that they would not budge (Satō Tatsuo Kankei Bunsho 45, p. 5).

24. Satō negotiated mostly with Kades and Hussey, with the help of Beate Sirota, the daughter of a Russian pianist who headed the piano department of the Imperial Academy of Music in Tokyo. Sirota was born in Vienna in 1923, and had spent ten years in Japan before emigrating to the United States in 1938. Although she was only twenty-two years old, with her competency in both English and Japanese, Sirota played a vital role in these negotiations (Satō 1955a, 172:13; Pharr 1987, p. 230).

it. But [the Japanese version] reads like the direct translation
of the American version. The [phrase] "We, the Japanese
people . . . " in the Preamble definitely rejects the present
Constitution, and it is not consistent with the present Article 73. We argued about what to do about this. We concluded that, although ultimately we have no choice but to
accept it, we would probably be able to change the wording
[of the text].

A second version is in Irie Toshio's recounting of the event to a group
of scholars at Tokyo University in the summer of 1954 (Irie 1976,
p. 215). He says,

At the Cabinet meeting on the afternoon of the 5th, we
discussed how to deal with this draft. The Americans had
said to us, "Publish this draft as the creation of the Japanese
government. We will announce at the same time that we
have approved it." Minister Matsumoto angrily said, "We
cannot possibly draft the Japanese government's version in a
couple of days. If the Americans plan to announce this, why
not let them publish it as they please?" To this, Minister
Mito and Minister Iwata said, "We cannot look the other
way." Chief of the Bureau of Legislation Ishiguro, Deputy
Chief Irie, and Chief Secretary Narahashi all said, "Under
the circumstances, we must not lose any time. We understand that this is an unsatisfactory situation, but Japan must
maintain its autonomy at all cost. So we think we have no
choice but to publish this draft as [the government's] own
proposal at the same time the Americans publish their [ver-
sion]. (My translation)

Thus Irie believes that the Americans delivered an ultimatum, but he
does not mention a specific time. Satō Tatsuo, on the other hand, does
not mention this incident in his accounts of the marathon.[25] He simply
says that the work at GHQ was completed at around 4 o'clock in the
afternoon of the 5th.[26] Justin Williams, who was on the staff of the
Government Section, confirms that the work was completed at 4 P.M.
(Williams 1979, p. 116).

Charles Kades also does not remember such an incident taking place
on the afternoon of March 5. He has no recollection of making such a
demand, and thinks that it could not have happened, because neither

25. Satō might not have known about it, since he was still at GHQ at 2:30 P.M. on March 5,
1946.
26. *Jurisuto*, August 15, 1955, p. 33.

he nor anyone else at the Government Section had the authority to issue such a demand without MacArthur's approval. Since MacArthur did not see the complete draft of the constitution until after six o'clock, he could not have issued such an order (Kades, pers. comm., September 20, 1988). Theodore H. McNelly also does not mention such an ultimatum. He says, "GHQ forwarded ten copies of the final English version to the Shidehara cabinet and *asked* whether they would accept it before the day was over."[27]

Thus, it is not clear what exactly transpired during the afternoon of March 5. It is also unclear whether GHQ stated that it would make the final draft public, if not that afternoon, then after MacArthur had approved it, whether or not the Japanese government was willing to release the Japanese version. But since the Americans had told Matsumoto and Satō, on the morning of the 4th, that the final version had to be prepared immediately; and possibly because they also remembered Whitney's statement on February 13 that MacArthur was willing to put the constitution to the people of Japan himself if the Japanese government did not do so; the Japanese concluded that the Americans would publish this draft if they did not act. They felt that they had no choice but to publish the Japanese version concurrently, and were worried about how best to deal with this critical situation.

As noted in Ashida's diary, the cabinet members felt that, although the new constitution stated that the right of governance resided in the people of Japan, legally speaking the nation was still being governed under the Meiji Constitution. That document gave the Emperor alone the authority to put amendments to the Constitution before the Diet. The Cabinet decided that the solution would be to ask the Emperor to issue an imperial rescript commanding the government to present the cabinet version to the National Diet. To this end, late that afternoon, they interrupted their meeting, and Shidehara and Matsumoto rushed to the Imperial Palace. The two ministers explained the situation to the Emperor, who approved the course of action they had outlined. The Japanese resolved the difficulty about the language of the Constitution by preparing a so-called outline of the document. The cabinet meeting finally ended at 9:15 P.M., reconvening the next morning to discuss that outline (Irie 1976, pp. 215–17; Matsumoto 1958, p. 26).

At 5:00 P.M. on March 6, the Cabinet finally released to the press

27. McNelly 1987, p. 83; emphasis added. In his letter to me of November 29, 1988, Charles Kades reconfirmed that GHQ "never expected, demanded, or even asked to have word from the Cabinet on whether it would sponsor the draft that same evening or later that night."

the outline of the new, democratic Constitution of Japan, along with
the imperial rescript mandating constitutional reform, and the Prime
Minister's statement accepting it. General MacArthur also issued a letter of support for the new Constitution (SCAP 1968, 2:657): "It is
with a sense of deep satisfaction that I am today able to announce a
decision of the Emperor and Government of Japan to submit to the
Japanese people a new and enlightened Constitution which has my full
approval." On the same afternoon, GHQ sent Hussey to Washington,
with the English version of the Constitution, on a special plane. The
outline of the new Constitution was printed in the morning papers of
March 7, for all Japan to read.[28]

The Americans were greatly relieved, but the Japanese officials were
somber. As Satō explained,

> When the work at GHQ was finished, General Whitney ap-
> peared for the first time, looking very relieved. He held our
> hands firmly and repeatedly thanked us. His joy was so great
> that I almost wondered whose constitution I had just helped
> create.
>
> In a marked contrast to his pleasure, however, my heart
> was heavier than ever, and filled with gloom, because I
> thought I was unable to preserve the imperial system that
> Minister Matsumoto worked so hard to save, and, in every
> other way, I had failed to satisfactorily fulfill this grave re-
> sponsibility. (Satō 1955a, 172:17; my translation)

The question of why MacArthur insisted that the American and Japanese drafters prepare the constitution in such great haste remains. The
two generally accepted reasons are the imminent FEC meeting discussed earlier, and Japan's first election since the end of the war, scheduled for April 10. MacArthur wanted the Constitution to be included
among the campaign issues. But were there any other reasons why Mac-
Arthur rushed the drafters into a 30-hour marathon? American documents do not shed light on this question, but Ashida (1986, 1:88–89)
mentions one factor that the prime minister and some cabinet members
believed might have influenced MacArthur.

On February 27, 1946, *Yomiuri-Hōchi*, another leading Japanese
newspaper, printed a front-page article raising the possibility of the Emperor's abdication. It reported that Russell Brines of the Associated
Press had met with a certain high-ranking official of the Imperial

---

28. The text, along with the imperial rescript, Prime Minister Shidehara's statement, and the
Japanese translation of MacArthur's message, is found in Shimizu 1962–63, 4:351–63.

Household Agency, who told him that the Emperor had expressed his desire to abdicate at an appropriate time to acknowledge his own responsibility for the war. In such a case, his younger brother, Prince Takamatsu, would probably act as regent until the Crown Prince came of age. The report also said that, while many members of the imperial family approved of the Emperor's abdication, among those opposed were Prime Minister Shidehara and the minister of the Imperial Household Agency. On March 4, 1946, *The New York Times* (sec. 6, p. 2) printed an interview with Prince Higashikuni Naruhiko, the Emperor's cousin and former prime minister, by the Kyodo News Agency, whose content was nearly identical. It said that the Prince had suggested to the Emperor three "timely opportunities" for his abdication: when the surrender was signed; when the Japanese Constitution was finally revised; and when a final peace treaty was signed. He did not know what the Emperor might do. He also said that, if the Emperor should abdicate, and if it was decided that the imperial system should continue, Prince Nobuhito Takamatsu, brother of Hirohito, probably would act as Regent until Crown Prince Akihito came of age. On the same day, *Yomiuri-Hōchi* (p. 1) published another report by an unidentified American journalist who allegedly had said that the Emperor's recent visits to various parts of Japan might have been in preparation for a possible national referendum on his position. The report indicated that, while the opinions of the top officers of MacArthur's headquarters regarding the Emperor's responsibility for the war was not clear, one of the reasons that the United States and Great Britain, in opposition to Australia, New Zealand, and others, favored not holding the Emperor responsible for Japan's war efforts, was his immense popularity among the Japanese people and his contribution as the only stabilizing factor of postwar Japanese society. These reports greatly worried Japanese government officials.

In his diary, Ashida recorded a detailed account of the events surrounding the Emperor at this time. First, on February 27, at the plenary session of the Privy Council, Prince Mikasa, the Emperor's youngest brother, said that because there was a great deal of debate about the status of the Emperor and the imperial family, the government should take decisive and courageous action to prevent some unfortunate and regrettable developments at a later time. "It would be extremely unfortunate if the government, adhering to some old ideas, failed to make some thoroughgoing policy changes that were necessary at this time." [29]

29. Ashida 1986, 1:82; my translation. I believe this extremely vague statement reflects Prince Mikasa's delicate position, as well as the Japanese tendency to be very conscious of their

As for the reports about the Emperor's abdication, Ashida wrote that the cabinet ministers were gravely concerned about the whole turn of events. Shidehara discussed these reports with the Emperor, and repeatedly said that they would do great harm to MacArthur. The minister of the Imperial Household rushed to Prince Higashikuni to reprimand him for lack of discretion (Ashida 1986, 1:88–89).

MacArthur may indeed have felt that this news could be used as additional ammunition by those members of the Far Eastern Commission, who were taking a stern attitude toward the Emperor and his wartime responsibilities. He may also have believed that any further delay would encourage extensive public debate about the position of the Emperor. By that time, MacArthur had decided that it was desirable to retain the Emperor. If so, it was ironic that a member of the imperial family, by suggesting the possibility of abdication, actually helped solidify both the Throne and the position of the Emperor himself. It is also noteworthy that, for the second time, the Japanese press influenced the making of the new Japanese Constitution.

One last note. The Japanese press did not know the true origin of the new Constitution, but there is evidence that it strongly suspected that the document was not a Japanese creation. Its translation flavor gives the secret away, but the press never mentioned this point. Immediately after the new Constitution was made public, the press submitted a list of questions concerning the new document to the Civil Information and Education section of GHQ. The list included the following two related questions:

> 9. Upon reading through the contents, it appears that the constitution is not Japanese; one gets the impression that GHQ has submitted the draft as a proposition to the Japanese government and that the latter merely translated it into Japanese. If this is true, was it done for the purpose of curbing political activity under terms of the new constitution? In other words, according to the new constitution, the Emperor system is supported. Will any anti-Emperor activity be considered contrary to the spirit of the constitution?

> 12. When General MacArthur says the constitution has his "full approval," does it mean the principles cannot be revised or that wording of small details can be revised?

---

position in the group when expressing opinions or preferences, and their sensitivity to guessing the unspoken intentions and desires of others. While it is not certain what Prince Mikasa meant by "the government should take decisive and courageous action," he might have been referring to a decision by the government that the Emperor should abdicate. If so, given his position, it is understandable that he would not state this explicitly, but merely let others guess what he meant.

The list was sent to the chief of the Government Section with a memorandum dated March 9, 1946. Whitney consulted with MacArthur, and the latter decided that the Japanese press should be referred to the Japanese government.[30] Although I have not come across any Japanese documents referring to these questions, if the government had to respond to the press, it must have requested that the press keep quiet. And it did until after the American occupation was finally terminated in 1952. It appears that the first article in which the true origin of the Japanese Constitution was revealed was in the April 1952 issue of the journal *Kaizō* (Koseki Shōichi, pers. comm., March 17, 1986).

## Translation and Translation Flavor

The "outline" of the Japanese Constitution made public on March 6 was written in the language of Meiji legal documents, called *kana-majiri-bun*. *Kana-majiri-bun* literally means "prose mixed with *kana*," and refers to prose composed in simple classical grammar, and written in the *katakana* syllabary, with a great many erudite, technical words in Chinese characters.[31] The extensive use of these characters made the Meiji Constitution, and prewar government documents in general, difficult for citizens with limited education to understand.[32]

Originally, when the Japanese government was preparing a complete text of the Constitution for the debates in the Diet, the officials had intended to use *kana-majiri-bun*. Not all Japanese approved, however. On March 26, an organization of concerned writers and scholars, the Association for the People's National Language Movement (Kokumin-no Kokugo Undō Remmei), submitted a series of recommendations to the Japanese government, suggesting (1) that the constitution be written in simple, colloquial Japanese limiting the number of Chinese char-

30. GHQ/SCAP Records (RG 331), Microfiche sheet no. GS (B)-643, Modern Political History Materials Room, National Diet Library, Tokyo. The original document is in box no. 2088, folder title/number: Publicity (6), National Archives of the United States, Washington, D.C.

31. The Japanese people first acquired a writing system in the sixth century when Chinese and Korean Buddhist monks decided to write Japanese using Chinese characters. The Japanese subsequently created two sets of syllabaries of 51 letters each, called *hiragana* and *katakana*. During the Tokugawa period, the bakufu used what is known as *hentai kambun*, composed in Japanized Chinese syntax and written entirely in Chinese characters, for official documents. For public announcements to be read by the less educated, the bakufu used *kana-majiri-bun*. By the beginning of the Meiji era, the government had ceased to use *hentai kambun*. All official documents, including the imperial rescripts, were being written in *kana-majiri-bun*. For a concise discussion of the development of the Japanese writing system in relation to its grammar, see Inoue 1979, pp. 243–49. Habien 1984, pp. 97–103, also gives a concise discussion on the development of the modern written style in the Meiji era. DeFrancis 1989, pp. 89–121, 131–43, gives a most interesting and illuminating discussion of the Chinese and Japanese writing systems.

32. In a letter to the editor on page 2 of the *Yūbin Hōchi* of July 14, 1873, a reader complained

acters and avoiding difficult ones altogether; (2) that punctuation marks and other orthographic devices used in ordinary written materials be employed; and (3) that the *hiragana* syllabary of ordinary prose, instead of the *katakana* syllabary, be used (Shimizu 1962–63, 4:132). One of the main proponents of this movement was a noted novelist, Yamamoto Yūzō.

Matsumoto was not pleased. He believed that using colloquial Japanese would diminish the dignity of the document, but not all government officials shared his concern. Watanabe Yoshihide of the Cabinet Bureau of Legislation felt that, in the atmosphere of democratization, various sectors of Japanese society would press for a revision of the language of the Constitution. Since the government had little control over the content of the document, he thought it would be wise to take the lead in the matter of format. Other officials held similar views. On March 21, nearly a week before the Association for the People's National Language Movement presented its petition, Watanabe approached Yamamoto Yūzō unofficially, asking him to write a draft of the constitution in colloquial language (Nagano 1983). Matsumoto finally decided to yield, not because he had been persuaded by their reasoning, but because he felt that time constraints would prevent him from producing a text in classical Japanese with a dignity of style and form appropriate to the nation's highest legal document. His draft would inevitably be awkward, and he thought it would be much easier to minimize the translation flavor if he adopted colloquial Japanese (Matsumoto 1958, pp. 26–27).[33]

So the new Japanese Constitution was written in colloquial Japanese, readable by all Japanese citizens, enhancing the democratic character

---

that the publications and public notices of the Meiji government had too many erudite words that were too difficult for uneducated ordinary citizens.

33. At the first plenary session of the House of Representatives on June 25, 1946, Kita Reiki-chi, of the Liberal party, criticized the beginning of the Preamble as having a "translation flavor." It reads: "We, the Japanese people, acting *through our duly elected representatives in the National Diet*, determined that we will secure for ourselves . . . " (Ministry of Justice translation). He asked why the italicized phrase in Japanese, *Kokkai-ni okeru seitō-ni senkyo sareta daihyōsha-o tsūjite*, could not be put in a straightforwad phrase *seitō-ni senkyo sareta Kokkai giin-o tsūjite*, "through our duly elected National Diet members" (Shūgi-in 1946a, 5:70, col. 4). One reason that Kita, and indeed other Japanese as well, would find the direct translation of the English phrase unnatural is the use of the passive "duly elected," and the phrase "representatives in the National Diet." The English phrase "duly elected" is concise, but the Japanese experession *seitō-ni senkyo sareta* is verbose and clumsy. Moreover, while the "representatives in the National Diet" conveys a different sense from "the National Diet members," the translation of the former, *Kokkai-ni okeru daihyōsha*, is again verbose and unfamiliar. In contrast, the translation of the latter, *Kokkai giin*, is a well-established common noun, at least as widely used as the comparable American expression, "congressmen."

of the Japanese government.[34] One result of this linguistic change was that all subsequent legal and government documents in postwar Japan have been written in the colloquial language.[35] In consonance with the Japanese tradition of collective responsibility, no single individual has been credited with this important decision, but it is looked upon as one of the memorable positive events surrounding the making of the Japanese Constitution.[36]

## The Constitutional Debates

All of the Japanese participants understood that the Americans had actually drafted the constitution. Nonetheless, it was necessary to maintain the facade of Japanese authorship, so that no one could challenge the legitimacy of the document. For the same reason, the Japanese legislative bodies created under the Meiji Constitution had to go through the motions of deliberation and ratification. That process began in the Privy Council, an advisory board to the Emperor, and then moved to the two bodies of the Imperial Diet—the House of Representatives, and the House of Peers—each of which formed both a special committee and a subcommittee to discuss the document.

Beginning on April 22, 1946, a twelve-member committee of the

34. It does, however, retain the old use of *hiragana* (*kyū-kana-zukai*).

35. The national statute book, called *Roppō Zensho* (A Complete Book of the Six Major Laws), thus includes both the postwar laws, written in the colloquial style in *hiragana*, and the old laws in the language of the Meiji Constitution, written in *katakana*.

36. Alfred Hussey (SCAP 1968, 1:107) claims that the Americans urged the Japanese to adopt colloquial language. He writes,

> Great difficulty was encountered over the choice of appropriate language. The legal language used in the Meiji Constitution was archaic, stilted, and inelastic and could not be read, much less understood by the ordinary man. It was considered undignified if not impossible to use the vernacular in a Constitution.

He goes on to say, in a footnote:

> Early in the discussion an attempt was made to work entirely in colloquial Japanese, but the Japanese vigorously protested the impossibility of such a procedure. Their protest lost [its] force when a draft in simple readable Japanese of the original Government Section proposal was discovered among some papers left after an early conference.

Justin Williams, another staff member, contradicts Hussey. He says (1979, p. 117),

> The epochal decision was to draw up the draft constitution in spoken Japanese instead of in the traditional literary style of legal language. Thenceforth the spoken language was used for promulgating all laws and ordinances. SCAP had nothing to do with the decision.

Charles Kades (1987, tape 5) also mentioned to me that he saw Shirasu Jirō take out a translation of the MacArthur Constitution in colloquial Japanese during the 30-hour marathon. Thus it appears that Hussey is mistaken.

Privy Council met eleven times. On the opening day, Minobe Tatsukichi, who has been characterized as "without question the best mind in
prewar Japan,"[37] argued against the new constitution, giving the following reasons: (1) When Japan accepted the Potsdam Proclamation, the
provisions for constitutional amendments specified in Article 73 of the
Meiji Constitution were nullified; (2) it was inappropriate for the Privy
Council to be asked for its opinion on and for the House of Peers to
debate a new constitution that abolished both institutions; and (3) it
was inconsistent for the new constitution, which was to represent the
will of the people, to be drafted by the government, approved by a Diet
that had a limited ability to amend it, and ultimately promulgated by
an imperial rescript (Murakawa 1986, p. 29). As compelling as these
reasons were, they attracted no overt support. On June 8, at a meeting
of the entire Privy Council in the presence of the Emperor, the council
accepted it by a majority vote (ibid., p. 191). The council gave its final
unanimous approval on October 29, after the completion of the entire
process at the Diet. Minobe and two other members were absent from
this last session (p. 234).

For the debates at the National Diet, the government had appointed
Kanamori Tokujirō (1886–1959) as "constitution minister," to serve as
the principal government spokesman. Kanamori had had a distinguished career in the government, and had once served as the chief of
the Bureau of Legislation of the Okada cabinet (1934–36). He was also
a constitutional scholar, whose published commentary on the Meiji
Constitution was severely criticized by conservatives for its sympathy
with Minobe Tatsukichi's constitutional theory mentioned earlier.[38]
Throughout the debates at the National Diet, which lasted for 114
days, Kanamori responded to interpellations well over one thousand
times.[39] Some of them lasted several hours, and a few several days. The
longest of Kanamori's answers lasted over an hour and a half.

On June 25, 1946, the plenary session of the House of Representatives of the 90th Imperial Diet was opened by an imperial rescript.
Prime Minister Yoshida introduced the draft of the new Japanese Con-

37. Najita 1974, p. 109. Najita gives a concise summary of Minobe's political theory of the
emperor as "instrument" of the constitutional order and the theory's role in the development of
early-twentieth-century Japanese politics (ibid., pp. 102–114).

38. The edition available at the National Diet Library is, Kanamori Tokujirō, *Teikoku Kempō
Yōkō*, 13th edition (Tokyo: Ganshōdō Shoten, 1928). It mentions that the original edition was
published in 1921, but no bibliographic information is given.

39. According to Shimizu Shin, there were more than 104 interpellators at the plenary sessions
and the hearings at the special committees of both Houses. See Shimizu 1962–63, vol. 4, appendix, p. 94.

stitution to the newly elected Representatives. This was followed by interpellations by party representatives lasting four days.[40] The Representatives then formed a special committee of 72 members, which debated the document in detail until July 23. At both the plenary sessions and the special committee hearings, interpellators presented a series of opinions and questions, initially covering the entire document, and later moving on to specific articles. The members did not argue the pros and cons of specific articles and revise them. That work was undertaken in a subcommittee of thirteen members that began meeting on July 25. During the next month, the subcommittee met fourteen times in closed session.[41] There, the members candidly discussed the constitution from beginning to end, paying close attention to the language of the draft, both in English and Japanese. They negotiated various amendments proposed by the parties, and made the majority of the eventual changes to the document. They also eliminated the translation flavor from various phrases, as best they could. The government consulted and negotiated with GHQ at every step of this process, the Americans insisting that the respective meanings of the English and Japanese expressions had to be very close, if not exactly the same.

On August 21, 1946, the special committee of the House of Representatives reconvened to discuss the subcommittee proposals. The Socialist party proposed additional amendments, but they were rejected by all other parties. Three days later, on August 24, the entire House of Representatives convened for a final vote. It began with a lengthy report of the proceedings by Ashida Hitoshi, the chairman of both the special committee and the subcommittee. In closing, Ashida, nearly overcome by emotion, said that he was deeply sorry that the nation and the people had been driven to this crisis because of misuse of the Meiji Constitution by a handful of extremists, and that it was the duty of this Diet to establish the new Constitution to serve as a basis for rebuilding Japan as a democratic and civilized nation (Shūgi-in 1946a, 35:505, cols. 1–3). Following the final statements by party representatives, the House of Representatives passed the newly amended Japanese Constitution by a vote of 429 to 8 (ibid., 525, cols. 1–5). Five of the eight opposition votes came from the Communists, who were opposed to the continuation of the imperial institution, and who claimed that the

40. The Liberal, Progressive, and Socialist parties each had two interpellators, and the Cooperative Democratic, and Communist parties each had one, as did the Committee for the Japanese Democratic Party. The Independents were represented by two members.

41. The chairman of the subcommittee, however, released summary reports regularly. Thus, newspaper reports were available.

Constitution did not go far enough in promoting individual rights and liberties.[42]

On August 26, 1946, the House of Peers began its hearings. Some of the nation's most distinguished legal scholars had been specially appointed to participate in the deliberations. After the plenary sessions, it, too, sent the document to a special committee, consisting of 45 members, which debated it for nearly a month. The first seven sessions dealt with general interpellations by various leading members, and these were followed by another nine sessions focusing on specific chapters. The committee then sent the document to a subcommittee of thirteen members, which debated in closed session for four more days. The subcommittee made only a few changes, enhancing, to a small degree, the democratic intent of this Constitution.[43] On October 5, the House of Peers debated the new Constitution for the last time in plenary session. Abe Yoshishige, the chairman of the special committee and the subcommittee opened the session with a lengthy report of the proceedings. Abe concluded that while he could not really take pleasure in the new Constitution, he hoped to work toward happiness in the future of Japan based on the positive spirits of the Constitution (Kizoku-in 1946a, 39:500, col. 3). Sasaki Sōichi, the man who assisted Prince Konoe in the initial stage of preparing for the new Constitution, argued against enactment, because he believed that this revision ignored the traditional sentiment of the Japanese people toward the fundamental character of the nation's political system. He said that it was important for those who opposed this Constitution to express their opinions for public record, particularly since GHQ not only allowed but encouraged the people to freely express their opinions on this document (508, col.

42. The Communist party did not participate in the debate at the subcommittee of the House of Representatives because it had too few Representatives to qualify for a seat. The July 27, 1946 issue of *Yomiuri Shimbun* reported that the Communists protested this, and presented amendments to the subcommittee, requesting it to discuss them (Satō, *Jurisuto*, March 15, 1956, p. 50).

43. In addition to changes in words and expressions, the subcommittee of the House of Representatives added eight clauses, five of which became new articles. The House of Peers added only three clauses, amending existing articles. Moreover, two of them were proposed at the House of Peers in compliance with requests from GHQ. One, in particular, had originated in the Far Eastern Commission (Satō, *Jurisuto*, November 1, 1957, pp. 43–46; see also p. 36 n. 47). Miyazawa Toshiyoshi later gave the following reasons why the House of Peers made so few changes: (1) the government officials strongly urged them to approve the document because of the government's difficult position; (2) the officials stressed that GHQ supported the document; and (3) the Peers realized that the document had popular support because it had been approved by the House of Representatives, whose members had been chosen in the election in which the constitution was an issue. The Peers thus decided that it was politically wise to support it (Satō Tatsuo Kankei Bunsho 638). See Shimizu 1962–63, 4:455–67 for the changes made at the House of Representatives, and pp. 531–33 for those added at the House of Peers.

3). Another member, Sawada Ushimaro, also gave an opposing statement. He said that Japan should wait until it regained complete independence before revising its constitution (515, col. 4). But other members spoke in its favor. At the conclusion of the deliberations on October 6, the House of Peers passed the new Constitution with more than a two-thirds majority (ibid., 40:541, col. 2–542, col. 3). Because the Peers had added a few amendments, the document was sent back to the House of Representatives for a final vote.[44]

As will be seen, the debates at the House of Representatives were markedly different from those at the House of Peers. The majority of the members of the House of Representatives had been elected to the Diet for the first time at the general election of April 10, 1946. Some of their debates included well-organized arguments and penetrating questions, but, on the whole, members' speeches—particularly those by the newly elected Representatives who lacked experience in parliamentary debate and, in some cases, political sophistication—were extremely long-winded, repetitive, and incoherent.[45] Kanamori's replies were often just as vague as those of the interpellators, for his role was to explain the new democratic principles in a way that would convince the Diet members that the essential spirit and substance of the Meiji Constitution were, for the most part, still intact. The Japanese government had no choice but to persuade the members of the National Diet to accept the document with as few changes as possible. Kanamori later said that he appreciated the members of the House of Representatives who tackled this important task with a genuine sense of commitment and devotion; there were some who were so overcome by emotion that their voices cracked. In contrast, the debate at the House of Peers was

44. The transcripts of both the plenary sessions and the special committee meetings of the House of Peers and the House of Representatives altogether comprise more than thirty-five hundred pages (see, respectively, Shūgi-in 1946a,b and Kizoku-in 1946a,b) There are two edited versions of the constitutional debates, which are useful for getting a general sense of the important issues. One is a four-volume study of the making of the Japanese Constitution by Shimizu Shin, who presents the debates at both Houses on each one of the 103 articles under major themes (Shimizu 1962–1963). Another is a twelve-volume study by the Commission on the Constitution, entitled, *Teikoku Kempō Kaisei Shingi-roku* (Kempō Chōsa-kai 1959). Finally, a series of 57 articles by Satō Tatsuo appeared in a bi-weekly law journal, *Jurisuto*, from May 1, 1955 to February 15, 1958 (cited throughout the notes as *Jurisuto*, with date and page, and in the bibliography as Satō Tatsuo, 1955–58). They were to constitute the third volume of his study, *Nihonkoku Kempō Seiritsu-shi* (1962–64). Satō gives an extensive discussion of the constitutional debates at the National Diet, with many quotes from the actual interpellations, as well as valuable summaries. In addition, the debate at the Privy Council is in Murakawa 1986, and that of the subcommittee of the House of Representatives is in Mori 1983.

45. Of the eleven party representatives who spoke at the plenary sessions, all but three (two from the Liberal party and one from the Progressive party) were first-time Representatives.

dominated by Japan's leading constitutional scholars, men knowledge-able not only about Japanese constitutional history, but also the legal traditions of Western nations. On the one hand, they were Kanamori's peers, who understood the government's predicament quite well. But they were also scholars, and they did not hesitate to point out to Kana-mori that they were not convinced that the Meiji tradition was alive in the new, democratic Constitution. Some of them presented truly im-pressive arguments. Kanamori had approached the House of Peers with considerable perturbation, and he did not appreciate some of their com-ments, finding them overly pedantic and disagreeable, making his al-ready difficult task even more unpleasant (Kanamori 1947, pp. 7–11; 1962, pp. 9–11, 14–15).

GHQ and the Far Eastern Commission kept a close watch over the debates.[46] Japanese officials met with GHQ staff several times, and ne-gotiated intensely several important issues. By then, however, the Americans were no longer in total control. MacArthur and the FEC were in a continuing battle over the proposed constitution, and in one instance, GHQ yielded to FEC pressure, asking the Japanese to add a new clause.[47]

On November 3, 1946, the new Constitution of Japan was promul-gated with great fanfare.[48] It went into effect on May 3, 1947, which has since been established as a national holiday, Constitutional Me-morial Day.

## Postscript

In 1956, four years after the termination of the American occupation of Japan, the House of Representatives officially sealed the record of the

46. The Cabinet Bureau of Legislation prepared a summary of each day's debate, which was then translated into English and submitted to GHQ (Satō, *Jurisuto*, September 15, 1956, p. 50). For a general discussion on FEC and SCAP, see Satō Tatsuo Kankei Bunsho 617 and 618. See also, U.S. Department of State 1947, which includes several important memoranda highlighting the disagreements between the two agencies.

47. In its policy decision of July 2, 1946, FEC stated, "That the prime minister and the ministers of state, all of whom shall be *civilians* and of whom a majority, including the prime minister, shall be selected from the Diet, shall form a Cabinet collectively responsible to the legislature" (U.S. Department of State 1947, p. 66; emphasis added). GHQ repeatedly requested that the Japanese add this clause to the new constitution, and thus the subcommittee of the House of Peers coined a new word, *bummin*, to stand for "civilian," and added to Article 66 "The prime minister and other ministers of state have to be civilians" (*Naikaku sōri-daijin sono-ta-no kokumu daijin-wa, bummin-de nakere-ba naranai*) (Satō 1955a, 180:26; idem., 186:16–19; Satō, *Jurisuto*, November 1, 1957, pp. 43–45).

48. At the top of the front page of *Mainichi Shimbun* of November 4, 1946 is a photograph of the Emperor and Empress in a carriage, surrounded by a mass of people in the Imperial Palace Plaza. The caption says, "The New Constitution is Now with the People" (*Shin-kempō Ima-zo*

deliberations at the subcommittee meetings. Today, only its own members can read those documents at the National Diet Library, and even they are not allowed to take notes or copy any of the transcripts. In 1980, Mori Kiyoshi, a member of the House of Representatives, learned that the National Diet Library had obtained from the National Archives and Records Service in Washington, D.C., a complete copy of the English translation of the minutes of the meetings, which had been submitted to GHQ at that time. Believing that this was a record that should be made available to the Japanese public, Mori, with the assistance of Murakawa Ichirō and Nishi Osamu, published a complete Japanese translation of this English translation (Mori 1983). In an effort to provide as accurate an account of the meetings as possible, Mori spent many hours at the National Diet Library, reading and making mental notes of important details, which he then incorporated into his translation (Nishi, pers. comm., February 7, 1985). As a result, in my opinion, this translation reads much more naturally and in line with the style of the constitutional debates elsewhere than the English version.[49]

Why did the House of Representatives seal this historic document from the Japanese people? The only reasonable explanation, though unnecessary by 1956, was to conceal the true origin of the Japanese Constitution. That origin was openly publicized in the American press as early as June 25, 1946, when *The Christian Science Monitor* (sec. 2, R) printed an article entitled "Reluctant Japanese Accept Constitution Dictated by MacArthur." Those Japanese who had access to American newspapers must have known about it. Indeed, as mentioned earlier, the Japanese press suspected this on March 6, 1946, when it first saw the outline of the new Constitution. Nevertheless, the Japanese press kept quiet until April 1952, when *Kaizō* published a discussion by Ashida Hitoshi and three former members of the Constitutional Research Group (Ashida et al. 1952, pp. 13–25).

---

*Kokumin-to Tomo-ni Ari*). Below is a photo of the ceremony at the House of Peers, where the Emperor read the imperial rescript promulgating the new Constitution.

49. I have read the transcripts of the 4th, 5th and 7th meetings of the subcommittee, obtained from the National Archives, Washington, D.C. (The 90th Session of the Imperial Diet, The House of Representatives, Minutes of the Sub-Committee on the Bill for Revision of the Imperial Constitution, no. 4 [July 29, 1946], no. 5 [July 30, 1946], and no. 7 [August 1, 1946], RG 331 SCAP, box 2088, National Archives). The only other record of the meetings of the subcommittee is a series of articles by Satō Tatsuo, in which he gives a day-to-day account of the debates, using his own notes and newspaper articles reporting the events (*Jurisuto*, March 1–August 1, 1957).

*Two*

# THE MEIJI RESTORATION

Japan's first constitution was given to the Japanese people in the name of the Emperor in 1889. It did not provide for the limited government and protection of individual rights that Americans associate with constitutional government, and thus was quite different from the constitution created in 1946. Nevertheless, there are some underlying continuities, both in the process of drafting and in the general conception of government, which will help to illuminate the Japanese response to the MacArthur Constitution. To understand these continuities, we must go back to the beginnings of modern Japanese history, the founding of the Tokugawa government in 1603, as it was during the Tokugawa period that the basic patterns of modern Japanese politics took shape.

I will begin with a brief discussion of the Tokugawa political, social, and economic systems, and the ideas that were used to justify them. I will then turn to the Meiji Ishin, which is normally translated as the Meiji Restoration,[1] to show how the government established by the Restoration leaders continued some of the most basic features of the Tokugawa regime, even though the Restoration was in many ways a sharp break with the past. These continuities help to explain the manner in which the Constitution was drafted twenty years after the Restoration. Finally, I will discuss three of the most influential thinkers of the Meiji era, focusing on their attitudes toward political rights, and the relationship between the government and the people. They interpreted the concept of political rights in terms of their own Confucian intellectual tradition, and thus reached an understanding of the ideas involved that was quite different from the prevalent Western view of

---

1. The term *ishin* normally carries the sense that something is renewed. As applied to the Emperor, it reflects the increased prominence the Meiji leaders gave to the imperial institution as part of their efforts to revitalize the Japanese state and nation. Since the Emperor had been of little political significance for several centuries, the term "restoration" is somewhat misleading.

the matter. Their interpretations will help us understand the Japanese debate over the new Constitution more than a half-century later.

## The Tokugawa Order

In 1603, Tokugawa Ieyasu (1542–1616) unified Japan by military force, and together with the other daimyo, or feudal lords, who supported him, established a central government, the Tokugawa bakufu, in Edo, present-day Tokyo.[2] Although the new government was not fully secure until 1615, the creation of the Tokugawa bakufu marked the beginning of 250 years of relative peace and stability for Japan. During this period of virtually complete isolation from the outside world, many of modern Japan's fundamental political ideas and patterns of political behavior developed. The most important of these for our purposes were an autocratic, bureaucratic government, and a pattern of political thought emphasizing a harmonious and hierarchical social order, with an educated ruling class that was supposed to govern in the interests of the nation as a whole.

To establish a strong and stable government, Ieyasu initially confiscated the estates of the daimyo who had opposed him, and distributed them among his loyal followers. He placed these followers strategically throughout the country, so that they might watch over those untrustworthy and potentially hostile daimyo, known as *tozama*.[3] The bakufu ruled its own *han*, or fief, and many of the largest cities directly, but left the actual administration of the other *han* in the hands of the daimyo themselves. The bakufu did lay down general rules regulating the conduct of the entire military class, the *bushi*. Eventually these regulations developed into an elaborate code of behavior, including distinctions in permitted behavior among the different ranks of the bushi. It also imposed heavy restrictions and obligations on the daimyo, who were required to provide manpower and funds for the bakufu's various construction projects. They had to obtain permission to repair their own castles, and were also required to reside in Edo for a period of time each

2. The term bakufu refers to the military government that actually ruled feudal Japan, distinct from the imperial court in Kyoto. It was first established by Minamoto-no Yoritomo in 1185, in Kamakura, thirty miles west of Tokyo. After consolidating his rule, Yoritomo had the Emperor officially appoint him shogun, commander of the Kamakura bakufu, in 1192. In the late sixteenth century, there was a brief period when there was no individual powerful enough to claim the title of shogun, but Ieyasu had himself named to that post after the establishment of the Edo bakufu in 1603.

3. The *tozama daimyō* (literally, "outside lord") had either been neutral or had fought against Ieyasu in the great battle of Sekigahara in 1600, and recognized him as their overlord only after his victory.

year. The latter practice, called *sankin kōtai*, also required them to leave their wives and children in Edo when they returned to their *han*. This hostage system helped keep the daimyo under control.

During the sixteenth century, many of the daimyo had begun developing administrative procedures to help them rule their *han* more effectively.[4] Many of the methods adopted by the bakufu extended and improved those administrative procedures, so that by the end of the seventeenth century a strong and well-entrenched bureaucracy had grown up. Ever since this time, Japanese government has been characterized by a powerful central bureaucracy.

At the time of Ieyasu's triumph, Japanese society, in general terms, comprised four classes—bushi, peasants, artisans, and merchants. The social order was not rigid, however, and movement between classes was possible, particularly during the sixteenth century, when the country was racked by civil wars. The bakufu saw this mobility as a threat to social stability, and tried to freeze the social order by making membership in the four classes hereditary and permanent. The bushi became a privileged civil elite, running the Tokugawa administrative machine, and those of the *han* as well. The bushi class itself was arranged hierarchically, and limited movement between its internal levels was possible, though even this type of mobility was not favored. Beneath the bushi came the peasants, who were regarded as the foundation of the entire social system, because they grew the rice that was the main source of wealth. By turning the bushi into civil administrators, and requiring them to live in castle towns and cities, the bakufu was able to separate the bushi from the peasantry, and thereby discourage the development of strong local landholders who might lead rural uprisings. Artisans were considered less valuable than peasants, but because they made items useful to the bushi, this class was ranked right below the peasants. The merchants were consigned to the bottom of the social hierarchy, because they were regarded as unproductive.

Japanese social structure had always been hierarchical, so the bakufu policy was not a radical innovation, but simply reinforced existing tendencies. The insistence on a fixed and rigid social hierarchy, however, was ultimately counterproductive, as it made it difficult, if not impossible, for the bakufu to cope effectively with social and economic

4. John Whitney Hall (1961) gives an interesting case study of the province of Bizen in the southwestern part of Japan, showing how its administrative organization and procedures developed from the fifteenth to the seventeenth centuries. Hall contends that developments in Bizen were characteristic of what was happening in other parts of Japan, and shows how the methods and techniques of rule foreshadowed the procedures developed by the bakufu.

change. While it lasted, though, it taught the Japanese to think about society, and their own position in it, in terms of a clear and fixed series of ranks.

This vision of society found ready support in Confucian thought. The Japanese had been familiar with Confucian ideas since the eighth century, but had never tried to apply them to solve governmental problems (Sansom 1958–63, 3:71–72). During the Tokugawa period, however, a Japanese variant of neo-Confucianism quickly and easily became the reigning ideology. Chinese neo-Confucianism saw the ideal society as an organic hierarchy reflecting unchanging universal principles of order.[5] This world view was elaborated in the writings of philosophers favored by the bakufu, particularly Hayashi Razan (1583–1657). The following passage provides a succinct summary of his views:

> Heaven is above and earth is below. This is the order of heaven and earth. If we can understand the meaning of the order existing between heaven and earth, we can also perceive that in everything there is an order separating those who are above and those who are below. When we extend this understanding between heaven and earth, we cannot allow disorder in the relations between the ruler and the subject, and between those who are above and those who are below. The separation into four classes of samurai, farmers, artisans and merchants, like the five relationships [of ruler and the subject, father and son, husband and wife, older and younger brother, and friend and friend], is part of the principles of heaven and is the Way which was taught by the Sage (Confucius). (Lu 1974, 1:236)

The emphasis on loyalties and obligations arising out of human relationships fit well with the principles of loyalty, self-sacrifice, and other military virtues prevalent among the bushi, virtues which they continued to cultivate through military education, even though they had become primarily administrators of the new civil order. The stress on an ordered hierarchy of classes was also important, as it confirmed the bushi in their own role as an educated elite, and justified the maintenance of a rigid status system.

Neo-Confucian teaching predominated in the early years of Tokugawa rule primarily because it closely matched the social order that the bakufu was trying to create. From the beginning, however, there

---

5. Chinese neo-Confucianism is generally attributed to the twelfth-century Chinese philosopher, Chu Hsi.

were competing schools of Confucian thought, and the bakufu did not try to suppress them so long as they did not threaten or challenge Tokugawa rule.

One element in the Confucian tradition, particularly emphasized in the writings of Ogyū Sorai (1666–1728), was the desirability of cultivating benevolence and wisdom in political rulers. Sorai believed that those virtues could only be developed among members of a ruling class, and thought that the king or ruler should promote men who acquired them to the ranks of bureaucracy in order to bring peace and security to the people (Maruyama 1974, pp. 90–91). This aspect of the Confucian thought, neglected in the writings of the favored neo-Confucianist school, later proved to be of great importance. Not only was it used to justify the Restoration, it also helped foster among its leaders a strong, elitist sense of responsibility to rule the nation well for the benefit of the people (Minamoto 1973, pp. 25–26). The top-ranking bureaucrats, politicians, and business leaders in contemporary Japan still conceive of their roles in these terms.

When the bakufu was first created, large numbers of bushi found that some education was necessary to handle their new administrative responsibilities, so bakufu schools were established to educate their children. In time, education spread to other classes through tera-koya, temple schools run by bushi, and Buddhist priests (Nihongo-no Rekishi 1963–66, 5:344–56). By the beginning of the eighteenth century, large numbers of people in the other classes had become literate, and had adopted the Confucian ideas of the bushi.[6]

The bakufu retained the Emperor as the spiritual head of the country. The imperial court had long before lost its political power, and on the surface it is not easy to see why the bakufu did not simply eliminate it. But this idea seems not to have occurred to them. The tradition of reverence for the Emperor as the spiritual leader of Japan was still present throughout most ranks of society. Any attempt to abolish the institution might well have aroused considerable opposition, and provided the tozama daimyō with an excellent reason for revolt. Ieyasu and his successors probably also recognized that the Emperor could lend considerable legitimacy to bakufu rule, so they made generous financial contributions to the court. But the bakufu was careful to control this source of legitimacy by preventing the daimyo from having any direct contact with the court, lest they manipulate the Emperor for their own political purposes. The Emperor, himself, "was kept under a close if respectful

---

6. By the end of the Tokugawa period, nearly 45 percent of the men, and 15 percent of the women in Japan were literate, principally due to these schools (E. Reischauer 1981, p. 85).

surveillance, his activities and ceremonies rigorously circumscribed by bakufu regulations" (Norman 1975, pp. 121–22).

From the late seventeenth century on, another group of intellectuals, the *kokugaku-sha* (scholars of national studies), provided the Emperor with additional support. The *kokugaku-sha* advocated the revival of Shintoism, and emphasized both the ancient Japanese literary tradition, and the mythical origin of Japan and the imperial family found in the ancient chronicles. In the late eighteenth century, they severely criticized both the Confucian ideology and the bakufu. Those criticisms eventually became politically significant, because of their emphasis on reverence for the Emperor, and his role as the head of Japan, perceived as one household (Aruga 1966–71, 4:324–25; Minamoto 1973, pp. 206–7). In the end, this revival contributed to the downfall of the bakufu by giving added legitimacy to those who opposed the rule of the bakufu in the name of the Emperor.

In the West, the best-known aspect of Tokugawa rule is the policy of exclusion that cut Japan off from virtually all contacts with Western nations. Initially, Ieyasu had favored the expansion of trade as a potential source of revenue for the bakufu. His successors, however, were not risk takers, and chose to bring this trade, and other contacts, to a complete end in 1641. The reasons for this exclusion policy are not entirely clear, but the bakufu may have feared that Western powers would use both trade and Christianity to meddle in Japanese affairs.[7] Christian believers were concentrated in the southwest, where several powerful *tozama han* were located. The daimyo who ruled these *han* might also have used trade to strengthen themselves economically to the point at which they could have challenged the bakufu. Apparently the bakufu decided that exclusion was necessary to protect the peace and prosperity of Japan. In addition to fiercely persecuting Christians, they issued orders preventing ships or people from leaving Japan, as well as forbidding Japanese living outside the country from returning. The bakufu allowed a small amount of foreign trade to be conducted through Nagasaki, a city they ruled directly. Only those Western nations that did not send missionaries were allowed to participate in that trade, however, and in practice that meant only the Dutch. Thus, for more than 200 years, the only direct contact the Japanese had with the West came through this small window of trade in Nagasaki.

The bakufu was initially successful in establishing a stable political

---

7. The persecution and elimination of Christianity seem to have been adopted for political reasons. This policy was not proposed by the Buddhists, and Buddhist priests did not play an important role in the persecution (Sansom 1958–63, 3:44).

order, isolated from potentially disturbing outside influences. But in the long run, contradictions at the very center of the new social and political order undermined it. As Totman (1981, p. 158) puts it,

> It was the contradiction between a polity that was from its inception based on a complex economy and intricately linked social order and a theory of a state that envisioned society in terms of a single diffuse status hierarchy rooted in a simple agrarian economy.

Even when it was formulated, the theory did not adequately describe social reality; with the growth of cities, the development of commerce and a national market, and the resulting changes in village life, it became more and more divorced from reality. Yet, when the bakufu officials made their sporadic efforts to reform the system, they always thought in terms of restoring the old order, with the inevitable result that their efforts were inadequate to deal with the conflicts and problems generated by social and economic change. In consequence, they gradually lost support throughout the country.

At the beginning of the Tokugawa era, the economic foundation of government policy was a rice economy based on small scale production organized by villages. In the seventeenth century, these villages resembled organic communities, organized hierarchically, and controlled by hereditary leading families. Ordinarily, a competent village head, when supported by village opinion, could rule absolutely, with little outside help. The pressures to conform within the village were formidable, and helped to solidify this control (T. Smith 1959, pp. 59–64). The rise of cities and the expansion of commerce, however, gave the village populace new economic alternatives—such as leaving the village, or producing goods for the new urban markets—and new patterns of land ownership developed. Internal conflicts became less manageable, and periodic crop failures and famine exacerbated these problems. Both the number and intensity of rural disorders increased during the late eighteenth and early nineteenth centuries, and the bakufu was unable to develop effective policies to deal with the growing rural violence.

The bakufu demonstrated similar ineffectiveness in its relations with merchants. Merchants had supported the Tokugawa rulers in the seventeenth century, despite being relegated to the lowest rank in the social order, for they correctly realized that political stability would lead to commercial prosperity. As merchant wealth increased, however, tensions between bushi and merchants also grew. The bakufu, the daimyo, and the bushi all became increasingly dependent on the financial resources of the merchants, but at the same time, the bakufu insisted on restricting merchant activities, and denying them social status and political power commensurate with their economic contributions. Nor were they able to protect merchants from the violence periodically directed against them in the cities. Ultimately, the merchants abandoned the bakufu, and threw their financial support behind the Restoration leaders challenging Tokugawa rule.

Similarly, the bushi, particularly in the lower ranks, slowly weakened in their allegiance to the bakufu. Dependent on a fixed stipend of rice that often yielded insufficient cash to meet their needs, they gradually became impoverished, and were forced to rely on loans from wealthy merchants to meet their expenses. As economic power shifted to merchants and landowners, the bushi directed their resentment and hostility both at those who held economic power and at the bakufu leaders who had allowed control of society to shift away from the bushi class. As their feudal loyalties weakened, they began to look for alternative structures of political loyalty. Eventually, many found such a standard by rallying behind those who professed to act in the name of the Emperor.

Thus, the bakufu proved themselves unable to govern effectively. Not only were they unable to control disorder both in the countryside and the cities, they also gradually alienated their main supporters. It took an external threat, however, to bring the system to the verge of collapse.

Throughout the eighteenth century, it had become increasingly clear that the policy of exclusion was unrealistic. By the middle of the nineteenth century, Western powers were expanding their political and economic influence in Asia. Britain's rapid penetration into China, and its easy victory in the Opium War, jolted the bakufu, forcing them to acknowledge the possibility of Western military threats to Japan's security. The country also faced growing pressure from the Russians in the north, and increasing demands from Western powers that Japan permit foreign trade. In 1854, Commodore Perry's notorious "black ships" finally forced Japan to open its doors to the West, demonstrating to the Japanese that they were too weak to resist foreign military pressure. Japan was compelled to establish relations with Western nations, granting them commercial and political concessions in a series of unequal treaties.

Even before Perry forced Japan to trade with the West, a growing number of Japanese believed that the bakufu should relax its policy of exclusion. Some merchants, anxious to engage in foreign trade, wanted an end to commercial restrictions. Also, the pursuit of the so-called Dutch studies, beginning in the middle of the eighteenth century, led to the growth of a body of scholars, within and without the bakufu, interested in gaining access to Western scientific knowledge. In the nineteenth century, a number of these men recognized the significance of science and technology for building a strong national defense. But the growing interest in Western knowledge provoked a strong reaction among Confucian scholars. The conservative factions of the bakufu, suspicious of change, encouraged hostility toward the West, and took punitive measures against some of those who advocated Western learning. Ironically, this hostility was later turned against the bakufu, when it was forced to grant economic and political concessions to the foreigners.

When Perry made his initial demands, the bakufu was thrown into confusion. Unable to reach a consensus on a course of action, the bakufu asked both the daimyo and the imperial court for advice. Involving the Emperor and the court in political deliberations had far-reaching consequences, because it provided the enemies of the bakufu with an alternative center of loyalty around which they could build opposition to the government. The concessions forced on the bakufu, and the ensuing presence of foreign communities on Japanese soil stimulated the growth of anti-foreign opinion, and led to demands to resist Western pressure, and "expel the barbarians" (jōi). This slogan was quickly linked to another, "revere the Emperor" (sonnō). Several of the tozama daimyo—Satsuma, Chōshū, Tosa, and Hizen—had gradually built up a political alliance against the bakufu, and the leaders of this alliance deliberately stimulated this anti-foreign sentiment in order to undermine bakufu authority. The slogan sonnō jōi became the rallying cry of dissident elements. Because the dissidents framed their challenge in terms of loyalty to the Emperor, the bakufu found it impossible to reply effectively.

The lower-ranking bushi, weakened in their loyalty to the feudal system, and joined by many rōnin—those bushi without lords—took the lead in the restoration movement. With the financial support of the merchants, and acting in the name of the Emperor, restoration leaders were able to defeat the bakufu rather easily. On October 14, 1867, the fifteenth shogun, Tokugawa Yoshinobu, resigned, and 250 years of feudal rule came to an end.

## The Restoration

The leaders of the Restoration shared some important similarities in background and experience. They were all from the lower strata of the

bushi class, and had received the standard Confucian-oriented education. The majority of them had also been educated by the bakufu school
of Western learning, starting with Dutch studies, and moving on to the
study of English and French. As young bureaucrats, several of them had
accompanied the bakufu envoys to Europe and the United States, and
had gained some firsthand knowledge of Western political, social, and
economic systems. They were men of exceptional talent and foresight
who understood that the government needed a thorough housecleaning
if Japan was to transform itself into a strong modern nation that would
gain the respect of the Western powers. Beyond this general goal of
modernizing and strengthening Japan, however, they were not guided
by a specific set of ideas, or a particular vision of society.

After defeating the Tokugawa armies, the Restoration leaders' most
immediate necessity was to create a strong central government that
could industrialize Japan and build its military strength. They began in
1871 by replacing the old *han* with a new system of prefectures, ap-
pointing many of the former daimyo as governors. The elimination of
the *han* weakened the status of the bushi, who no longer had lords to
serve. The introduction of universal military service in 1873 reduced it
further, by denying them a special and exclusive role in the social order.
The gradual elimination of the old feudal structure alarmed some of the
more conservative Restoration leaders, who had a more limited aim of
replacing Tokugawa rule with that of other leading daimyo. Saigō Takamori of Satsuma, and a few others left the government in 1873, when
the rest chose to concentrate on reform at home rather than launch a
military expedition against Korea. The discontented bushi engaged in
a number of uprisings against the new government, and eventually ral-
lied around Saigō, who led the famous Satsuma Rebellion of 1877, in a
desperate effort to retain his own power base. The rebellion was crushed
by the new national army after six months of bloody fighting, and with
it the last resistence to the newly emerging Japanese state collapsed.

During the same period, the Meiji oligarchs encouraged rapid economic growth to build up Japan's military strength. They realized that
they could not rely on private capital to invest heavily in critical stra-
tegic areas, so they used government revenues to develop engineering,
mining, munitions, metallurgy, and other heavy industries. They did
rely on private enterprise for railroad construction, but watched its development carefully, giving assistance when needed. Eventually they
sold the state industries to private individuals for ridiculously low
prices, but they continued to watch over the economy to ensure that it
developed in a manner consistent with the government's goals. Ever

since, the Japanese government has attempted to channel economic energies in directions consistent with government policy.

Throughout this early period, Japan managed to industrialize mostly on its own, without relying on foreign loans. The decisive reason was fear of the dangers arising from dependence on foreign capital. The Meiji leaders did not want to repeat "the unhappy experiences of Egypt and Turkey, which had mismanaged foreign capital introduced into their countries and so had invited foreign intervention" (Norman 1975, p. 223).

Japan's rapid and costly industrialization did not bring economic relief to the peasants and small merchant-landowners. While the government protected the wealthy financier-industrialists, it relied on a heavy land tax to raise the capital necessary to develop industry.[8] Moreover, the price of rice, the main source of income for small landowners, fell drastically. Government policies created widespread discontent in the countryside, and the small landowners and peasants who carried the economic burden of industrialization eventually formed the social base of the Jiyū-tō (Liberal party). This short-lived opposition party was, however, too weak to change the direction of the government policy.

## Party Politics, the Popular Rights Movement, and Constitutionalism

Once Tokugawa resistance had been suppressed, virtually all of the first generation of oligarchs recognized that it would eventually be necessary to broaden the new regime's political support.[9] They were very interested in Western constitutional governments, but agreed that their first task was to secure internal order and establish an effective centralized administration.

In November 1871, Iwakura Tomomi and two other oligarchs, Ōkubo Toshimichi, and Kido Takayoshi, accompanied by several other officials, left on a two-year mission to Europe and the United States, hoping to learn about Western governmental systems, and to gain a revision of the notorious unequal treaties forced on the Tokugawa government. Their diplomatic mission was a failure, both because the Western nations strongly resisted, and the Japanese were inexperienced and inept negotiators. At that point, Ōkubo and Kido realized that Japan had

8. From 1875 to 1879, the land tax accounted for 80.5 percent of national revenue. Even in late 1880s, after the government reduced the tax as a conciliatory move, small landowners were providing 69.4 percent of the nation's revenue (Norman 1975, p. 281).

9. The most important of these leaders were two court nobles, Iwakura Tomomi and Sanjō Sanetomi, and former bushi from four of the old han—Kido Takayoshi of Chōshū, Ōkubo Toshimichi and Saigō Takamori of Satsuma, Itagaki Taisuke and Gotō Shōjirō of Tosa, and Soejima Taneomi and Etō Shimpei of Hizen.

to adopt a constitutional government to gain respect from Western nations.

Following the return of the Iwakura mission, a political crisis developed over the issue of whether Japan should try to expand its influence overseas, or concentrate on domestic reforms and modernization. The oligarchs who had stayed behind were preparing to send troops to Korea, but Iwakura, Ōkubo, and Kido opposed them, favoring domestic reform instead. The Iwakura faction won, and several of its opponents, including Saigō Takamori, and Itagaki Taisuke, left the government. Itagaki and his followers then presented the government with a *kempaku-sho*, or petition, calling for a popularly elected assembly. This injected a new element into the discussions. The government had considered the idea of a popularly elected assembly as early as 1872, but had not decided on a definite plan of action before the crisis. After Itagaki's defection, however, government leaders had to deal with an enduring and articulate opposition demanding political reform. The Satsuma Rebellion reinforced their sense of concern, but at the same time allowed them to give the question greater attention, since the government's victory indicated that their efforts to create a strong central government had been successful.

Itagaki's initial efforts produced no lasting results. He and the petitioners formed the Aikoku-kōtō (Patriotic Public party), the first Japanese political party; but it collapsed within two months. Itagaki then organized the Risshi-sha (Society to Establish One's Ambitions), which soon reorganized into the Aikoku-sha (Patriotic Society), to pursue the same aims. The government decided that the best strategy to control this nascent opposition was to persuade Itagaki to return to the government, which he did in March 1875. Shortly afterwards, the Aikoku-sha dissolved, and with it Japan's first attempt at party politics came to an end. One reason is that Itagaki's followers were mostly disaffected former bushi, with little additional popular support. Itagaki soon left the government a second time, and proceeded to organize another, more successful opposition.

Between 1879 and 1884, this movement, called the Jiyū Minken Undō, The Popular Rights Movement,[10] became the main force outside the government demanding the opening of a representative national assembly. The movement eventually led to the formation of the Jiyū-tō (Liberal party) in 1881. The Jiyū-tō gained considerable support among wealthy landowners and merchants throughout the country, primarily because they were being forced to shoulder a disproportionate share of

10. The literal translation of Jiyū Minken Undō is "freedom and people's rights movement."

the burden of Japan's rapid industrialization. As the movement accel-
erated, however, so, too, did the government's repressive measures.
The Meiji rulers strengthened existing laws regulating the press, prohibited political parties from organizing local groups, tightened the laws
pertaining to public meetings and associations, and forbade educational
and industrial associations from taking part in political activities. The
government was also successful in splitting the Jiyū-tō leadership. Itagaki and Gotō Shōjirō had unwisely left for Europe on a year's study
tour, secretly financed by the Mitsui Company. When this fact became
public, it caused considerable dissension among the remaining leaders.
By 1884 the Jiyū-tō had dissolved, and the liberal movement came to
an end (Tōyama 1985, pp. 125–54).

While Itagaki was trying unsuccessfully to build a strong opposition
party around the issue of a national assembly, the government was conducting a similar debate within its own ranks. The issue came to a head
in the spring of 1881, after both Kido and Ōkubo had died. The
younger generation of oligarchs all agreed that it would be necessary to
draft a constitution and establish a national assembly. Only Ōkuma
Shigenobu, however, wanted to move quickly. He advocated a British-
style parliamentary system, and surprised his colleagues by calling for
the opening of a national assembly within a year. The others, headed
by Itō Hirobumi, argued for a Prussian model, to be created at a much
slower pace. Itō wanted to be sure the new government was firmly established before risking the creation of a national assembly. Ōkuma
lost, and was ousted from the government, allowing Itō to proceed with
his plans. Ōkuma then founded a new political party, the Rikken
Kaishin-tō (Constitutional Progressive party), which joined the Jiyū-tō
in calling for a national assembly.

In October 1881, at the direction of the government, the Emperor
issued a rescript calling for the establishment of the national assembly
in 1890. Itō and his associates then embarked on a year-long study tour,
traveling first to Berlin, where they met with Rudolf von Gneist and
Albert Mosse; and then to Vienna, to receive lectures from Lorenz von
Stein. These German scholars reinforced Itō's authoritarian views, urging the Japanese to establish a strong monarchy, and have the Emperor
give a constitution to the people. Upon his return, Itō first undertook
administrative reforms necessary for the new constitutional government
he had in mind. In July 1884, the government revised the Peerage Law
to prepare for the establishment of a House of Peers, open to the former
daimyo, court nobles, and the leaders of the Meiji Restoration. In 1888,
it also created the Privy Council, for the purpose of discussing and
adopting the constitution that was soon to be drafted. Itō then formed

a cabinet, and became the first prime minister. Cabinet government was therefore established before the new constitution, and did not owe its existence to it.

From June 1887 to March 1888, Itō and three others worked in complete secrecy with a German scholar, Carl Friedrich Hermann Roesler, to draft a constitution for Japan. Their work was unknown, not only to the ordinary people of Japan, but also to the other members of the government. When they had finished their work, from June 1888 to January 1889 the thirty members of the Privy Council, representing a wide variety of opinions and perspectives, discussed and debated the new constitution in the presence of the Emperor. They modified nearly fifty of the original seventy-six articles, and finally adopted the document that became Japan's first modern constitution. The Constitution of the Empire of Japan was promulgated on February 11, 1889, as a gift of the Emperor to his subjects.

The Meiji Constitution established the Emperor as the sovereign ruler of the Japanese Empire. It also created a bicameral national assembly, the Diet, with a House of Peers, and a popularly elected House of Representatives, to be chosen by an electorate representing about one percent of the total population (*Nihon-no Rekishi* 1959–61, 11:83).

Japan received its first constitution more than twenty years after the collapse of the Tokugawa shogunate. By that time, the Meiji rulers had created a centralized bureaucratic government, which the Constitution helped to legitimize. The Constitution was a gift from the rulers to the people rather than a response to popular demand, and represented a continuation of the Japanese tradition of governmental action in the best interests of the nation, as determined by the government leaders.

### The Japanese Understanding of the Concept of Rights

In Western thought, rights normally imply corresponding duties on the part of others. If an individual has the right of free speech, the government has a duty not to interfere with the exercise of that right. Similarly, property rights imply that others have duties not to interfere with the protected uses of the property. But not all obligations and responsibilities in Western societies are linked to rights. Parents, for example, have nonspecific obligations to provide proper care and upbringing for their children, but the children do not have a corresponding set of specific rights that they can demand of their parents. The proper upbringing of a child depends on the quality of care and education it receives in the entire range of family activities. Parents have a moral responsibility to provide that upbringing, but that responsibility cannot be reduced to a specific set of rights that a child may legitimately demand. In fact, to define the relationship in terms of rights could, by limiting the responsibility of parents, encourage them to give inadequate care to their children.[11]

The emphasis on nonspecific obligations is an important aspect of Japanese ethical thought. Two ideas central to the Japanese ethos during the long feudal era were the concepts of *on* and *giri*. *On* refers to a nonspecific sense of indebtedness and gratitude in hierarchical relationships, particularly of the bushi toward his lord (called *chū*) and of a child toward its parents (called *kō*) for their benevolent care and sacrifice. This concept is expressed in writings as far back as eighth-century Japanese legends, but during the Tokugawa era, the idea of *on* toward one's ancestors, lord, and parents gained prominence in Japanese Confucian teachings (S. Sakurai 1971, pp. 77–98). The Chinese had always placed priority on *kō*, filial piety, but the Japanese Confucians all taught that *chū*, loyalty to one's lord, overrode *kō*. Aruga (1966–71, 4:323–24) attributes this to the strong emphasis the Japanese had historically placed on the importance of the social functions of individuals. An individual had the obligation to serve his lord and parents, not simply as individuals, but as figures who personified (or occupied) important social positions. But his obligation to his lord would supersede the obligation to his parents.

*Giri* is another concept of obligation in Confucian teaching. In Chinese, *giri*[12] meant the correct way for a man to follow, particularly in relations between a feudal lord and his subjects. It appears that a Buddhist monk first introduced this word to the Japanese during the Kamakura period (1185–1333). However, it, too, became important among the bushi class only during the Tokugawa period (S. Sakurai 1971, pp. 175–78).

As Tokugawa society matured, merchants began to adopt the values of the bushi class, including the idea of *giri*. Among merchants, however, *giri* was understood as the obligation to repay a kindness shown by someone who was of equal status, or to keep a promise. In other words, the meaning of the word *giri* shifted from the more general sense of proper conduct, which included the concept of obligation, to obligation itself.[13] As its use spread among the merchant class, *giri* came to be linked to *ninjō*, which has a wide range of meaning, extending from

11. In an insightful article, Onora O'Neill (1988) discusses the problems inherent in defining the children's welfare in terms of positive rights.

12. All Sino-Japanese words are given in their Japanese pronunciations.

13. Ruth Benedict (1946, p. 116) translated *on* as "obligations passively incurred," and *giri* as "duty." Takie Sugiyama Lebra (1976, p. 91) gives a similar description: "From the donor's point

"sympathy," "empathy," and "compassion," to "love between a man and a woman." By the middle of the seventeenth century, the expression *giri-ninjō* had become the most popular theme of Japanese theater. *Giri* referred to a person's obligation to repay indebtedness, while *ninjō* referred to the other's compassion or benevolence in receiving it (S. Sakurai 1971, pp. 178–86; Minamoto 1969, chapter 3).

As the illustration of the responsibilities of parents toward children shows, responsibilities and obligations do not always imply corresponding rights in the party to whom they are owed. While a person may have *on* and/or *giri* toward another, the beneficiary does not have the right to demand performance of that obligation in specific ways. In fact, demanding performance violates *giri*. Moreover, the beneficiary is expected to temper any expectations of performance with benevolence, or *ninjō*.

More generally, the emphasis on *on* and *giri*, rather than on rights, reflects a profound difference in the way the Japanese view the relationship of the individual to society. The Japanese never see themselves primarily as individuals, but as participants in social relations with other people, and they identify with roles they are expected to perform. They do not emphasize their claims against their group or community so much as their obligation to contribute to the smooth and harmonious functioning of society. As with the obligations of parents to children, these obligations are nonspecific, and depend to a considerable extent on the nature of the context (Noda 1976, pp. 174–75).

In contrast, Americans conceive of most social relations as a matter of choice, so they tend to see social obligations as voluntary or contractual, and limited by the act of choice that brought them into being (Varenne 1977, pp. 40–41). Should social demands and obligations become too heavy, an American may feel that society is infringing on his rights, or autonomy.

These contrasting views of social relations carry over even more strongly to beliefs about government. Historically, Americans have defined their relationship to government largely in terms of rights and duties. From an American perspective, therefore, the Meiji Constitution was defective in not providing effective protection for individual rights. Although the Constitution defined certain rights, these rights were gifts of the Emperor rather than inherent in the people. The government could limit those rights, and there were no provisions in the Constitution stating what those limits were. In addition, the executive

---

of view, *on* refers to a social credit, while from the receiver's point of view, it means a social debt." She translates *giri* simply as "social obligations" (p. 46).

branch of the government was to a considerable extent independent of the Diet.

For the Japanese, however, the Meiji Constitution was consistent with their view of social relations, and their acceptance of a hierarchical social order as natural and desirable. As we have already noted, the Cabinet had been established prior to the Constitution, and the Constitution did not give the Diet much control over it. Itō, along with most Japanese, distrusted political parties, seeing them as self-interested factions, unconcerned with ruling for the benefit of the nation as a whole.[14] They did their best to ensure that the rulers, rather than the majority party, retained the power to organize the government. Both their attitude toward individual rights, and their distrust of political parties were natural consequences of standard Confucian views about the obligations and responsibilities of rulers.

As noted earlier, one of the teachings of Ogyū Sorai and his followers, neglected by the neo-Confucian schools, was that the virtues of wisdom and benevolence were acquired only by the political rulers. It was the king's responsibility to select those who had developed special talents, promote them into the ranks of the bureaucracy, and "make them work for the peace and security of the people" (Maruyama 1974, pp. 90–91). Ronald Dore (1985, pp. 208–9), in discussing ideas about the responsibility of benevolence in rulers, elaborates on this Confucian attitude toward authority as follows:

> In a society which starts from the premise of original virtue, as Confucian societies did, it is possible for things to be different, especially since Confucian writings devote not as much time, it is true, but some time, to underlining the duties of benevolence in rulers as well as the duties of obedient loyalty in subordinates. They promise—though naturally Emperors and Shoguns did not dwell on the fact—that a ruler who fails in benevolence will very properly be overthrown by popular revolt, for if the people are so oppressed that they rise in rebellion then this will be proof that the mandate of heaven has been withdrawn. The word usually translated as benevolence, of course, does not mean welfare paternalism, but rather a general sense of responsibility for others and for the social order, an abstention from greed,

---

14. It is worth noting that many of America's Founding Fathers had a similar view of organized opposition to the government. Madison's well-known comments about factions in *Federalist* no. 10 reflected the conventional wisdom of the time, and Americans did not begin to see political parties as legitimate and necessary institutions until some time after the establishment of the U.S. Constitution (J. Miller 1960, chapter 7).

concern for the interests and dignity of subjects, a concern for justice, tempered with the optimistic faith which puts more reliance on the judicious use of rewards than on punishments.

In Tokugawa Japan, rebellions were "always protest rebellions, based on the Confucian premise that rulers could be and *ought to be*, benevolent, and that a desperate life-risking protest might call them back to the path of virtue" (Dore 1985, p. 209). The *on* relationship between the ruler and the ruled was parallel to that of a parent and child. Therefore, just as the relationship between parent and child cannot be defined by a set of specific obligations, it was not possible for the Japanese to delineate the relationship between ruler and ruled in terms of a list of rights and duties. When the ruler failed to fulfill his obligations, it was difficult for the ruled to say exactly how he had failed. They could only say that he did not rule as well as he should have.

The Meiji Restoration fit this pattern. It was the work of a talented group of bushi determined to revitalize Japanese government, acting for what they believed to be the best interests of the country as a whole. The Tokugawa bakufu had proved itself increasingly ineffective over a long period of time. The initial aim of the Restoration leaders was to create a government capable of ruling effectively and building the strength and prestige of Japan. The subsequent dismantling of the feudal political structure was a response to the needs of the moment, as perceived by the leaders, rather than a preconceived goal. Moreover, although there was widespread discontent before the collapse of the bakufu, there was no popular movement for a new political order based on a different set of governing principles.

The Restoration brought extensive social and political change, but it is important not to lose sight of the significant continuities as well, particularly the reliance on and deference to leadership. Sansom (1970, p. 185) points out that one reason why the Restoration was so successful was that the Japanese had long been trained to respect authority, and the privileged classes were still moved by a strong sense of responsibility and loyalty to their leaders. Traditional views concerning social hierarchy remained strong despite the abolition of feudal institutions and the accompanying social rules and duties. There had been no movement for social and political equality during the Tokugawa era, and such a movement did not arise as a result of the Restoration. The old habits of deference to social superiors continued virtually unabated.[15]

---

15. In his autobiography, Fukuzawa Yukichi (1966, pp. 243–44; 1980–81, 10:233), one of the most prominent intellectuals of the Meiji era, recalls an incident that occurred while he and

## Three Significant Intellectual Figures

Evidence of continuity of Confucian ways of thinking is found in the writings of Japanese thinkers who introduced into Japan the Western political philosophy of rights. Japanese intellectuals had developed a keen interest in Western political thought and constitutional government during the latter part of the Tokugawa era, when the bakufu was struggling to reform its entrenched feudal system. [16] They were exposed to the language of rights for the first time in William Martin's Chinese translation of Henry Wheaton's *Elements of International Law*, published in 1864. Martin sometimes used an ancient Chinese word, *kenri*, composed of the characters *ken*, meaning "power," and *ri*, meaning "advantage/interests/profit," and sometimes simply the character *ken* to translate "right"; and a relatively new word, *gimu*, for "duty." In the Japanese translation published in Edo the following year, the Japanese adopted these two Chinese expressions (Noda 1979, pp. 4, 11, 22).

The Japanese learned about the American Revolution and the U.S. Constitution from Elijah Coleman Bridgeman's two-volume history of America, written in Chinese in 1861. Fukuzawa Yukichi (1835–1901) provided the first Japanese translation of the U.S. Constitution, including most of the Bill of Rights, in his enormously popular *Seiyō Jijō* (The Conditions of the West), published in 1866. [17] The following year Tsuda Mamichi (1829–1903) published *Taisei Kokuhō-ron* (Treatise on the Laws of the Occidental Countries), consisting of notes on the lectures he received from Simon Vissering (1818–1888), a noted Dutch scholar and professor at Leyden University, while he was on the bakufu mission to Europe during 1862–65. [18] Both Tsuda and Fukuzawa tried to assimilate the concept of rights to the Confucian idea of *bun*, which usually

his family were walking along the seashore near Kamakura in the early 1870s. A mounted farmer, recognizing Fukuzawa as a *shizoku* (former bushi), immediately jumped off his horse and began apologizing profusely. Fukuzawa had to order him to remount. Even though the government had abolished the rule that only a bushi might ride a horse in public, Fukuzawa was exasperated to discover that this farmer continued to follow the old customs, fearing the anger of the bushi.

16. Beckmann (1957, p. 26) notes that, as early as 1843, the daimyo of Echizen *han* had the Dutch constitution translated.

17. Fukuzawa wrote *Seiyō Jijō* after his trip to the United States in 1861 as part of the bakufu envoy, and his trip to Europe the following year. Two hundred and fifty thousand copies of this book were sold immediately (Shimizu 1971–74, 1:145). Together with *Gakumon-no Susume* (An Encouragement of Learning; see Fukuzawa 1969; 1980–81, vol. 3) published in a series of seventeen small books during 1872–76, it became a classic. Several million copies of the two books were sold during the Meiji era (Najita 1974, p. 88).

18. Tsuda Mamichi was one of the first Japanese to study Western law. Along with Fukuzawa, he was one of the most active intellectual leaders of the Meiji era, but unlike Fukuzawa, he also participated actively in the government throughout his life.

refers to one's role or share in society. But this effort reveals a fundamental misunderstanding of the Western concept.

In the preface to *Taisei Kokuhō-ron*, Tsuda says that the original meaning of the terms "droit," "right," and "recht," was *shōjiki*, "the correct way," but that it had acquired various other meanings. The first two illustrate his understanding of rights:

1. It is the opposite of *gi*, "duty," and [one] should translated [it] as *ken*. For example, the borrower has *gi* to pay, and the lender has *ken* to demand/request this. This usage is most common in legal studies, and therefore, [one] should translate *hō-gaku* (legal study) also as *ken-gaku* (study of rights).
2. [One] should translate [right] as *bun*. Each individual has his *bun*. It is the child's *bun* to succeed his father at his death. Selling and buying are the *bun* of a merchant, and planting is the *bun* of a farmer. Others may not contest them. (Meiji Bunka Kenkyū-kai 1967–74, 13:68–69; my translation)

Had he confined himself to the first illustration, his exposition would have been consistent with the standard American understanding of rights. But the meaning of *bun* in the second illustration is "part," "role," or "share," so Tsuda seems to be suggesting that a person's rights (and duties) are associated with his social role. Such usage implies that rights vary according to social position, an idea that is inconsistent with the prevalent Western view that all people have equal rights, whatever their place in society.

Tsuda's discussion of the rights of the people against the state reveals further difficulties. To begin with, he entitles this discussion *Kokka-ni Taishite Jūmin Yū-suru Tokoro-no Tsū-ken*: "The Rights that the People have in Relation to (*taishite*) the Nation." The Japanese expression *taishite* is ambiguous. It is usually translated as "to," "toward," or "in contrast to," and does not necessarily convey the strong sense of opposition that the English word "against" does. Thus, it is not clear how well he understood the idea that rights are limits placed on governmental action by the people.

He also uses the compound *tsū-ken*, as well as *kenri*, and *ken*, to stand for "rights." It is not clear whether he intended to distinguish *tsū-ken* from the other two translations of the word. The first four definitions of rights show that he is thinking at least partially in Confucian terms. In my translation, they read as follows:

1. The right (*tsū-ken*) of the people is that the state (*kokka*) should first accomplish the original intent of establishing

the body politic (*kokka*). With the resources under its management, the state (*kokka*) should increase the happiness of the entire nation, maintain its sovereignty, protect the people's rights and peace (*kenri-heian*), maintain order and courtesy in the nation, unify the people, promote mutual nurturing, and thus increase the national welfare. The people can require these of the state (*kokka*).[19]

2. The various rights (*shoken*) listed above, which the people require of the state (*kokka*), are the public duties (*kōgi*) and public responsibility (*kōmu*) of the state (*kokka*).[20] However, these duties (*gimu*) are the duties (*gimu*) of the state (*kokka*) in Confucianism, so it is difficult to regard them as promises of the state (*kokka*) by law. Therefore, the people should not demand them of the state (*kokka*) by legal arguments.

3. But the people have fundamental rights (*honken*) in relation to (*taishite*) the nation (*kokka*) and can exercise them. At times, they should protect them by legal arguments.

4. [One] should list the fundamental rights (*honken*) of the people in the nation's (*kokka's*) constitution and protect them. But the law determines when the people should forgo them for the welfare of the nation (*kokka*). (Meiji Bunka Kenkyū-kai 1967–74, 13:85)

He then goes on to enumerate several fundamental rights, such as independence, freedom of thought, speech and writing, and the right to petititon the government. These comments reveal that Tsuda understands rights as a blend of Western and Confucian ideas. While he recognizes certain basic individual rights, he stresses the "right" of the

19. The word *kokka* has various meanings in Japanese. For instance, *Kenkyusha's New Japanese-English Dictionary* (4th ed. 1974, p. 893) gives "state," "country," "nation" and "body politic" in this order. *Hōritsu-gaku Shō-jiten* (Abridged Dictionary of Legal Study; 1972, p. 319) gives "territory" (*ryōdo*), "the people" (*kokumin*), and "sovereign power" (*tōchi-ken*). Japanese does not distinguish these ideas clearly, so the translation is my interpretation of Tsuda's meaning.

The distinction between state and nation, state and community, or state and society is a commonplace in Western political thought. With that distinction it is easy to develop the idea that the rulers are, in some sense, the servants of the ruled, and that the people have rights against the state. Conversely, without that linguistic distinction, it may be difficult to conceive of state and society, or state and nation, as different entities. As we have already seen, in Confucian thought the state or government is not clearly distinguishable from the people, at least in part because they are not supposed to be distinct.

20. Tsuda separated the two characters, *gi* and *mu* of *gimu*, meaning "duty," and combined each with *kō* in *kō-gi* and *kō-mu*. Although it is difficult to determine how Tsuda differentiated the meanings of these two characters, I have translated them as "public duty," and "public responsibility," respectively. *Kōmu*, in contemporary usage, means "public service," or "official business," and a compound, *kōmu-in*, denotes "civil servant." *Kōgi* is not a commonly used word.

people to have the government rule for the benefit and well-being of the people, and the society as a whole. The government has a corresponding nonspecific obligation to rule in this manner, much as parents have an obligation to provide for the well-being and upbringing of their children. Tsuda recognizes that these claims are Confucian in nature, and should not be pursued by legal means.[21] Justified legal claims can be based only on rights protected by law, but even these rights are subordinate to the general welfare, as determined by law. While such a conception of rights represents an advance over the previously unlimited rule sanctioned by the Confucian tradition, it is far more Confucian than Western in spirit. Indeed, the lack of precision in the relationship between the government and the people reflected in the title of Tsuda's discussion appropriately illustrates, in a manner no doubt unintended by him, the interesting mixture of the Western and Confucian ideas expressed in this chapter.

Fukuzawa Yukichi was the most prominent man of letters during the Meiji period, and in many ways the most liberal. The central theme running through most of his writings was the importance of self-reliance, both in individuals and the nation. His political writings are free from the suspicion of partisan bias, since he consistently refused to join or adhere to any political party.[22] Yet even Fukuzawa retained Confucian elements in his thought—ideas that did not fit well with his notion of limited government. This Confucian strain emerges from time to time in his translation of the Constitution of the United States, suggesting that he did not thoroughly understand some of the key concepts of American democracy.

One example is the idea of checks and balances among the three branches of the government. Article 2, Section 2 of the U.S. Constitution states that the president must gain the "advice and consent" of the Senate in making certain key appointments. Fukuzawa's translation suggests that, while he did not look upon the president of the United States as the same as the Emperor, he did not understand that the Founding Fathers were determined to check his power. Section 2 reads, in part:

> He [The president] shall have power, by and with the advice
> and consent of the Senate, to make treaties, provided two-
> thirds of the Senators present concur; and he shall nomi-

---

21. O'Neill (1988) makes the same point in her article on children's rights.

22. Fukuzawa founded Keiō Gijuku, in Edo, in 1858. This small school for Dutch studies eventually became Keiō University, Japan's most prestigious private university. Fukuzawa devoted his life to educating and enlightening the Japanese people in preparation for modern life.

nate, and by and with the advice and consent of the Senate, shall appoint ambassadors, other public ministers and consuls, judges of the Supreme Court, and all other officers of the United States.

Fukuzawa's translation reads as follows:

The president will confer with (*shōgi shi*) the members of the Senate, and in case two-thirds of the senators concur, make treaties with foreign nations. Also he has the right to appoint, in conference with (*shōgi shi*) the members of the Senate, ambassadors, other public ministers and consuls, judges of the Upper Court, and other officers of the United States.[23] (My translation)

His use of the term *shōgi shi*, which simply means "engage in conference," or "confer," is ambiguous, and suggests that Fukuzawa did not grasp the significance of the phrase "advice and consent," with its two distinctly different terms. He may not have understood that the president need not accept the advice of the Senate, but could not act without its consent.

Another example is the translation of the Second Amendment, which fails to convey the sense that the people place explicit limits on the government's power:

A well regulated militia being necessary to the security of a free state, the right of the people to keep and bear arms shall not be infringed.

His version, in my translation, reads:

Because it is urgently necessary for people to maintain a militia in a nation where laws are lenient, [one] should permit (*yurusu-beshi*) everyone of the people to keep and bear arms.[24]

This translation implies that, if and when laws are strict, the government could legitimately prevent the people from bearing arms. It fails to recognize that the Constitution does not qualify this right, which is inherent in the people.

23. *Daitōryō-wa, Jōin-no gijikan-to shōgi shite, gijikan-no zen'in sambun-no-ni dōi sure-ba, gaikoku-to jōyaku-o musubu beshi. Mata, Jōin-no gijikan-to shōgi shite, gaikoku-e kensa suru shisetsu, minisutoru, konshuru, oyobi Jōkyoku-no saibanshi, sono hoka Gasshū-koku-no sho-yūshi-o meizuru-no ken ari* (Fukuzawa 1980–81, 1:155).

24. *Hōritsu-no kan naru kuni-ni oite-wa gōhei-o yashinau koto kin'yō naru-ga yue-ni, kokumin mina buki-o takuwae buki-o tazusaeru-o yurusu-beshi* (Ibid., 1:158).

Fukuzawa's next influential book, *Gakumon-no Susume* (An Encouragement of Learning), published in 1872, gives a systematic explanation of the proper role of the government and its relationship to the people. It provides a far more complete picture of Fukuzawa's views on limited government, and shows that he did not grasp the importance of institutional checks on power that are so crucial in the U.S. Constitution. He says (1980–81, 3:89) that civilization does not rise from either the government or the people alone, but succeeds or flourishes where the the government and people stand side by side. Each has a function, or *shokubun*, to perform. The word *shokubun* consists of *shoku*, meaning "vocation," and *bun*, meaning "share," or "function," and it is probably most appropriately translated as "responsibility." [25] Fukuzawa advocates very limited responsibilities for the government, something like the "watchdog" state of nineteenth-century British liberalism. The government is the representative, or proxy (*myōdai*) of the people, and should handle affairs according to popular wishes. Its function is merely to provide order by arresting criminals and protecting the citizens. But the people must obey the laws created by their own representatives. They have the responsibility of establishing a government to protect them, and then of firmly abiding by the laws that provide this protection (ibid., 3:91–94).

Fukuzawa gives little attention to the problem that worried the Americans—how to protect the citizens and their rights from the government. A government strong enough to protect the people is also strong enough to oppress them, but Fukuzawa does not see the danger of governmental abuse of power. He likens the nation to a commercial company, with the government as the manager or head of the company, chosen by its members. The people are the masters, for they appoint government officials to serve as managers. But Fukuzawa (ibid., 3:102) gives the people no controls over the managers, and states that, if government officials engage in misconduct, the people must not complain. The proper remedy is that the people should always pay attention to governmental affairs. When there are things that worry them, they must warn the officials kindly, and quietly, without hesitation, discuss the matter with them. He apparently believes that if the people are always vigilant, and discuss matters as soon as there is any suspicion

25. Chapter 7 (ibid., 3:99–106) is entitled "Kokumin-no Shokubun-o Ron-zu" (Discussing the People's Shokubun). David A. Dilworth and Umeyo Hirano, in their translation of this book, use "duties" to stand for *shokubun* (Fukuzawa 1969, p. 41). To me, "duty" conveys the idea of specific obligations. I believe that Fukuzawa had a more general, nonspecific idea in mind.

that officials are acting inappropriately, real abuse of power will not occur. Thus, he does not see the need for the people to have the means of controlling, replacing, or punishing undesirable government officials.

Fukuzawa deals with governmental oppression in a similar manner. The people have three ways to deal with a government that violates its own boundary (*bungen*)—they can abandon their sense of integrity and submit to the government, fight against it using force or power, or adhere to their rightful principles at the risk of their lives. Fukuzawa recommends the third alternative. He believes government officials will eventually come to understand the people's plight, and will repent and reform themselves (ibid., 3:102–5).

Fukuzawa's recommendation shows that, although he advocated a limited government, his reasoning was quite different from that embodied in American democracy. Rather than fearing excessive power, he simply believed that the government had a limited role to play. Perhaps he shared the Confucian premise of original virtue, and trusted that the government would ultimately rule the nation for the welfare and benefit of the people. Such trust probably made it difficult for him to appreciate the American concept of rights and limited government, even though he understood that greater freedom would encourage self-reliance and autonomy.

The final writer to be considered is Ueki Emori (1857–1892), one of the most radical thinkers of the Popular Rights Movement, and the leading theorist of the Jiyū-tō.[26] Unlike Tsuda, who actively participated in governmental affairs, and Fukuzawa, who stayed out of the government and concentrated on educating the people to become responsible citizens, Ueki devoted himself to party politics, promoting the rights of the people against the government, in the belief that the people and the government had different and incompatible interests.[27]

26. Ueki decided to enter politics in 1874, at the age of seventeen, when he first heard Itagaki speak in his home town in Tosa. Unlike his predecessors, who had to learn French and English to read Western political philosophy, Ueki never had to learn these languages. By the 1870s, there were translations of most works of Western political thought, and he apparently read Rousseau, Bentham, Spencer and others in translation (Ienaga 1955, pp. 9–25).

27. In an article entitled "Jimmin-no Kokka-ni Tai-suru Seishin-o Ronzu" (On the Spirit of the Relationship Between the People and the Government), which appeared in the journal *Aikoku Shin-shi* on November 12, 1880, Ueki says, "The government and the people have different interests, and they are incompatible. It is very good for the nation (*kokka*) that its government and the people have different interests." (Meiji Bunka Kenkyū-kai 1967–74, 14:120; my translation). It is noteworthy that in this and many other writings, Ueki uses the term *jimmin* to refer to "the people." This term connotes "the people who have liberted themselves from oppressors" (see chapter 5, pp. 189–90). Nevertheless, as will be shown in the remainder of the discussion on Ueki, his ideas on the relationship between the Emperor and the people, and his use of expressions, are not entirely consistent with the above comment.

Moreover, he espoused the radical idea that the people had the right to overthrow a government that failed to adhere to the constitution and protect the rights and liberties of the people.[28]

Despite his emphasis on natural rights, Ueki did not advocate a pure form of popular sovereignty, but joint sovereignty of the Emperor and the people. He stated this view in *Minken Jiyū-ron* (A Theory of Popular Rights and Freedom), written in 1879:

> The constitution (*kempō*) is the nation's law, or the fundamental law and is the foundation of the state. First, the people and the Emperor should consult each other and determine broadly what rights and duties the Emperor and the people should have, respectively. [The constitution] will then outline the ways of governing, which the Emperor and the government cannot change as they please, and according to which they will perform respective responsibilities (*shokubun*). (Meiji Bunka Kenkyū-kai 1967–74, 2:190; my translation)

Thus, he distinguished both the Emperor and the people from the government, with the implication that the government derived its authority from the Emperor and the people acting together.[29] This view also appears in an essay published in 1880, in which Ueki encouraged the people, who were not aware of their proper role in politics, to ask the monarch directly for a national assembly.

> [I]f the people want a national assembly, they should go to the monarch and say, "We would like to have a national assembly, so give us permission to establish one." They should simply ask for it. But the awareness of the people is not sufficiently developed, so they are confused about the notion (*ryōken*) of the ruler and the ruled (the proper relationships of the ruler and the ruled) . . . The people do not know what they are, so some of them even think that individuals do not have the right to request the establishment of a national assembly because it is a national matter (*zenkoku*) (ibid., 14:117; my translation).

This passage also clearly implies that Ueki regarded the Emperor as a higher source of authority than the people themselves.[30]

The same idea reappears in the constitution he drafted at the height

28. Article 72 of Ueki's draft constitution. See p. 64 n. 32.

29. In this article, Ueki uses the term *kimi* to refer to the emperor, and *tami* to refer to the people. These are traditional terms, with no connotation of the ruler and the ruled in opposition to each other.

30. Here, Ueki uses *jimmin*, which is incongruent with the idea he is expressing.

of the Popular Rights Movement in the late summer of 1881, when various private individuals and groups were formulating constitutions.[31] It is an elaborate document, consisting of 220 articles in fifteen chapters. In one sense, it is a remarkably democratic constitution, listing thirty-five individual rights and liberties, most of which are included in the present Japanese Constitution. Among them is the right of the people to overthrow the government and establish a new one when the government violates the constitution, destroys their rights and liberties, and subverts the founding intent of the nation (Article 72).[32] No other constitution drafted at this time contained a similar statement of rights. Such a right is obviously not legally enforceable, but it indicates that Ueki had grasped the Western idea that rights are absolute limits on the government. The document has some nondemocratic features as well, since it calls for a hereditary emperor who apparently is jointly sovereign with the people, and is to have considerable power (Article 97).[33] Ueki provides only some weak checks on the emperor's power.

The proposed government consists of three branches, the legislative, executive, and judiciary. The legislative branch, called Rempō Rippō-in (Federal Legislative Council), is to be popularly elected (Articles 114 and 141).[34] The legislative council appoints and fires judges (Article 187), so the judiciary is not independent of the popularly elected leg-

31. This draft constitution, entitled *Tōyō Dai-Nihonkoku Kokken-an* (The Draft Constitution of the Great Japan of the Orient), was originally thought to have been written by Nakajima Nobuyuki and Furusawa Shigeru in 1882. But Suzuki Yasuzō, a distinguished constitutional scholar who found a draft of the document among Ueki's personal papers, thought that the ideas it set forth were much too radical for either of the alleged authors, but were very much like those espoused by Ueki in various other writings. Therefore, he decided that Ueki wrote this constitution (Suzuki 1948, pp. 265, 285–87). It appears that there is no longer any dispute about the authorship of this constitution. Suzuki does not state exactly when the document was drafted. Inada Masatsugu says that it was written in the summer of 1881, basing his remarks on a passage from Ueki's diary (1960–62, 1:402, 424). The text included in appendix 5 is from Itō 1934, pp. 207–37.

32. ARTICLE 72. If the government freely violates the constitution, freely damages the freedoms and rights of the people, or goes against the intent of the founding of the nation, the Japanese people can overthrow it and establish a new government.

This and all the other articles that I quote in this chapter are my own translations. I have not provided translations for articles whose direct translations do not differ significantly from the text citations.

33. ARTICLE 97. If the present Emperor abdicates, the legitimate imperial descendents will succeed to the imperial throne. . . .

Ueki uses the term *kōtei* to refer to the emperor, and *jimmin* to refer to the people in this constitution. *Kōtei* is a curious choice, because it is ordinarily used to refer only to foreign emperors, such as the famous ancient Chinese emperor, Shi-kōtei (Shih Huang Ti, in Chinese), who unified that country in 221 B.C., and Napoleon I, the emperor of France.

34. ARTICLE 114. The legislative right of the Japanese federation belongs to its people.
ARTICLE 141. As for the federation council members, the Japanese people will directly elect them.

islature. The constitution places executive power in the Emperor, who appoints the prime minister and other ministerial officers (Articles 165 and 168).[35] But there is no clause giving the Emperor power to fire them. Moreover, the executive and legislative branches are mutually independent because their respective members cannot serve in the other branch (Articles 148 and 174). The Emperor's power is checked by the legislature, in that he is not allowed to discard existing laws and replace them with his own (Article 91). But since he is allowed to dissolve the assembly of the legislative council in cases of disagreement, the Emperor has considerable power over that branch of the government as well. Ueki does place a limit on the Emperor's power in such situations by stipulating that he must call new elections within sixty days. He cannot then dissolve the assembly on the same issue that led to the first dissolution (Article 94).[36] The constitution also states that when the Emperor has difficulty in implementing the decisions of the council (which presumably would also include disagreements with the council), he can request it to study the issue again (Article 95).[37] But it does not indicate what is to happen if the council reaffirms its original position. Moreover, the Emperor is above the law; he is not accountable for his actions and cannot be punished (Articles 75 and 76).

The result is an executive branch, headed by the hereditary Emperor, that is not directly accountable to the people, and is accountable to the legislative council only in limited ways. In practice, such an executive could obviously threaten the rights of the people. Even the theoretical right to overthrow the government may be limited, as Ueki apparently does not believe the people have the right to overthrow the Emperor. The only protection Ueki provides is the right to petition the government, and a vague provision that the Emperor must consult the legislative council on the matters of individual rights (Articles 68 and 87).[38] Thus, rather than give the people the right to appeal to the indepen-

35. ARTICLE 165. The executive power of the Japanese federation belongs to the emperor.
ARTICLE 168. As for the emperor's executive rights, he will appoint the prime minister, define various governmental responsibilities and establish respective ministries, and appoint their heads.

36. ARTICLE 94. If the emperor disagrees with the assembly of the legislative council, he can dissolve the assembly. When [the emperor] dissolves the assembly, he must notify the electoral districts within three days. He must have the people elect new representatives and reconvene the assembly within sixty days. [The emperor] cannot dissolve the new assembly on the same matter that had led him to initially dissolve the assembly.

37. ARTICLE 95. When the emperor finds it difficult to implement the decisions of the legislative council, he can request it to study the issue again, provided that he gives a detailed explanation for his request.

38. ARTICLE 68. The Japanese people can present a memorial to the government in their names, and have the right to petition in their behalf. Public companies can present a memorial in the name of the company.

dent judiciary, he permits them to appeal to the government, though in his earlier writing, quoted above, he encourages the people to appeal directly to the emperor. It is not clear how such an appeal to the government or the emperor would work. The people might be able to control the legislative council through elections, but they would have little control over the emperor, who could dissolve the assembly of the legislative council.

Thus, despite his affirmation of individual rights, Ueki failed to provide adequate protection for the people by controlling the emperor and the executive branch of the government. He was probably well aware of the limited role of the Emperor in politics; along with the other Meiji reformers, he had a strong sense of loyalty and devotion to him, and did not see the need to curtail his powers, either against other branches of the government, or the people. His primary concern was the other branches of the government, which he knew from his own experience could become oppressive.

## Summary

From the beginning of the seventeenth to the middle of the nineteenth centuries, Japan was ruled by the Tokugawa bakufu. During these 250 years of peace and stability in virtual isolation from the outside world, the bakufu built a strong central bureaucracy in Edo, and kept the feudal domains throughout the country under strict control. The Emperor was retained in Kyoto, ostensibly as the spiritual head of the nation, giving legitimacy to the bakufu, but with no real political power. The Tokugawa government was overthrown partly because the bakufu was incapable of adjusting its policies to the emerging political, social, and economic forces, and partly because the Western powers in Asia made it impossible for Japan to remain secure in isolation.

The Meiji Restoration was staged by a group of bushi of unusual competence and foresight. These leaders brought the Emperor to the center of politics, and rapidly transformed Japan into a militarily strong, industrialized, modern nation. They were men with a strong Confucian belief in loyalty to the new leader, the Emperor, and an elitist sense of responsibility to rule the nation for the interests of the nation as a whole. They carried out reforms in a manner consistent with the pattern of government established by the Tokugawa bakufu, first establishing a central national government with a powerful bureaucratic

---

ARTICLE 87. The emperor cannot alone decide matters related to the rights of the people. . . . He must consult with the legislative council. Without discussion by the legislative council, decisions cannot be put into effect.

administration that continued and strengthened the bureaucratic rule established by the bakufu. Only after the government had been securely organized did they create a constitution, and a bicameral national assembly with an elected lower house. They did not provide this constitution in response to popular demand; rather, they realized that some form of constitutional government was essential to achieve their ends, and they chose a form that was consistent with the Tokugawa tradition and their own sense of responsibility for guiding the nation. Thus, the Meiji leaders established a new political system, and created various new social and economic institutions in a manner congenial to them, operating them in ways that were faithful to Tokugawa patterns of ideas and behavior.

The writings of the Meiji intellectuals who introduced the Japanese people to Western political philosophy and systems of government reveal that they failed to understand some of the key concepts of the Western political philosophy of individual rights: the relationship between the government and the people, and separation of powers among the branches of government. They interpreted those ideas in ways that were meaningful within their Confucian intellectual heritage, with its ideas of social hierarchy and the responsibility of leaders to rule the nation in the interests of the nation as a whole. The Meiji Restoration was in many ways a sharp break with the past, but in many other ways, it was a revitalization of the values of the Tokugawa social order.

## Three

# THE ROLE OF THE

# CONSTITUTION

### The Illocutionary Force of the Constitution

A constitution is the product of a particular political tradition and historical circumstances. Within this context, each constitution is written in a language that speaks to its audience in a particular way. It has an illocutionary force, be it commanding, asserting, promising, or committing, which reflects both the relationship between the government and the people and the role of the constitution in that country.[1] In this chapter, I will compare and contrast the language of the two modern Japanese constitutions with that of the U.S. Constitution, showing the similarities and differences in the ways those documents speak to their respective audiences. The contrast between the U.S. Constitution and the English version of the current Japanese Constitution on the one hand, and the two Japanese constitutions in Japanese on the other, illustrates important differences in the roles of the government and the constitution in the two societies.

I will begin with a brief review of the creation of Japan's two modern constitutions to point out one striking similarity between them. Next, I will sketch the creation of the U.S. Constitution to demonstrate how

---

1. "Illocutionary force" is a technical term in the philosophy of language, first introduced by J. L. Austin (1962) in connection with the phrase "illocutionary act." These terms were later refined by John R. Searle (1970) and have become standard terminology in speech act theories. When analyzing sentences in isolation, linguists and grammarians classify them as declarative, interrogative, etc., strictly on the basis of form. In actual use, speakers use these different types of sentences to perform different types of speech acts. For instance, when someone says "Close the window," the speaker has used an imperative sentence to perform the illocutionary act of commanding. The sentence type, however, does not always determine the nature of the illocutionary act. For instance, when a wife says to her husband, "I will be home by six o'clock," she may either be predicting that she will be home by six o'clock, or she may be promising to be back by then. In this instance, we would say that the illocutionary *act* that the wife has performed in saying what she did would have the illocutionary *force* of either a prediction or a promise, depending on the circumstances in which she utters it. See McCawley 1981, pp. 205–15, for a concise and clear discussion.

its language represents the people's commitment to create a democratic government, and their command to that government not to infringe their rights and liberties—a reflection of the special conception Americans have of their government. I will then demonstrate how, in creating a democratic constitution for the Japanese in 1946, the Americans used, to a considerable extent, the language of their own Constitution. This, however, resulted in an inconsistency in the illocutionary force of the Japanese Constitution as drafted in English, because the ostensible intention of the Americans was incompatible with their actual intention and actions. Finally, I will show how the Japanese drafters, in expressing democratic principles in Japanese, were able to change this constitutional language so that it would speak to the Japanese people, for the most part, in a manner similar to that of the Meiji Constitution. The Japanese version acknowledges the creation of a democratic government, and sets forth the shared responsibility of the government and the people to adhere to and promote their newly acquired democratic ideals for the good of the nation.

### The Process of Making the Two Japanese Constitutions

The Meiji leaders created Japan's first modern constitution primarily to win Western recognition of Japan as a modern nation, worthy of their respect, and thereby to gain a revision of the unequal treaties that Western nations had forced on the Tokugawa government. By the late nineteenth century, most leading European nations were constitutional monarchies, and the Japanese correctly realized that Japan had to adopt a constitution to persuade the Western powers to regard Japan as an equal.

A constitution was in the back of the Meiji rulers' minds almost from the beginning of the Restoration, but they first devoted their energies to creating the political and economic institutions necessary for modernizing the nation. Fifteen years after the overthrow of the Tokugawa government, once the first generation of leaders had consolidated its power, established a functioning governmental bureaucracy, and started the country on the road to industrialization, the younger leaders were ready to think about a constitution.

In March 1882, Itō Hirobumi and his associates went on a three-month tour of Europe to study European constitutions. In Berlin and Vienna, they conferred with German constitutional scholars, who advised them to establish a strong monarchical system by means of a constitution given to the people by the Emperor—advice that reinforced Itō's own authoritarian inclinations. After returning to Japan, Itō first

reorganized the government, becoming Japan's first prime minister in
1885. Then, from June 1887 to March 1888, he worked on the Meiji
Constitution in complete secrecy, with the help of three Japanese advisors, Inoue Kowashi, Itō Miyoji, and Kaneko Kentarō, and a German
scholar, Carl Friedrich Hermann Roesler. Itō purposely avoided any
participation by his political opponents, fearing that if he even allowed
them to debate it in the National Diet, he would not be able to establish the imperial constitution he envisioned (Akita 1967, pp. 63–66).
On February 11, 1889, Itō and his associates promulgated the Constitution of the Empire of Japan in the name of the Emperor.

As Tōyama Shigeki (1985, p. 23) puts it, the Meiji Constitution was
"a book of instructions to be taken to heart, setting forth the fundamental rules of politics and governmental affairs for the rulers of the
nation" (my translation). The Japanese leaders assumed both the authority and the responsibility of ruling in the name of the Emperor, for
the good of the nation as a whole. The Japanese people themselves had
nothing to do with its creation, although they participated in the grand
celebration of its enactment. The great majority did not even know
its contents (Gluck 1985, pp. 42–49; Koseki Shōichi, pers. comm.,
March 17, 1986). If they thought about it at all, they simply assumed
that the government bureaucrats and constitutional scholars had the
task of studying the new Constitution, and steering the nation according to its directions.

The process of creating Japan's second modern constitution exhibits
some striking parallels. In 1946, the Americans, like the Meiji oligarchs, decided on the basic principles of the new government, and
gave the Japanese a new constitution reflecting those principles. A
handful of individuals in MacArthur's headquarters, who aspired to
transform Japan into a democratic nation acceptable to the Americans
and the other allies (excluding the USSR), drafted the initial version.
Japanese government officials negotiated with them in secrecy until the
two sides agreed on a document that could be made public. Unlike the
members of the First Imperial Diet, the members of the 90th Imperial
Diet, in 1946, had a chance to debate the Constitution, but they played
no part in formulating it, and made only a few minor changes in its
text. Once again, the ordinary people of Japan did not participate directly, and had no voice in selecting the principles incorporated in the
document. The new Constitution was promulgated by imperial mandate, following the procedure specified in the Meiji Constitution. It was
presented to the Japanese people in the name of the Emperor, just as
the Meiji Constitution had been, a half-century earlier. Democracy was
thus imposed on the Japanese from above.

## The Creation of the U.S. Constitution

The creation of the Constitution of the United States is a very different story. After their victory in the Revolutionary War, the Americans tried to govern themselves under the Articles of Confederation. In the eyes of many, this experience was unsatisfactory, and there was considerable sentiment in favor of revising the Articles to strengthen the central government. A convention to be held in Annapolis in September 1786 for the purpose of revising the Articles failed to attract enough state delegates to constitute a quorum. Those who did attend proposed that invitations be sent, requesting the states to send delegates to another convention, in Philadelphia, next year. When the delegates to the Constitutional Convention gathered in Philadelphia in May of 1787, however, they immediately set about establishing an entirely new form of government rather than reforming the Articles of Confederation. They drafted the new constitution as a compact, not between the existing government and people, but between the people and a new government, to be created by the people for their own benefit.

The delegates themselves had not been elected by the people, and could not claim to represent the people or the nation as a whole. Therefore, the Constitution provided that it would not become effective until ratified by popularly elected, special conventions in nine states. Gordon Wood (1969, pp. 306–43) argues that it was the invention of these constitutional conventions that was the most original American contribution to the practice of democratic government. They provided a mechanism by which the people, through elected representatives, could participate in deciding how they would actually be governed. It was certainly a remarkable effort to give the citizens of the various states an important voice in the formation of their government. After the ratification, the Americans could justly claim to have created a government that in some sense exhibited popular sovereignty.[2]

The Preamble of the Constitution forcefully proclaims that the people of the United States are creating a government to serve certain definite purposes:

> We, the people of the United States, in order to form a more perfect union, establish justice, ensure domestic tranquillity, provide for the common defence, promote the general wel-

---

2. Of course, this is an oversimplication or, as Edmund Morgan (1988) would put it a "fiction." The story of how ratification was actually accomplished in the state conventions is well told by Forrest McDonald (1965). The political maneuvering to obtain the delegates' votes will dispel any illusions that the ratification was the direct expression of public opinion. Moreover, many Americans, including Native Americans, blacks, and women, had no vote.

fare, and secure the blessings of liberty to ourselves and our posterity, do ordain and establish this Constitution for the United States of America.

Yet, Americans had serious misgivings about government, having recently rebelled against a government that many of them regarded as oppressive. Therefore, they created a government of strictly limited powers. For many Americans, even this limited government seemed too dangerous. To secure the ratification of the Constitution, its proponents promised, and later secured, the adoption of the Bill of Rights, consisting of the first ten amendments to the Constitution. The end result was a government whereby the people agreed to commit themselves to a certain form of political organization, and surrendered some of their rights and liberties to the government for the sake of protecting the remainder of their freedoms. That commitment is expressed through the use of the modal "shall" throughout the Constitution.

The English modal "shall" is used in at least four distinct senses. Sometimes it is used simply to refer to an event in the future, as in "I shall go to church on Sunday." In other contexts, it is used to express the speaker's commitment to do something. Thus, in the example just given, the speaker may be expressing his determination to go to church on Sunday. When the speaker says "You shall go to church on Sunday," on the other hand, he may be expressing his determination or commitment to get his addressee to go to church on Sunday. In still other cases, such as "Thou shalt not kill," the commitment is expressed as a command, or the imposition of an obligation, with the implication that the speaker has the power to enforce that command or obligation. Finally, in some situations, the statement of command may be weak or even missing. Legal documents, such as contracts, often express obligations by the use of "shall," where the context is one of obligation created by mutual agreement rather than by command. The precise sense that the speaker intends cannot be determined from the linguistic form alone; that sense becomes clear only from the context in which it is uttered.[3]

The U.S. Constitution uses "shall" in the second and third senses, that is, to express the people's commitment to creating a democratic government, and to command the government not to violate their rights and liberties.[4] Article 1, Section 1 is an example of the use of "shall" to state a commitment:

3. The specification of the precise meanings and uses of the English modals, "shall," "must," "may," etc., has been one of the major topics of contemporary semantics and pragmatics, and linguists have not yet reached a consensus on many questions.

4. Austin (1962, pp. 150–58) initially identified "shall" as one of the verbal expressions used in utterances that have a "commissive" illocutionary force, committing the speaker to a certain

> All legislative powers herein granted, shall be vested in a Congress of the United States, which shall consist of a Senate and House of Representatives.

By this statement, the American people commit themselves to place all legislative powers in Congress.

The First Amendment provides an example of command:

> Congress shall make no law respecting an establishment of religion, or prohibiting the free exercise thereof; or abridging the freedom of speech, or of the press; or the right of the people peaceably to assemble, and to petition the Government for a redress of grievances.

In this article, the people command the government not to encroach on the various freedoms mentioned.

The U.S. Constitution is remarkably consistent in its use of "shall." All instances fall into one of these two categories. The clauses creating the institutions of government convey the "commitment" sense, while the clauses protecting rights express the "command" sense. The result is a document whereby the people commit themselves to a particular form of representative democracy, and then command that government not infringe on those rights and liberties they have retained for themselves. The institutions created provide the means by which the people can change both the representatives and the institutions if the government does not follow those commands. Thus, both in theory and in linguistic expression, sovereign power resides in the people of the United States.

## The American Draft of the Japanese Constitution

Unlike the framers of the U.S. Constitution, who had several months to debate their ideas, and Gouverneur Morris, a superb literary craftsman, to compose the final version of document, the Americans in 1946 had only one week to prepare the initial version of a democratic constitution for Japanese. Initially, they had delegated this task to the Japa-

---

course of action, and Searle (1979, pp. 1–29) later refined the idea. F. R. Palmer (1986, p. 115) notes that this usage is restricted to sentences with only a second or third person subject, as in "You shall go to the circus" and "John shall have the book tomorrow"; how strongly these statements are interpreted, that is, whether they are intended and accepted simply as a promise or threat, depends on the context. It appears Austin and Searle would regard the utterance of sentences with "shall" conveying both what I call the "commitment" sense and the "command" sense as having commissive illocutionary force. Since my purpose is to clarify the uses of "shall" in the Constitution, I will distinguish sentences with "shall" having the illocutionary force of commitment from those having the force of command.

nese government, but found that they could not trust its officials to prepare the kind of document they had in mind. They wanted to educate the Japanese people in democratic principles, as well as establish popular sovereignty on their behalf. So they drafted a constitution that, in effect, presented some of their own principles of limited government as a gift to the Japanese.

In addition to their own Constitution, the New Deal was another influence on the American drafters. Unlike Americans of the late eighteenth century, who feared government, and therefore tried to impose strict limits on what it might do, the principal American drafters of the Japanese Constitution were New Dealers, who believed that government might take an active role in promoting the welfare and security of its citizens. Many of them saw themselves as playing a similar role in Japan. Thus they included Article XXIV, proclaiming that "laws shall be designed for the promotion and extension of social welfare."[5]

These circumstantial differences were enough to ensure that this "American" constitution would be quite different both in tone and in content from the one created by their forefathers. But Americans in 1946 believed in the universal appeal of American democracy, including the principle of limited government. It apparently did not occur to MacArthur, or to many other Americans, that there was any contradiction in imposing democracy on another nation, or that many Japanese might not select democracy, as understood in the United States, if given a free choice. MacArthur himself provides an articulate illustration of this mentality in a letter written on February 14, 1948:

5. Article XXIV included provisions for free universal education and social security. There is evidence that the members of the Committee on Civil Rights were overly zealous about teaching and reforming the Japanese people, and tried to include a great many of their own democratic ideas and ideals that were inappropriate for a Japanese constitution. The members of the Steering Committee repeatedly had to convince them to tone down the original draft. The following passage in the record of the meeting of the Committee on Civil Rights with the Steering Committee on February 8, 1946 is a good illustration:

Colonel Rowell [of the Steering Committee] objected that the setting-up of a complete system of social welfare was not part of the Government Section's responsibility. Insistence upon these provisions might cause so much resentment that the Japanese Government might reject our constitutional draft in toto. Mr. Wildes answered that we do have the responsibility to effect a social revolution in Japan and that the most expedient way of doing so is to force through with the Constitution a reversal of social patterns. Colonel Rowell answered that you cannot impose a new mode of social thought upon a country by law (Takayanagi et al. 1972, 1:206).

Charles Kades (1987, tape 1) told me that the Americans were influenced by their New Deal experiences, but he also pointed out that Milo E. Rowell was a very conservative Republican, and that the GHQ staff was a blend of liberals and conservatives.

The pattern of my course in the occupation of Japan lies deeply rooted in the lessons and experience of American history. For here I have merely sought to draw therefrom the political, economic, and social concepts which throughout our own past have worked and provided the American people with a spiritual and material strength never before equalled in human history.

There is no need to experiment with new and yet untried, or already tried and discredited concepts, when success itself stands as the eloquent and convincing advocate of our own—nor is there factual basis for the fallacious argument occasionally heard that those high principles upon which rest our own strength and progress are ill-fitted to serve the well-being of others, as history will clearly show that the entire human race, irrespective of geographical delimitations or cultural tradition, is capable of absorbing, cherishing and defending liberty, tolerance and justice, and will find maximum strength and progress when so blessed. (SCAP 1968, 2:785)

It is not surprising that, in drafting the Japanese Constitution, the Americans adopted ideas from the U.S. Constitution. It is also not surprising that, since they were imposing these ideas on the Japanese, and since they did not approach their task from a consistent, well-thought-out view of government, the Americans could not create a document with a consistent illocutionary force. Unfortunately, not only did the American and Japanese drafters preserve the diction of the initial American version in all subsequent English versions of the constitution during the negotiations, but the Japanese government has preserved it, for the most part, in the current translation prepared by the Ministry of Justice in 1958.[6]

The Preamble in the current English "translation," which differs only slightly in punctuation and wording from that in the initial American version, begins as follows:

We, the Japanese people, acting through our duly elected representatives in the National Diet, determined that we shall secure for ourselves and our posterity the fruits of peaceful cooperation with all nations and the blessings of liberty throughout this land, and resolved that never again

6. There is no "official English translation" of the Japanese Constitution (Itoh and Beer 1978, p. 256). The excerpts in this book, except where otherwise noted, are taken from the translation of the Ministry of Justice.

shall we be visited with the horrors of war through the action of the government, do proclaim that sovereign power
resides with the people and do firmly establish this Constitution. Government is a sacred trust of the people, the authority for which is derived from the people, the powers of
which are exercised by the representatives of the people, and
the benefits of which are enjoyed by the people. This is a
universal principle of mankind upon which this Constitution
is founded. We reject and revoke all constitutions, ordinances, laws and rescripts in conflict herewith.

The use of "shall" expresses the Japanese people's apparent determination to bring about certain desired states of affairs. "Shall" is used extensively, but not exclusively, throughout the main text in English.

I will focus my attention on the language of Chapter 3, "Rights and
Duties of the People," because it is in this section that the predominant
idea of the U.S. Constitution, the notion that the people command
their government not to abridge their rights and liberties, is most significant. The drafters' attempt to incorporate this American principle
into the Japanese Constitution, however, created some difficulties in
the illocutionary force of the English text. Among the thirty-one articles of this chapter, only fifty-six of the seventy-one main clauses use
"shall" and "shall not."[7] Moreover, the uses of "shall" are inconsistent.
The remaining fifteen use verbal expressions other than "shall." Eleven
are simple declarative sentences in the present tense, asserting certain
rights, liberties, and duties. Three have a different modal, "may," indicating permission, and one has "must," a modal of necessity, or obligation.[8] The inconsistencies in usage, reveal the actual intentions of
the American drafters, and prevent the English version of the Constitution from expressing a consistent view of government.

The clauses using "shall" in Articles 31 through 40 set forth procedural rights of individuals; they are, for the most part, straightforward:

---

7. Not all of the seventy-one clauses are independent sentences. In some instances, two
clauses are conjoined within a single sentence by a comma or a semicolon. I have also included
one instance (from Article 37) of a restrictive relative clause. With six exceptions, however, all
are translated into separate sentences in Japanese. In one instance, the Japanese version has divided one English sentence into two clauses; thus, it has altogether seventy-two relevant clauses.

8. The sentences in the simple present tense are found in the following articles: 14 (9); 15
(14, 15, 16); 18 (23); 20 (25); 21 (29); 23 (34); 28 (46); 29 (47); 36 (60). The sentences with
"may" are found in: 17 (21); 29 (49); 40 (71). The one sentence with "must" is in 34 (57). The
first number is the article number, and the number in parenthesis is the number I have assigned
to each clause. See appendix 3 for the English and Japanese texts of the articles of Chapter 3, with
the numbers assigned to clauses.

ARTICLE 31. No person shall be deprived of life or liberty, nor shall any other criminal penalty be imposed, except according to procedure established by law.

ARTICLE 32. No person shall be denied the right of access to the courts.

ARTICLE 33. No person shall be apprehended except upon warrant issued by a competent judical officer which specifies the offense with which the person is charged, unless he is apprehended, the offense being committed [sic].[9]

These articles express the citizens' commands to the government not to violate fundamental procedural rights.

The more problematic uses of *shall*, as well as the use of the simple present tense, are found in the first twenty-one articles, which guarantee substantive rights and liberties. They raise a number of questions. First, the function of the articles using the simple present tense is ambiguous. Consider the following examples:

ARTICLE 20. Freedom of religion is guaranteed.

ARTICLE 21. Freedom of assembly and association as well as speech, press and all other forms of expression are guaranteed.

ARTICLE 23. Academic freedom is guaranteed.

ARTICLE 28. The right of workers to organize and to bargain and act collectively is guaranteed.

ARTICLE 29. The right to own or to hold property is inviolable.

These articles have an assertive force, but they do not say who is to guarantee them, or against whom they are guaranteed.[10] The articles granting procedural rights are clearly directed against the government, since it is the government that creates and administers criminal law. But these articles could be directed against private groups and individ-

9. In the original American version, the final phrase read as: "unless he is apprehended while he is committing a crime" (Article 30). Satō notes that when the officials of the Liaison Office of the Ministry of Foreign Affairs and the Cabinet Bureau of Legislation were modifying the English text to fit the final Japanese version passed by the National Diet, they changed it to "unless he is apprehended, the offense being committed." He recalls that the change was suggested by the officials of the Ministry of Justice, who believed that the American version was too strict (*Jurisuto*, February 15, 1958, p. 45).

10. The First Amendment to the American Constitution protects freedoms that could be threatened by private as well as governmental action by specifying that "*Congress* shall pass no law. . . ." The agentless passive in these articles leaves the scope of the protection unclear.

uals. Are they intended as restraints on private actions that violate rights and freedoms? And who is imposing the restraints? I suggest that the articles make better sense if they are interpreted as assertions of rights by the Americans on behalf of the Japanese. From that point of view, these articles tell the Japanese people what rights they have, or should assert, and leave it to the Japanese to determine how they are to be applied in particular contexts.

Some of the articles using "shall" are problematic from the American perspective of popular sovereignty and individual rights:

> ARTICLE 11. The people <u>shall</u> not be prevented from enjoying any of the fundamental human rights. These fundamental human rights guaranteed to the people by this Constitution <u>shall</u> be conferred upon the people of this and future generations as eternal and inviolate rights.

To begin with, the two sentences are rhetorically inconsistent. Unlike the articles just mentioned, the first sentence commands someone not to interfere with fundamental human rights. Presumably this is the government, though it can also be read more broadly to include private groups and individuals. But the second sentence then confers them on the people. Who is doing the conferring? If the people already possess these fundamental rights and liberties, it is odd to say that the government confers them, especially if the people must be protected against governmental abuse of power. Nor does it make much sense if we assume that the Japanese take their freedoms and rights for granted as "natural" and inalienable, as Americans often do. But the two sentences in the article gain both consistency and sense if we recognize that the American authors are commanding and instructing the Japanese government, and at the same time educating the people about the constitutional guarantees protecting their rights.

Similarly:

> ARTICLE 13. All of the people <u>shall</u> be respected as individuals. Their right to life, liberty, and the pursuit of happiness <u>shall</u>, to the extent that it does not interfere with the public welfare, be the supreme consideration in legislation and in other governmental affairs.

This clearly instructs the Japanese government to respect the fundamental rights and liberties of the people. But the article only serves a rhetorical function if we assume that the Japanese take for granted that they have these rights. It is of dubious legal value as well. If other articles do not protect individual rights, it is not clear what Article 13 would add. The limitation that the right to life, liberty, and the pursuit of happiness, shall not interfere with public welfare, could even be used to restrain the exercise of individual rights. Of course, to the Americans, the article was obviously not intended as rhetoric, so it seems best to interpret it as an educational statement.[11]

Article 12 is even more problematic from the viewpoint of popular sovereignty:

> The freedoms and rights guaranteed to the people by this Constitution <u>shall</u> be maintained by the constant endeavor of the people, who <u>shall</u> refrain from any abuse of these freedoms and rights and <u>shall</u> always be responsible for utilizing them for the public welfare.[12]

Who is issuing the command, and how is it to be enforced? This article makes sense only as rhetoric, insisting that the people use their freedom responsibly. It is hardly consistent with the notion that the primary threat to rights comes from government action. Clearly the Americans are instructing, and even commanding the Japanese people, placing a heavy responsibility on them.

The first paragraph of this next article falls in the same category:

> ARTICLE 24. Marriage <u>shall</u> be based only on the mutual consent of both sexes and it <u>shall</u> be maintained through mutual cooperation with the equal rights of husband and wife as a basis.
>
> With regard to choice of spouse, property rights, inheritance, choice of domicile, divorce and other matters pertaining to marriage and the family, laws <u>shall</u> be enacted from the standpoint of individual dignity and the essential equality of the sexes.

Article 24 expresses a social policy and/or aspiration for social change. Again, who is giving the command to whom? How is the first sentence to be enforced? The entire paragraph makes more sense if it is read as a pledge by the Japanese people to the Americans (or to themselves) to bring about marriages in which partners are equal, or an instruction or command by the Americans to the Japanese to bring about such a social change.

---

11. The original MacArthur version shows even more obviously that the Americans were commanding the Japanese government to respect the rights of the citizens: "Article XII. The feudal system of Japan shall cease. All Japanese by virtue of their humanity shall be respected as individuals. Their right to life, liberty and the pursuit of happiness within the limits of the general welfare shall be the supreme consideration of all law and of all governmental affairs."

12. The clause after the comma, "who shall refrain from any abuse . . . ," is a nonrestrictive relative clause containing two instances of "shall." This can be rephrased as "and [the people] shall refrain from abuse of these freedoms and shall always be responsible."

To summarize, the American drafters of the Japanese Constitution had a much different idea of the proper role of government than had the framers of the U.S. Constitution. Unlike their forefathers, they believed that government should play a positive role in promoting democratic ideas, and in providing for social welfare. In part, they were compelled to adopt such an attitude because they did not believe the Japanese were capable of creating a constitution expressing democratic ideas, but this approach also fit well with their own ideas of government. Consequently, they wrote a constitution intended in part to guarantee the rights and liberties of the Japanese people against governmental action, and in part to instruct the Japanese in democracy and popular sovereignty. Despite the crucial historical and circumstantial differences between their forefathers and themselves, the Americans tried to incorporate many of the ideas and principles of their own Constitution. But these ideas and principles were inconsistent with the reality of imposing democracy and popular sovereignty on a people unfamiliar with these practices. As a result, the English text of the Constitution, which uses to a significant degree language similar to that of the U.S. Constitution, includes some articles rhetorically inconsistent with American democratic principles, and lacks a consistent illocutionary force.

## The Japanese Text of the Constitution

The Meiji government was established and operated by the leaders of the Restoration, who assumed they had both the authority and responsibility to build a strong modern nation. They governed in the name of the Emperor, and for the good of the nation as they understood it. The Meiji Constitution was an important aspect of this effort. A handful of individuals created it and gave it to the people of Japan in the name of the Emperor.

The language of the Meiji Constitution reflects its origin by its consistent assertive illocutionary force. The imperial rescript proclaiming it sets the tone by asserting the reasons why the Emperor has chosen to grant his subjects the Constitution:

> Having, by virtue of the glories of Our Ancestors, ascended the Throne of a lineal succession unbroken for ages eternal; desiring to promote the welfare of, and to give development to the moral and intellectual faculties of Our beloved subjects, the very same that have been favoured with the benevolent care and affectionate vigilance of Our Ancestors; and hoping to maintain the prosperity of the State, in concert with Our people and with their support, We hereby promulgate, in pursuance of Our Imperial Rescript of the 12th

day of the 10th month of the 14th year of Meiji, a fundamental law of the State, to exhibit the principles, by which
We are guided in Our conduct, and to point out to what Our
descendants and Our subjects and their descendants are forever to conform. [13]

The main text of the Constitution, consisting of seventy-six articles,
lays out the principles of the new governmental system in a series of
assertions, expressed in sentences in the simple nonpast tense. In standard usage, this tense implies that the situations exist presently and/or
will exist in the future. Chapter 2, "Rights and Duties of Subjects,"
consisting of fifteen articles, maintains the same illocutionary force
throughout. All articles use declarative sentences in the nonpast tense,
beginning with *Nihon shimmin* (Japanese subjects). The following articles, in my own translation, are illustrative:

ARTICLE 20. Japanese subjects have the duty to serve in the
Military, according to the provisions of law.

ARTICLE 22. Japanese subjects have the liberty of choosing
their residence and moving, within the limits of law.

ARTICLE 23. Japanese subjects will not be arrested, detained,
tried or punished, except according to law.

ARTICLE 29. Japanese subjects have the liberty of speech,
writing, publication, public meetings and association, within
the limits of law.

The consistent use of the illocutionary force of assertion in the Constitution thus reinforces the historical reality that the government had
assumed the responsibility of ruling on behalf of the nation, and granted
the citizens such rights as it saw fit.

In 1946 the new Japanese Constitution was drafted by a handful of
individuals, and, once again, given to the Japanese people. This time,
however, the Japanese drafters were government officials who were not
totally in control. They found themselves leading the nation under the
direction of the Americans in the aftermath of an unconditional surrender. Drafting a new constitution was one of their apparent responsibilities, but they had little real power in creating the new government.

The Japanese drafters were naturally extremely careful in choosing
language for the Japanese text of the Constitution. We have seen that
the English text had an inconsistent or ambiguous illocutionary force.

13. Beckmann 1957, p. 150. Appendix 4 contains the complete Japanese text of the Meiji
Constitution. Beckmann calls the quoted paragraph the Preamble to the Constitution. As the text
indicates, it is actually the second part of the imperial rescript, promulgating the Constitution.

The Japanese text achieves far greater consistency by setting forth the structure of the governmental institutions as assertions. Many of the articles guaranteeing individual rights and liberties are also assertions. It expresses other such articles as commitments, reflecting the commitment of the government, joined by the people, to respect democratic principles and fundamental rights. Thus, in the Japanese text, the people do not command the government not to infringe their rights and liberties. Although this change was contrary to some of the Americans' intentions, it reflects the reality of the enactment of this document much more faithfully than the English version. Moreover, the Constitution was, and still is, far more congenial than the English version to Japanese views about the function of a constitution, and the proper relationship between the government and the people. In the Meiji era, the government assumed the responsibility of running the nation. In the new, democratic era, the people joined the government in sharing the responsibility of transforming the nation into a democracy. This idea of shared responsibility is quite different from the American notion of limited government.[14]

The difference in the illocutionary force of the two versions largely came about during the period between the 30-hour marathon negotiations at the beginning of March and in the middle of April, when the Japanese drafters presented a full version to the Cabinet for debate. In changing the language of the Constitution from the classical style to modern colloquial Japanese, and polishing the phraseology of the hastily prepared outline, the Japanese drafters reworked the entire document, and created a constitution that was more consistent with their own tradition. Because of the subtlety of the changes, however, I believe that the Japanese did not deliberately set out to change the illocutionary force of the document. Rather, they made stylistic and grammatical changes simply by following their keen sense of language, and their familiarity with the Meiji Constitution and the Japanese tradition of government responsibility. I have found no evidence of any discussions of this issue among them.

The changes were largely of two kinds—different choices of modality, and a change in sentence pattern from the English passive to the Japanese topic-comment construction in the active voice.

### Modality

The change in illocutionary force, from command and commitment in the English text to assertion in the Japanese version, was accomplished

---

14. See chapter 5 for further discussion.

by replacing the English modal "shall" with the simple nonpast tense form. Japanese has two kinds of tense markers, -u/ru, the nonpast, and -ta/da, the past. Sentences in the nonpast tense can ordinarily refer to either habitual or future activities. For instance, the Japanese expression for "to go to school," gakkō-e ik (school-to go), followed by the nonpast marker -u, as used in Watashi-wa gakkō-e ik-u, can mean either "I go to school habitually," or "I will go to school." Likewise, "to study," benkyō su (study do), followed by -ru, as in John-wa benkyō su-ru, can mean either "John studies regularly," or "John will study."

The Japanese drafters used declarative sentences in the nonpast tense extensively to translate articles using "shall" in English. In Chapter 3, fifty-two of the seventy-two relevant clauses are in this form.[15] This is almost as many clauses as those that use "shall" in English. Only ten of these clauses were simple declarative sentences in the present tense in the English version.

Of the remaining twenty clauses, fifteen translate "shall" using the Japanese expression comparable to "must" or, more appropriately, "have to," and its negative form. These include the one instance of "must" and thirteen instances of "shall" in the English version. They also used this expression for one clause in the simple present tense in English.[16]

English uses two modals, "must," and "have to," to express necessity and obligation, but their meanings are not identical. "Must" and "have to" differ in terms of speaker involvement. For instance, when a father says to his child "You must go," he is obligating his child to go, but when he says, "You have to go," he may simply be stating that it is necessary for the child to go (Palmer 1986, pp. 103–4).[17] The sense of necessity implied by "have to" could be the result of a command or obligation, but it is also used to convey the idea that, if you want to attain certain purposes, it is necessary that you take certain actions. "Have to," in the latter sense, is usually an objective expression, since

15. Clause 43 of Article 27 reads in English, "All people have the right and the obligation to work." In the Japanese version, this is divided into two clauses—"All people have the right to work, and [they] bear the obligation to work (43a, 43b). Thus the Japanese text has altogether seventy-two relevant clauses.

16. The thirteen instances where "shall" and "shall not" have been changed to "has to/must" and "has to not/must not" in Japanese are: 12 (4, 5); 15 (17); 19 (24); 20 (26, 28); 21 (30, 31); 24 (35, 36, 37); 25 (39); 27 (45). The one where "must" appears in the English version is 34 (57), and the one in the present tense is 29 (47).

17. One piece of evidence that Palmer gives in support of this distinction is that "have to" has a past tense, but "must" does not. The latter cannot be used to refer to a past action because the speaker can only obligate someone to do something in the future. In ordinary usage, however, the distinction is not as clear as Palmer says, particularly in sentences with a third-person subject.

it is the situation that demands or requires a certain action. In contrast, "must" is a more subjective expression, since it is usually the speaker or a third party who is trying to compel action. Thus, "You must go" ordinarily implies a much stronger sense of command or obligation than "You have to go."

Japanese also has two expressions conveying a sense of necessity or obligation that are in some ways comparable to "must" and "have to" in English. They are -nakere-ba ike-nai and -nakere-ba nara-nai, respectively. The former expression, in sentences such as John-wa ika-nakere-ba ike-nai, literally means "If John does not go, [it] will not be good." It can be translated as "John must go." This expression implies that the necessity is based on the speaker's subjective evaluation or understanding of the situation, and therefore, it can be intended as a command.[18] In contrast, the latter expression in John-wa ika-nakere-ba nara-nai literally means "If John does not go, [it] will not become." It implies that the situation, rather than the speaker's evaluation, necessitates, or obligates John to go, and thus is comparable to "John has to go." Because it does not entail the speaker's subjective judgment, this expression normally cannot be intended as a command.[19] The importance of this distinction lies in the Japanese drafters' use of -nakere-ba nara-nai and its negative form, -te-wa nara-nai, to stand for the "shall" of command. By this choice, they virtually eliminated the sense of command crucial to the English version.

Finally, there are three instances of "may," meaning permission, and two of "shall," in English, which appear as koto-ga deki-ru in Japanese.[20] The Japanese expression koto-ga deki-ru is closer to "can" than "may." It simply implies that John has either the possibility of going or the ability to go. Translating those English sentences with the "may" of permission into those with koto-ga deki-ru has the effect of weakening the authority of the speaker. Changing the "shall" of commitment or command in English to koto-ga deki-ru has the same effect.

In sum, the extensive use of the simple nonpast tense form, the use

18. The common negative imperative form in Japanese is -ike-nai as in Tabete-wa ike-nai, "Don't eat!"

19. The difference between the two expressions in Japanese also appears in the accepted uses of the respective past tense forms. The past tense form of -ike-nai is -ike-nakat-ta, and that of -nara-nai is -nara-nakat-ta. However, while the latter is quite common, the former sounds rather contrived in the ordinary usage. This is another piece of evidence that the former is parallel to "must" and the latter "have to" in English, because "must" in English also does not have the past tense.

20. The sentences with "may" translated by koto-ga deki-ru are found in 17 (21); 29 (49); 40 (71). The two with shall translated by the same expression are in 37 (64) and 38 (67).

of -*nakere-ba nara-nai* to stand for "shall," and the choice of *koto-ga deki-ru* to stand for "may" and "shall" in the Japanese text of the Constitution, have virtually eliminated the sense of the people's authority to command the government, found in the English version. But since neither the Japanese government nor the people had much real power in creating this document, these modals better reflect the actual process of forming the Constitution.

Let us first look at the articles expressing procedural rights in the final ten articles of Chapter 3. In the English version of articles 31 through 40, containing twenty-one clauses, eighteen use "shall" in the sense of command. Of those, all but two (which were changed to *koto-ga deki-ru*) are translated into Japanese using the simple nonpast tense. This has changed the illocutionary force of the articles. To quote two examples, the English versions read:

> ARTICLE 31. No person shall be deprived of life or liberty, nor shall any other criminal penalty be imposed, except according to procedure established by law.
>
> ARTICLE 32. No person shall be denied the right of access to the courts.

In these articles, the people are commanding the government not to restrict their individual rights and liberties without due process of law. The Japanese versions, in my translation, read as follows:

> ARTICLE 31. No person is/will be [21] deprived of life or liberty, except according to procedure established by law. Also, no other criminal penalty is/will be imposed [on any person], except according to procedure established by law. [22]
>
> ARTICLE 32. No person is/will be denied the right of access to the courts.

Much like the Meiji Constitution (though with more limited scope), these articles simply assert that these procedural rights will not be denied. Presumably the government takes the responsibility for protecting them, or for not denying them. While the sense of command is lost,

---

21. I give both the present and the future forms in English in the remainder of the chapter to emphasize the ambiguity. In other instances I have chosen to translate it in the tense appropriate to the context.

22. In this and all other instances where the English version uses "No person shall . . . ," the most literal Japanese version would be something like "Any person does/will not . . ." Since this is an awkward translation, I have compromised by using the English pattern, changing only the verb phrase.

the actual language is faithful to the historical context because it was not the Japanese people who were placing limits on the government.

The uses of "shall" implying the commitment of the people to democratic institutions were also changed to straightforward assertions. For instance, the English versions of Articles 41 and 42 in Chapter 4, "The Diet," say,

> ARTICLE 41. The Diet shall be the highest organ of state power, and shall be the sole law-making organ of the State.
>
> ARTICLE 42. The Diet shall consist of two Houses, namely the House of Representatives and the House of Councillors.

The Japanese versions, in my translation, read:

> ARTICLE 41. The Diet is/will be the highest organ of state power, and is/will be the sole law-making organ of the state.
>
> ARTICLE 42. The Diet consists/will consist of two Houses, the House of Representatives and the House of Councillors.[23]

These clauses simply assert the basic powers and structure of the Diet under this Constitution.

The change from "shall" in the sense of command to the simple nonpast tense form in Japanese, also had an important effect in those articles expressing positive rights that were problematic in English. The English version of Article 11 states,

> The people shall not be prevented from enjoying any of the fundamental human rights. These fundamental human rights guaranteed to the people by this Constitution shall be conferred upon the people of this and future generations as eternal and inviolate rights.

The Japanese version, in my translation, reads:

> The people are not/will not be prevented from enjoying any of the fundamental human rights. These fundamental human rights that this Constitution guarantees are/will be conferred upon the people of this and future generations as eternal and inviolate rights.

The English version suffered from an inconsistency between the drafters' ostensible and actual intent. The Japanese version is free of that

---

23. The literal translation of Article 41 is "As for the Diet, [it] is/will be the highest organ of the State, and is/will be the sole law-making organ of the State. Likewise, Article 42 is "As for the Diet, [one] constitutes/will constitute this by the House of Representatives and the House of Councillors." See the discussion on the topic-comment construction in Japanese in the next section.

problem. It is a straightforward assertion that the people are and will be guaranteed their fundamental human rights. In fact, the inverted order of the two sentences gives a more natural progression of the two ideas. The article still leaves it unclear, however, who or what is conferring the rights, though it is presumably the government.

Similarly, the first sentence of Article 13 is an assertion. The English version is,

> All of the people <u>shall</u> be respected as individuals.

The Japanese version, again in my translation, states:

> All of the people <u>are/will be</u> respected as individuals.

Here, too, the American intent of instructing and/or commanding the Japanese government to respect the people as individuals is appropriately transformed into an assertion that (presumably) the government will respect the rights of the people.

The second important change in modality is the Japanese use of "have to" to translate "shall." This change also had an interesting effect. The articles that were problematic from the American perspective of popular sovereignty are no longer so problematic once the sense of command is lost. For instance, the first paragraph of Article 24, which reads in English,

> Marriage <u>shall</u> be based only on the mutual consent of both sexes and <u>it shall</u> be maintained through mutual cooperation with the equal rights of husband and wife as a basis.

reads in Japanese:

> Marriage <u>has to</u> be based only on the mutual consent of both sexes, and <u>it has to</u> be maintained through mutual cooperation with the equal rights of husband and wife as a basis. (My translation) [24]

As we have seen, the English version is most naturally read as an instruction or command to the Japanese to bring about marriages of equal partners. The Japanese translation is the government's (and possibly the people's) acknowledgment of the necessity of bringing about social change in the new, democratic era. It states that equality between the sexes is the basis of marriage, and exhorts the Japanese to maintain this relationship.

---

24. In the Japanese version, the first clause ends in a simple conjoining verbal form *shi* as in *Kon'in-wa, ryōsei-no gōi-nomi-ni motozuite seiritsu shi*, making it ambiguous whether or not it should be interpreted as a simple nonpast form, or *nakereba nara-nai*. In my view, it should be the latter.

Another example falling in the same category is the third paragraph of Article 27. The English version says,

Children <u>shall</u> not be exploited.

Since most use of child labor would occur in the private sector, it is hard to interpret this article as a command to the government not to exploit children. It could be read as a command to private employers, but it can also be viewed as an American command to the Japanese people not to exploit children. The Japanese version, in my translation, reads,

As for children, [one] <u>has to</u> not exploit [them].[25]

Thus, it is simply an acknowledgment by the Japanese people (and perhaps the government) that children should not be exploited, and reads more like a moral obligation rather than a legal limitation. There are, however, other instances where the government is clearly instructed about its obligations, although again the instruction does not come from the people. Two examples are found in the final paragraph of Article 20 and the second paragraph of Article 25. In my translation, they read as follows:

ARTICLE 20: . . . The State and its organs <u>have to</u> not engage in religious education or any other religious activities.

ARTICLE 25: . . . In all spheres of life, the State <u>has to</u> endeavor to promote and extend social welfare and security, and public health.

The use of "have to" in Article 20 clearly expresses a sense of objective necessity that the government and the people observe this principle. The provision in Article 25 is largely rhetorical, and tells the government to pursue certain general goals. The people are not the source of the necessity in either article. The sense of command found in the Bill of Rights is absent.

Turning to the third change in modality, the use of "can" in the Japanese version in place of "may" in the English text, has also created an important difference in the illocutionary force of the two versions. Articles 17 and 40 were originally introduced by the Japanese, and then translated into English. In my translation, the two articles read as follows:

---

25. The negative form that we need is the one that parallels *must not*. Since it does not exist, I have decided to use the awkward expression, *has to not*. This is additional evidence that the distinction between *must* and *have to* cannot simply be explained in terms of speaker involvement, as Palmer suggests (1986, p. 103).

ARTICLE 17. Every person can request redress as provided by law from the State or a public entity, if one has suffered damage through the illegal acts of any public officials.

ARTICLE 40. Any person, if acquitted after having been arrested or detained, can request redress from the state, as provided by law.

In translating these articles into English, "can" (*koto-ga deki-ru*) was replaced by "may":

ARTICLE 17. Every person may sue for redress as provided by law from the State or a public entity, in case he has suffered damage through illegal act of any public official.

ARTICLE 40. Any person, in case he is acquitted after he has been arrested or detained, may sue the State for redress as provided by law. (Ministry of Justice translation)

The Japanese versions do not convey the speaker's authority to grant the rights expressed; they only state a possibility. Moreover, unlike the English phrase "sue for redress," which clearly indicates that there will be legal remedies, the original Japanese articles use *(baishō-o/hoshō-o) motome-ru,* "seek (redress)," which only suggests that the people will have the opportunity to seek compensation from the government by some means in appropriate circumstances. It is also interesting that the Japanese versions use two different expressions, *baishō* and *hoshō* to stand for "redress" in the two articles. In legal usage, *baishō* generally refers to compensation for failure to pay one's debts or fulfill one's legal obligations, such as failure to honor a contract. In contrast, *hoshō* generally refers to compensation for damage to or the taking of property arising out of the legitimate exercise of public power, such as the condemnation of private property for public purposes.[26] Thus, the use of *hoshō* in Article 40 is an extension of its normal legal use. Not all injury to property rights is compensable, so the use of *hoshō* suggests that a citizen is entitled to compensation in some limited circumstances, whose boundaries are not clearly defined.

The third example, the third paragraph of Article 37 in which "shall" has been changed to "can," also seriously undermines the American intent of granting a right to the people. The English version reads:

At all times the accused shall have the assistance of competent counsel.

26. *Hōritsugaku Shō-jiten* (An Abridged Dictionary of Jurisprudence), edited by Hideo Fujiki, Hiroshi Kaneko, and Kōji Shindō (Tokyo: Yūhikaku, 1972), pp. 290, 610.

The Japanese language, in my translation, reads:

> The accused <u>can</u> have the assistance of qualified counsel at all times.

There is one instance in which the English text grants the government more power than the Japanese version. The third paragraph of Article 29 reads in English,

> Private property <u>may</u> be taken for public use upon just compensation therefor.

The Japanese article, in my translation, reads,

> As for private property, [one] <u>can</u> use this for public use upon just compensation.

The English version explicitly gives the government permission to take private property for public use, but the Japanese text only suggests such a possibility.[27] This is the only place where the English version seems to provide the government with greater power than the Japanese.

My interpretation of the Japanese version of the Constitution as a document in which the government asserts its responsibility to establish democracy is substantiated by statements of both the liberal and conservative members of the Diet, as well as Kanamori Tokujirō, the chief government spokesman in the constitutional debates. The Japanese recognized that the new Constitution incorporated both the eighteenth-century American democratic principles of limited government, and the twentieth-century idea that government should take positive action to promote social welfare. They welcomed the latter idea because, drawing on the traditional Japanese view of government as similar to a responsible parent, they believed that it was the responsibility of the government to look after the welfare of the nation. They also believed that the Constitution was a sacred book, a textbook for the political education of the people, and thus should express aspirations for a better future for the people and the nation. Some of them wanted to expand these provisions of the Constitution. The following two exchanges between Diet members and Kanamori illustrate these points.

On June 26, 1946, the second day of the plenary session at the House of Representatives, Suzuki Yoshio, a leading member of the Socialist party, said,

---

27. The fifth instance of "can" appears in the second paragraph of Article 38, "As for confessions made under compulsion, torture or threat, or after prolonged arrest or detention, [one] cannot use these as evidence." The negative form, *koto-ga deki-nai*, conveys almost as strong a sense of denial as *shall not*, which the English version uses.

I dare say that this draft constitution does a fairly good job in expressing the people's liberties, rights and duties in some detail. But if one looks at it carefully, while it does a satisfactory job in guaranteeing political liberties, such as the right to life, freedom of speech, religion, communication, etc., it includes very few clauses specifying rights and duties of the working class, such as protection of home life, communal life, and economic rights that are generally demanded in modern nations. . . . You might say that to guarantee food for the workers . . . is a moral obligation to be carried out by legislative policy, but if so, then Articles 11 and 12 merely express excellent political morality. "As for the freedoms and rights guaranteed to the people by this Constitution, [the people] have to maintain these by their constant endeavor"—this is really a moral provision. "All of the people will be respected as individuals. As for the right to life, liberty, and the pursuit of happiness, to the extent that it does not interfere with the public welfare, [this] will be the supreme consideration in legislation and in other governmental affairs"—[this is] really a moral provision. In the past there was a time when, aside from guaranteeing political liberty, a constitution honored merely the technical rules of governmental operations. But modern constitutions such as the Weimar Constitution of Germany, the Constitution of the Soviet Union, the draft of the French Constitution, and the draft of the Chinese Constitution all include a great many cultural, social and economic rights and duties. They give the impression that they are the great sacred books (*ichidai kyōten*). . . . At this epochal juncture of constitutional revision, we would like to make this [a document containing] guidelines for the people, which will include a great many provisions regarding cultural, social, and economic rights of the twentieth century, and the freedoms of the nineteenth century; and also their great sacred book. (Shūgi-in 1946a, 6:92, col. 4–93, col. 1) [28]

Suzuki went on to suggest that several specific principles be added to the Constitution. Kanamori replied that while he appreciated the Socialist party's amendments, the government could not accept them at that time (94, cols. 2–3).

On August 27, 1946, at the plenary session of the House of Peers,

---

28. This passage, and all the other passages quoted from the debates at the National Diet in the remainder of the book, are my own translations.

Makino Eiichi expressed very similar ideas about both the government's responsibility to the people and the Constitution as a text for the political education of the people. First he indicated how nineteenth-century laissez-faire ideas had led to social problems in the twentieth century:

> The idea of fundamental human rights began in the state bills of rights in the United States, then in the declaration of human rights in France, and then in various constitutions of the nineteenth century. This idea belongs to the nineteenth-century legal theory that assures that the state has the passive duty of noninterference with individual rights and liberties. This established nineteenth-century individualism and liberalism, and developed into the principles of free competition and nonintervention of the state in the lives of individuals, leading to the prosperity of that century. But this prosperity also led to social problems, making it necessary for states to take responsibility for solving them. Contemporary states have to go further than nineteenth-century states and become twentieth-century constitutional governments. We call them the cultured/civilized nations (*bunka-koku*). (Kizoku-in 1946a, 24:260, col. 4)

Makino went on to say that the new Constitution did not express strongly enough the twentieth-century idea of government's responsibility to provide for the welfare of the people:

> The government might say that the ideals of the cultured nation are sufficiently represented. If one reads the draft constitution carefully, one cannot help but think that it has a nineteenth-century spirit. Article 11 (current 12) of the government's draft indicates that the freedoms and rights have to be maintained by the constant endeavor of the people, and Article 12 (current 13) says that the rights of the people will be the supreme consideration in legislation and other governmental affairs. . . . But it does not adequately express the idea that the state should take active responsibility for the fulfillment of the right to life for all people. I would like to see the government's cultural responsibility clearly stated in the beginning of Chapter 3. My impression is that this draft takes a passive stand toward fundamental human rights. It guarantees the minimum requirements for the government, but it does not establish guiding principles for the future development of the nation. I cannot help but characterize this constitution as an old-fashioned document, far too limited to serve as the people's

sacred book, the people's textbook. The Constitution should not stop at the minimal starting point for the life of the people. It has to express the fundamental principles of the overall developmental scheme for the people (261, cols. 1–3).

Kanamori replied that while he basically agreed with Makino's idea of governmental responsibility, the role of the Constitution was to express only the fundamental principles of the government, and that the government's immediate task was to establish principles that the majority of the Japanese people could agree on (Kizoku-in 1946a, 25:277, cols. 3–4).

Consistent with the idea that the government had responsibility for promoting the welfare of the nation, the Japanese also made important changes in the original American article guaranteeing social welfare. They broke it into three separate articles, added new clauses, and measurably strengthened the ideas of social welfare expressed in the Constitution. The original American version read as follows:

> ARTICLE XXIV. In all spheres of life, laws shall be designed for the promotion and extension of social welfare, and of freedom, justice, and democracy.
> Free, universal, and compulsory education shall be established.
> The exploitation of children shall be prohibited.
> The public health shall be promoted.
> Social security shall be provided.
> Standards for working conditions, wages and hours shall be fixed.

The Japanese turned the first sentence into a separate article, and prefaced it with an aspirational clause asserting the right to maintain minimum living standards. In my translation, they read as follows:

> ARTICLE 25. All people have/will have the right to maintain minimum standards of wholesome and cultured living.
> In all spheres of life, the State has to strive for the promotion and extension of social welfare and security, and of public health.

They created a second article on the right to equal education, greatly expanding it. In my translation, it states:

> ARTICLE 26. All people have/will have the right to receive an equal education corresponding to their ability, as provided by law.
> All people are/will be obligated to have all boys and girls

under their protection receive ordinary education as provided by law. Such compulsory education is/will be free.

In a third article they imposed a duty on the people to work and included rest as a condition of work:

ARTICLE 27. All people have/will have the right to work and
bear/will bear the duty [to work].
   As for standards for wages, hours, rest, and other working
conditions, [one] determines/will determine them by law.
   As for children, [one] has to not exploit them.

Thus the Japanese expanded the duty of the government to provide for
social welfare, even though these articles expressed aspirations that
would be difficult to enforce in a court of law.[29]

Finally, the Japanese reinforced the responsibility of the government
for its citizens by adding two new articles, Articles 17 and 40 discussed
above, to provide remedies for illegal official acts and mistaken arrests.
The first was proposed by the Socialist party and the Club of Nonaffiliated Members, and the second one was suggested by both the Socialist
and the Progressive parties. In my translation, they read as follows:

ARTICLE 17. Every person can request redress as provided by
law from the state or a public entity, if one has suffered damage through the illegal acts of any public official.[30]
ARTICLE 40. Any person, if acquitted after having been arrested or detained, can request redress from the state as provided by law.[31]

In his report on the proceedings of the subcommittee before a plenary
session of the House of Representatives on August 24, Ashida Hitoshi
explained that these articles were added to the Constitution to protect

29. As mentioned above (n. 5), some members of the Committee on Civil Rights were eager
to include their own ideas about the promotion of social welfare in the Constitution. The Japanese
had the same idea, though coming from a very different perspective.

30. The Socialist party proposal simply read, *Nanibito-mo kōmuin-no kōhō-jō-no fuhō-kōi-ni
taishite kuni-ni songai-baishō-o motomeru koto-ga dekiru* (Every person can request redress from the
state for the illegal acts of any public official) (Mori 1983 p. 419; my translation). The one by the
Club of Nonaffiliated Members read, *Nihon kokumin-wa kōmuin-no fuhō-kōi-ni yoru songai-ni taishite
baishō-o yōkyū suru kenri-o yū suru* (Japanese nationals have/will have the right to redress from the
state for damage suffered through the illegal acts of any public official) (ibid., p. 426; my
translation).

31. The Socialist party proposed that *Menzai-sha-ni taishite-wa kuni kore-ni hoshō suru* (As for
an acquitted person, the state compensates/will compensate [the person for] this) be added to
Article 35 (Mori 1983, p. 419; my translation). The Progressive party proposed a similar amendment to Article 35 that read as follows: "Any person who has been acquitted after being arrested
or detained has the right to redress as provided by law" (ibid., p. 415; my translation). The
subcommittee of the House of Representatives adopted the latter, but changed "has/will have the

the people and provide appropriate redress in cases where it had not been previously available (Shūgi-in 1946a, 35:504, col. 1). But the Americans, reading only the English version, apparently saw implications that the Japanese had not intended. According to the Japanese record, Kanamori and other Japanese officials asked Charles Kades to comment on Article 40 when the two sides met on July 23. Kades said that he was worried that this clause might encourage the courts to declare suspected criminals guilty, rather than acquit them (Satō Tatsuo Kankei Bunsho 184).[32] However, Kades later told me that the Americans were concerned about the possibility of the state opening itself up to a large number of lawsuits, "giving the lawyers a heyday" (1987, tape 2).

In sum, these procedural and substantive changes in the social welfare clauses reinforced the linguistic changes in the Constitution, so both the form and content of the new Constitution became more consistent with the Japanese political tradition.

## Topic-Comment Construction

The majority of the sentences in the English text of the Constitution are written in what is known as the agentless passive, with the subject noun phrase representing either a human subject or a nonhuman subject. In Chapter 3, thirty-nine out of seventy-one sentences are of this type. Of those, twenty-three have a nonhuman subject noun phrase representing rights, liberties, and duties, for instance, "Academic freedom is guaranteed." The remaining sentences have a subject noun phrase representing people, for instance, "All of the people shall be respected as individuals." Because the use of passive sentences in Japanese is much more restricted than in English, the Japanese drafters resorted to using what some linguists call the *topic-comment* construction in translating fifteen of the thirty-nine sentences. These include eight sentences with a subject noun phrase representing rights and liberties. There are two other English sentences that do not use the agentless

---

right to receive redress" (*sono hoshō-o ukeru kenri-o yū suru*) to "can request redress from the state" (*kuni-ni sono hoshō-o motomeru koto-ga dekiru*).

32. In its proposal published on December 26, 1945, the Constitutional Research Group also included the clause "The State should amply indemnify a person who is acquitted" (Satō 1962–64, 2:787; my translation). When Milo E. Rowell submitted his evaluation of this proposal to Whitney on January 11, 1946, he said "It is strongly recommended that this section be deleted. Experience in Japan has shown that, in order to protect the State's funds, police and prosecutors will go to extreme lengths in obtaining confessions in order to avoid acquittals. It is believed that, so long as this provision remains, it is an added incentive to use illegal means to convict every person accused of crime" (Takayanagi et al. 1972, 2:32, 34).

passive that are also translated by the topic-comment construction in Japanese.[33]

The use of this construction in articles expressing fundamental rights and liberties is significant because it implies that the government and people are affirming and guaranteeing rights and liberties that are already familiar and well understood. By suggesting that the Constitution is simply protecting rights that already exist, the language of the document may have contributed to the ultimate acceptance of democratic principles.

Before discussing the effects of this grammatical change, it will be helpful to explain the topic-comment construction. I will give three illustrations, using a single sentence, to show how new information, in contrast to old or shared information, is conveyed in English, and then translate them into Japanese.

In English, intonation is one way to distinguish shared information from new information in a conversation. For instance, suppose I am talking about the wide range of literary interests of Japanese young people today. I might say, "My niece reads Eco." If I utter this sentence with a sustained high pitch, it indicates that the entire sentence provides new information to the listener, as an illustration of the type of books that some Japanese young people are reading. In contrast, if I have already been talking about my niece's literary interests, I will utter the same sentence with a raised pitch only on "Eco." In this second case, my niece's interests are the topic of the conversation, and "Eco" is a comment which gives new information to my listener. Finally, if I have been talking about "Eco," I will use the same sentence, but utter "My niece" with a high pitch, because that phrase provides the new information; it is a comment on the topic, "Eco."

In Japanese, the functional distinction between a sentence used to give the listener an entirely new piece of information and a sentence used to make a comment about a familiar subject matter or topic is usually not marked by intonation. Instead, Japanese uses two syntactic markers, the subject marker, -*ga*, and the topic marker -*wa*, respectively.[34] Japanese will translate the single English sentence given above in three different ways, depending on what piece of information in the

33. The eight clauses are: 15 (17); 19 (24); 20 (25); 21 (29, 30, 31); 23 (34); 28 (46). The two additional ones are: 26 (42) and 29 (47).

34. The precise meanings and uses of Japanese postpositions, -*ga* and -*wa* are notoriously difficult. Traditional grammarians and linguists have categorized them in various ways, but have not yet agreed on a definitive characterization. In contemporary generative linguistics, Kuroda 1965, and Kuno 1973, were the first to give useful explications, which have served as the basis of all later studies.

sentence is new. Two of the three sentences use the topic-comment construction.

In translating the first illustration, "My niece reads Eco," where the entire sentence provides new information, I will begin with *Watashi-no mei-ga* (Japanese is a verb final language):

> *Watashi-no mei -ga Ekō -o yomi -mas -u.*
> I 's niece-Subj. Eco-Obj. read-Polite-Nonpast

Using -*ga* with the subject noun phrase alerts the listener that the entire sentence will be new information. In Japanese, this sentence is a declarative sentence, which does not use the topic-comment construction.

When only a part of the sentence is new information, however, I will use the topic-comment construction. Thus when I have already been talking about my niece's literary interests, I will replace -*ga* with *wa* and say,

> *Watashi-no mei -wa Ekō -o yomi -mas -u.*
> Topic Obj.

Using -*wa* tells the listener that I am talking about my niece, which is shared information. She is the topic of the sentence, and the predicate then provides new information. The third sentence illustrates how the topic-comment construction works when we have been talking about Eco. To indicate that Eco is the shared information, I will bring the object noun phrase, *Ekō-o*, to the beginning of the sentence, replace the object marker, -*o*, with topic marker, -*wa*, and say,

> *Ekō -wa watashi-no mei -ga yomi -mas -u.*
> Topic Subj.

Again, the -*wa* signifies shared information. The literal translation of the sentence is "Eco, my niece reads," which is an unnatural English sentence. A better, but still awkward expression in English would be "As for Eco, my niece reads [him]." In Japanese, however, this construction is perfectly natural. It is the basic form of the topic-comment construction that the Japanese drafters adopted to translate agentless passive sentences in English.

In Chapter 2 of the Meiji Constitution, "Rights and Duties of Subjects," all of the articles specifying rights and duties are in the topic-comment construction in the active voice, beginning with *Nihon shimmin-wa* (Japanese subjects-Topic marker). For example,

ARTICLE 22. Japanese subjects (*Nihon shimmin-wa*) have the liberty of choosing their residence and moving within the limits of the law. (My translation)

The topic noun phrase *Nihon shimmin-wa* indicates that the Emperor, the ostensible grantor of the Constitution, is addressing Japanese subjects who are familiar. The predicate grants the liberty of choice of residence and moving, and since the predicate is new information, it carries the impliction that the rights themselves are new. Thus, the grammatical structure of the article is consistent with the actual circumstances of the creation of the Meiji Constitution, which specified the rights and duties of the citizens for the first time in Japanese history.

When the Japanese drafters prepared the so-called March 2 version, which Matsumoto and Satō took to GHQ on the morning of March 4, 1946, they followed the Meiji example by writing the majority of the articles in Chapter 3 in the active voice, with a topic noun phrase referring to the people: *Subete-no kokumin-wa* (All of the people-Topic marker). As mentioned earlier, however, during the 30-hour marathon of March 4 through 6, the Americans objected to the Japanese version of this chapter, because it eliminated several key American ideas. They insisted that the two sides rework it, using the American draft as the basis, and the Japanese had to agree. The Japanese drafters did their best in translating the English sentences into Japanese. Nonetheless, the one stylistic feature that undoubtedly stood out as problematic in the English text was the extensive use of the agentless passive.

The passive voice in Japanese works much differently from that in English.[35] One can usually translate an English passive with an animate subject into a Japanese passive sentence. "The boy was praised by his teacher" can easily be translated into a Japanese passive, *Shōnen-wa sensei-ni home-rare-ta*. But some English sentences with an inanimate subject or topic, for instance, "These dishes have been washed," cannot be expressed naturally in the passive in Japanese. One problem concerns tense and aspect.[36] The verb in the simple present tense in a

35. It is often said that the ordinary passive construction in Japanese is a relatively new development due to the influence of English. I mentioned this point in an earlier version of this discussion (Inoue 1986, p. 207). However, Japan's distinguished grammarian, Yamada Yoshio (1908, pp. 375–80) notes the presence of passive sentences in the literary works of the Heian Period (794–1185), attesting to its long use in the Japanese language.

Japanese also has another passive construction known as the "adversative passive." This construction has no syntactic parallel in English. A sentence using this structure typically takes a noun phrase with an animate entity, followed by subject marker *-ga* or topic marker *-wa*. It is often used to indicate that the person or other animate entity is adversely affected by the event. An example is *Watashi-wa inu-ni shin-are-ta*, which is often translated into English as "I had a dog die on me," or "My dog died on me." A more literal translation would be "I was died on by my dog."

36. In contrast to the term *tense*, which indicates the time the activity or state denoted by the verb occurs, the term *aspect* typically indicates its duration or completion. In English, for instance,

passive sentence conveys the so-called "habitual" sense. Unlike its active counterpart, it does not express a clear sense of either the present or the future situation. This causes no difficulty in cases where the subject noun phrase in English represents "the people" or "no person." For instance,

> ARTICLE 13. All of the people shall be respected as individuals . . .

is translated into the topic-comment construction in the passive voice in the nonpast tense:

> Subete-no kokumin -wa      kojin    -to shi-te sonchō
> all    's people -Topic individual   as     respect
> s -are -ru.
> do-Pass. Nonpast

The Japanese sentence says that all people are or will be habitually respected as individuals. It does not command anyone, but simply expresses the idea that respect for the individual is the normal state of affairs.

But the habitual sense of the passive creates a problem in cases where the topic noun phrase refers to a right or liberty. For instance, Article 13, "Academic freedom is guaranteed," can be translated directly into Japanese as:

> Gakumon -no jiyū    -wa      hoshō   s -are -ru.
> learning 's freedom -Topic guarantee-do-Pass.-Nonpast

The English clause, "Academic freedom is guaranteed" means that the circumstances in which academic freedom exists will prevail. The Japanese counterpart does not communicate such a clear idea. Without an adverbial phrase specifying a time period, it only conveys the vague sense that academic freedom will be guaranteed when an issue arises. To express a clear idea of an existing state of freedom, we must use the nonpast progressive, hoshō s-are-te i-ru (is being guaranteed).

The Japanese translation of the agentless passive with "shall," which takes "have to," is less ambiguous about the prevailing state. For instance, the official English version of Article 19,

> Freedom of thought and conscience shall not be violated

---

"I ran" is in the simple past tense, indicating that the speaker's running occurred at some point in the past. But "I have run" is in the present perfect, indicating that the running has been completed. When the running is going on at the time of utterance, the speaker would use the present progressive, "I am running."

can be translated into a Japanese passive sentence *Shisō oyobi ryōshin-no jiyū-wa okas-are-te-wa nara-nai* (Freedom of thought and conscience has to not be violated). This type of expression, however, is not commonly used in Japanese.

The Japanese drafters solved the problem of translation creatively. They adopted the topic-comment construction with an object-noun phrase in the beginning of the sentence, followed by an active sentence including an object pronoun "this" (*kore-o*). To illustrate, using an agentless passive sentence in English, "The tree was cut [by someone]," is first changed into an active sentence, "[Someone] cut the tree." Next, the object-noun phrase, "the tree," is brought to the front of the sentence, "The tree, [someone] cut," or "As for the tree, [someone] cut." Finally, a pronoun referring to the object noun phrase is added at the end. The sentence now reads, "As for the tree, [someone] cut this." The Japanese used this construction to translate eight of the seventeen passive sentences beginning with a right or liberty, as well as two others. Thus, the Japanese versions of Articles 19 and 23 read as follows:

> ARTICLE 19. As for freedom of thought and conscience, [one] has to not violate <u>this</u>.
>
> ARTICLE 23. As for academic freedom, [one] guarantees/will guarantee <u>this</u>.

This change had an interesting and significant consequence. In the Japanese text, some of the most important individual rights and liberties are now expressed in a manner that suggests that they are familiar to the Japanese people. Moreover, by using the additional reference to the rights by *kore-o* (this-Object marker), these sentences affirm them much more strongly than other articles in which the sentence starts out with a topic noun phrase representing the people, either in the passive or the active voice. Here are four more examples of articles expressing rights and liberties, in my own translation:

> ARTICLE 20. As for freedom of religion, [one] guarantees/will guarantee this to everyone.
>
> ARTICLE 21. As for freedom of assembly and association, speech, press and all other forms of expression, [one] guarantees/will guarantee this.
>
> ARTICLE 28. As for the right of workers to organize and to bargain and act collectively, [one] guarantees/will guarantee this.
>
> ARTICLE 29. As for the right to own property, [one] has to not violate this.

The Japanese articles not only imply that the individual rights and liberties regarded by Americans as critically important are already familiar to the people, but they also guarantee them emphatically. By insisting that their own version be used as the basis of Chapter 3, the Americans inadvertently led the Japanese to express some important rights as identifiable and familiar concepts, and at the same time to emphasize the necessity of protecting them.

An exchange between Kanamori and Matsuzawa Kenjin, of the Socialist party, at the House of Representatives on July 18, 1946, substantiates my linguistic explanation. Matzuzawa asked what difference there was between the articles that state that the people have rights and those which state that the rights are guaranteed.

> I would like to ask whether there is any difference in the meanings of the [following] expressions, or whether they are simply a matter of different usage, so that there is no difference in meaning. For instance, one article says "All people have the right to work," and another says "As for academic freedom, [one] guarantees this." Is there any difference in significance between the ones that state *kenri-o hoshō suru* ([one] guarantees the right) and others that simply say *kenri-o yū suru* ([the people] have the right)? (Shūgi-in 1946b, 16:302, col. 3)

Kanamori replied,

> As for the difference between those articles that state [*kenri-o*] *hoshō suru* and those that state *kenri-o yū suru*, there is a splendid (*kasha-na*) difference. *Kenri-o yū suru* literally is a declaration that one has the right. On the other hand, *kenri-o hoshō suru* means that such a right exists and that [one] would not violate it arbitrarily. It takes the right as given, and that the government will not unjustifiably violate it. So in the end the two might convey similar senses, but there could be a slight difference in the way the government might restrict these rights, or express its position toward them (ibid., col. 5).

Kanamori was unable to articulate that it is not the verb phrase *hoshō suru* (guarantees) alone, that carries the emphatic meaning. Rather, it is the entire sentence, with an object noun phrase in the beginning of the sentence, followed by *kore-o hoshō suru* ([one] guarantees this), which implies that the government and people guarantee an existing right. Nevertheless, my linguistic analysis clearly fits with Kanamori's native intuition.

Matsuzawa provided additional evidence for this explanation with his comments about Article 28, "As for the right of workers to organize and to bargain and act collectively, [one] guarantees this." He interpreted this article to mean that the state or government would actively guarantee this right and eliminate obstacles to its free exercise.

> You say there is some difference. But when the people read this article with *hoshō suru* ([one] guarantees), they will interpret [it to mean] that they have the right to bargain and act collectively, and that when someone violates that right, the state will actively and literally guarantee their right, and actively eliminate the obstacle and support them. If one does not interpret *hoshō suru* in that sense, it would be exactly the same as *kenri-o yū suru* ([the people] have the right). I think the government has to recognize the people's rights and actively and earnestly support them. I would like to have your response (302, col. 5–303, col. 1).

Kanamori agreed with Matsuzawa, but he did not want to commit himself to a specific legal interpretation of this particular right. Therefore, he replied that the floor of the National Diet was different from a classroom of a course in law, and that he could not elaborate on the political and legal implications any further (303, cols. 1–2).

### Summary

Not only is a constitution the product of a particular political tradition and historical circumstances, it also is expressed in a language that speaks to its audience with a particular illocutionary force. The U.S. Constitution was created by the Founding Fathers, who were determined to establish a government that endorsed popular sovereignty and protected individual rights and liberties. Through the consistent use of the modal "shall," the U.S. Constitution conveys the people's commitment to a representative government and their command to their government not to abridge their rights and liberties. The Meiji Constitution had an entirely different illocutionary force, reflecting the Japanese government's assertion, in the name of the Emperor, of both its authority and its responsibility to govern the nation for the welfare and benefit of the people.

The English and Japanese texts of the Constitution of 1946 convey different illocutionary forces. The English version is partly written in language similar to that of the U.S. Constitution. The majority of the articles referring to the democratic form of government read as if the Japanese people are committing themselves to the new government on their own initiative. Likewise, many articles referring to individual rights and liberties read as if the people are commanding the government not to infringe them. Other articles, however, speak with a different illocutionary force. This inconsistency reflects the circumstances of its drafting. The document was not created on the initiative of the Japanese people. Rather, it was written by Americans who sought to give the Japanese people a democratic form of government, to instruct them about the rights and liberties to which they were entitled, and to command the Japanese to guard them. It is hardly surprising, therefore, that the Americans were unable to maintain a consistent illocutionary force similar to that of their own Constitution throughout their draft of the Japanese Constitution.

In creating a text in their own language, the Japanese modified the wording and included a few new articles. The result is a document with a more consistent illocutionary force. In the Japanese text, the people do not command the government not to infringe their rights and liberties. Instead, it affirms the responsibility of the Japanese government to establish a democratic government, and the people and the government together affirm the necessity of protecting individual rights and liberties. Thus, this text continues in a significant way the political tradition of Meiji Japan, in which the government took the authority and responsibility to govern the nation well. But it adds an important new element: the participation of the people in the political process. The language of the new Constitution, in form and content, says that the government, joined by the people, undertakes the responsibility to create a democratic government, and to safeguard the citizens' rights and liberties.

The difference in the illocutionary force of the Japanese and English texts of the new Japanese Constitution came about partly because neither version was created as the "translation" of the other in the strict sense of the term. The Americans and Japanese worked on the document concurrently much of the time. In later years, the English version has been treated as the translation of the Japanese Constitution. Since this "translation" does not accurately convey the meaning of the Japanese version, particularly the commitment of the Japanese to their own brand of democracy, a new translation of the document would seem to be appropriate.

*Four*

# RELIGIOUS FREEDOM
# AND THE SEPARATION OF
# RELIGION AND STATE

ARTICLE 20. As for freedom of religion, [one] guarantees this to all. Religious organizations have to not receive any privileges from the State, or exercise any political authority.

No person will be compelled to take part in any religious act, celebration, rite or practice.

The State and its organs have to refrain from religious education or any other religious activities. (My translation)

The Americans, as well as other Allied powers, regarded freedom of religion and the separation of religion and state as critical to the transformation of Japan into a democratic nation. They were, of course, correct in assuming that religion played a central role in the Japanese political system. But the Americans did not realize how vastly Japanese tradition differed from their own. They did not know or understand that the Japanese people had never been concerned about religious freedom in ways familiar to the West, because their concept of God was much different from the Christian conception, and because most Japanese did not adhere to an exclusive system of religious belief. Also unlike the West, Japanese religions, and particularly Shintoism, did not have an institutionalized church to support, or come into conflict with the state. Consequently, the issue of religion and state in Japanese society was much different from that in the United States. To help understand the critical issues, I will begin with a brief account of the relevant features of the history of Japanese religion. I will then discuss the historical background of religious freedom and separation of church and state in the United States to show how greatly the American experience differs from that of the Japanese. Finally, I will examine how the Americans and Japanese negotiated these issues in the drafting of the Constitution, and how the Japanese Diet members debated them. Because of the differences in tradition, the debate did not raise general questions about church and state, but focused on specific questions about the consequences and ramifications of the new article.

# The Japanese Religious Tradition
## Ancient to Early Modern Times

Over the past two thousand years, the Japanese have been influenced by three different religious traditions: the native Japanese religion called Shinto, and two others imported from China in ancient times, Buddhism and Confucianism. Confucianism, which is perhaps better characterized as an ethical system than a religion, did not gain prominence until the rise of the Tokugawa bakufu in the seventeenth century. Shintoism and Buddhism, on the other hand, have coexisted in relative harmony from the very beginning. Shintoism never developed an institutionalized church or a theology. After Buddhism was introduced, it quickly became the favored religion of the aristocracy, but there was never any effort to eliminate Shintoism or challenge the Emperor's position as the spiritual leader of the nation. In fact, the two religions borrowed rituals and practices from each other, and neither tried to gain the exclusive allegiance of the Japanese people. While there have been instances of religious intolerance, with one or two exceptions, no religion or sect has tried to claim that it had the true faith to the exclusion of others. These characteristics—the religious role of the Emperor, the syncretism of Buddhism and Shintoism, and the relative absence of claims to exclusive truth—have given Japan a religious tradition quite distinct from that of Western nations, one which gives a different significance to the issues of religious freedom and separation of church and state.

By about A.D. 300, the Japanese people had formed kinship groups called *uji*, which were alliances of families, in the Yamato Plain near present day Osaka and Nara. They worshiped natural phenomena such as mountains, trees, and water, and, in the belief that the spirits of the deceased could bring fortune or misfortune to the living, they worshiped them, and cared for them at their graves. It also became customary for politically and socially influential families to choose well-known and powerful figures of another family in the distant past as their "pseudo-pedigree ancestors" or "ancestors of origin." They enshrined these ancestors, and worshiped them to enhance their political power and prestige. Leaders of the *uji* induced their members to worship them as their *uji-gami*, tutelary deities.[1]

By the sixth century, the ancestors of the present imperial family had risen to prominence as the most powerful and prestigious *uji* of Japan.

---

1. Aruga Kizaemon (1967) uses the term "pseudo-pedigree ancestor"; Robert J. Smith (1974, pp. 6–12) uses "the ancestor of origin" in his discussion based on Aruga's study.

The family chose as its ancestor of origin Amaterasu-ō-mikami, the Sun Goddess, and enshrined her at the Ise Shrine near Nara. According to legend, the grandson of the Sun Goddess descended from heaven, married a daughter of the leader of a local *uji* and became the ruler of the region. Their great-grandson conquered the nation and became Emperor Jimmu, the first emperor of Japan.[2] Emperor Jimmu, though a mythical figure, became the founding ancestor of the imperial family, from whom the direct and unbroken lineage of Japan's imperial family continues to the present day. The family's ancestor of origin, Amaterasu-ō-mikami, became the highest tutelary deity of the people and the nation. This is the mythical origin of the divinity of the Japanese emperor (Aruga 1967, pp. 177–78; *Nihon-no Rekishi*, vol. 1).

The Japanese emperor had a dual role from the very beginning. In his secular role, he was the head of state, and in the early centuries of Japanese history he had substantial political power. But as a descendant of the Sun Goddess, though not a god himself, he was also the high priest of the nation, who alone could be purified to worship her (Aruga 1966–71, 4:345–46). The religious practices of the early Japanese people, centering on purification ceremonies and worship of ancestors, were later called *Shintō*, "the way of the gods."

In the middle of the sixth century, two other important religious and ethical traditions, Buddhism and Confucianism, were brought to Japan from China, and Buddhism in particular flourished among the aristocrats. But the Japanese eventually reduced their heavy reliance on the Chinese culture, and developed a religious culture that was distinctly Japanese. Buddhism and Shintoism began to borrow ideas and practices from each other. Until the arrival of Buddhism, Shinto deities had no earthly representations. Soon, however, Buddhist carvers began to carve statues of these gods. Some were housed in Shinto shrines, while others were placed in Buddhist temples along with statues of buddhas (*Nihon-no Rekishi* 3:65).

Buddhism had a number of different philosophical schools of thought, but this side of the religion had little appeal for the Japanese, who were more interested in religious practices and ceremonies. Shintoism concentrated on ritual and purification, and had no church organization or developed theology, so there were no grounds for doctrinal disputes. Buddhist theologians argued that the Shinto gods were manifestations of the Buddha nature, and the Shinto priests, in turn, claimed that

---

2. The two chronicles in which the mythical stories of the imperial origin of Japan are told are *Kojiki* (Record of Ancient Matters), completed in 712, and *Nihon Shoki* (Chronicles of Japan) written in 720.

their deities were also the protectors of Buddhism in Japan. By the tenth century, the distinctions between the two religions had blurred considerably, and a blend of doctrines and practices had developed which reinforced the existing political order.

In the initial stages of the feudal era, a new form of Chinese Buddhism, Zen, which emphasized meditation and strict self-reliance in attaining salvation, gained adherents among the emerging bushi class. The influence of Zen Buddhism stimulated Shinto priests to emphasize inner purity. In particular, the Shinto priests at Ise Jingū, the imperial shrine, stressed that deities disliked evil deeds, and were pleased by honesty, uprightness, and sincerity (Bellah 1985, pp. 63–69). Thus, syncretism continued as the two religions developed.

When Tokugawa Ieyasu established the bakufu in Edo, for the first time in Japanese history Confucianism became the main force in the political, as well as the spiritual life of all classes of the Japanese people. Fujiwara Seika (1561–1619), and his disciple, Hayashi Razan (1583–1657), both Buddhist monks who left the priesthood for Confucianism, developed the Japanese variant of neo-Confucianism that provided an ideological justification for the rigid, hierarchical social order of the Tokugawa bakufu. Their doctrine became the dominant school of thought, but there were a number of competing schools as well. The bakufu had not adopted an official ideology, and did not insist on ideological conformity. So long as intellectual disagreements did not lead to political movements against the bakufu, they took no action to suppress either those who challenged neo-Confucian thought, or their doctrines.

The one apparent exception to this attitude was the treatment of Christians. During the reign of the third Tokugawa shogun, Iemitsu (1604–1651), the bakufu adopted a policy of seclusion, and Japan severed virtually all of its contacts with the outside world. European Christian missionaries were expelled, and their Japanese converts were mercilessly persecuted. But this persecution was probably politically, rather than religiously, motivated. Buddhists did not originate the policy of persecution, and Buddhist priests did not take an active part in it (Sansom 1958–63, 3:44). The bakufu was probably afraid that the European Catholic missionaries and Japanese Christians would challenge the bakufu. To ensure that there were no new Christian converts, and to keep a record of the population, the bakufu instituted a requirement that every household be affiliated with a Buddhist temple—a policy that profoundly changed the role of Buddhism in Japanese society. Buddhist temples became identified with funerals and memorial services for the members of its registered households, and

began to play a central role in the ancestor worship that had previously
been practiced at Shinto shrines. Buddhist priests ceased to make efforts
to teach and spread their religion. Since governmental protection and
contributions from the member households ensured the economic basis
of temples, it was easy for them to become complacent (*Nihon-no Reki-shi* 8:182–83).

Thus, over the course of more than a thousand years, Buddhism and
Shintoism evolved together, intermingling their religious practices,
rituals and beliefs. The Japanese have never been particularly interested
in abstract philosophical thought, and made no effort to keep the religions distinct, or to develop an exclusive theology. Neither Buddhism
nor Shintoism promoted a strong set of ethical principles or code of
conduct, so when neo-Confucianism became the dominant strain of
thought under the Tokugawa bakufu, the Japanese saw no conflict between its ethical principles and the ideas of Shintoism and Buddhism.
The two religions found that such ethical concerns as they had were
quite compatible with neo-Confucian ideals.

### The Meiji Restoration, Religion, and the Emperor

Throughout the Tokugawa period, the Emperor remained both head of
state and high priest of Shinto. Though he may have been neglected
both as political and religious leader, he was never explicitly rejected.
The Meiji Restoration, in one sense, was an attempt to "restore," or
revitalize the ancient Japanese tradition by placing both political and
religious authority in the Emperor. In early Japanese history, the imperial family had established its political dominance and then linked itself to the mythical ancestors of origin to enhance its prestige and
power. To gain the support of the people for their program of modernization, the Meiji oligarchs tried to revitalize the prestige and authority
of the Emperor by enhancing and emphasizing his illustrious mythical
origin. They initially attempted to separate Buddhism from Shintoism,
and make Shintoism the national religion. Although this effort failed,
the oligarchs did succeed in reviving the Emperor's authority through
the avenue of education. The government taught Japanese children the
Confucian ideas of loyalty and filial piety, and, by emphasizing that the
Emperor was the head of Japan as a household, the father of the nation,
they were able to develop considerable loyalty to the Emperor and the
government that exercised power in his name.

The Emperor had ceased to exercise any real political power by the
eleventh century, but the imperial institution was never eliminated,
because the Emperor was an important source of legitimacy for the secu-

lar political system. Everyone understood that the Emperor was merely a figurehead in secular politics, but spiritually he was the highest and sole head of the national household (Aruga 1966–71, 4:345–46). For this reason, the Emperor's prestige has been effectively used to reaffirm the unity of the nation in crises. During the final years of the Tokugawa bakufu, the shogun had turned to the Emperor for advice, and the new order, created in 1868, was a "revitalization" in the name of the Emperor. Similarly in 1945, during the final days of World War II, the Emperor played a key role in bringing the war to a close.

During the Meiji Restoration, the Emperor was drawn into the center of political life, but this did not mean that he, himself, became powerful. The Meiji oligarchs carefully educated the young Emperor, who was enthroned at the age of sixteen, so that he would effectively serve as the symbolic center of the new state. The Emperor received lectures from leading scholars on Western political philosophy, as well as *kokugaku* and the Confucian ideas of the responsibility of the ruler (A. Tanaka 1979, pp. 252–54). But the oligarchs had no intention of giving him actual political power.[3]

At the beginning of the Restoration, the ordinary people, who had lived under the reign of the Tokugawa bakufu for more than 250 years, did not show much interest in or respect for the Emperor. A German doctor, who went to Japan in 1876 to serve as the Emperor's attending physician and professor of medicine at Tokyo Imperial University, lamented the people's lack of interest. In his diary on November 3, 1880, he recorded:

> The Emperor's birthday. It distresses me to see how little interest the populace take in their ruler. Only when the police insists on it are houses decorated with flags. In default of this, house-owners do the minimum. (Baelz 1932, p. 62)

The Meiji rulers took a number of steps to change the Emperor's status in the eyes of the Japanese people. One of the most successful was simply to make him more visible. During the first twenty years of his reign, Emperor Meiji traveled extensively to various parts of Japan. At each stop, he stayed at the home of the local leader, met with citizens, and visited the courthouse and the teachers' college. Afterward, the local government would build a monument commemorating his visit. All this was part of the government's effort to improve the image

3. Tanaka Akira (1979, pp. 253–54) says that the government was careful not to let the Emperor's Confucian teacher, Motoda Eifu, and the Imperial Household Agency gain too much influence in formulating the role of the emperor.

of the Emperor as the leader of the new political order (A. Tanaka 1979, pp. 235–43).

The Meiji oligarchs had to institute radical changes in Japanese political, social, and economic institutions to transform Japan into a modern, industrial nation, changes that would have been impossible without the widespread support, or at least the acquiescence, of the Japanese people. To this end, they emphasized that the Emperor was the head of Japan as if it were a single household, so that the Emperor and the people were united in spirit, *kummin ichinyo*, and the nation was jointly ruled by the Emperor and the people, *kummin dōchi*.[4] They initially tried to rely on the Emperor's dual role as the head of both the religious and secular realms by establishing Shintoism as the national religion, and strengthening the Emperor's role as the head of the national religion.

One aspect of this program was separating Shintoism from Buddhism, "purifying" it by severing all its ties with Buddhism at the imperial court. All buddhas and other Buddhist sculptures were removed from the court, and the imperial household was forced to end its association with Buddhist monasteries. Thus a relationship that had begun at the time of the Yamato court was brought to an end.[5]

The government also tried unsuccessfully to bring about similar radical changes in the religious life of the ordinary people. It ordered that all buddhas housed in Shinto shrines be removed. Many Buddhist monks serving in temples within the compounds of tutelary shrines were forced to give up their positions and return to secular life. The government encouraged the people to hold funerals at Shinto shrines rather than at Buddhist temples. But after more than fifteen years of controversy and great confusion, the Meiji government saw that its policy was not succeeding, and was finally forced to abandon the idea of establishing Shintoism as Japan's official state religion. The people were simply not willing to give up their long tradition of syncretism (see M. Sakurai 1971, pp. 21–54).

One other reform that the government initiated but did not complete

4. Ōkubo Toshimichi said in his opinion on the constitution drafted in 1873, "Constitutional monarchy is a joint government of the ruler and the people; it is a limited monarchy. . . . When the people and the government are united, modernization will not be fruitless. This shall be the foundation of our nation and the basis of our government" (Beckmann 1957, p. 113, appendix 2).

5. During the Tokugawa era, the imperial family consisted of the Emperor's immediate family and four other households. The members of the family who were not in line to become head of one of the four households joined Buddhist monasteries. The government abolished this custom, and those who were already in monasteries returned to secular life, with new titles, and established new households (M. Sakurai 1971, p. 25).

was an attempt to gain control over the land which had belonged to the old *han*, or fiefs. During the 1870s, the government decreed that the properties of institutions such as public schools and hospitals throughout the nation belonged to the central administration. The government also gained control of the grounds and forests of both Shinto shrines and Buddhist temples, and then leased these properties to their respective users rent-free. Later the government relented somewhat, and attempted to return ownership of land to those Buddhist temples that requested it, but World War II intervened, and the transfer was never completed (Umeda 1971, pp. 271–75; Woodward 1972, pp. 117–20). As will be seen, this became a great concern of religious leaders in 1946.

The Meiji government was more successful in linking the Emperor to education, particularly in the teaching of ethics in schools. The centerpiece of its program was the Imperial Rescript on Education, promulgated in 1890. It drew on Confucian ideas of loyalty and filial piety, but linked them to the Emperor as the father of the nation. It also encouraged Japanese subjects to maintain harmonious relationships within families and communities, and work toward building a harmonious and prosperous nation:

> Know ye, Our Subjects:
>
> Our Imperial Ancestors have founded Our Empire on a basis broad and everlasting and have deeply and firmly implanted virtue; Our subjects ever united in loyalty and filial piety have from generation to generation illustrated the beauty thereof. This is the glory of the fundamental character of Our Empire, and herein also lies the source of Our education. Ye, Our subjects, be filial to your parents, affectionate to your brothers and sisters; as husbands and wives be harmonious, as friends true; bear yourselves in modesty and moderation; extend your benevolence to all; pursue learning and cultivate arts, and thereby develop intellectual faculties and perfect moral powers; furthermore advance public good and promote common interests; always respect the Constitution and observe the laws; should emergency arise, offer yourselves courageously to the State; and thus guard and maintain the prosperity of Our Imperial Throne coeval with heaven and earth. So shall ye not only be Our good and faithful subjects, but render illustrious the best traditions of your forefathers.
>
> The Way here set forth is indeed the teaching bequeathed by Our Imperial Ancestors, to be observed alike by Their Descendants and the subjects, infallible for all ages and true

in all places. It is Our wish to lay it to heart in all reverence,
in common with you, Our subjects, that we may thus attain
to the same virtue. (Lu 1974, 2:70–71)

For the next fifty-five years, until the end of World War II, this document was read aloud in full by school principals throughout the nation
on various ceremonial occasions, and "was made the subject of countless exegeses, and its sentiments worked into textbooks of ethics and
morals used in the primary and secondary schools" (R. Smith 1983,
p. 11). This educational progam achieved considerable success, and the
Emperor became the center of reverence and adoration of most ordinary
Japanese people, many of whom came to see him as the head of Japan,
united as a single household.

### The Meiji Constitution, Freedom of Religion, and Separation of Religion and State

The oligarchs considered the Meiji Constitution another means of
strengthening the Emperor's position. Following the European model of
the king as God's vicar on earth and the spiritual head of the nation,
Itō characterized the Emperor as "sacred" and "inviolable" in the Constitution. However, he chose the word *shinsei*, from an ancient Japanese
literary text, to stand for "sacred," thereby drawing on the traditional
Japanese idea of the Emperor's purifying role in religious ceremonies,
asking for the tutelary deities' protection of his nation. The drafters of
the Constitution also included a clause granting freedom of religion,
realizing that such a provision was crucial for getting the Western
nations to agree to revise the unequal treaties. They had no difficulty
giving the people this right, because they believed that religion was a
matter of the heart, and not of direct concern to the government. They
did, however, worry about the implication of this clause for the Emper-
or's role in education, and the potential difficulties for public officials
who might be required to participate in Shinto ceremonies at the imperial court. The government finally found a way out of these difficulties
by splitting Shintoism into two different categories—ordinary sectarian
Shintoism (Kyōha Shinto) and shrine Shintoism (Jinja Shinto). Kyōha
Shinto referred to new sects that were periodically founded, primarily
in rural Japan, by individuals guided by special spirits.[6] The government
decided that the Bureau of Religion would oversee those sects. The
shrines that housed ancestral deities and other deities related to the

---

6. The best known ones are Tenri-kyō, founded in 1838 by Nakamura Miki, a farm-woman in
Nara; and Konkō-kyō, founded in 1859 by Kawate Bunjirō, another farmer in Okayama.

founding of the nation, on the other hand, were included in Jinja Shinto, and the Bureau of Shrines would administer and support them.[7] Thereafter, the government made the odd claim that the shrines belonging to Jinja Shinto were public, and not religious, institutions. Ceremonies and rituals performed at these shrines, therefore, were public, and not religious, performances.

As we have seen, the Meiji reformers looked to Europe for a suitable model of government and constitution. They learned that most leading European nations, although constitutionalized, were still monarchies ruled by hereditary sovereigns. They also saw that "the essence of monarchy lay in its association with the forces of religion," although by then the political thought of Western nations had been largely secularized (Watkins 1946, p. 311). Much of the ceremony of Western monarchies was also religious in origin. With some variation in choice of expression, European constitutions stated that the king's person was sacred and inviolable. The writers of the Meiji Constitution drew on the divine origin of the Emperor, seeking to equate him with European kings, and to define his status in language parallel to that in European constitutions. But they did not forget their own traditional view of the Emperor.

Evidence of their intention to include Japanese ideas is found in a document which was apparently distributed to the members of the Privy Council at the constitutional hearings. This document, simply headed "References" (Sanshō), records sources for most of the articles included in the Meiji Constitution, as well as some illuminating commentaries.[8] Article 3 of the Meiji Constitution reads, *Tennō-wa shinsei-ni shite okasu bekarazu*, "The Emperor is sacred and inviolable" (my translation). As sources for this article, the "References" first list two ancient books, *Nihon Shoki* (A chronicle of Japan), and *Man'yō-shū*, Japan's oldest collection of poetry, compiled around 760. The four quotes from these sources describe the mythical origin of Japan and the imperial throne.

---

7. Umeda (1974, p. 24) divides Shinto into two types, national Shinto (Kokka Shinto) and sectarian Shinto (Kyōha Shinto). National Shinto is further divided into Shinto at the imperial court (Kyūtei Shinto) and shrine Shinto (Jinja Shinto). Since the Meiji government failed in its effort to make Shintoism the national religion, however, it seems inappropriate to use the term "Kokka Shinto."

8. For the text, see Shimizu 1971–74, 3:331–424. The document was discovered in the study of Itō Miyoji, secretary to the chairman of the council, and one of the drafters of the Constitution, after his death in 1934. Shimizu Shin included it in his book, *Teikoku Kempō Seitei Kaigi* (Meetings on the Making of the Imperial Constitution), published in November 1940. The book was banned shortly thereafter, however, so the document also remained undisclosed for several years. It is now at the National Diet Library in Tokyo (Shimizu 1971–74, 2:331).

But the word *shinsei,* "sacred," appears only in the first item from *Nihon Shoki:* "Heaven was created, then Earth was formed. Thereafter the sacred ones were born between them" (my translation).[9] Eight European sources follow, all of which define the sanctity of kingship (Shimizu 1971–74, 2:335–36). It turns out that the Japanese sentence is identical to the first half of the Japanese translation of the corresponding article in the Austrian, Spanish, and Portuguese constitutions (ibid., p. 336).

But the two religious traditions are quite different, as are the corresponding roles of the king and the emperor. The Christian God is more like an earthly ruler, laying down laws or commands for his subjects to obey. As God's representative, the sovereign not only had the sanction of God, but could also claim to implement God's rule. This possibility is absent in Shintoism. The Shinto gods may protect the inhabitants of earth from danger, and Shinto rituals are performed to secure this protection. But they do not 'rule' the earth in the same way that the Christian God does. As mentioned earlier, the Emperor is the link between the gods and the Japanese people through his divine ancestry, but only in the sense that he alone can perform the purifying rituals and pray for their protection of the nation and its people. Other than prescribing rituals, the priest does not lay down rules or codes of behavior for believers. He is not the gods' agent or representative, only an intermediary.

For modern readers, this idea might not seem important. Should the British queen be called "sacred," it would have no effect either on the form of government or substantive legislation. Things were still quite different in the nineteenth century, however. In Europe, sanctity of kingship was designed "to make people believe that resistance to the authority of the monarch was not only a crime to be punished in this life but also a sin to be punished throughout eternity" (Watkins 1946, p. 312).

Itō Hirobumi had doubts as to whether Japan could properly be called an empire. But Lorenz Von Stein reassured him:

> Japan is a natural empire and the natural emperor cannot be moved, just as heaven and earth cannot be moved. This is what is important of Japanese national polity. There are people who call themselves members of the Japanese People's

---

9. In Aston's translation, published in 1924 and reissued in 1972, this sentence reads: "Heaven was therefore formed first, and Earth was established subsequently. Thereafter Divine Beings were produced between them" (p. 2).

Rights party, and who try to gradually change the national polity. For what reason? . . . People have no right to dispute the idea of national polity by their whims. . . . The Japanese Emperor is not a man-made institution. The Emperor is a natural emperor, so it is easy for him to govern his nation. Thus, the government should rest assured. The government should not worry about the various ideas of the People's Rights party and the like. It would suffice for the government to pay attention to expressing its position clearly. Napoleon, the first emperor of France, was a great man, but he became the emperor by exercising power. Thus people, in return, used power to remove him, obtained the control of the government, and established sovereignty of the people. The Japanese polity is a beautiful one of which Germany is envious. (Meiji Bunka Kenkyū-kai 1967–74, 1:524–25; my translation)

This view was most congenial to Itō and the other Meiji leaders, who had no interest in or intention of introducing democracy in Japan. But there is nothing in the Japanese concept of *shinsei* that is inherently antidemocratic. The Emperor can play his purifying role in any type of state or regime whatsoever. His celebration of Shinto rites is similar in some respects to the rituals of state performed by the remaining Western monarchs. But the Emperor did not have a church hierarchy behind him, since Shinto is not an organized religion. Thus, there would be no official "church," as there was in some Westen nations. The drafters of the Meiji Constitution, by defining the role of the Emperor in terms of European constitutional models, inadvertently planted the seeds of later misunderstanding between the Japanese and Americans.

The drafters had an easier time with the issue of religious freedom, which they granted in limited form in Article 28:

Japanese subjects have freedom of religious belief, within limits not prejudicial to peace and order and not antagonistic to their duties as subjects. (My translation)

The "References" give twelve European sources (Shimizu 1971–74, 2:369–70). As expected, there is no Japanese source. The Japanese drafters included this clause in the Constitution because they had learned that Europeans considered such a clause important. In his commentary, Itō writes,

In medieval Europe, when religion was at its height, there were conflicts and bloodshed due to the mixing of religion and politics. . . . Today, however, although there are nations with state religions and social and educational systems built on a particular religious sect, there is no government that does not give individuals legal freedom to worship religions of their choice. . . . It is impossible not to regard freedom of religion as a great and beautiful product of modern civilization.

He then continued,

Faith is a matter of heart, but law and order require that general constraints be placed on public expressions of one's heart, such as rituals, proselytizing, speaking in public, and organizing meetings. (ibid., 3:540; my translation)

The Meiji leaders were not afraid to allow ordinary people freedom of belief for, as we have seen, Japan does not have a strong tradition of religious intolerance. They were mainly concerned about the consequences of public expression of belief for social order.

Another concern was the relationship between religion and the state, and more specifically, the government officials' participation in official functions involving ceremonies at the imperial court. When this article was introduced in the Privy Council, it generated much debate. One of the more vocal members, Sasaki Takayuki, told Itō Miyoji that this article did not affect ordinary citizens, but might affect government officials who had a duty to participate in ceremonies at the imperial court. Presumably referring to Christianity, he said that there were religions which did not allow believers to participate in rituals of other religions. Under the provisions of this article, if a member of such a religious group happened to be a government official, but refused to worship at these ceremonies, he should not be considered to be violating his duty as an official. Moreover, it should not be construed as disturbing peace and order. He asked, however, whether the government would accept this interpretation (ibid., 3:244). Itō denied that there was a difficulty, saying that Sasaki's query did not involve a matter of religion, but that of public service regulations. He said,

The freedom of religion expressed in Article 28 is not an unqualified freedom, but a limited one. To list some of the limits, the people must not disregard their duties, and exercise of this freedom should not disturb social order, or interfere with freedom of individual beliefs. According to this Constitution, Japanese subjects have freedom of belief as long as they do not overstep these limits. Thus this clause represents a constitutional right of the subjects. It does not apply to government officials. A government official's participation in ceremonies at the imperial court is a matter of public service regulations, and is not covered by the Constitution (ibid., pp. 244–45; my translation).[10]

Another member, Torio Koyata, said,

> The drafters must have included this clause after careful consideration of its consequences. Of course, for ordinary citizens, the restrictions that Mr. Itō explained would be sufficient. Even if they do not worship (reihai) at the imperial festivals (chōtei saishi), one can say that that will not jeopardize the national polity or their duties as citizens. However, if a cabinet member or a government official acts in such a way, it will be regarded as improper in respect to his duty as a subject, and a rejection of the national polity. How will the government deal with such a case? (ibid., p. 245; my translation).

Itō Hirobumi responded that no one could predict the government's policy on religious freedom a hundred years hence; cases such as the ones brought up by the members would have to be resolved when they arose. The article was passed with eighteen affirmative votes, presumably out of a total of thirty (ibid., p. 246).[11]

Eleven years after the promulgation of the Meiji Constitution, the Japanese government made three important policy changes concerning religion, partly to combat criticisms from Western nations that used the Japanese government's negative attitude toward Christianity to resist its repeated attempts to revise the unequal treaties of the 1850s. First, the government officially included Christianity in the list of religions practiced in Japan. It also issued an order prohibiting religious teachings and ceremonies in public schools. These actions were presumably undertaken to impress the Western nations. The third and by far the most important change, was the government's decision, mentioned above, to classify Jinja Shinto shrines as public institutions. In the spring of 1900, the government renamed Shaji-kyoku (the Bureau of Shrines and Temples) Shūkyō-kyoku (the Bureau of Religions), and placed private shrines under its jurisdiction. But it placed shrines supported by government funds under a newly created unit, Jinja-kyoku (the Bureau of Shrines); the priests and other employees at these shrines became public officials. Thus, the government in effect redefined these shrines to

---

10. Such a case actually occurred several years later. In 1891, a distinguished Japanese Christian, Uchimura Kanzō, then an instructor at a public high school, refused to bow while the Imperial Rescript on Education was being recited, and was subsequently dismissed from his post (Nihon-no Rekishi 11:82).

11. Shimizu (3:31–33) does not give the number of opposition votes. He only gives the names of thirty councillors who participated in the constitutional hearings at the Privy Council.

be public, nonreligious institutions, making it possible for public schools to include shrine worship as part of the teaching of ethics without violating the constitutional right of religious freedom. This also made it possible for the national and local governments to sponsor various traditional festivals, where the people worshiped ancestral deities, and asked for their protection, and allowed public officials to attend them as part of their official functions (Umeda 1971, pp. 49–50). From then on until the end of World War II, Jinja Shinto became the quasi-national religion.

## Freedom of Religion and Separation of Church and State in America

In the West, religious freedom has traditionally involved two related issues: freedom of conscience, and the relationship between church and state. Religious doctrines or ideas have always been of concern to political leaders, because such ideas could either lend legitimacy to the regime or lead believers to oppose the political order. When religious thought is closely linked to a strong church organization, however, it acquires far greater political significance. Church organization can reinforce the legitimizing force of religious ideas by insisting on and maintaining uniformity of doctrine. In the West, this was not simply a theoretical concern. Since the end of the Roman Empire, political disputes involving religion had been a constant feature of political life. Thus it is not surprising that most seventeenth-century European governments maintained a close alliance with a single established church. Nor is it surprising that they were concerned about religious dissent. Not only could religious dissenters provide a potential challenge to the legitimacy of the government, their church could also form an organized base of political opposition.

Some of the earliest settlers of the American colonies were religious dissenters who, nonetheless, brought with them the idea that the community should have a single, established church. Yet virtually from the beginning, the colonies were distinguished by religious diversity and pluralism. Different religious groups established their own communities, each with its own church; dissenters in a particular community often moved away and established a new community and a new church in another location, only to be faced with further disagreements in their new settlement. It soon became obvious that no colony could effectively insist on and impose a single, established church, however much it may have aspired to such a condition.

By the Revolutionary period, the colonists generally believed that "religion was a matter between God and the individual; that government possessed no intrinsic powers over matters of religion; and that when secular powers interfered in religious affairs, they exceeded their authority, violated religious liberty, and corrupted both Church and State" (Curry 1986, p. 190). Yet they "did not bring their accepted theories of Church and State to bear on the numerous ways by which governments did exercise jurisdiction in religious matters, and they continued to maintain the Christian Protestant society inherited from colonial times" (pp. 190–91). Catholics were often not allowed to hold public office, and they complained about it. Americans engaged in extensive discussions about church and state, and debated whether states should support religious establishments—ministers and church buildings. Those opposed argued that an individual "could not be compelled to attend religious worship, but neither could one be forced to pay for the worship one chose to attend." Thus the colonists argued for freedom of choice in religious matters, but expected most people to choose a form of Protestant Christianity (pp. 190–91).

By 1789, Americans "largely believed that issues of Church and State had been satisfactorily settled by the individual states. They agreed that the federal government had no power in such matters" (ibid., p. 194). Robert Rutland (1962, p. 88) summarizes the issue of religious freedom in American states at the time of the ratification of the Constitution as follows:

> No single issue among the various points covered by the bills of rights caused so much discussion or legislative action as freedom of religion. All citizens could expect equal treatment under the bills of rights except those whose religious convictions placed them in the minority. Thus a Congregationalist, Baptist, Catholic, and Anglican might have joined to support guarantees of a free press or trial by jury; but when it came to the matter of complete freedom of religion, a stirring argument and perhaps a bloody nose or two were likely. Legal incrustations upheld the established church in many of the new states. *The drive to gain religious freedom, therefore, was in fact an effort to separate church and state completely* [emphasis added]. This meant that in New England the various splinter groups of Protestantism were arrayed against the established Congregational church, while in the South the dissenters toiled to sever state support from the older Anglican churches.
>
> Foremost among the groups demanding unequivocal religious freedom were the Baptists. Their historic aversion to official ties between church and state was based on the con-

viction that civil authorities who touched religious affairs
were transgressors in a field reserved "for Christ [who] only
is the king and lawgiver of the church and conscience."

Many of the supporters of the Constitution promised to add a bill of
rights to win over those who distrusted the proposed new federal government. When James Madison was seeking a seat in the House of
Representatives, he made such a promise to ease the fear of Virginia
Baptists that the federal Constitution provided insufficient protection
for religious freedom. Once elected, Madison "informed the House that
he considered himself 'bound in honor and in duty' to present and advocate amendments" (Curry 1986, pp. 198–99). After much debate,
Congress passed the Bill of Rights, including the First Amendment,
which reads:

Congress shall make no law respecting an establishment of
religion, or prohibiting the free exercise thereof; or abridging
the freedom of speech, or of the press; or the right of the
people peaceably to assemble, and to petition the Government for a redress of grievances.

The issue of church and state has another important aspect. In Western thought, religious and ethical beliefs are often intimately connected, and particular moral codes or ideas are closely linked with
specific religions. This makes it possible for Americans to distinguish
between religious education and education about religions, even
though the distinction may not be clear in specific instances. Religious
education usually means teaching the doctrines and ethical principles
of a particular faith, with the intention and expectation that the students will believe them. Education about religion, on the other hand,
means teaching students about the history, practices and beliefs of different religions. The teacher remains neutral, presenting each religion
in an "objective" manner, without encouraging the students to adopt a
particular religion or set of ethical beliefs. Americans thus believe that
separation of religion and state naturally leads to divorcing religious
education from public education.

But in specific situations Americans have not always been able to
agree on the application of the principle of separation of church and
state, especially in connection with education. In 1947, shortly after
the Americans at MacArthur's headquarters in Tokyo wrote the draft of
the Japanese Constitution, the proper relationship between the two became a matter of controversy in the United States. *Everson vs. Board of
Education*, 330 U.S. 1 (1947) raised the issue of whether a local school
district could reimburse parents for the expense of busing their children

to parochial schools. The Supreme Court held that the government could not finance religious educational institutions:

> The "establishment of religion" clause of the First Amendment means at least this: Neither a state nor the Federal Government can set up a church. Neither can pass laws which aid one religion, aid all religions, or prefer one religion over another. (330 U.S. at 15)

Critics of this decision contended that "the amendment was intended only to ban a state religion—an exclusive government preference for one religion," arguing that the government should be allowed to give nonpreferential assistance to all religions. Yet Curry (1986, pp. 207–8) writes that, in 1789, "not a shred of evidence exists to verify that anyone wanted the new government to have any power in matters of religion."

## The American Approach to Freedom of Religion in Japan

Americans went to Japan with a deeply felt conviction that the Japanese government should not restrict individual religious freedom. They looked upon its promotion of Shrine Shintoism and the emphasis on the divinity of the Emperor, both before and during the war, with profound suspicion. The following passage from a State Department memorandum expresses this view:

> The occupation authorities should in all of their treatment of and their contacts with the Emperor refrain from any action which would imply recognition of or support for the Japanese concept that the Japanese Emperor is different from and superior to other temporal rulers, that he is of divine origin and capacities, that he is sacrosanct or that he is indispensable. They should permit absolute freedom of discussion, except where there may be incitement to breaches of peace, of political as well as other subjects.[12]

GHQ also took a strongly negative view, illustrated by the following passage:

> It has been stated that the basis of all political authority is the acquiescence of the individual member of the state. However obtained, it is the vital ingredient. It is the people who, in the last analysis, determine what form their government takes. The rulers of Japan were well aware of this. The

---

12. Quoted from a memorandum prepared by the Inter-Divisional Area Committee on the Far East of the Department of State on May 9, 1944 (U.S. Department of State 1965, p. 1254).

knowledge of that basic truth guided their conduct and influenced their every action. It was because of this knowledge
that they enlarged Shinto into a state religion that glorified
the Japanese State as symbolized by the Emperor and por-
trayed the sublimity of unquestioning obedience to an ever
loving and ever watchful temporal and spiritual ruler, the
divine parent of an earthly family, by this means deepening
and strengthening the already powerful unifying force of emperor worship. It was because they were afraid that acquiescence might be withdrawn that they developed a police
system which inquired into every intimate detail of the private life of every subject, that watched, regulated and op-
pressed, that acted swiftly and summarily whenever danger
to the state appeared to threaten—acted without regard for
human rights and with no concern for law. . . . The Imperial Japanese Government arrogated unto itself the position
of guides of the people's morals, keepers of the people's conscience and arbiters of the people's destinies. The people
were not consulted. (SCAP 1968, 1:88)

The Americans took several steps to return religious freedom to the
Japanese people. First, on December 15, 1945, GHQ issued a lengthy
directive to the Japanese government, commanding disestablishment of
"state religion":

The sponsorship, support, perpetuation, control and dissemi-
nation of Shinto by the Japanese national, prefectural, and
local governments, or by public officials, subordinates and
employees acting in their official capacity are prohibited
and will cease immediately.

The directive listed twelve specific practices, including the maintenance of shrines with public funds, and gave the following reasons for
banning them: (1) to free the Japanese people from direct or indirect
compulsion to believe or profess to believe in a religion or cult officially designed by the state; (2) to lift from the Japanese people the
burden of compulsory financial support of an ideology which has contributed to their war guilt, defeat, suffering, privation, and present de-
plorable condition; (3) to prevent a recurrence of the perversion of
Shinto theory and beliefs into militaristic and ultra-nationalistic pro-
paganda designed to delude the Japanese people and lead them into
wars of agression; (4) to assist the Japanese people in a rededication of
their national life to building a new Japan based upon ideals of perpetual
peace and democracy (SCAP 1968, 2:467–69). Thus, GHQ officially
determined that shrines were religious institutions, used by the Japanese

government to promote ultranationalistic war efforts. They therefore compelled the government to sever its links with shrines and cease supporting them with public funds.

MacArthur's staff also believed that Shintoism, like Christianity, had a theory, if not a theology, or set of doctrines, and had little doubt that separation of religion and state naturally led to divorcing religious education from public education. The GHQ directive of December 15, 1945, quoted earlier stated,

> h. The dissemination of Shinto doctrines in any form and by any means in any educational institution supported wholly or in part by public funds is prohibited and will cease immediately.
> (1) All teachers' manuals and textbooks now in use in any educational institution supported wholly or in part by public funds will be censored, and all Shinto doctrine will be deleted. No teachers' manual or textbook which is published in the future for use in such institutions will contain any Shinto doctrine.
> (2) No visits to Shinto shrines and no rites, practices, or ceremonies associated with Shinto will be conducted or sponsored by any educational institution supported wholly or in part by public funds. (ibid., 2:467–468)

As a follow up, GHQ issued a second directive on December 31, ordering an immediate suspension of courses in *shūshin* (moral training in filial piety and loyalty to the Emperor and the nation), as well as courses in history and geography in all Japanese schools, public and private. They ordered the Ministry of Education to prepare a new set of textbooks on those subjects, and to submit them to GHQ for approval as soon as possible. The Americans looked upon *shūshin* as intimately linked to Shinto doctrine, and militaristic and ultranationalistic ideologies, and tried to prevent its resurgence.[13]

Finally, the Americans played a decisive role in bringing about the Emperor's renunciation of his divinity in the famous rescript of January 1, 1946. As was mentioned earlier, the Japanese government was gravely worried about the position of the Emperor in postwar Japan. Thus, the government asked the Emperor to travel to various parts of

---

13. A GHQ memorandum to the Japanese government, which bans history and geography, as well as *shūshin*, says " . . . inasmuch as the Japanese Government has used education to inculcate militaristic and ultranationalistic ideologies which have been inextricably interwoven in certain textbooks imposed upon students, it is hereby directed that . . . " (AG 000.8 [31 Dec 45] CIE). National Diet Library, Modern History Materials Room.

the war-torn nation, and personally encourage people in their efforts to rebuild their lives and the nation. This contributed considerably to creating a new, "democratic" image of the Emperor both in Japan and abroad (Satō 1962–64, 2:898–99). The Emperor, himself, was thinking about ways to change his image. According to Shidehara Kijūrō's biography, in late fall of 1945 the Emperor indicated to the Prime Minister that renouncing his divinity might be necessary if he was to be accepted as the emperor of the new democratic nation. He even expressed his desire to announce it in a rescript in the beginning of the year (Shidehara Heiwa Zaidan 1955, pp. 666–67). The Japanese, however, took no action.

It was an American who took the initiative. One day in late November, 1945, a member of the Religions Division of the Civil Information and Education Section of GHQ, Lieutenant Colonel Harold G. Henderson, was talking with R. H. Blyth, an Englishman serving as an unofficial liaison between the Imperial Household and GHQ.[14] Henderson told him that the Americans had to "eradicate their [Japanese] false notions of national and especially Imperial superiority due to divine descent." He further suggested that an imperial rescript would be a possible way to bring about this change. Upon the urging of Blyth, Henderson drafted a statement to this effect. Blyth took this draft to the Imperial Household. The following day, Blyth came back to GHQ with "a copy of the essential part of the proposed rescript, which turned out to be [Henderson's] formula with the change of only one word."[15]

---

14. Blyth had become a member of the faculty of Gakushūin, a school for the children of the imperial family and the peerage, shortly before this event.

15. Blyth's proposed rescript is as follows.

> *This is a New Year, a New Year for Japan, a new world with new ideals, with Humanity above nationality as the Great Goal.* Altruistic love stems from the love of nature, of family and of nation, and provides the foundation to the love of mankind.
>
> In our country love of family and love of nation have always been very firm. Today we should endeavor to work toward love of mankind. The ties binding the Emperor and the people have always been especially strong, but they are not derived from only myths and legends nor the mistaken idea that the Japanese people are of divine descent (descendants of the kami), superior to all the people, and destined to rule them. This bond of trust and love is the produce of thousands of years of mutual affection and devotion.
>
> Loyalty has always characterized our political as well as religious life. Loyalty has been our supreme value, and it shall be so for ever. If loyalty to nation be broader than that to family, so loyalty to mankind is greater than that to a nation. The present condition of society, prevailing unemployment, stagnation of foreign trade, and hardship of maintaining your life are Our great sufferings. But let Us endeavor to reconstruct our cities, let us make work for everybody, and let us produce necessities for our life. Let us proceed to build our new and free nation of Japan, and join in the society of friendly nations in the world. Let us prove to the world our uncomparable courage, our noble loyalty, our ability in reconstruction and our love of

MacArthur approved this statement, and Blyth took it back to the Imperial Household (Woodward 1972, pp. 318–19). Blyth apparently handed this draft to the Japanese and urged them to have the Emperor renounce his divinity (Maeda 1963, p. 76). It is not clear exactly what happened between this time and the middle of December, when the Emperor's rescript was prepared by the Japanese officials. According to Minister of Education Maeda Tamon, Shidehara, on December 23, showed him a statement in English, and told him that an English professor at Gakushūin named Blyth had urged that the Emperor renounce his divinity as a New Year's present to the people. Shidehara asked Maeda to draft an imperial rescript in secret. Maeda drafted it in consultation with a few close colleagues and the Emperor himself.[16]

On January 1, 1946, the Emperor issued the rescript. While the complete Japanese version includes the main ideas expressed in Blyth's proposed rescript, it does not include his (and presumably Henderson's) final statement unequivocally renouncing the Emperor's divinity: "His Majesty disavows entirely any deification or mythologizing of his own Person" (Woodward 1972, p. 319). But the renunciation is sufficiently clear to leave little doubt. The rescript in translation stated in part,

> We stand by the people and we wish always to share with them in their moments of joys and sorrows. The ties between us and our people have always stood upon mutual trust and affection. They do not depend upon mere legends and myths. They are not predicated on the false conception that the Emperor is divine and that the Japanese people are superior to other races and fated to rule the world. (SCAP 1968, 2:470)

MacArthur issued the following statement on the same day:

> The Emperor's New Year's statement pleases me very much. By it he undertakes a leading part in the democratization of his people. He squarely takes his stand for the future along liberal lines. His action reflects the irresistible influence of a sound idea. A sound idea cannot be stopped (ibid., 2:471).

---

ideals. Let us thus make our contribution to the welfare and orderliness of mankind.

*His Majesty disavows entirely any deification or mythologizing of his own Person* (quoted from Woodward 1972, p. 319).

Woodward states, "This is a translation of Junji Togashi's Japanese translation of Blyth's draft in *Sunday Mainichi*, 10 Jan 62. The sentences at the beginning and end are italicized in the original English."

16. T. Maeda 1962; Satō 1962–64, 2:892–93; Woodward 1972, pp. 265–68. According to Shidehara's biography, compiled by the Shidehara Peace Foundation, however, Shidehara himself drafted it on December 25, 1945 (Shidehara Heiwa Zaidan 1955, p. 667).

The Emperor's renunciation of his divine status had a curious consequence for the issue of separation of religion and state. The Americans
were opposed to so-called state Shinto, with the sacred emperor as its
high priest. The Emperor of Japan was not only the spiritual head of
the Japanese nation, but also the head of the secular state. The prestige
and authority he acquired as a spiritual leader thus added to his authority as head of state. The actual leaders of Japan had taken advantage of
the Emperor's prestige to launch a devastating war in his name. By
leading the Emperor to proclaim that he was only human, the Americans eliminated the keystone of "state Shinto" because the Emperor
had, in effect, renounced the myth that justified his claim to be spiritual
head of the nation. State Shinto became a sect no different from other
popular Shinto sects. From the American viewpoint, the Emperor's own
personal belief in Shintoism did not matter, as he and his family would
simply have been believers in that religion. This effectively resolved
the issue of the merging of religion and government in Japanese society.

If the negative attitude of the China specialists in the State Department, as well as that of the hostile Allies, had prevailed in formulating
the postsurrender policies, the Emperor might have been forced to abdicate, and the imperial institution might have been eliminated. That,
too, would have automatically eliminated one of the essential components of "state Shinto." This more radical approach proved to be unnecessary; by keeping the monarchy intact but having the Emperor
renounce his divine origin, the Americans accomplished, in theory at
least, virtually the same result. But the Americans apparently did not
consider the logical significance of the Emperor's renunciation. They
wanted to make certain that state Shintoism would never again revive,
so they built additional guarantees into the Constitution.[17]

When the Americans prepared the initial version of the Japanese
Constitution in February, 1946, they included the following article on
religious freedom as part of Chapter III, "Rights and Duties of the
People":

> ARTICLE XIX. Freedom of religion is guaranteed to all. No
> religious organization shall receive special privileges from the
> State, nor exercise political authority.
>   No person shall be compelled to take part in any religious

17. Kades told me that he agreed with my analysis, but said that it did not occur to him or
any other GHQ staff to think the matter through. They were just eager to make certain that there
wouldn't be a revival of state Shintoism. He said, "We wanted to not only close the door on state
Shintoism, [but also] to throw the key away so that it couldn't be opened" (1987, tape 3). I have
found no discussion of the logical significance of the imperial rescript in the SCAP materials.

acts, celebrations, rites or practices. The State and its organs shall refrain from religious education or any other religious activity.

In addition, they included the following in Chapter VII, "Finance":

ARTICLE LXXXIII. No public money or property shall be appropriated for the use, benefit or support of any system of religion, or religious institution or association, or for any charitable, educational or benevolent purposes not under the control of the State.

The minutes of the meeting between the Civil Rights Committee and the Steering Committee provide further evidence that some American drafters not only did not understand the relationship between the state and religion in Japanese society, but also mistakenly thought that religious organizations wielded considerable power. To quote,

7. As originally written Article XIII not only guaranteed freedom of religion but expressedly forbids all ecclesiastics from political activity of any kind. The Steering Committee questioned both the wisdom and the practicality of the latter provision. Colonel Kades objected that the denial of political activity to ecclesiastics involved the denial to them of freedom of speech and press as well. A special prohibition of this kind has no place in a Constitution, which should be a Bill of Rights, rather than a Bill of Restrictions.

Colonel Roest stated that this Article was designed to prevent the abuse of spiritual authority to political ends. Japan has been a priest-ridden country for generations, and political tyranny has been reinforced by the threat of spiritual punishment. It must be made clear to the Japanese that no political authority is attached to any ecclesiastical organization.

Commander Hussey agreed that people are persuaded to political action by the authority of the church, but pointed out that this is a matter of individual conscience, unlikely to be corrected by constitutional provision or statutory law. The further provision that "no religious body will be recognized as such if under the disguise of religion, it should stir up and practice antagonism to other or should weaken instead of strengthen public order and morality" could be used to justify the suppression of any new religious sect because it might disturb the established public order. On the one hand the Drafting Committee forbids ecclesiastical penetration into politics but on the other, it condones State interference with religion.

The article was shortened and amended by the Steering
Committee to read as a straight forward guarantee of freedom
of religion and the separation of church and state. (Takayanagi et al. 1972, 1:200, 202).[18]

It is interesting that at a time when the precise meaning of religious
freedom was a matter of considerable controversy in the United States,
the Americans in Japan drafted an article guaranteeing freedom of religion, and providing for complete separation of religion and state, in
language which seemed to allow no possibility whatever of nonpreferential assistance to religious institutions.

## The Creation of the Japanese Version

As we have already seen, when Matsumoto Jōji and the members of the
Constitutional Problem Investigation Committee began their work in
the fall of 1945, they took the stance that the Meiji Constitution was,
for the most part, a valid and satisfactory document. But there is evidence that the government and the committee were worried about the
status of Jinja Shinto even before the GHQ directive prohibiting its
practice. A memorandum in Satō Tatsuo's file on constitutional revision, dated October 22, 1945, includes the following passage about Article 28 of the Meiji Constitution:

> There are problems related to *jinja*. One solution might be
> to entirely eliminate their religious character. There also is a
> possibility of moving the *jinja* administration to the Ministry
> of Imperial Household and treating the ceremonies as the
> private activities of the imperial family, making the religion
> itself the private religion of the imperial family, and letting
> the people worship as they desire. (Satō Kankei Bunsho 1;
> my translation)

In one of the liberal versions of its draft constitution, the committee
included a clause on the separation of religion and state that read, "As
for the privileges that the shrines have enjoyed, these will be abolished"
(Satō 1962–64, 2:490; my translation). As might be expected, the
committee had no problem with freedom of religion. Its various versions all included modified versions of the Meiji clause that states,
"Japanese subjects have freedom of religious belief, within limits not

18. The copies of the minutes of the Government Section conferences on the preparation of
the draft constitution, held during February 5–11, 1946, are also available in the Justin Williams
Papers at the East Asia Collection, University of Maryland Libraries, College Park, Maryland
(Record no. 33). I thank Mr. Frank J. Shulman for sending me a copy of the version (dated
16 December 1947) kept at that time by Justin Williams of the Government Section.

prejudicial to peace and order, and not antagonistic to their duties as subjects" (Article 28; my translation). As might also have been expected, these tentative versions did not include a clause prohibiting the appropriation of public money or property for religious institutions. With regard to Article 3 of the Meiji Constitution, "The Emperor is sacred and inviolable," the committee eventually settled for change in the word to stand for "sacred" from *shinsei* to *shison* in its conservative version (ibid., p. 551).[19] But it appears that the committee never reached a consensus on the liberal version of this article (ibid., p. 568).[20]

What were the ideas of the private groups and individuals, some of whom were strongly advocating democratizing the Japanese Constitution? It is interesting that almost all proposals included a clause guaranteeing religious freedom, but none included separation of religion and state. The one possible exception came from the Constitutional Research Group. In their initial outline of late November 1945, they mentioned this issue, and in the second version, they included the clause, "Separation of religion from the state and schools."[21] The third draft contained a similar idea: "Shrines, temples and churches will be separated from the state."[22]

When they publicly announced their final text on December 26, however, the clause had disappeared.[23] It is not clear whether the group eliminated this clause because there was no support for the idea among the members, or whether they realized that the GHQ directive ten days earlier had effectively accomplished this, so that there was no need to stipulate it in the constitution.

On February 8, 1946, when the Matsumoto committee submitted its first version to GHQ after the fiasco of the *Mainichi* scoop, it only had the changes that had been included in the earlier, conservative proposals. Article 3 of the Meiji Constitution had been changed to:

> The Emperor is majestic (*shison*) and inviolable. (My translation)

19. *Tennō-wa shison-ni shite okasu bekarazu.* The difference in meaning between the two words is subtle but significant. The word *shinsei* consists of two characters with similar meaning, *shin* meaning "god" and *sei* meaning "saintly." *Shison* consists of *shi* meaning "surpassing all else," or "supreme," and *son* meaning "noble," "majestic," "holy/sacred." Thus, while both of these expressions can be translated as "sacred," the former conveys a clearer sense of the emperor's suprahuman origin.

20. Satō (1962–64, 2:485–627) gives a detailed discussion of the activities of the Matsumoto committee and various drafts of the constitution.

21. *Shūkyō-no kokka narabi-ni gakkō yori-no bunri* (Satō 1962–64, 2:805; my translation).

22. *Jinja bukkaku kyōkai-wa kokka yori bunri seraru* (Satō 1962–64, 2:810).

23. The complete text of this version is given in Satō 1962–64, 2:784–89.

Article 28 had been simplified to:

> Japanese subjects have freedom of religious belief within lim-
> its not prejudicial to peace and order. (My translation)

The committee had included no clause regarding separation of religion
and state.

When the Japanese returned to GHQ on March 4 with a revised
version based on the American draft, they had eliminated Article 3 of
the Meiji Constitution. They also had combined two sentences of Article XIX of the American version that had read, "Freedom of religion
is guaranteed to all. . . . No person shall be compelled to take part in
any religious acts, celebrations, rites or practices" into "All of the
people have freedom of religious belief, and [they] will not be forced to
engage in worship, prayer or any other religious acts." Thus their Article 18 (formerly 28) at this stage read as follows:

> All of the people have freedom of religious belief, and [they]
> will not be forced to engage in worship, prayer or any other
> religious activities.
>
> Religious organizations cannot participate in politics or be
> given special privileges from the state.
>
> The State and its organs cannot practice religious edu-
> cation or engage in any other religious activities.[24] (My
> translation)

The Japanese also included Article 97 (current 89), which contained
ideas similar to Article LXXXIII of the American draft:

> ARTICLE 97. The State or the local public entities cannot
> appropriate money or other public property to religious or-
> ganizations. This also applies to any other charitable, edu-
> cational or other activities not under the control of the
> State.[25] (My translation)

But at the 30-hour marathon, the Japanese version of the first sentence
of Article 18 was discarded, and was replaced by one comparable to the
original American draft. Thus, the clause in the outline form published
on March 6 read, "As for religious freedom, [one] has determined to

24. *Dai-jū-hachi-jō. Subete-no kokumin-wa shinkyō-no jiyū-o yū-shi, reihai kitō sono-ta shūkyō-jō-no kōi-o kyōsei seraruru koto nashi. Shūkyō dantai-wa seiji-ni kan'yo-shi, mata-wa kuni yori tokken-o fuyo seraruru koto-o e-zu. Kuni oyobi sono kikan-wa shūkyō kyōiku-no jisshi sono-ta shūkyō-jō-no ka-tsudō-o nasu koto-o e-zu* (Shimizu 1962–63, 4:341).
25. *Dai-kyūjū-nana-jō. Kuni-mata-wa chihō kōkyō dantai-wa shūkyō-ni kan-suru dantai-ni taishi kinsen sono-ta-no zaisan-o shusson suru-koto-o e-zu. Kuni-no kanri-ni zoku-sezaru jizen, kyōiku sono-ta kore-ni rui-suru jigyō-ni taishi mata onaji* (ibid., 4:348).

guarantee it to all persons, and no religious organization should receive any privileges from the State, nor exercise any political authority"[26] (my translation). The remainder of both Articles 18 and 97 (Article 89 in the final version) were likewise rewritten to conform to the sentence patterns used in the American text. The Japanese government was thus forced to adopt the initial MacArthur version of Articles XIX and LXXXIII nearly in their entirety.

## The Debate at the National Diet

The draft constitution proposed to the National Diet by the government in late June 1946 included the following article:

> ARTICLE 18. As for freedom of religion, [one] guarantees this to all. Religious organizations have to not receive any privileges from the State, nor exercise any political authority.
>
> No person will be compelled to take part in any religious act, celebration, rite or practice.
>
> The State and its organs have to not engage in religious education or any other religious activity. (Shūgi-in 1946a, 5:64; my translation)

The most significant debates on this article (current 20) took place at the House of Representatives special committee hearing on July 16, and at the House of Peers special committee hearing on September 17 and 18. These debates demonstrate that the Japanese had difficulty appreciating the significance of the American idea of religious freedom, separation of state and religion, and noninterference by the state in religious education. The leading Diet members were far more concerned about maintaining public order than protecting the citizens' religious freedom. The members were also greatly concerned about the separation of religion and state. They pressed the government to admit that the shrines belonging to shrine Shintō, which it had classified as nonreligious institutions, were indeed religious institutions, and therefore could not receive preferential treatment under the new Constitution. They did not understand the meaning of "religious education" and pressed the government to assure them that it was not the same as "education about religions." The debate on religious education was, in one way, the most interesting one, illustrating the difference in the nature and the role of religions in the Japanese and American societies.

---

26. *Dai-jūhachi-jō. Shinkyō-no jiyū-wa nanibito-ni taishite-mo kore-o hoshō suru koto-to shi ikanaru shūkyō dantai-mo kokka-yori tokken-o ukuru koto-naku katsu seiji-jō-no kenryoku-o kōshi suru koto nakaru beki koto* (ibid., 4:353).

I will discuss the debates under four topics, illustrating the most significant points with representative quotations: individual religious freedom, separation of religion and state, noninterference by the state in religious education, and religion and its relationship to freedom of conscience and morality.

### Freedom of Religion

As for freedom of religion, [one] guarantees this to all. . . .
    No person will be compelled to take part in any religious act, celebration, rite or practice.

The Meiji government had not worried about guaranteeing religious freedom to ordinary people because, unlike the Christian God, buddhas and Japanese deities do not teach moral views that might challenge the secular rulers. As we have seen, its main worry concerned granting religious freedom to government officials. Such freedom meant allowing them to challenge official rules of conduct concerning participation in Shinto ceremonies at court, which might disturb the order of governmental affairs.

In contrast, the members of the House of Representatives in 1946 worried about the article's relation to public order. On July 16, 1946, at the special committee hearing, one member, Inoue Tokumei of the Cooperative Democratic party, who was a Buddhist priest, asked how the government would deal with individuals who took advantage of religious freedom to disturb social order. He began by asking whether the freedom was absolute.[27]

INOUE: Article 18 says "As for freedom of religion, [one] guarantees this to all." Does this mean absolute freedom?

Kanamori replied,

The expression "absolute freedom" can mean various things, so, I cannot answer immediately. This guarantee is linked to Article 11 [current 12].[28] But I do not think believing in a particular religion will interfere with public welfare. So I think, in reality, religious freedom is close to being absolute.

Inoue pursued his real concern about social order:

I believe religion is something that should develop freely and naturally without protection or restriction by the state. But

27. For the discussion that follows, see Shūgi-in 1946b, 14:261, col. 5–262, col. 2.
28. Article 12. As for the freedoms and rights that this Constitution guarantees to the people, [the people] have to maintain these by their constant endeavor. The people also have to refrain from abusing these [rights], and have the responsibility to always use them for the public welfare (my translation).

at the level of religious knowledge and religious sentiment, the Japanese people lack the ability to evaluate appropriately superstitions, perverse religions and the like. This Constitution guarantees religious freedom. But if there is a religion that interferes with the peace and happiness of society, by what means will the government control it?

The Minister of Justice, Kimura Tokutarō, replied,

If someone oversteps [societal] bounds in the name of religious freedom and disturbs people and destroys the peace and order of the society, such an individual will be subject to control.

This issue drew more attention in the House of Peers. On September 17, at the special committee hearing, Yūki Yasuji raised the same issue with the government representative:

Speaking of religion, if there is a definition, or a set of guidelines as to what constitutes religion, then we can withhold the guarantee or impose restrictions according to an established set of criteria. But there is no such definition in this article. So I fear that one can believe in anything and call it a religion. As long as one keeps one's belief to oneself, or talks about what one believes in, there is no harm done. Once the believers begin to proselytize and mobilize a large number of people, there could be cases disruptive to social order and harmful to the lives of the citizens and the environment. . . .

Minister Kanamori, you explained, by quoting Article 11 (current 12), that while [the government] guarantees all kinds of freedom to the people by this Constitution, they should not abuse them. [The people] have the responsibility to use them for the public welfare. Therefore, your previous explanation was that religious freedom, too, comes with the duty not to abuse it, and that the Supreme Court will determine whether the activities of the believers of a given religion violate their responsibility and are therefore unconstitutional. But I think it will be difficult for the Supreme Court to determine that certain religious practices are unconstitutional and to restrict them. I assume that the police, or an investigative agency will expose them, and through due process, those cases will be brought up to the Supreme Court. But such a process will take years. By the time the Supreme Court has decided that a particular religion is perverse and harmful to the nation and the public welfare, the religion itself will probably have disappeared without a trace.

If a given belief survives for years, it might have some value. But the ones that are harmful are the ones that take advantage of a particular time, arouse people in economic distress, spread some unthinkable teachings among them and disturb social order. This Constitution guarantees freedom, but I think we have to prevent its abuse. . . . I would like to ask if the government has any other measures of control besides Article 11. (Kizoku-in 1946b, 15:21, cols. 1–4)

Kanamori replied with a vague discussion of what constituted a religion and ignored the issue of public order:

I cannot define what constitutes a religious belief. However, I think it means that in the heart of every human being, there is an element of faith, and when an individual forms an emotional relationship with the will of a suprahuman being, a religious faith emerges. Such a feeling cannot be evaluated rationally—that is something special. This Constitution takes the stand that such a matter should be placed outside [the jurisdiction of] the state as a political system as much as possible (ibid., 22, col. 4)

On the following day, Sasaki Sōichi brought up some specific questions related to the state's ability to control religious practices:[29]

For instance, the present Constitution permits war, but the new Constitution forbids war. Suppose there is a religion that advocates wars. Is it the case that the government will not be able to censor such a doctrine on the grounds that it opposes national policy?

Kanamori replied that if such a doctrine affected the welfare of the general public, it would be within the state's function to control such a group. Sasaki continued,

Suppose a religious group has holy water presented to the altar and then given to the believers. The water is unsanitary and might even contain mosquito larvae. In another case, there may be a religious group that engages in all night wild dancing. Can the government control such activities that are part of the doctrines and rites of a particular religion?

Kanamori said that such matters are within the concerns of public welfare, so the government would have to interfere. Sasaki and Kanamori continued:

29. For what follows, see Kizoku-in 1946b, 16:3, cols. 2–5.

SASAKI: May I understand then that, under this Constitution, too, the government can place constraints on religious freedom from the point of view of public welfare?

KANAMORI: That is correct.

SASAKI: In controlling such matters, can government officials deal with them as administrative matters and control them, even if there is no law specifying them? Or, should there be laws for such matters? Can the government deal with them only on the basis of this clause in the Constitution? Or, should there be laws according to which the matters will be treated?

KANAMORI: I think a relevant code is necessary.

SASAKI: Under the present Constitution, no law is necessary to control such cases. Under the present Constitution, it is understood that when citizens jeopardize public order, or violate their duties as subjects, the government can control them without specific laws. If my interpretation of the current Constitution is wrong and Mr. Kanamori's interpretation is correct, then, freedom of religious belief will be under a stricter control in the new Constitution than under the present one, will it not?

KANAMORI: I believe freedom of religious belief must not be more strictly controlled under the new Constitution, and such is not the case. I believe that, under this Constitution, there is a principle that limiting the individual's freedom of action requires specific laws, even when that is done within the limits allowed in the Constitution.

In their final exchange,[30] Sasaki asked Kanamori if individuals have the freedom not to disclose their beliefs:

SASAKI: Can the government ask what religion an individual believes in?

KANAMORI: I am not prepared to answer precisely, but I would interpret it to be a violation of this clause for the government to compel an answer against the will of the individual.

SASAKI: I agree completely. What about, for instance, an item in the national census? Can the government require individuals to answer an item on religious affiliation? That is a matter of administrative law, so the purpose is different. The government can do it, can't it?

KANAMORI: I have a feeling that if we force someone who

30. Kizoku-in 1946b, 16:4, cols. 3–4.

vehemently refuses to do so, we will violate the law. But as
long as there is no one who has such a complicated ideology,
then, I think things will go smoothly.

No one at the National Diet asked whether or not the two clauses in
this article would finally protect individual freedom of worship, as the
Americans had intended. Rather, they were concerned with specific
instances where the freedom might be abused or come into conflict with
other important principles.

### Separation of Religion and State

Religious organizations have to not receive any privileges from the
State, or exercise any political authority.

As mentioned earlier, when the Emperor renounced his divinity, the
Emperor in effect gave up his role as the high priest of "state Shinto,"
or shrine Shinto. This meant that the only remaining issue of significance was the relationship between the shrines and the state. The
Americans had determined that those shrines classified by the Japanese
fifty years earlier as nonreligious institutions were actually religious in
nature, and that the government had misused them for its ultranationalistic war efforts. So they included a clause in Article 19 of their draft
prohibiting the state from giving them preferential treatment.

The debates are interesting for the light they shed on the Japanese
understanding of separation of religion and state. There was virtually
no discussion of the general principle. The Diet members did ask why
the article was included, but did not ask why the separation of religion
and state was significant. Nor did they discuss or question the wisdom
of including such a principle in the new Constitution, even though
neither the government nor the private groups had thought to include
such a clause in their initial versions. Rather, they spent most of their
efforts puzzling over the history of the change in status of the shrines.
This may seem to be a rather insignificant issue to absorb so much time
and effort. But, apart from the Emperor, support of shrines was the only
remaining instance of state support of religion. After shrines, there was
nothing left to discuss.

On September 18, Baron Matsudaira Narimitsu of the House of Peers
opened the lengthy debate, pointing out that the purpose of this clause
was to prevent a future government from imposing a particular religion
on the people that would emphasize ultranationalistic ideology:[31]

---

31. For what follows, see Kizoku-in 1946b, 16:1, col. 1–2, col. 1.

ARTICLE 20 (formerly 19) is unique in this Constitution not because of its content, but because, unlike all the other clauses which will go into effect after the enactment, this clause is already in effect. The reason is the GHQ directive prohibiting Shinto shrines [from receiving preferential treatment]. . . . The purpose of this article, as I understand it, is to prevent the government's imposition of a particular religion that emphasizes ultra-nationalistic ideology—I take all the sentences after the one expressing individual freedom of religion to be addressed to that problem. I would like to ask if there is any other ideological issue or purpose in this article.

Kanamori avoided responding to Matsudaira's question. In a circuitous statement, he eventually admitted that shrine Shinto was a religion and that the government would not give it any preferential treatment:

What the revised Article 20 guarantees is fundamentally no different from the existing clause [in the Meiji Constitution]. But we have to admit that, in its application, there will be a major gap between the two. As I mentioned yesterday, this revision means that the state's activities will be limited—the state will not do everything. . . . The state does not make light of religion—in spirit, it respects religion. But the state will not interfere with it as part of governmental affairs. . . . As I said yesterday, it is virtually impossible for the state to determine, from an administrative point of view, whether a given religion is a proper (tadashii) religion. . . . Thus this Constitution does not address itself to whether or not shrines are religious institutions. If it is a religion, this article applies. The issue of whether or not the shrine system is a religion has long been controversial among practioners. Generally, it can be regarded as a religious system. That is the reason behind the recent administrative acts. . . . The difference between the current Constitution and the new one is that the former guarantees religious freedom, but does not prohibit the government from having a hand in it to some extent. Therefore, while the government cannot prohibit people from believing in a certain religion, it can give one religion preferential treatment to the degree that it does not constrain individual freedom. For instance, giving special treatment to the superintendents of Shinto shrines and Buddhist temples is not a governmental regulation, but, from a broader perspective, it is an act of the state. We are recognizing the principle that the state will take no positive action toward religions in the future. That principle is reflected in the clause "Religious organizations have to not receive . . . ," and the third clause (the State and its organs have to refrain from religious education . . . ). These are the only differences [between the old and new articles]. These clarify the [government's] position toward religions. That is all.

Matsudaira pursued:

I have always thought that shrine belief (*jinja shinkō*) was a religion . . . so now, is it correct to understand that there are two frames of reference in protecting individual freedom of religion, one the welfare of the public and the other the separation of religion and state?

Kanamori simply replied that that was correct.

A second member, Tadokoro Miharu, pursued the issue of the status of Shinto shrines further. He began his lengthy statement with a historical discussion:

The issue of the status of shrines went through a series of debates between the government and both houses of the Diet, and it was finally concluded about the time the Religious Organization Law was passed that shrines were not religious institutions, but were institutions for praising (*sonsū*) the nation's ancestors. (Kizoku-in 1946b, 16:7, col. 1)

After stating that the Religious Organization Law was revised several times, and in the process was made so liberal that there was practically no governmental intereference with the activities of religious organizations, he asked,

Why is it that when the war ended, that law was immediately repealed? Why did the government take such an action? (ibid., col. 4).

Kanamori could have replied that the law was repealed because of the GHQ directive. Instead, he suggested (cols. 4–5) that the law did discriminate, implying that the shrines were religious in nature, though not saying so directly:

My own interpretation of the situation is that that law probably did discriminate. It did not recognize all religious organizations, but rather, it recognized certain ones and protected them. . . . As I said to Mr. Matsudaira earlier, the new Constitution is the same as the present one in that it guarantees religious freedom. But it also has an additional clause that the government will take a detached position—it

will not actively or passively influence [any religion]. . . .
From this new perspective, the status of the shrines is being
given a new interpretation.

That afternoon, when the minister of education, Tanaka Kōtarō,
returned to the House of Peers, the members reopened the discussion
of the status of shrines. Baron Matsudaira took the floor once again: [32]

> Until recently it was understood that shrines were not reli-
> gious institutions, and therefore, the legal status of shrines
> was very ambiguous. What is their status now?

Tanaka replied,

> As you say, until now the government treated the shrines
> administratively as nonreligious institutions. Following the
> spirit of the Potsdam Proclamation, and as required by the
> GHQ directive, shrines and the state have been separated.
> Therefore shrines are now being treated as religious corpo-
> rations. [33] But when we look at the actual operation of differ-
> ent shrines, there are some that have registered themselves
> as religious corporations, and others which have not. I think
> it will depend on individual shrines. In any case, however,
> there no longer is a relationship between the shrines and the
> state. Those institutions that desire to be recognized as reli-
> gious corporations will be treated as such and will receive
> the same treatment as other religious organizations.
> MATSUDAIRA: I assume that shrines must first of all register as
> religious corporations. But is there a time limit within which
> the shrines are to register?
> TANAKA: I don't think there is a time limit.
> MATSUDAIRA: What about the property that belongs to
> shrines? I assume the shrines must register as corporations.
> Otherwise, they will not be able to own property. Is that
> correct?
> TANAKA: I should correct my previous statement. The regis-
> tration period ended on August 1. . . . Those shrines that
> have registered are treated as belonging to the same category
> as [religious] corporations according to the Civil Code, and
> can become property owners. But those that did not cannot
> own property as religious organizations.

Thus, Tanaka inadvertently revealed that the government was unable
or unprepared to deal with this new, imposed change. Baron Matsudaira

---

32. Kizoku-in 1946b, 16:12, col. 1–13, col. 2.
33. The Japanese word is *hōjin*, "legal person." "Corporation" seems to be the best translation.

went on to discuss further the long and intimate relationship between villages and their tutelary shrines in Japanese society and asked how the new idea of separation of religion and state would affect this relationship:

> Matsudaira: As you know, there is the *uji-gami* in Japanese *jinja shinkō* (shrine belief) and the shrine at which the deity is worshiped. The shrine has its members called *uji-ko* (*uji-*children). As I understand it, the relationship between the *uji-gami* and the *uji-ko* is varied, but initially the *uji-gami* was the founding ancestor of the clan who was worshipped by its members. If you look at the existing groups, there are instances where the *uji-ko* and others in the territory have formed a community, a village. . . . So there are cases in which the membership of the *uji-ko*-group, protected by a particular *uji-gami*, coincides exactly with the membership of the village, a public organization. I assume that the *uji-ko*-group is free to conduct religious activities, if it is a private group. But if such a group coincides with a public group, would such activities as a festival of the *uji-gami*, or collecting donations, be considered as the state, or its local unit, engaging in a religious activity?

Tanaka gave a good answer, distinguishing the public and private activities of the villages:

> We will have to know more in detail about individual cases, but I don't think there will be any problem in the members of a local public community forming a separate group and engaging in festivities. But the festivals are not held by a public group. They are organized by a private group, most or all of whose members happen to belong to the public unit as well.

Finally, a third member, Matsumura Shin'ichirō, after yet another lengthy exchange with the Minister of Education, pointed out that as long as there was no objective set of criteria by which a given belief system could be established as a religion, the new clause on freedom of religion would ultimately not be able to eliminate the possibility of the government calling shrines nonreligious institutions and forcing people to worship there.[34]

> MATSUMURA: I am not satisfied with your response about the status of the shrines. The Japanese government has traditionally maintained a policy of merging religion and state. I

34. For what follows, see Kizoku-in 1946b, 16:15, col. 4–16, col. 5.

would like to ask the Minister of Education where the idea
of separation of religion and state is expressed in this article.

Tanaka could simply have said that the prohibition of state support of
religious organizations expressed in this article means separation of state
and religion. Instead, he said,

> That depends on in what circumstance and in what kind of
> spirit the idea of merging religion and state is interpreted.
> The spirit that a particular religion should not be protected
> by the government, or in other words, that the government
> should treat all religions fairly, in other words, the spirit that
> denies a national religion—that, I think, is amply expressed
> in Article 18 (current 20).

At this point, Matsumura asked Tanaka rather casually why it was necessary to separate religion from state. Tanaka did not directly address
the issue. Instead, he said,

> It is because that is one of the fundamental political princi-
> ples of modern civilized states, and in Japan, considering our
> past experiences, we see a need for it. Of course, officially,
> there has been no state religion. It is because the shrines, in
> reality, have acquired the characteristics of a state religious
> institution.

Matsumura returned to the nature of shrines, saying,

> I understand. That is the key point. So you do admit that
> shrines have been treated as religious institutions.
> TANAKA: This issue relates to what constitutes a religion. To
> leave the theological problem of whether shrines are really
> religious institutions to specialists, from the viewpoint of
> ceremonies and other matters at shrines and the feelings of a
> large number of worshipers about shrines, shrines have a
> considerable amount of religious character. And it is unde-
> niable that those shrines have had specially close ties with
> the state.
> MATSUMURA: The issue has become very clear. Despite the
> fact that shrines have had the characteristics of religious in-
> stitutions in appearance and content, they have been labeled
> "nonreligious institutions" because the state has been, in a
> way, forcing shrine worship on people. If we say shrines are
> religious institutions, forcing people to worship at them
> would violate the freedom of religion guaranteed by the pres-
> ent Constitution. That is the reason that [we] had labeled
> shrines as nonreligious institutions. Is that correct?
> TANAKA: You are absolutely correct.

Matsumura pursued the point further:

> That is the reason why this issue is extremely important. Up
> until now, when [the government] guaranteed religious free-
> dom, it also insisted that shrines were not included [in the
> category of religious institutions]. Now it says that shrines
> are religious institutions—[its interpretation], shall we say,
> has become fairer. . . . I think that the previous interpreta-
> tion was biased. It's not that the definition of religion has
> been broadened. The reason why this problem arose is
> shrines give the impression of being religious institutions.
> What do you think?
> TANAKA: If you claim that shrines have the atmosphere of
> being religious institutions, and therefore, this problem
> arose, I admit you are correct.
> MATSUMURA: This has an important consequence. I now
> would like to turn to Minister Kanamori. The clauses follow-
> ing "As for freedom of religion, [one] guarantees this to all"
> have all been newly added to Article 20. What motivated
> you to add them?

Kanamori took the floor and said,

> The clause beginning with "Religious organizations" has
> been added because there have been tendencies for such in-
> stitutions to function as religious organizations [reflecting]
> the state's position. Those clauses clarify that such activities
> are not desirable.

Matsumura continued:

> I think that that was included not because of a vague notion
> that [such organizations] might arise, but because such a ten-
> dency already exists. Since Japan has maintained the posi-
> tion of not recognizing a state religion, to say that there is a
> possibility means that such organizations already exist. Does
> it not?
> KANAMORI: It has the dual function of clarifying that the
> existing organizations have functioned in such a way, and
> that they should not work in such a way in the future.

Matsumura at this point shifted his attention from the function of religious organizations back to the status of shrines:

> The future is not relevant. What I am focusing on is what
> currently exists. I understand [your point] clearly. What I
> fear is the possibility of [the government] reinterpreting the
> definition of religion, and forcing shrines on the people,

claiming once again that shrines are not religious institutions. . . . I would like to ask the Minister of Education
now, if [shrines] are not religious institutions, what are they?
How have they been classified so far?

Tanaka could simply have replied that they were religious institutions,
but instead he said,

I believe that they have continued to exist simply as places
of *sūkei* (reverence, paying respect [to gods and ancestors]).

Matsumura was not satisfied:

To say that [shrines] are places to pay reverence (*sūkei*)
doesn't make sense. Let me give my interpretation. I think
that this [shrine worship] was necessary for maintaining
peace and order in the state. But now we should act on the
assumption that such a thing is not necessary for the maintenance of peace and order. [Unless we take this view], if the
idea arises again that it is harmful not to maintain such a
system [shrine worship], there is a potential danger that the
state will distort the definition of religion once again, claim
that shrines are not religious institutions, and force it on the
people. I would like your opinion.[35]

Tanaka replied that what he said earlier, presumably referring to his
interpretation of shrines as places of *sūkei*, was simply the reason for the
legal status of shrines, and he did not intend to refer to the deeper
political implications of this issue. Matsumura then ended his comments by virtually accusing Tanaka of evading the question:

I will not pursue the point about our past practices any further. But I think you understand precisely what I am saying.
[The government] had no choice but to take the route of
"maintenance of peace and order." It had to say that worshiping the sublime [at a shrine] was not a religious act. If it
had been a religious act, then it would have meant that the
state was illegally forcing people to worship at shrines. I once
asked a shrine administrator what the nature of the shrines
was. He said, "They are not religious institutions. Shrines
are shrines." That is not an answer. [The nonreligious status
of shrines] had a legal effect, (it made it possible for the gov-

---

35. Matsumura uses the pronominal expressions "this" (*kore*), "such a thing" (*sōyū mono*),
and "that system" (*sono seido*), without identifying what they refer to, leaving his meaning somewhat ambiguous. But I think this is the only interpretation that gives the passage a meaning
consistent with his entire exchange with Tanaka.

ernment to impose shrine worship on the people without violating the Constitution).[36] That is my interpretation, and I don't think I am wrong. I am afraid, from now on, we will have no choice but to depend on the court to decide what is a religion. . . . I believe it is not good to take such an ambiguous stand as the one that the Ministry of Education has taken so far, that is to say that those shrines that have registered would be regarded as religious institutions, and those that have not would not be treated as such. I ask you to give a thorough consideration on this matter.

Thus, the questions from the members of the Diet repeatedly demonstrated that separation of religion and state was not an idea of the Japanese government. The government did not explain the reasons why the article was added to the Constitution, and some of the Diet members seemed to have a better understanding of the point of the clauses than the government spokesmen. One member also exposed the weakness of the clause. The Japanese thus confirmed that the new clause in the Constitution might not guarantee separation of religion and state in the way the Americans had intended. Their own government had declared that those shrines were not religious institutions less than fifty years earlier, and now the Americans had redefined them. There was certainly no guarantee that the label could not be changed in a future round of political conflict. The vague responses of the government spokesmen gave no assurance that they fully accepted the new categorization. The Diet members saw this clearly, but could not get the government spokesmen to admit it.

Finally, Japanese religious leaders and the Diet members representing their interests raised one other pratical question. They, too, did not raise questions about the general principle of separation of religion and state. But they were greatly worried about the practical consequences of this clause in relation to Article 89:

> ARTICLE 89. As for public money or other property, [one] has to not expend or appropriate this for the use, benefit, or maintenance of any religious institution or association, or for any charitable, educational, or benevolent enterprises not under the control of public authority. (My translation)

As mentioned earlier, the Meiji government had nationalized the properties of Shinto shrines and Buddhist temples and then leased them to their respective users rent-free. Later, the government began to return

---

36. The sentence is incomplete, but I think this is the only interpretation that is consistent with his argument in this entire passage.

ownership to those Buddhist temples requesting it, but World War II intervened, and the program was never completed. On May 23, 1946, the Nihon Shūkyō Remmei (Religions League of Japan), representing the Shinto, Buddhist, and Christian leaders, submitted a petition to the government asking for clarification of both Articles 20 and 89.[37] The religious leaders feared that the government, after severing its ties with religious institutions, might simply claim ownership of their properties, and not give them the right to demand their return. They were also worried that it might mean the end of government protection of shrines, temples, and churches by such means as tax exemptions and rent-free use of grounds (Satō Tatsuo Kankei Bunsho 113).

On July 3, 1946, at the special committee hearing of the House of Representatives, Ōshima Tazō, of the New Light Club, expressed these anxieties, requesting the government's interpretation of Article 85 (current 89) in reference to the state-owned properties of religious institutions. Tanaka assured him that Article 85 did not imply that the religious institutions would lose their historically vested property rights. To quote,

> ŌSHIMA: There are two provisions on religion, Article 18 (current 20) and Article 85. According to Article 18, no religious organizations can receive privileges from the state. Similarly, Article 85 says, "As for public money or other property, [one] has to not expend or appropriate this for the use, benefit, or maintenance of any religious institution or association, or for any charitable, educational, or benevolent enterprises not under the control of public authority." I would like to ask you about this provision. Will it deny, for instance, the currently recognized privilege of tax exemption for the properties of shrines and temples? If under this provision shrine and temple grounds, which are nominally state properties, will be completely taken away from them, that will result in unjustifiable oppression of temples and shrines throughout the country. The temple and shrine personnel are gravely concerned about this. I would like to hear your interpretation. (Shūgi-in 1946b, 4:56, cols. 4–5)

Tanaka replied,

> As you know, the grounds belonging to shrines, temples and churches and other properties were established as such (gov-

37. In *The Allied Occupation of Japan 1945–1952 and Japanese Religions*, William Woodward (1972, chapters 18 and 19) gives a concise discussion of the Religions League of Japan and the attitude of the Civil Information and Education of GHQ toward it and other religious issues during the occupation.

ernment property) in the beginning of the Meiji [era]. Since
then there have been changes, but this is a problem today.
According to our interpretation, Article 85 is not intended
to take away the vested rights [of temples and shrines]. Even
though the properties are state-owned under current law, historically, [the shrines and temples] have vested rights. We
understand that [Article 85] does not intend to take away
those rights (ibid., 57, col. 1).

On July 16, in his lengthy interpellation, Satō Gisen of the Liberal
party, who was a Buddhist, referred to the same issue, and asked the
government to deal with the issue decisively, to ease the minds of the
religious leaders.

> SATŌ: The Minister of Education . . . has clearly said that
> Article 85 does not intend to take away vested rights. I think
> a clear solution has to be found regarding the grounds of the
> shrines which have now become religious organizations. . . .
> I would like the opinion of the Minister of Education. . . . I
> would also like to ask about the forests that are under the
> custody of temples and shrines. . . . I think there clearly is
> need for [the government] to reopen the possibility of trans-
> ferring them back. The religious organizations are extremely
> disturbed and worried—they are even saying that this is a
> matter of life and death for them. (Shūgi-in 1946b, 14:260,
> cols. 2–3)

Once again, Tanaka gave assurances that the vested rights of the shrines
and temples would be protected:

> I will respond to the issue of government-owned temple
> grounds. In view of the spirit of the constitutional draft, I
> would like to make clear that the vested rights of shrines
> must be protected, and the vested rights of temples over
> their grounds must be protected. There is no reason to think
> that the rights of shrines will be violated because shrines,
> which were not religious institutions, have now become so.
> Shrines will be treated in the same way [as all other religious
> institutions] when the new laws are created. The same holds
> for the forests that have been under the custody of shrines
> and temples (ibid., col. 4).

Thus, the religious leaders did not inquire about the general principle
of religion and state, but were primarily worried about the property of
their institutions. The government had to assure them that severing its
ties with religious institutions did not mean that the government would
seize their property.

## Religious Education and the State

The State and its organs have to refrain from religious education or any other religious activity.

As noted earlier, eleven years after the promulgation of the Meiji Constitution, when the Meiji government classified the shrines of shrine Shinto as nonreligious institutions, it also issued an order prohibiting religious teachings and ceremonies in public schools. This was another attempt to impress upon the West that Japan adhered to the policy of separation of religion and state (Umeda 1971, pp. 49–50). But it did not mean that, in 1946, the Japanese knew what the Americans meant by religious education. In fact, the debate at the National Diet reveals that the Japanese did not understand what the constitutional prohibition against religious education meant, or why it was necessary to include a clause prohibiting state support of religious education in public schools. But the government spokemen were able to convince the members who raised questions about religious education that the clause did not prohibit the teaching of religious sentiments through religious examples.

The Japanese had difficulty distinguishing the two because that distinction does not fit well into the Japanese religious tradition. The Japanese do not tie ethical principles to particular religions, partly because Japanese religions do not emphasize doctrines or theology. Instead, they emphasize character training through various religious teachings. Shintoism does not have church organization or theology. Teaching Shintoism is teaching the proper rituals of worshiping deities. Japanese Buddhism also has ceremonies, but places greater emphasis on practices, such as meditation, that teach self-discipline and character improvement, to permit one to better cope with life. Even Christianity, and Christian education in the schools and universities affiliated with Catholic and Protestant sects in Japan, are much different from those in America. Japanese Christians, who are, on the whole, highly educated, do not emphasize theology or interpretations of the Bible, but rather focus their attention on conducting their life properly as Christians. Again, the emphasis is on developing character. Their efforts are often directed toward helping others, and one consequence is that Japanese Christians, who currently constitute less than one percent of the population, have been far more influential than their number would suggest in fields such as medical and social welfare services, and education, particularly women's education.[38] Lastly, most Japanese people

---

38. I received seven years of education at so-called Protestant mission schools, and was an active member of a church for several years thereafter. I do remember clearly that students were

participate in ceremonies and rituals of more than one religion, and try to learn from all of them.

Japanese leaders were worried about the decline of morality among people in the aftermath of the catastrophic defeat and devastation of their land. Japan, in 1946, was in chaos—black markets were operating everywhere, people had difficulty in getting enough food, and parks and railway stations were filled with homeless and starving orphans and adults. Everyone seemed to be out for himself. Serious moral decay threatened Japanese society, and nihilistic attitudes were frequently expressed. The political leaders knew that the heavy emphasis on Shintoism, and loyalty to the Emperor, symbolized in rituals such as children bowing in the direction of the Imperial Palace and to the Emperor's picture at schools, and visiting shrines to worship the tutelary deities of the nation and the people, were no longer permissible. But they believed that the teachings of various religions were essential to cultivating character traits such as spirituality, compassion, ethical values, and a sense of responsibility for rebuilding one's family, community, and the nation. These characteristics were not linked to any specific religion, but might be cultivated by the study of more than one religion. Thus, "religious education" might include study of different religious traditions rather than teaching a single religion exclusively.

It is not easy to decide whether this type of education is "religious education" or "education about religions," as it has characteristics of both. The distinction does not really work well when applied to the Japanese experience. Nonetheless, the Japanese used this distinction to reach an understanding of the third clause that would allow the state to sponsor character training.

The Diet members, particularly in the House of Representatives, were puzzled as to why the government would not take the lead in fostering "religious education," and repeatedly asked if "religious education" was the same as "education about religions." They sought confirmation from the government spokesmen that this clause did not prohibit the teaching and cultivating of shūkyō-teki jōsō, the literal translation of which is "religious sentiments." By that term they were referring to "cultivating the spiritual emotions and empathy," or "cultivating appreciation for the spiritual aspect of life," which would also

---

required to attend worship services and Bible classes. Theology, however, was not emphasized. I did not realize how ignorant I was about Christian theology and doctrinal controversies within Christianity until I attended a public hearing on abortion in Honolulu in 1969. I was astounded by the impassioned testimonies of the Protestant and Catholic clergy, as well as ordinary citizens, and realized for the first time that the Christianity I had been taught in Japan was vastly different from that of the United States.

include teaching children moral and ethical principles, the right way to lead their lives.

I will begin with the debate at the special committee hearing of the House of Representatives on July 16, 1946. Satō Gisen of the Liberal party began by stating his understanding of religion in American democracy:

> Although it does not appear in the words of the Constitution, I believe that the democratic nations of the world, particularly the United States, are built on a strongly religious foundation. When the Puritans went to the New World on the Mayflower, they made promises to God on the Atlantic Ocean—the spirit of those promises, I believe, runs through the American Constitution. At that time, those people promised to build their society entirely on their religious convictions. The Americans still have not lost that spirit. Reading the writings of Washington, Lincoln, and various other presidents of the United States, I feel their devotion and prayers to God. Religion is the foundation of democracy, and it is the foundation of justice in the world. It is not an exaggeration to say that American democracy is a backbone enveloped by the flesh of religion. One can betray people, but one cannot betray gods and buddhas. Their pledge to the Constitution was not made in front of people, but God. . . . What kind of religious conviction is behind this Constitution, which is to serve as the basis for rebuilding our nation? The theory of the Divine Emperor is dead. Cabinet members will no longer go to the Ise Shrine to report [to the Sun Goddess] their new appointments. I wonder what kind of religious convictions the Prime Minister and other members of the cabinet have as individuals. I wonder what kind of religious foundation they are trying to incorporate. Of course, I go along with the notion that what belongs to God should be rendered unto God, what belongs to Caesar should be rendered unto Caesar, and religion and state should be separated. But that does not mean that religion is not necessary for politics. A statement such as "religious belief is a personal matter" would encourage ordinary citizens to take religion lightly. There is no other nation among the civilized nations where young men and women pay so little attention to religion as do the Japanese. . . . I would like to ask the Minister of Education your thoughts and policies regarding religion at this time when we are about to establish this Constitution as the foundation of civilized Japan. (Shūgi-in 1946b, 14:255, cols. 1–4)

Tanaka replied:

> There is a reason for the separation of religion and state ex-
> pressed in Article 18 (current 20). However, that does not
> mean that it denies the importance of religion in human life.
> I would like you to read [this Constitution] as expressing re-
> spect for the people's liberty and thought . . . In the cultural
> and educational policies of our nation, we must respect reli-
> gion more than ever. The current decline of people's morals,
> as you pointed out, comes largely from their lack of respect
> toward gods, and a numbing of their conscience so that they
> think they can do anything when they are not seen. . . . I
> am convinced that the best and most powerful remedy for
> this moral decay is religion. . . . So regarding the interpre-
> tation of Article 18, those who think that religion should be
> respected might be concerned about the implication of the
> statement, "The State and its organs have to refrain from
> religious education or any other religious activity." As I un-
> derstand it, however, this does not mean that the state
> should remove teaching about religion, and religious enrich-
> ment, from education. The state has to respect all religions
> equally, however, and should not emphasize one religion, or
> one sect of religion, to the exclusion of others. . . .
>
> Within the sphere of school education, we would like to
> include stories that would inspire students such as those
> about the world's principal religions, biographies of great men
> of religions, etc. We would like to foster students' interest
> in religion and increase their appreciation (ibid., 255 col.
> 4–256, col. 2).

That afternoon, Satō requested Tanaka's response on the precise nature
of the limits on religious activities in public schools:

> I would like you to respond clearly and precisely once again
> because this is a very serious matter. You said that the clause
> "The State and its organs . . ." applies only to public
> schools, and that private schools are permitted to hold reli-
> gious activities. But it is very difficult to determine exactly
> to what extent public schools can touch on religious issues.
> Unless that limit is established, religious education will
> weaken. For instance, is it acceptable for the alumni associ-
> ation of a public school to hold Zen meditation sessions, or
> to offer a special course on Christianity? Can the principal
> of the school participate in such an activity? Perhaps it is not
> acceptable to preach a particular faith in the classroom. But

I would like you to clearly state that it would be acceptable to discuss religion as a way of building the character of students, so the educators of the nation can pursue [their work] actively. I think we shouldn't be afraid. To mention my humble experience, I have taught *shūshin* for fifteen years at Kobe Maritime High School. I am a Buddhist. I have talked about my own convictions from the podium, although it might not be appropriate for me to urge students to believe them. . . . Without such strong convictions, we cannot really give truly [meaningful] views on life and the world to the young people who are lost. Many young men died in the bottom of hell in this past war. Forgive me for blowing my own horn, but those students who, by miraculous fortune, have come back, said to me that what I had told them about religion hit them when they were hovering between life and death. A former graduate said to me that he was convinced that what I had told them from the podium about the absolute salvation from within greatly helped those friends who died. I was greatly moved and grateful for the work that I had devoted my life to (ibid., 257, col. 5–258, col. 1).

Tanaka replied that it was perfectly acceptable for public schools to offer religious programs as extracurricular activities, as long as the school did not restrict itself to one religion. He said that the Ministry of Education would, in fact, encourage activities such as alumni groups inviting various religious authorities for lectures, and that he saw no problem with the principal of a public school initiating or actively participating in such activities (ibid., 258, cols. 4–5).

The same afternoon, another member, Matsuzawa Kenjin of the Socialist party, raised another important question. He asked the government spokesmen whether or not private schools could compel students to participate in religious activities. To Americans, such a question is strange, to say the least, because the whole point of the First Amendment is to protect the individual's freedom of beliefs against the state. It turns out, however, that Matsuzawa's question was legitimate, because of the wording of the second clause of Article 18, which states, "No person will be compelled to take part in any religious act, celebration, rite, or practice." This clause is ambiguous. In conjunction with the third clause of Article 18, it can be read as a restriction on the state. But taken alone, it can be construed that neither the state nor the private institutions can compel individuals to take part in religious acts, celebrations, rites, or practices. The discussion is interesting because the government spokesmen apparently agreed that the clause applied to private schools. Had they understood the American intent, they could have handled the question simply by saying that the clause referred only to government activities.

Matsuzawa first asked Kanamori whether students in religious schools could be compelled to attend religious activities:[39]

> The second clause says "No person will be compelled to take part in any religious act, celebration, rite or practice." I think that it will be appropriate for religious schools to require students to participate in those religious activities that have been approved by the government. Am I right?

Kanamori responded:

> As you see, this clause says "No person will be compelled to take part in. . . . " So the problem will be whether the individual students are compelled to participate in religious activities. But since the students have entered the school knowing about them, I do not think that such a case will be regarded as "compelling them to take part."

But Matsuzawa was not satisfied, and repeated the question, requesting an answer from Minister Tanaka. Tanaka responded vaguely that forcing students to participate in religious activities against their will would be counterproductive:

> Considering the nature of the schools, the Ministry of Education recognizes that, for instance, Christian schools would encourage students to attend Bible classes or masses as extracurricular activities. But to force students to attend them would be contrary in principle to the basic nature of religion. However, as Minister Kanamori mentioned earlier, I believe there will be no confusion in reality, because the students enter such schools knowing about the special nature of the institutions. It's possible that the students would change their minds and decide not to participate in religious activities. To force such students to attend them would be counterproductive because, ultimately, we have to respect each individual's conscience.

Matsuzawa persisted,

> I would like to confirm this point once again. For example, would the school be going too far if it takes attendance at the worship service?

---

39. For the following, see Shūgi-in 1946b, 14:261, cols. 1–4.

Tanaka replied,

> If it is a theological seminary where religion is the subject matter that is studied from scholarly perspectives, that is one thing. But if it is only a matter of religious education, then, I think it would not be appropriate to force it on the students.

At the fourth and fifth meetings of the House of Representatives subcommittee, at the end of July, despite Chairman Ashida's assurance that "religious education" meant "teaching of a particular religion such as Catholicism or Judaism," and not "teaching about religions," the members made two specific proposals to amend Article 18. One was to amend the clause to read, "The state has to refrain from religious education or any other religious activity prejudicial to one religion or sect" (Mori 1983, p. 154; my translation). This would have allowed the government to assist all religions equally, and would have resolved all doubts about the legitimacy of education about religions. The other would have achieved the same result by specifically allowing the teaching of religious sentiments by changing the clause to read, "The State has to refrain from religious education or any other religious activity, but, as for the teaching of religious sentiments, this does not apply" (ibid., p. 179). In the end, however, the debate was terminated without any clear argument for or against the proposed amendments, and no change was made.[40]

The government spokesmen assured the members of the House of Representatives that teaching about various religions and religious leaders was not only desirable, but important for cultivating religious sentiments, or enriching the students' spiritual life. Moreover, the Ministry of Education would encourage such activities in schools as long as they did not limit themselves to one religion.

At the special committee hearings of the House of Peers in mid-September, the Peers discussed this clause along the same lines. On September 17, Baron Shirane Matsusuke made a long statement in which he said that he believed education, and particularly cultivating religious faith (shūkyō-teki shinkō) in people, was central to rebuilding Japan as a democratic nation. He was concerned that the third clause of Article 20 appeared to be a very "negative" clause, representing a policy of noninterference and noncaring. He went on to pose some pointed questions on the application of this clause.

---

40. See Mori 1983, pp. 153–61, 179–81.

SHIRANE: The third clause says "The State and its organs. . . ." My reading of this clause is that the Ministry of
Education and public schools must not engage in religious
activities. I haven't quite understood the existing policy that
allows private schools to engage in religious education but
does not allow the public schools to do likewise, but let's put
that aside. I fear that this clause will be a great obstacle to
religious education in the future. . . . For instance, wouldn't
this clause be violated if a biography of a renowned Buddhist
monk is included in a public elementary school textbook?
Wouldn't it be a violation of this clause for the Minister of
Education or some other government official to attend the
graduation ceremony of a mission school, and give a con-
gratulatory speech to students who have received an education based on a particular religion? We have various social
welfare programs built on religious beliefs. They've all done
excellent jobs. Can the Minister of Welfare attend their
meetings and give words of praise in reference to their work
based on their religious beliefs? The spirit behind this clause
may be that [the government] must not engage in sectarian
education and other activities, which I think is one interpretation. If that is the spirit of this law, isn't it better to include
a clear statement to that effect? How about amending this
clause to read, "The State and its organs have to refrain from
education and activities limited to one religion or one sect,"
or "The State and its organs have to not engage in sectarian
education, or any other sectarian activities"? Frankly, rather
than amending it, I think we should eliminate the third
clause from Article 20, for the future of the development
of Japan's religious education. (Kizoku-in 1946b, 15:23, col.
5–24, col. 2)

In a long and circuitous response, Kanamori made an interesting distinction between religious education and cultivating religious sentiments. He said that the third clause of Article 20 prohibits the state
and its organs from participating in religious education, because religious education could not be conducted in a nonsectarian manner. But
religious sentiment was a different matter, and the government desired
people to cultivate such sentiments. He assured Shirane that he believed that public school textbooks could include biographies of cele-
brated monks, and that government officials could attend meetings of
social agencies with religious affiliations, and give speeches without violating the third clause of Article 20 (ibid., 24, col. 2–25, col. 2).

In the final exchange between Sasaki Sōichi and Kanamori, Kanamori spoke of his own religious experience, providing a good example of the Japanese understanding of religious experience and religious education.

> SASAKI: I agree with the principle that the state should not engage in religious education. As you know, I think there have been mistakes made in the past in the application of the current Constitution. What you say about the problem of religious education versus the teaching of religious sentiments seems clear enough, but it really is not. My point is whether it is possible to cultivate religious sentiment without referring to a particular religion. It does not seem possible today to cultivate religious sentiments without reference to particular religions. I'd like to hear your opinion. (Kizoku-in 1946b, 16:4, col. 1)
>
> KANAMORI: Well, this issue will pose considerable difficulty in actual practice. But in drawing a boundary between religion and state, we expect difficulties. I don't know what educators think, but from my personal experience, I think it is possible. I don't believe in one particular religion, but I think I have gone through a few paths in cultivating religious sentiments. So I think it should be possible (ibid., cols. 1–2).

Since Japanese religions are not closely linked to ethical principles, religious education does not mean teaching the doctrines and ethical principles of a particular faith. Both the Diet members and the government officials believed that ethical principles that could be taught through examples of religious practices would be vitally necessary for cultivating spirituality and a sense of responsibility for rebuilding the war-torn nation. Thus, the Diet members asked the government spokesmen whether the third clause in Article 20, prohibiting religious education in public schools, would be the same as prohibiting education about religions. The government spokesmen tried to assure them that the government had no intention of prohibiting the public schools from teaching about religions. Tanaka said that the Ministry of Education would in fact encourage schools to teach about religions. But they were able to give these assurances only by using a distinction between religious education and education about religions that did not fit well with their own tradition.

### Religion, Freedom of Conscience, and Morality

For Americans, religious freedom has always involved "freedom of conscience," the ability of individual citizens to believe and worship as they choose. To reinforce freedom of religion, the Americans included a clause on freedom of conscience in their own draft of the Japanese Constitution:

> ARTICLE XVIII. Freedom of thought and conscience shall be held inviolable.

This clause was included in the final Japanese version:

> ARTICLE 19. As for freedom of thought and conscience, [one] has to not violate this. (My translation)

The Japanese had difficulty grasping not only the significance of this article, but also its obvious relationship to religious freedom. On September 17, Makino Eiichi, of the House of Peers, asked Kanamori the meaning of freedom of thought and conscience and its relationship to other freedoms. He said,

> Next I will move to the relationship between Article 19 [on freedom of thought and conscience], Article 20 [on religious freedom] and Article 23 [on academic freedom]. The expression "freedom of thought and conscience" seems clear enough, but is really not clear to us. . . . "Freedom of expression" in Article 21, and "academic freedom" in Article 23—they seem to be repetitive, and I cannot quite grasp the relationship among the three. (Kizoku-in 1946b, 15:28, col. 3)

Kanamori's reply to Makino contributed little to clarify the issue:

> I think these three freedoms can be distinguished in the center of thinking. But on the periphery, these ideas could be indistinguishable. We can begin with freedom of thought, then go to freedom of speech, and finally to academic freedom . . . , but we simply distinguished the these ideas in the center and expressed them. (ibid., col. 4)

The following day, Sasaki Sōichi pursued this issue. He said,

> I would like to ask you the precise legal consequences of Article 19, "As for freedom of thought and conscience, [one] has to not violate this," and Article 20, "As for freedom of religion, [one] guarantees this to all." The reason I ask is that freedom of thought and conscience, and that of religious belief, are not something that the people possess because the government gives them to the people. We naturally possess such freedoms as human beings. For the Constitution to say that they have to not be infringed, we have to have an explanation of what these basic human freedoms mean in law. (Kizoku-in 1946b, 16:2, col. 4)

In response, Kanamori said (ibid.):

> As the words of this clause indicate, it means that the state
> does not place unreasonable restraints on them. This is re-
> garded by scholars as passive freedom (*shōkyoku-teki jiyū-
> ken*).

He might simply have said that the point of the article was to prevent
the government from trying to punish people who hold dissenting or
unpopular beliefs.

Little else was said about freedom of conscience. But in the general
discussion on Chapter 3 at the House of Representatives special committee hearing on July 15, there was one important exchange between
Miura Toranosuke of the Liberal party and Minister Kanamori that re-
lates indirectly but significantly to the issue of religion, ethics, and morality in the new democratic nation. It went as follows:

> MIURA: Is the idea of ancestor worship, which is the central
> element in the morality of Japanese people, being discarded?
> KANAMORI: This Constitution does not have any clause de-
> termining the role of ancestor worship.
> MIURA: I am raising the question because this Constitution
> does not address that issue. I think that the ideas of loyalty
> and filial piety, and the responsibility to care for one's family,
> are the basis of Japan's traditional morality. Although Chap-
> ter 3 of the Constitution supposedly specifies the people's
> rights and duties, as for the duties, there is only the people's
> duty to provide elementary education. All the other clauses
> specify the people's rights, freedom, and equality. I would
> like to ask your opinion regarding traditional Japanese
> ethics.
> KANAMORI: This Constitution has no intention of changing
> the moral principles of the Japanese people. However, there
> are practical specifics of morality that should have been criti-
> cized in the past, but were not. I think they should be criti-
> cized. The results of this scrutiny are the new clauses on the
> household system and marriage. But these are not supposed
> to change the people's morality. Rather, the legal system is
> changed in relation to the people's examination of moral
> principles.
> MIURA: I believe that morality is the foundation of building
> a peaceful and democratic nation, and it must, as a matter
> of course, be raised. Without morality, there will be no
> democratic or cultured nation. It is regrettable that this
> Constitution does not have a clear statement about morality.

I think it will be desirable for the government to clarify more
positively the issue of law having to do with morality.
KANAMORI: It is assumed that this Constitution respects morality. . . . In the past, however, moral principles tended to
be imposed on people. Article 17 (current 19) of this Constitution says, "As for freedom of thought and conscience,
[one] has to not violate this." The issue of morality [in the
new Constitution] is determined on the basis of respect for
human beings. In a sense, there is a possibility that a fairly
great change will occur in the way the nation's morality is
treated. (Shūgi-in 1946b, 13:242, col. 3–243, col. 1)

Kanamori tried to dispel fears about the disappearance of traditional
moral values, but, in the end, he was forced to admit that changes
might very well come. In law, at least, the moral principles of Japanese
society were being replaced by the new American concept of rights and
liberties, and freedom of thought and conscience obviously raised the
possibility that some individuals, at least, would challenge these traditional principles. Kanamori could only hope that traditional values
would survive within the new legal framework.

## Summary

The Americans, as well as other Allies, regarded freedom of religion
and separation of religion and state as critical to the democratization of
Japan. They believed that the Japanese government had imposed shrine
Shinto on its citizens, severely curtailing their freedom of religious belief, and enabling it to launch a war of aggression in the name of the
Emperor. Their task was to dismantle the state religion, eliminate the
Emperor's divinity, and grant freedom of religion to ordinary Japanese
citizens. But the Americans did not realize the vast difference between
their own religious tradition and that of the Japanese. They did not
know that religious freedom had never been a significant issue for the
Japanese people, nor did they realize that they had largely achieved
their goal of separating "state" Shinto from the state when the Emperor
announced that he was not a god. They also did not know how the
Japanese would interpret the phrase, "religious education," or how disruptive its complete removal from the schools might be, for the teaching of moral and spiritual values essential to rebuilding Japan.

For their part, the Japanese did not fully understand the point of the
new religious clauses in the Constitution. They did not discuss the general idea of separation of religion and the state because this had never
been a significant issue in Japanese history. Instead, the debates focused
almost entirely on the status of shrines, which was, after the Emperor,

the most important way in which the government had attempted to use religion to control the Japanese people. The most critical question for the Japanese probably involved the third clause of Article 20, proscribing religious education. The Diet members and the government spokesmen agreed that this allowed the state to conduct education about religions, as opposed to religious education, even though such a distinction did not fit well with the Japanese traditions. This allowed the government to have a role in teaching morality, and particularly character training. But the debates did not show Japanese understanding of how religious education, or education about religions, might relate to the general principle of religion and the state.

Finally, the Japanese did not ask whether or not the traditional values of ancestor worship, loyalty, and filial piety would be affected by Article 20, partly because they had difficulty understanding the intimate link between religious freedom and freedom of conscience that the Americans took for granted. Nonethless, one exchange between a member of the House of Representatives and Kanamori suggested that Kanamori understood that the new Constitution would challenge the moral values of traditional Japan. That issue will be discussed in more detail in chapter 6.

*Five*

# THE EMPEROR

ARTICLE 1. The Emperor is the symbol of the State and the unity of the People, and this position is founded on the will of the People in whom sovereignty resides.

ARTICLE 3. All acts of the Emperor in matters of state require the advice and approval of the Cabinet, and the Cabinet is responsible therefor. (My translation)

By far the most important issue for the Americans, in planning for the postwar administration of Japan, was the fate of the imperial institution and Emperor Hirohito.[1] Surprisingly, however, they had not formulated any definitive policy on this question by the end of the war. This allowed MacArthur to take the initiative. Soon after he arrived, MacArthur was persuaded that it would be unwise to remove the Emperor. Although some of the allies objected, and some within the American government wanted to try the Emperor as a war criminal, MacArthur's views prevailed.

The State Department had begun to consider this problem seriously in the spring of 1943, nearly two and a half years before Japan's surrender. By the end of May of that year, they had completed their first paper, "Status of the Japanese Emperor." After reviewing the arguments both for termination and continuation of the imperial institution, they concluded that "the survival of the emperorship would be a potential asset of great utility as an instrument not only for promoting domestic stability, but also for bringing about changes desired by the United Nations in Japanese policy."[2] The majority of the Japan specialists at

---

1. In modern times, Japan established the tradition that the accession of a new emperor begins a new era, marked by a new name. While an emperor reigns, he is called *Tennō Heika*, or simply *Tennō*; subsequent to his death, he is referred to by the name of his era. Thus Emperor Hirohito, who died on January 7, 1989, is now referred to as *Shōwa Tennō* (Emperor Shōwa). "Hirohito" (his given name) and "Emperor Hirohito" are rarely used in Japan, but since it is a name familiar to Westerners, I will use it from time to time.

2. Notter Files, Box 63, T-315 of May 25, 1943, "Status of the Japanese Emperor," quoted in Ward 1987, p. 4.

the State Department supported this view, although some important figures, such as Assistant Secretary of State Dean Acheson, were opposed. From this time on, throughout all of 1944, discussions of the various options regarding the treatment of the Japanese emperor, including specific instructions as to how Emperor Hirohito and his family should be treated, continued among the State Department planners.

From the beginning of 1945, with the end of the war in sight, the State-War-Navy Coordinating Committee began preparations for a military government in Japan. Initially, the military took a negative attitude toward retaining the Emperor. The State Department did not present a counterproposal, and for various reasons, no one took action on the issue until the fall of 1945. Thus, when General MacArthur arrived from Manila on August 30, 1945, the United States government had not yet adopted a policy regarding the Emperor (Ward 1987, pp. 9–11).

On September 18, 1945, Richard B. Russell, a Democratic senator from Georgia, introduced a joint resolution in Congress declaring that the United States should try the Emperor of Japan as a war criminal.[3] The resolution was referred to the Committee on Military Affairs, but nothing came of it. On October 6, 1945, the SWNCC subcommittee on the Far East finally produced a report (SWNCC-55/3) concluding that Emperor Hirohito was subject to arrest, trial, and punishment as a war criminal, and that MacArthur should gather evidence and send it to the Joint Chiefs of Staff, together with his recommendation as to when the proceedings against the Emperor could be started. This position, which contrasted so starkly with that of the State Department, was mitigated by the acknowledgment that an immediate move on this matter by the Joint Chiefs of Staff would be inappropriate, and that it was up to MacArthur to determine the proper time for such proceedings (Ward 1987, p. 11).

But Assistant Secretary of War for Air, Robert A. Lovett, quickly intervened, and urged that SWNCC reconsider its report. He said,

> The tone of the discussion . . . seems to me to be susceptible of the interpretation that Hirohito should be tried regardless of what the available evidence may be, if that is desirable as a matter of policy. I feel that the principle should be regarded as firmly settled that the trial of war criminals, so far as participated in by the United States, should be a judicial matter, and that proceedings should be initiated only where the evidence warrants. In a paper which recommends collecting

3. *Congressional Record* 91, pt. 7 (September 11, 1945 to October 18, 1945), pp. 8671–80.

the evidence, it seems to me to be premature to decide what will be the action taken when the evidence is collected. Thus far, I am aware of no adequate collection of the evidence with respect to Hirohito's actions, and certainly no dispassionate appraisal of any such evidence has been made.[4]

SWNCC subsequently retracted the document, and took no further action on the issue.

What was General MacArthur's own opinion regarding the Emperor? While the "U.S. Initial Postsurrender Policy for Japan" (August 29, 1945) and "Basic Directive for Postsurrender Military Government in Japan Proper" (November 3, 1945) were being prepared, MacArthur expressed his opinion to General Marshall that the occupation should not prematurely intervene in the Japanese governmental system:

> Limitation in occupation forces dictates a maximum utilization of existing Japanese governmental agencies and organizations. Control of the population by these agencies is highly effective and under favorable circumstances it is believed they can be employed to our material advantage. Premature dislocation of governmental machinery would involve an undesirable augmentation of forces and multiplication of the difficulties of control (dated July 27, 1945).[5]

MacArthur was not eager to bring the Emperor before a war crimes court, or to abolish the imperial institution, particularly after the Emperor visited him at the embassy on September 27, 1945. MacArthur says that, before the visit, he "had an uneasy feeling he might plead his own cause against indictment as a war criminal." But contrary to his expectations, the Emperor said to him, "I come to you, General MacArthur, to offer myself to the judgment of the powers you represent as the one to bear sole responsibility for every political and military decision made and action taken by my people in the conduct of war." MacArthur recalls:

> A tremendous impression swept me. This courageous assumption of a responsibility implicit with death, a responsibility clearly belied by facts of which I was fully aware, moved me to the very marrow of my bones. He was an Emperor by inherent birth, but in that instant I knew I faced

4. National Archives, Diplomatic Section, Record Group 353, Box 15, quoted in Ward 1987, p. 12.

5. MacArthur Memorial Library, Norfolk, Va., War Department Messages: 1001 to 1094 from April 29 to August 2, 1945, quoted by Ward (1987), p. 15.

the First Gentleman of Japan in his own right. (MacArthur
1964, p. 288)

MacArthur thus came to believe that the Emperor should be retained,
not only for utilitarian purposes, but also because he was deeply impressed by the Emperor as an individual.

But the issue was still not settled. Anticipating the possibility that
"American and Allied public opinion would ultimately oblige the occupation authorities to charge the Emperor with the commission of war
crimes and thus bring about a trial," the Joint Chiefs of Staff radioed
MacArthur on November 29, 1945, and instructed him to "gather information and evidence relating to the Emperor's possible war guilt"
(Ward 1987, p. 15). When MacArthur finally responded to this directive on January 25, 1946, he said:

> Since receipt of WX 85811 investigation has been con-
> ducted here under the limitations set forth with reference to
> possible criminal actions against the emperor. No specific
> and tangible evidence has been uncovered with regard to his
> exact activities which might connect him in varying degree
> with the political decisions of the Japanese Empire during
> the last decade. . . .
>
> If he is to be tried great changes must be made in occupa-
> tional plans and due preparation therefor should be accom-
> plished in preparedness before actual action is initiated. His
> indictment will unquestionably cause a tremendous convul-
> sion among the Japanese people, the repercussions of which
> cannot be over-estimated. . . .
>
> The whole of Japan can be expected, in my opinion, to
> resist the action either by passive or semi-active means.
> They are disarmed and therefore will represent no special
> menace to trained and equipped troops; but it is not incon-
> ceivable that all government agencies will break down, the
> civilized practices will largely cease, and a condition of un-
> derground chaos and disorder amounting to guerrilla warfare
> in the mountainous and outlying regions result. I believe all
> hope of introducing modern democratic methods would dis-
> appear and that when military control finally ceased some
> form of intense regimentation probably along communistic
> lines would arise from the mutilated masses. This would rep-
> resent an entirely different problem of occupation from the
> one now prevalent. It would be absolutely essential to greatly
> increase the occupational forces. It is quite possible that a
> minimum of a million troops would be required which would

have to be maintained for an indefinite number of years. In addition a complete civil service might have to be set up on practically a war basis embracing an indigent civil population of many millions. . . .

The decision as to whether the emperor should be tried as a war criminal involves a policy determination upon such a high level that I would not feel it appropriate for me to make a recommendation; but if the decision by the heads of state is in the affirmative, I recommend the above measures as imperative (ibid., p. 16).[6]

It is not clear what effect MacArthur's comments had in changing the negative attitude of the Americans about the Emperor, but his threat of a massive increase in the American troops in Japan did work. Ward (ibid.) says,

Questions of justice aside, even the possibility that such a move might entail the stationing of "a minimum of a million troops" in Japan "for an indefinite number of years" was calculated to strike terror into the hearts of the American military leadership, which was already under the strongest political and public pressure to repatriate and demobilize America's armed forces with the greatest possible speed.

So the Emperor of Japan remained on the throne.

## The Emperor in the Japanese Constitution

The staff of MacArthur's headquarters were not quite certain what legal status the Emperor should have in the new democratic era. Convinced that sovereignty, which had been lodged in the Emperor in the Meiji Constitution, had to be transferred to the people of Japan, they determined that the Emperor's power be severely curtailed, so that he would merely be the symbol of the state, "deriving his position from the sovereign will of the People, and from no other source" (MacArthur Constitution, Article I). The Japanese were also gravely concerned about the fate of the Emperor. When government officials saw these views incorporated in the MacArthur draft, they were stunned, for they felt that the very foundation of their nation was at stake.

In this chapter I will discuss this most central issue in the making of the Japanese Constitution, focusing attention on three problems of

6. Ward says (1987, p. 40 n. 29), "The radiograms involved are JCS to MacArthur, WARX-85811 of November 29, 1945, and MacArthur to WARCOS-JCS, CA 57235 of January 25, 1946. These may be found in National Archives, Record Group 218, Box 117, CCS 091.11 Japan, sec. 1."

translation. Two of them concern the selection of appropriate Japanese words for certain English expressions that the Americans insisted on incorporating into the Constitution: the phrase "advice and consent," used to describe the position of the Emperor in relation to the Cabinet, and the term "popular sovereignty," as interpreted by the Japanese. The third problem was the interpretation of the Japanese term, *kokumin*, chosen to stand for "the people." The Americans were adamant that the Japanese select a precise translation of both "advice and consent" and "popular sovereignty," and the Japanese finally yielded to American wishes. The Americans did not pay much attention to the Japanese choice of the word *kokumin*. But the Japanese debated its meaning at great length, for to them the meaning of this word was directly related to whether or not they could believe that the fundamental character of their nation had changed. Interestingly, the issue underlying the Japanese semantic debate on *kokumin* was exactly the same as the choice of the proper Japanese word for "popular sovereignty," about which the Americans were extremely sensitive. But because of the difference in the meanings and usages of the two expressions in the American and Japanese political contexts, each side apparently failed to understand the other's concern.

## "Advice and Consent"

ARTICLE 3. All acts of the Emperor in the matters of state require the advice and approval of the Cabinet, and the Cabinet will be responsible therefor. (My translation)

### A Historical Perspective on "Advice and Consent"

One of the most distinctive features of the American political system is the separation of powers. Fear of uncontrolled political power, and particularly executive power, was a potent force in the events leading up to the American revolution, and suspicion and distrust of government entrenched itself as a dominant theme in American political thought from that time onward. When the Founding Fathers drafted the Constitution, they sought to protect the people from the power of the new national government by splitting its functions among three branches, making it difficult, if not impossible, for one branch to act without the others' consent. One means of checking executive power was to require the president to gain the advice and consent of the Senate in making certain key appointments. The recent rejection of a nominee to the Supreme Court was an impressive demonstration of how the Senate, by withholding consent, can thwart the president. The Senate's action was, of course, controversial, and many believed that the senators should not have rejected a nominee simply because they disagreed with his judicial philosophy. Yet none could doubt that the Senate's action was legitimate. Americans of all political persuasions understand that "advice and consent" means that the Senate has the power to block presidential actions.

The Americans were uncertain of the appropriate legal status for the Japanese Emperor, but they were convinced that one of the evils of the Meiji Constitution was the fact that the Emperor's power, or power exercised in his name, was not limited in any significant way. They firmly believed that Japan had been governed by the Emperor and the men surrounding him with "complete despotism." A passage from the report of the Government Section of GHQ amply reflects their attitude:

> It has already been pointed out that the so-called Meiji Con-
> stitution provided none of the safeguards or the guarantees
> customarily found in the organic law of a modern state. The
> Japanese state, as has so often been pointed out, operated as
> a government of men rather than of laws. All authority
> stemmed from the top—a supreme ruler upon whom every
> Japanese subject depended, to whom he looked, for whom
> he lived. The agents of that ruler governed with complete
> despotism. Their authority could not be challenged for two
> excellent and eminently practical reasons. There was no fo-
> rum sufficiently exalted to assume jurisdiction, for that would
> be to permit questioning His Imperial Majesty; and there
> were no laws in the Western sense of the word to define in
> clear and unequivocal terms the relationships between the
> subject and his government. (SCAP 1968, 1:92)

They were convinced that, to prevent the Emperor and his subordinates from exercising despotic power, it was necessary to severely curtail the political power of the Emperor himself. For the Americans, one obvious solution was a constitutional check on his powers. Therefore, in the MacArthur draft, they included the following article:

> ARTICLE III. The advice and consent of the Cabinet shall be
> required for all acts of the Emperor in matters of state, and
> the Cabinet shall be responsible therefor.

Furthermore, Article VI listed nine state functions to be performed by the Emperor on behalf of the people, with the advice and consent of the Cabinet. But did the Japanese understand the American idea of checks and balances, especially when the Emperor was involved? Throughout its long recorded history, from A.D. 300 until its defeat in 1945, Japan had never been occupied by a foreign power. During this entire period, Japan had an unbroken line of emperors as its formal head of state. In the earliest years, the emperors actually ruled, but in the course of time, gradually lost political power. By the eleventh century, the emperor's councillors exercised the powers of the court, and the emperor was little more than a figurehead. Eventually, various military factions seized power from the councillors. Nevertheless, for religious and political reasons, none of the subsequent military rulers tried to abolish the imperial institution, and the emperor continued to be the symbolic leader of the nation, though perhaps only dimly perceived as such by many. When Tokugawa Ieyasu unified the country in the early seventeenth century, he left the fiction of imperial rule intact, and his successors continued this policy. The emperor was so politically insignificant that, until the end of the Tokugawa era, many ordinary Japanese may have been ignorant of his existence. But he retained sufficient prestige and authority among the ruling elite that when the leaders of the Meiji Restoration overthrew Tokugawa rule, they made their revolution in the name of the Emperor Meiji, claiming they were "restoring" the Emperor to his rightful place. The Meiji Constitution was promulgated in the name of the Emperor, and Article 5 appeared to grant him legislative power:

> The Emperor exercises the legislative power with the consent (*kyōsan*) of the Imperial Diet. (My translation)

But Article 55 made it clear that the Emperor could not exercise independent power:

> The respective Ministers of State will advise (*hohitsu shi*) the Emperor, and be responsible for it.
> All laws, Imperial Ordinances, and Imperial Rescripts of whatever kind, that relate to the affairs of the State, require the countersignature of a Minister of State. (My translation)

And in fact, all significant decisions, though made in the name of the Emperor, were made by the Meiji oligarchs.

The Americans misunderstood the actual position of the Emperor, probably in part because Japanese policy, during the prewar years and through the war, was so emphatically carried out in the name of the Emperor. To an outsider, the Emperor might have been viewed as an active participant, since he was present when the Cabinet deliberated and decided any important question. But the Emperor never actively participated in the discussions. Rather, he sat silently while the Cabinet members deliberated among themselves, except on very rare occasions, such as the eve of Japan's surrender, when the Prime Minister specifically asked the Emperor to express his opinion to break the deadlock. Only when the Cabinet had reached a consensus was he asked to give his approval, which he never withheld.[7] The Japanese had a word, *hohitsu*, meaning "assistance/advice to the Emperor," to describe this situation. This word, used in Article 55 of the Meiji Constitution, meant in practice that the ministers of the state took full responsibility for all decisions, while leaving the Emperor with ostensible authority, and the great prestige that went with the imperial office.

The Americans apparently did not understand or appreciate the actual position of the Emperor.[8] One possible reason is that the Japanese distinguish formal position and actual power far more readily than Americans do. In most Japanese organizations, leadership positions customarily go to individuals with the longest period of service in an organization. The person who is at the head of an organization receives very high social prestige, whether or not he is a capable leader. In some cases, a leader may have little actual power, or may rely so heavily on his subordinates that a few highly capable subordinates wield the actual power in the organization. Nevertheless, leader continues to receive great deference from these same subordinates (Nakane 1970, pp. 64–68).

But, while the formal leader receives great prestige, he usually must accept responsibility for the actions of the organization as well, whether

7. In his book, *Seidan* (The Sacred Decision), Handō Kazutoshi says that Emperor Hirohito made the decision to remain firmly above politics at the time of the June 1928 assassination of Chang Tso-lin, of Manchuria, by the Kwantung Army officer, Colonel Kōmoto Daisaku. At that time, the Emperor expressed to Prime Minister Tanaka his extreme displeasure over the Cabinet's inability to censure Kōmoto, who acted independently, and against the wishes of the government. The Emperor's actions eventually led the Tanaka cabinet to resign. Prince Saionji Kimmochi, the last of the Meiji oligarchs, advised the young Emperor that the Emperor of Japan held a position similar to that of the British constitutional monarch, and therefore should not express his opinions on matters of state. From that time, until the end of World War II, the Emperor maintained his neutrality and his silence. He spoke only when he realized that it was necessary for him to do so to save the nation from utter destruction (Handō 1985, pp.101–4). It is not clear whether the Emperor could have exercised any influence over governmental policy had he attempted to assert himself.

8. In fact, part of the blame may have been due to the unfortunate translation of the Japanese term *tennō* as "emperor," rather than "king." Robert J. Smith, a distinguished scholar who specializes in Japanese anthropology, says that in the early years of the Meiji period, translations of official documents used the term "head of state" to refer to the emperor. Later, the Meiji leaders changed the term to "emperor." To "the foreign reader, the word 'emperor' conjures up images of pomp and the public display of immense wealth and power, both quite antithetical to the role and functions of the *tennō* throughout most of Japanese history" (R. Smith 1983, p. 13).

It is conceivable that if the term *tennō* had been translated as "king," Americans of 1946 might have understood his role in Japanese society much more accurately than they did. Neither the Japanese officials, nor Americans knowledgeable about Japanese history, explained to MacArthur's staff that they should think of the Emperor as being more like British king than Napoleon. Of course, such an explanation might not have worked.

or not he had anything to do with the actual decisions. Thus, it is very common for the head of an organization to resign when some disaster or organizational misconduct occurs.[9] When Emperor Hirohito called on MacArthur, and offered to assume full responsibility for Japanese conduct during the war, he was acting as a proper Japanese leader would have been expected to act.

The Emperor was an extreme example of this separation of prestige and power. As John Toland (1970, p. 23) says,

> Theoretically the Emperor had plenary power; all state decisions needed his sanction. But according to tradition, once the Cabinet and military leaders had agreed on a policy, he could not withhold his approval. He was to remain above politics and transcend party considerations and feuds, for he represented the entire nation.

Certainly the Emperor understood his role in this manner. Even at the end of the war—when Emperor Hirohito played an unprecedented and decisive role in bringing it to a close—he did not act alone. When Baron Suzuki Kantarō took over the premiership in April 1945, at the urging of the Emperor himself, he knew that the Emperor was anxious to end the war and prevent further casualties. Suzuki secretly decided to take the responsibility for closing the war while trying to maintain the nation intact, and deliberately and carefully worked toward that end.[10] In the final hours of the war, Sakomizu Hisatsune called a meeting of the Cabinet, with the top military leaders, in the presence of the Emperor, on August 10. Ordinarily, such a meeting would be called by the Emperor in response to a joint request by the Prime Minister and the military leaders. But Sakomizu was afraid that the military leaders would refuse to go along, so with the tacit approval of Suzuki, he submitted a request for a meeting to the Emperor in the Prime Minister's name alone. In the course of the meeting, when it became clear that the Cabinet could not reach a consensus, the Prime

9. When pilot error caused a Japan Air Lines plane to crash at Haneda Airport on February 9, 1982, killing twenty-four passengers and injuring more than one hundred, the president of JAL apparently immediately expressed to the Minister of Transportation his intention to resign (*Asahi Shimbun*, 14 February 1982, p. 1). In the end, however, several top executives stepped down, allowing the president to stay on (ibid., May 25, 1982; May 31, 1983). Because many Japanese felt that it would have been honorable for the president to resign immediately, the issue of his resignation lingered on for months after the accident (ibid., September 11, 1982).

10. Sakomizu Hisatsune, chief cabinet secretary of the Suzuki cabinet, states that Suzuki gave him the clear impression that when the Emperor asked Suzuki to be prime minister, Suzuki understood this to be the Emperor's wish (Sakomizu 1964, p. 151).

Minister took the unprecedented step of asking the Emperor to express
his opinion. The Emperor then told the military leaders that he agreed
with the decision to surrender to spare the nation further casualties.
Once he had stated his opinion, the military leaders could not oppose
him, and the decision was made. Sakomizu prepared the draft of the
imperial rescript proclaiming Japan's defeat, the Cabinet members debated it and made a few minor changes, and finally all the ministers
countersigned it on the night of August 14, Japan time. Shortly thereafter, General Anami, the minister of the army, took his own life to
stop further opposition by younger officers. By this act, he accepted
personal responsibility, both for the Army's insistence on the continuation of the war, and for Japan's catastrophic defeat (Sakomizu 1964,
pp. 145–316; Tsunoda 1980, pp. 116–265).[11]

At the war's end, the Japanese people fully realized that the military
had miscalculated Japan's military and economic strength, and that the
government, controlled by the military faction, had steered the nation
into the catastrophic war. To be sure, the military had taken all its
actions in the name of the Emperor. But in 1946 most Japanese understood, and still do today, that the *actual* responsibility rested on the
men surrounding the Emperor, and not on the Emperor himself. They
believed that the way to prevent the nation from repeating this catas-
trophe was to keep a close watch over the government leaders, not the
Emperor, so that they would act responsibly for the good of the nation.
It was the Cabinet that had to be checked, not the Emperor.

### The Negotiations Between the Americans and the Japanese

On the morning of March 4, 1946, when the Japanese presented their
own version of the constitution, modeled after the MacArthur Constitution, they had translated the phrase "advice and consent" using the
Japanese expression, *hohitsu*, which the Meiji Constitution used in Article 55 (The respective Ministers of State will advise [*hohitsu-shi*] the

---

11. From an American perspective, the Emperor was not responsible for the war because he
was largely a figurehead, and had no influence or control over the decision to attack the United
States. If he were to be held responsible, it would be for failing to act when he might have had
some influence. From a Japanese perspective, however, his actions or omissions were beside the
point. The Emperor was the symbolic leader during this disastrous period, so it was quite appropriate for him to take responsibility for the consequences. When the Emperor visited MacArthur,
he came in his role as Emperor, not as an individual. I believe MacArthur mistook the Emperor's
offer to assume responsibility for the war as the act of an individual, and not the act of a person
carrying out a duty appropriate to his role. The Japanese people could not have imagined that he
would go to MacArthur and beg for his own life. That would have been an unthinkably dishon-
orable thing for him to do.

Emperor, and be responsible therefor; my translation). The new article read:

> ARTICLE 3. All acts of the Emperor in the matters of state require the *hohitsu* of the Cabinet. The Cabinet will take the responsibility therefor.[12] (My translation)

Article 7 listed nine specific state functions to be performed by the Emperor, with the *hohitsu* of the Cabinet. As we have already noted, *hohitsu* refers to the "advice" the Cabinet gives to the Emperor. Since the Emperor could not ignore or reject this advice, to state that the Cabinet had to give its consent would have been superfluous.

When the Americans and Japanese began the 30-hour marathon negotiations, the Americans immediately noticed the use of *hohitsu* and vehemently opposed it. In fact, had they properly understood the Emperor's position, they might have insisted that the Emperor have the power to give or withhold consent, since it was the unchecked power of the Cabinet that had led the nation into war. But the Americans did not have this understanding, so they insisted that the Japanese phrase had to include a term equivalent to "consent." Matsumoto argued that, according to the new Constitution,[13] the Emperor could not act without the advice of his ministers, so *hohitsu* would suffice. But the Americans would not budge. Angry and frustrated, Matsumoto excused himself, and did not return to the negotiating table that day. The debate continued, with Satō serving as the sole legal authority on the Japanese side (Matsumoto 1958, p. 22).

Later in the evening, on the advice of Frank Rizzo, a staff member with some knowledge of Japanese, Charles Kades, the chief negotiator on the American side, suggested *kyōsan*, a term used in Article 5 of the Meiji Constitution, which reads, in my translation,

> The Emperor exercises the legislative power with *kyōsan* of the Imperial Diet.

Satō rejected the term, however, saying that it was an archaic expression inappropriate for the new Constitution. Kades then proposed another word, *shōnin*, a formal but more common word meaning "approval." Satō felt that *shōnin* would not be regarded as deferential enough to express the Cabinet's "consent" to the acts of the Emperor,

12. *Dai-san-jō. Tennō-no kokuji-ni kansuru issai-no kōi-wa naikaku-no hohitsu-ni yoru-koto-o yō-su. Naikaku-wa kore-ni-tsuki sono-seki-ni ninzu* (Shimizu 1962–63, 4:340).

13. Matsumoto simply said *kempō* (the Constitution), so it is not entirely clear whether he meant the new Constitution or the Meiji Constitution.

so he rejected it as well. He suggested *sandō* as an alternative. *Sandō* consists of *san* (praise/honor) and *dō* (same), so it literally means something like "agreement in praise," although contemporary usage does not convey a clear sense of deference. Rizzo consulted a dictionary and confirmed its meaning. The two sides thus agreed on the phrase *hohitsu-sandō* (assist/advise the Emperor and respectfully approve his acts). The Americans replaced "consent" with "approval" in their own version. The matter was settled, or so it seemed (Satō 1955a, 172:14).

After the so-called outline of the new Constitution of Japan was made public on March 6, 1946, the Japanese government prepared its full version to be presented to the Cabinet. When changing the language of the Constitution from the classical style to the written form of colloquial Japanese, the Japanese officials altered vocabulary as well. Included among these alterations was *hohitsu-sandō*, which was changed to *hosa-to dōi*. *Hosa* means simply "assistance," and is often used in an everyday expression such as *kachō hosa* (assistant manager); *dōi* literally means "the same thought," or "agreement"; and *to* is "and."

The Japanese officials chose the new phrase because they regarded it as more democratic. In his personal notes, Satō says that this change was motivated by the criticisms in newspapers that *hohitsu-sandō* was too archaic, and difficult to understand (Satō Tatsuo Kankei Bunsho 67). The Japanese often use the term "democratic" to refer to situations in which a person of high status deals with one of lower status with consideration and respect, as if there were no difference in rank. For instance, a company supervisor who listens to his supervisees' opinions and treats them as if they are his equals is considered "democratic." The Japanese thought that replacing *sandō* with *dōi*, to refer to the Cabinet's consent, would democratize the relationship between the two without impairing the Emperor's status. But, of course, it ignored the central American concern, which was to place an institutional constraint on the Emperor's power.

On April 18, the day after the Japanese government made public the new colloquial version of the Japanese Constitution, Kades requested a meeting with Japanese officials to discuss the various changes that they had made, among them "advice and approval." Kades, along with Joseph Gordon, a translator on the GHQ staff, said that they had conducted a small survey concerning the Japanese understanding of the word *dōi*, and had been told by five informants that it was a word used between two equals. Kades told Satō that if the Japanese could not find a better word, they would have to add a phrase such as "under the authorization of the Cabinet," to express clearly the notion that the Cabinet was superior to the Emperor. Satō says that he was very surprised by Kades' sharp tone. Kades raised his right fist high and said, "This is the Cabinet"; he then placed his left fist below it and said, "This is the Emperor." Satō pointed out to Kades that *dōi* was a term used in the Civil Code to refer to a househead's consent to the marriage of a son under the age of 30, where the relationship is clearly not equal. But Satō also realized that Americans would not understand the special position of the Emperor in relation to the Japanese people. He asked for time to find a more suitable word, but Kades told him that there was no time to ponder, for GHQ had to send a telegram containing errata to the Far Eastern Commission as soon as possible. Finally, Satō proposed that they adopt *shōnin*, the term that the Americans had suggested at the 30-hour marathon. Kades agreed. As for *hosa*, Kades said that that was not appropriate, because, as he understood it, its primary sense was "assistance," and not "advice" given by someone below to one above. Satō replied that he regarded the choice of *hosa* over *hohitsu* as an attempt to democratize the document, but then suggested that they drop it altogether. Kades responded that eliminating it would imply that the Cabinet would not have an active role in advising the Emperor. Satō finally pointed to *jogen* in a dictionary and suggested that it be adopted. Having looked up the word in another dictionary, Kades and Gordon agreed. Satō telephoned the Cabinet office, and, with the Prime Minister's approval, the matter was finally settled (Satō Tatsuo Kankei Bunsho 67; 1955a, 175:14–15). Article 3 in the new Constitution now read,

> All acts of the Emperor in matters of state require the advice and approval (*jogen-to shōnin*) of the Cabinet, and the Cabinet will be responsible therefor. (My translation)

The dispute between the Americans and the Japanese officials was over. But neither side had really understood the other. The Americans wanted to make sure that the Cabinet was, in a legal sense, superior to the Emperor, so they insisted on a phrase that would explicitly convey the idea that the Cabinet had to consent to any action the Emperor might take. Since the Emperor had never been able to act without Cabinet approval, the Japanese government saw no need for a new phrase. *Jogen-to shōnin* did not seem to them to create a substantive change in the government. But *hohitsu* was important to them, because it suggested that, in *form*, the Emperor remained superior to the Cabinet.

## The Debate at the National Diet

The debates in the National Diet indicate that the members did not appreciate the American intentions behind "advice and consent." Although some members understood that the formal position of the Emperor had changed, no one mentioned the principles behind checks and balances. Since they understood that the Emperor had no real power, they probably did not see the need for the new phrase. Their main concern was to persuade themselves that the meaning of the old word carried over to the new one.

To illustrate, on June 25, 1946, the opening day of the plenary sessions of the House of Representatives, Kita Reikichi of the Liberal party asked if the new phrase replacing *hohitsu* implied any change in the role of the Emperor in the new Constitution.

> Moving on to Article 3, . . . speaking of the essence of this article, it means that the Emperor has no legal responsibility. The Emperor has no need to take responsibility, as long as the ministers who are responsible for advising (*hohitsu*) [him] take legal and political responsibility entirely. However, in this Constitution, that stipulation is missing. I would like to ask what the government thinks about it. (Shūgi-in 1946a, 5:71, col. 3)

Kanamori assured him that there would be no change:

> Your question was that there is no stipulation that the Emperor has no responsibility, but you presume that such is still the case. You are entirely correct. As Article 1 shows, the Emperor is the symbol of the State and the unity of the people. He is at the center of the nation, and is colorless and transparent. There is no reason to place political responsibility on such a person. Why do we not stipulate this clearly? To do so is too obvious. Article 3 reflects the idea without clearly writing it down (ibid., 76, col. 2).

Kanamori simply reiterated the traditional view of the symbolic role of the Emperor, who had no actual responsibility for affairs of state.

On July 8, at the special committee hearing of the House of Representatives, Sakai Toshio, of the Cooperative Democratic party, made the same point, and asked about the responsibility of the Cabinet:

> It is clear from Article 3 that the Emperor is free of responsibility, and that the Cabinet takes responsibility on his behalf. But may I ask to whom the Cabinet is responsible and for what? Are you considering special laws specifying the duties of the ministers? (Shūgi-in 1946b, 8:132, cols. 1–2)

Kanamori replied,

> As you say, Article 3 simply says that the Cabinet is responsible and does not say to whom the Cabinet is respon-

sible. But various articles in the Constitution referring to the cabinet system indicate that the Cabinet is responsible to the National Diet, and through the Diet, to the people. Article 3 is an instance of the application of that [idea] (ibid., col. 2).

Sakai continued,

If we look at Article 95 (current 99), it says "The Emperor or the Regent . . . have the obligation to respect and uphold this Constitution." Suppose [the Emperor or the Regent] fails to fulfill this duty, what would happen? (ibid., col. 4).

Kanamori answered by indicating that the Emperor could not be held accountable:

It is clear that, according to Article 95, the Emperor has the obligation to respect and uphold this Constitution. It is logically possible for the Emperor not to fulfill that obligation. But even in such a case, I should say that the Emperor will not be responsible (col. 5).

His response reinforced the idea that the Emperor's position had not changed.

On July 12, Yamazaki Iwao, of the Progressive party, did make reference to the new choice of words. His exchanges with Kanamori[14] are noteworthy:

Article 55 of the present Constitution says, "The respective Ministers of State will advise (hohitsu shi) the Emperor, and be responsible therefor." The draft says naikaku-no jogen-to shōnin (advice and approval of the Cabinet). Why did you distinguish jogen and shōnin from hohitsu?

Kanamori replied that there was no difference, but his explanation is vague:

I think there is no substantial difference between hohitsu and jogen-to shōnin. But the meaning of hohitsu is not clear—ho means "assist" and hitsu also means "assist," so it is "assist-assist."[15] It is not appropriate for accurately capturing the actual workings of democratic politics. Moreover, this word is very difficult. Taking account into these two factors, we adopted the easier and more accurate terms, jogen and shōnin.

14. Shūgi-in 1946b, 11:191, col. 5–192, col. 4.
15. In Sino-Japanese word formation, it is common to see two-character expressions where the characters have similar meanings.

Yamazaki continued,

> I think *jogen* precedes *shōnin*. Was there any reason for sepa-
> rating the two?

Kanamori responded that the phrase meant that the Cabinet would
sometimes take the initiative, while at other times it would be the
Emperor:

> I don't know if *jogen* precedes *shōnin*. What I can say clearly
> is that *jogen* means that the Cabinet forms an opinion and
> presents it to the Emperor. *Shōnin* implies the Cabinet
> takes a passive role. In other words, the former means that
> the Cabinet works actively, and the later means that it
> works passively. I cannot tell you immediately which pre-
> cedes which.

Kanamori thus appears to have missed completely the American intentions behind the new Japanese words. Yamazaki then pointed out that
the status of the Emperor had apparently changed:

> From the point of view of constitutional law, we learned that
> a monarchy is an institution of direct rule, and also a dicta-
> torial one. In this draft, however, it appears that the Cabinet
> has an advantage [over the Emperor]. It appears that the
> position of the Emperor as an autocratic institution has been
> somewhat eroded in Article 3 of this draft. I would like to
> hear your opinion on this.

Kanamori simply repeated the 'proper' interpretation of the advisory
responsibilities of the ministers to the Emperor in the Japanese political system, and said that the new phrase meant exactly the same as
the old word:

> Within the present political framework, it is already the case
> that the Emperor's actual work is somewhat constrained by
> the ministers of state, and their exercise of authority. The
> weakness of the term *hohitsu* is that it simply means "assis-
> tance." One could interpret it as implying that the minister
> would advise the Emperor, and that it would be acceptable
> for him to sit and do nothing when the Emperor does not
> accept it. But according to accepted constitutional theory, it
> is not sufficient for a minister simply to advise. *Hohitsu*
> means that a minister would give advice to the Emperor and
> urge him to accept it. Such a practice helps to facilitate the
> proper functioning of constitutional government. Therefore,
> if one interprets it (*hohitsu*) in that way, one can conclude
> that, politically, the rather exact expression, *jogen-to shōnin*,
> is no different from *hohitsu* in its content.

Yamazaki pursued the point, asking Kanamori for further clarification:

> Article 55 (of the Meiji Constitution) states, "All laws, imperial ordinances . . . that relate to the affairs of the State require the countersignature of a Minister of State." Is the responsibility of a minister in Article 3 of this draft to be shown by his countersignature also?
>
> KANAMORI: There is considerable room for differences of opinion over the nature and value of countersignatures in the present Constitution. . . . In the new Constitution, we have emphasized the practical act of advice and consent (*jogen-to shōnin*). But as a matter of law, nothing has been written about the relationship of Cabinet members toward a document provided with their advice and consent, and signed by the Emperor.[16] We intend to establish laws, which might be called laws of formality, which will clarify who will countersign, and in what circumstances.
>
> YAMAZAKI: I understand.

Thus, Yamazaki probably did recognize that the change in the choice of expressions implied that, under the new Constitution, the Emperor's power would be limited both in form and in substance. Kanamori managed to maintain an ambiguous position.

The next day, a fourth member, Kashihara Yoshinori of the Club of Nonaffiliated Members, raised a question from a different perspective, asking what would happen if the Emperor and the Cabinet disagreed (from an American point of view, this was an important question):

> Do you suppose there will always be agreement between the Cabinet's advice and the Emperor's perspective on the affairs of the state? Would the Emperor always agree with the Cabinet when it makes suggestions? Could there be some difference [of opinion]? (Shūgi-in 1946b, 12:214, col. 3)

Kanamori knew that, in practice, the Emperor alone hardly ever opposed the members of the Cabinet. So he simply stated that he expected that the Cabinet and the Emperor would always reach a consensus:

> I believe ultimately there will be agreement. The reason I say "ultimately" is because it is quite possible for disagreements to arise at the stage of advice, but when the final decision is made, there will be complete agreement (ibid.).

---

16. The text is difficult to translate accurately. Kanamori's point seems to be that the Constitution does not specify what the Cabinet must do once a bill has been signed by the Emperor, after receiving the advice and consent of the Cabinet. Some means must be established to formally mark the Cabinet's consent.

Finally, a fifth member, Kasai Shigeharu, brought up the Emperor's exceptional act in bringing the war to a close by overruling the military. Kasai, probably without knowing exactly what happened on the eve of Japan's surrender, asked Kanamori what would happen in such a case under the new Constitution (216, cols. 4–5). Kanamori once again evaded the question by saying he thought they would always reach an agreement:

> As is stated in Article 3, for all acts of the Emperor in matters of state, the advice and approval of the Cabinet is required, and the Cabinet takes responsibility for them. That is predicated on the principle that there is no difference in the position of the Emperor engaging in the affairs of state and the minister taking responsibility for them. We do not expect any discrepancy between the two. (216, col. 5)

When the draft Constitution was considered by the House of Peers, toward the end of the summer, some distinguished constitutional scholars also raised questions regarding the interpretation of *jogen-to shōnin*. They knew exactly what *hohitsu* meant in actual practice, and appeared to want to get Kanamori to admit that the change to the new phrase was unnecessary. They should also have understood what the phrase "advice and consent" meant in American constitutional history, but their comments and questions indicate that they either did not quite understand the American intentions, or deliberately avoided acknowledging them.

On September 5, 1946, Takayanagi Kenzō, a noted specialist in Anglo-American law, compared the British and Japanese political systems and said that, in brief, British constitutional history has been the story of the struggle between two groups—a small elite, and the majority of the people—over which group would serve as the advisory organ to the monarch (*hoyoku kikan*). In his view, under the new Constitution, Japan was to become a nation where, in place of a small elite, all the Japanese people were to become advisors to the Emperor:

> I think it is very fortunate for the Japanese people that, after the world-wide upheaval, the imperial institution has been kept intact. It is commonsensically apparent that there would have been a great deal of confusion without the imperial system. . . . The main object of this Constitution is to democratize the Japanese political system with the Emperor at the center—that is the central idea of this Constitution. (Kizoku-in 1946b, 5:16, cols. 2–3)

He continued,

> The idea expressed in Article 4 that the Emperor "does not have powers related to government," that is, he has no power to influence governmental affairs—this idea represents the system of modern constitutional monarchy. But, as I read the Constitution, it is not the case that the Emperor has no connection with the government. He formally participates in legislative, executive, judicial, and diplomatic affairs. The Emperor promulgates amendments to the Constitution, laws, cabinet orders, and treaties. In other words, enactment requires the Emperor's promulgation. . . . For all these acts of the Emperor, *jogen* and *shōnin* of the Cabinet is required, and the responsibility rests with the Cabinet. The Emperor has no responsibility. So the Emperor in this Constitution is a constitutional monarch, very much like the British King. . . . The big difference between the British constitution and this draft is that Britain has "representative democracy," and the Parliament, consisting of the King and the national assembly, is omnipotent, and constitutional laws can be abolished by a single law. In comparison, our constitutional draft also incorporates some elements of direct democracy as practiced in Switzerland. To look at this draft from the point of view of legal sovereignty, constitutional revisions will be proposed by the Diet, then submitted to a popular referendum and promulgated by the Emperor. So legal sovereignty rests with the Diet, the people, and the Emperor. From this point of view, I believe the British would say that legal sovereignty is shared by the Emperor, the National Diet and the people. . . . Ultimate political power, on the other hand, rests in the people, apart from the Emperor, as it does in Britain. If this observation is correct, this Constitution eliminates the military, who exercised power behind the imperial prerogative (*taiken*), and the influence of senior statesmen. The Prime Minister, representing the people, will take full responsibility. If you will permit me to use an old expression, he will "assist/advise" (*hoyoku*)[17] the imperial prerogative [in the name of the people]. In other words, all the people have become the advisory organ (*hoyoku kikan*), rather than a handful of individuals. The development of British constitutional history is the history of change in the [membership] of the advisory organ . . . From

17. *Hoyoku* is synonymous with *hohitsu* (*Kadokawa Kanwa Chū-jiten*, 1979:1069).

this point of view, this Constitution parallels the British constitution closely (18, col. 2–19, col. 2).

Immediately after Takayanagi, Makino Eiichi expressed his doubt that the new phrase appropriately captured the existing Japanese understanding of the role of the Emperor under the Constitution. He apparently understood that the Emperor's formal position had changed. He said,

> [The Article] says "*jogen* and *shōnin* of the Cabinet," or "advice and approval." I wonder if the phrase "the Cabinet advises the Emperor" accurately reflects the idea we have about the Emperor's position in the Constitution. In reference to the position of the Cabinet, is it appropriate to say that the Cabinet approves the acts of the Emperor? . . . There must be a Japanese word which represents [the idea] that the Cabinet advises the Emperor from below, and approves his acts from below. I would like to ask you to avoid the expression such as *jogen-to shōnin*, which makes one supect that it is a phrase used between two equals, or worse yet, the Cabinet is above the Emperor. (25, cols. 1–3)

Kanamori said that he, too, felt that the new phrase did not accurately reflect the Japanese people's feelings toward the Emperor, but that that was of secondary importance. Under the circumstances, they had no choice but to face reality, and make certain that the nation avoided past mistakes under this Constitution (29, cols. 3–4).

On September 10, Shimojō Yasumaro again raised the question of the difference between *jogen* and *shōnin*:[18]

> According to your explanation at the House of Representatives, *jogen* refers to cases when the Cabinet speaks to the Emperor. *Shōnin* refers to the Cabinet's approval of the Emperor's action. Isn't it sufficient to use either *jogen* or *shōnin*? For what reason have you used both?

Kanamori replied that, while conceptually the two were separate, he thought that there would be cases where one would not be able to tell how much was advice and how much was consent. To this, Shimojō said,

> I don't quite understand, but let's assume that the House of Representatives is dissolved according to Article 7. I think that when the Cabinet requests the Emperor to dissolve the House of Representatives, it goes into effect by that "ad-

---

18. Kikozu-in 1946b, 9:28, cols. 1–2.

vice." There is no need to approve the Emperor's act [of dissolving it] again. But is there a possibility that the Emperor would directly initiate a request, for instance, that the House of Representatives be dissolved, and the Cabinet would give its approval?

Kanamori replied that that was logically possible but was not certain if such a situation would arise in reality. The entire exchange suggests that neither of them had grasped the significance of "consent." Instead, they seemed to be concerned with the nature of the communications between Cabinet and Emperor.

This also emerges in the comments and questions by Sasaki Sōichi on the same day.[19] To an American, they are curiously off-target, and illustrate the difficulty the Japanese had in understanding the American intentions:

> I would now like to ask about the relationship between the Emperor and the Cabinet. . . . [Article 3 says] that the Emperor acts with *jogen* and *shōnin* of the Cabinet. Does this mean that, besides the Cabinet members, anyone could advise the Emperor? At any rate, I would like to ask how the new phrase differs from *hohitsu* in the present Constitution.

Kanamori replied,

> The consensus is that the new phrase means the same as *hohitsu*. But there is a wide variety of interpretations of *hohitsu*. Therefore, we have selected a less ambiguous expression to make the meaning clear.
> SASAKI: So that means anyone can advise the Emperor, although when it comes to *shōnin* of anyone other than the cabinet members, that would be a different matter.
> KANAMORI: I don't quite understand the point of your comment. I am placed in a rather ambiguous position, so I cannot say yes or no. There is nothing strange about [the Emperor] receiving advice in his personal relationships. But such advice would not have constitutional effect.[20]
> SASAKI: For instance, if the Emperor wishes to learn something about Japan's inflation, can he invite a professor of some university and ask him to explain Japanese economy and ask him how to deal with it?
> KANAMORI: If the Emperor wishes to gain information as an individual, there will be no problem.
> SASAKI: I understand. . . . So, this "advice" refers to requests

19. Ibid., 21, col. 5–22, col. 2.
20. Kanamori's reply is ambiguous, and this is the best sense I can make of his statement.

[by the Cabinet] to the Emperor to bring about certain practical affairs of state. Is that right?
KANAMORI: That is correct.

To conclude, the role of the Emperor in the new Constitution was
the most important issue for both the Americans and Japanese. The
Americans believed that one way to democratize the Japanese political
system, and to guarantee that Japan would never be governed despoti-
cally by the Emperor, was to place a check on his power by requiring
the advice and consent of the Cabinet for all his acts. Therefore, they
insisted that the phrase "advice and consent" be accurately translated
into Japanese to reflect the legal limitations on the Emperor's power.
The Japanese had a traditional word, *hohitsu*, which expressed their idea
of the proper form of communication between the Cabinet and the
Emperor. Since the Japanese Emperor never acted alone, and had no
real power under the Meiji Constitution, they saw little need for the
new phrase that they were forced to accept, and did not understand the
American intent behind "advice and consent." The Americans, on the
other hand, did not realize that the new phrase might actually threaten
the symbolic role of the Emperor by changing the formal relationship
between the Emperor and the Cabinet. The Japanese did their best to
persuade themselves that this had not happened.

## The General Election and the Government's Dilemma

On December 17, 1945, the House of Representatives passed a revision
of the election law of 1925. For the first time in Japan's history, women
were granted the right to vote and the right to run for and hold office.
The following day, the House of Representatives was dissolved. Early
in January 1946, MacArthur launched the first phase of an extensive
purge, removing and excluding from office individuals whom GHQ regarded as culpable of significant wartime activities. The Progressive
party lost 238 out of its 270 former members in the House of Representatives. The Liberal party lost 28 of its 46 members, and even the Socialist party lost half of its representation. On April 10, 1946, Japan's
first truly popular election was held, in which 37 million Japanese voters
elected a total of 464 members. Nearly six weeks later, on May 22,
1946, Yoshida Shigeru established a coalition cabinet consisting of four
ministers from his own Liberal party, four from the Progressive party,
and four from the other groups.

The membership of the new House of Representatives was conservative. The only clearly identifiable nonconservative groups were the
95 members of the Socialist party and the five Communist party mem-

bers, together making up less than a quarter of the total membership. To be sure, many of the new members said they eagerly aspired to democracy, but for the most part they adhered to the principles of the previous political order, particularly the sovereignty of the Emperor, and were gravely concerned about the changes incorporated in the new Constitution.

The constitutional proposal of the Liberal party, made public on January 22, provided that the Emperor was to reign over the nation. Hatoyama Ichirō, the former head of the party, said at that time, "Our Emperor is in the line of emperors unbroken for ages eternal, and he reigns over the nation as the head of State. This is the conviction that our party holds, and our idea of national polity also lies here" (Satō 1962–64, 2:740; my translation). Similarly, the Progressive party stated in its outline that the Emperor reigned over the nation, with the assistance of the people and the laws established by the Constitution (ibid., 2:775). Even the Socialist party advocated the idea that the nation was ruled by both the government and the people, including the Emperor. Its proposal said that sovereignty resided in the state, and the community of people, including the Emperor (ibid., 2:780). The Communist party was the only party to declare that the imperial system had to be abolished and that sovereignty resided in the people. Later, however, they modified their position, saying that the party advocated the abolition of the imperial institution, but left open the question of whether the Imperial Household would continue (ibid., 2:772–73).[21] Yet, less than two months later, the coalition cabinet "produced" a democratic constitution, reducing the official status of the Emperor to a mere symbol. The new Cabinet members, though they shared the conservative views of their colleagues in the Diet, had no choice but to stand by its own ostensible creation, and try to persuade the Diet members to accept this Constitution.[22] How were they to deal with the sud-

21. Takano Iwasaburō was the only person to draft a constitution that espoused a presidential system. He stated, "Sovereignty of the Japanese state resides in the Japanese people," and "The head of state will be the president elected by the people" (Satō 1962–64, 2:850–51; my translation). However, Iwabuchi Tatsuo, who worked on the Constitutional Research Group draft constitution with Takano, later said (1961, pp. 4–5) that even Takano did not start out favoring abolishing the Emperor.

22. In his book on the making of the Japanese Constitution, published in March 1947, Kanamori Tokujirō says, in extremely circuitous language, that he sensed that the members of the House of Representatives thought that this Constitution was going too far, and that the position of the Emperor was not properly protected. Moreover, he thought that the majority of the Japanese people shared this sentiment, for they had sent those Representatives to the Diet to participate in the constitutional debate (1947, pp. 5–6). I believe that the fact that Kanamori saw fit to raise this point barely four months after the promulgation of the Constitution is an indication of how much resistance there was among the Japanese to this document.

den and radical change between their earlier views and the principles
embodied in the new Constitution? The government had a serious
problem, since its spokesmen could not admit that the Constitution
had been imposed by the Americans. They had to find a way to claim
that, although the formal locus of sovereignty had changed, nothing
fundamental about the Emperor's position had changed.

### "The People"

ARTICLE 1. As for the Empire of Japan, the Emperor, in a line
unbroken for ages eternal, reigns over it. (Meiji Constitution; my
translation)

The Americans, along with all the other allied nations, firmly believed
that, to create a new democratic government, the people, and not the
Emperor, had to be sovereign, and that this idea had to be clearly expressed in the Constitution. Thus, the Americans began the Preamble
of the Japanese Constitution as follows:

We, the Japanese People, . . . do proclaim the sovereignty
of the people's will and do ordain and establish this Constitution, . . . ,

and Article 1 stated,

The Emperor shall be the symbol of the State and of the
Unity of the People, deriving his position from the sovereign
will of the People, and from no other source.

The Japanese reaction to this change was by far the strongest of all
the constitutional controversies.[23] Unlike the change in the relationship between the Emperor and the Cabinet, the Japanese feared that
changing the locus of sovereignty from the Emperor to the people, or
more precisely, to the people in opposition to the Emperor, threatened
the fundamental character of the nation. In this section, I will discuss
how the Japanese wrestled with this radical change in connection with
the interpretation of the word *kokumin*, meaning "the nation's people."

23. Shimizu Shin provides some quantitative evidence of the importance of the issue of the
Emperor. In his comprehensive study of the debates at the plenary sessions and the special committee hearings of both Houses, Shimizu gives a list of page numbers of the transcripts in which
articles and major topics are discussed. The top three articles and topics are: Preamble (392 pages);
the debate on national polity, or the character of the nation (154 pages), and Article 1 (130). In
the list of numbers of interpellators on articles and topics, the largest number of interpellators, 57,
was on the Premable. The second largest was on Article 1 (35), the third was on Article 9 (29),
and the fourth was the question of national polity (26). Thus, looking at both the number of pages
on Article 1 and the national polity, and the number of interpellators on Article 1 and the national polity, the issue of the Emperor was clearly the most frequently discussed in the course of
the constitutional debate (Shimizu 1962–63, vol. 4 appendix, pp. 89–94).

The Americans had little interest in this controversy, partly because it was an issue dealing with the semantics of the Japanese language, and partly because they probably did not understand how the idea of popular sovereignty could confuse the Japanese.

## The "People" in American Democracy

Americans tend to equate democracy with popular sovereignty, and they often speak and act as if the meaning of the latter phrase were transparent. Yet the proper relationship between the people and the government, the rulers and the ruled, is a source of intense disagreement. Political figures of various persuasions have fought, and are likely to continue to fight, to capture the favorable connotations of the phrase "popular sovereignty" for their own policies or political arrangements. The struggle to capture this slogan is a persistent theme in American political history.[24]

Kenneth Burke (1973, p. 110) has an interesting discussion of the Bill of Rights that illustrates the changing relationship between ruler and ruled in American history:

> Our Bill of Rights, for instance, is composed of clauses that descended from two substantially different situations. First, as emerging in Magna Carta, they were enunciated by the feudal barons in their "reactionary" struggles against the "progressive" rise of central authority. Later, in the British Petition of Right and Bill of Rights, they were enunciated by the merchant class in their "progressive" struggles against the "reactionary" resistance of the Crown. It is in this second form that they came into our Constitution.
>
> BUT:
>
> Note this important distinction: in the British Bill of Rights, they were defined, or located, as a resistance of the *people* to the *Crown*. Thus they had, at this stage, a strongly collectivistic quality, as the people were united in a common cause against the Crown, and the rights were thus dialectically defined with relation to this opposition. The position of the Crown, in other words, was a necessary term in giving meaning to the people's counter-assertions.
>
> In the United States document, however, the Crown had been abolished. Hence, the dialectical function of the Crown in giving meaning to the terms would have to be taken over by some other concept of sovereignty. And the

---

24. In *Contested Truths: Keywords in American Politics Since Independence*, Daniel T. Rodgers (1987, pp. 84–92) gives an insightful history of different interpretations of "the people" in American politics, and specifically discusses changes in the interpretation of "popular sovereignty."

only sovereignty within the realm covered by the Constitution was the *government elected by the people*. Hence, since
the opposite "cooperates" in the definition of a dialectical
term, and since the sovereignty or authority against which
the rights were proclaimed had changed from that of an an-
tipopular Crown to that of a popularly representative government, it would follow that the quality of the "rights"
themselves would have to change. And such change of quality did take place, in that the rights became interpreted as
rights of the people as *individuals or minorities* against a government representing the will of the people as a *collectivity*
or *majority*.

Thus, initially the people saw themselves as a collective body, opposed
to an alien government. In the revolutionary period, it was the British
government—more particularly, the king—that was responsible for
oppressing the Americans. Having overthrown this alien rule, the
Americans had to reconstitute their government and seek to protect
themselves from oppression in the future. But this meant protecting one
part of the people against another. Although the Americans may not
have recognized it at the time, this gave a very different color to the
notion of popular sovereignty, since it placed unspecified limits on the
sovereign that were to be the occasion of continual and bitter dispute
in the future. If the concept of popular sovereignty is contested within
a single political tradition, it is to be expected that it will be even more
susceptible to different interpretations across political cultures.

Like popular sovereignty, the word "democracy" is the subject of
widespread disagreement, particularly where the vastly different political traditions of the Allies were concerned. In the Potsdam Proclamation, the Allies stated, "The Japanese government shall remove all
obstacles to the revival and strengthening of democratic tendencies
among the Japanese people." But the Americans alone occupied Japan,
so it was largely an American conception of "democracy" and "people"
that was built into the new Japanese Constitution. Nonetheless, because they retained the Emperor, the democratic government that the
Americans conceived bears considerable resemblance to the British system, where the monarch is ceremonial head of state. This caused no
problems for the Americans, who were used to thinking of Great Britain as a democracy. Their main concern, as we have seen, was to make
sure that the Emperor had a purely symbolic role, like that of the British
monarch, and wielded no political power. Since the Japanese people
elected the Diet, the Americans never thought to ask how the idea of
a ceremonial head of state fit with the notion of popular sovereignty.

For the Japanese, however, it was not so simple. The new Constitution placed the Emperor within a radically different form of government, forcing the Japanese to think about the Emperor in new and very different ways.

The Japanese had to make a similar adjustment in thinking about the relationship of the people to the Emperor, but they had to do it in a far shorter time than the American colonists, and within an intellectual framework foreign to their own tradition, not of their own choosing. It is not surprising that they ran into problems.

The most formidable was the change from a legendary, divine Emperor to one who is the creation of the Japanese people. Article 1 of the new Constitution reads:

> The Emperor is the symbol of the State and the unity of the
> People, and this position is founded on the will of the People
> in whom sovereignty resides.

The language of this article appears to blend two different political traditions. On the one hand, the Emperor is the symbol of both the government and the people. As we have seen, this idea has deep roots in Japan's historical experience. On the other hand, the article says that the Emperor's position is founded on the will of the people, as if the people in some sense deliberately chose to have a hereditary emperor.[25] This was consistent with the American fiction that the Constitution was the expression of "the will" of the Japanese people. And in fact, the article *did*, in one sense, reflect the will of the people, since most Japanese wanted to retain the imperial institution, and continue to revere their Emperor. Such an explanation, however, is hardly consistent with the American notion of popular sovereignty, since the Japanese did not elect their Emperor, could not remove him from office, and were never asked whether they wanted to retain the imperial institution. This was probably of little concern to the Americans, who only wanted an Emperor with no political power, whose only role was to be symbolic head of the state and nation. By changing the form of the Constitution, they thought they were changing the substance of the

25. In Article II of the MacArthur Constitution, the Americans stated, "Succession to the Imperial Throne shall be dynastic and in accordance with such Imperial House Law as the Diet may enact." The word "dynastic" was translated as *seshū*, meaning "hereditary," in its initial translation by the Ministry of Foreign Affairs, and was never questioned (Miyazawa and Satō 1954, appendix, p. 5). The present Constitution thus states, "The Imperial Throne is hereditary and succession is in accordance with the Imperial House Law passed by the Diet" (my translation). It is not clear if the Americans simply meant that the successive emperors are to come from the present Imperial family, or that the throne should be hereditary as well.

imperial institution. But, as we have seen, the prewar Emperor had very little power to begin with, so the new Constitution brought little substantive change.

The Japanese, on the other hand, worried about the form of the Constitution, for although the Emperor's *power* remained substantially the same, his symbolic position seemed to be considerably weakened. It had, in fact, been diluted by the separation of religion and state, as we saw in the previous chapter. Thus it was especially important that it not be diluted further by making him the creature of popular will. Their concern emerges in the debates over the proper word for "people," and the discussion of the relationship of the Emperor to the people. Fortunately, the ambiguities inherent in trying to combine popular sovereignty with a hereditary monarchy gave the Japanese enough room to persuade themselves that the imperial institution had not changed significantly. Perhaps they were right.

### The Japanese Translation of "People"

The Meiji Constitution referred to the people as *shinmin*,[26] reflecting the imperial system created by the Meiji rulers. *Shinmin* is a Sino-Japanese expression consisting of *shin*, meaning "one who serves the ruler" and *min*, meaning "ordinary persons" or, simply, "people." It clearly implies a government both distinct from and superior to the people, a conception that obviously did not fit with the American notion of popular sovereignty. American-style democracy required the Japanese to abandon their historical tradition of oligarchic rule in the name of the Emperor. What did the Japanese think, and how did they deal with this?

At first they resisted. On December 22, 1945, at the fifth meeting of the Matsumoto committee, the members debated whether *shinmin* ought to be replaced by a different term, *kokumin*. *Koku* means "nation," so *kokumin* is a more neutral term than *shinmin*, meaning "people of the nation." As was mentioned earlier, the Matsumoto committee tried to retain as much of the spirit and substance of the Meiji Constitution as possible. Thus, greatly concerned about the potentially serious consequences of replacing the old word clearly implying imperial rule with a more neutral one, they decided to retain *shinmin* (Satō Tatsuo Kankei Bunsho 7). The first version, submitted to GHQ by the Japa-

---

26. According to the Hepburn system of romanization, n followed by *m*, *b* and *p* is spelled with m. Thus *shinmin* and *jinmin* should be spelled as *shimmin* and *jimmin*, respectively. In order to discuss the meanings of *shin* and *jin* apart from *min*, however, I have chosen to spell them with an *n* in both cases.

nese government on February 8, used that word (Shimizu 1962–63, 4:314).

Interestingly, when the Ministry of Foreign Affairs prepared its translation of the MacArthur draft, first shown to the cabinet members on February 25, it had translated the word "people" as *jinmin*, consisting of *jin* (person(s)/national) and *min* (people) (Miyazawa and Satō 1954). Looking at the two components, this expression appears to be a fairly neutral term. But in contemporary Japanese, it has the strong connotation of "people who have liberated themselves from oppressors." It appears frequently in socialist and Marxist literature, and is often used to refer to people in labor movements in the Western world.[27] Curiously enough, Japanese translators have long thought that the same term is also appropriate to refer to the American people.[28] But among the political parties and private individuals that prepared their own versions of the new Constitution in the winter of 1946, the only group that used *jinmin* was the Japanese Communist party. Even the Socialist party avoided it (Satō 1962–64, 2:736–860). Popular sentiment was clearly against the term *jinmin* with its Marxist connotations. Thus, when the Japanese government officials prepared their second version, based on the MacArthur Constitution, they rejected *jinmin* in favor of *kokumin*. On the one hand, the change from *shinmin* to *kokumin* enhanced the democratic nature of the Constitution, and indicated that the Japanese political system was breaking away from the old hierarchy of the Emperor and his subjects. But, on the other hand, as we will see, *kokumin* was a deliberate choice that made it possible for the government to insist that the Meiji political tradition was not totally dead, and helped elicit much-needed support for the new, democratic Constitution among the conservative members of the National Diet.[29]

GHQ did not complain about the Japanese choice of *kokumin*. How-

27. For instance, Great Britain's People's Charter of 1837 is translated as *Jinmin Kenshō*, and the "Front Populaire" of Europe of the 1930s, as well as more recent popular-front movements, is called *jinmin sensen*.

28. The standard Japanese translation of Abraham Lincoln's famous phrase, "government of the people, by the people, for the people," from the Gettysburg Address, is *jinmin-no, jinmin-ni yoru, jinmin-no tame-no seiji*. Likewise, Nishikawa Masami's translation of the American Constitution, included in Samuel E. Morison's history of America, uses *jinmin* throughout. See Morison, Samuel E., *Amerika-no Rekishi* (*The Oxford History of the American People*, 1965), translated and edited by Nishikawa Masami et al. 1971, 3:438–53).

29. Satō says, in one of his memoranda, "The difference between *jinmin* and *kokumin* is a matter of usage, and [we] cannot say decisively that the two are the same or different. [We] adopted *kokumin* because (1) we wanted to emphasize the sense of the people as members of the state, and (2) we thought that *jinmin* would convey a sense of the people in exclusion and opposition to the Emperor" (Satō Tatsuo Kankei Bunsho 84; my translation).

ever, Thomas Arthur Bisson, an advisor to the Government Section, says (1983) that the staff of the translation pool of the Government Section warned Whitney and Kades that the choice of the Japanese word for "the people" was important, and that *jinmin*, and not *kokumin*, was the appropriate translation. Whitney and Kades ignored their plea, and the Japanese succeeded in adopting *kokumin*.[30]

### The Emperor as a Kokumin

Once the Japanese government had decided on the more neutral term *kokumin* to replace *shinmin*, they had to face the most serious problem of all—how to define the relationship between the Emperor and the *kokumin*. The government could have adopted what to an American is an eminently sensible position: in his official role, the Emperor is separate from the people, but as an individual he is not. For example, the Queen of England is, in some sense, representative of the community as a whole, and as such it would be very odd to speak of her as just another citizen of Great Britain. Yet if one were to speak of the British people as opposed to the American people, it would be quite appropriate to think of her as one Briton among many. So the Queen is both one of the people and also apart from them; it all depends on the context. The Japanese, however, did not want to make such a clear distinction. In fact, their position that nothing fundamental had changed depended on *not* making this distinction.

From the end of May through the middle of June, the cabinet members conferred with Irie Toshio and Satō Tatsuo, of the Bureu of Legislation, to formulate the government's replies to potential questions from the floor. Now that sovereignty had formally been shifted from the Emperor to the people, was the Emperor completely excluded from exercising any sovereign powers, and if so, what would his role be in the new democratic era?

---

30. Bisson 1983, pp. 247–48. After Bisson's death, Mrs. Bisson gave the original Bisson manuscript in English, entitled "Reform Years in Japan 1945–47," to Professor Nakamura Masanori to translate and publish in Japan. It was subsequently published under the title *Nihon Senryō Kaisō-ki* (Recollections on the Occupation of Japan). I am grateful to Professor Shōichi Koseki for obtaining a portion of this manuscript from Professor Nakamura. Since I do not have access to the English version (which never was published), I have simply summarized the Japanese version of Bisson's discussion.

Kades told me that he accepted the Japanese choice of *kokumin* for three reasons. First, it was MacArthur's policy "that revision should take place in such a way that the Japanese could view the resulting document as a Japanese product." Second, Kades himself was "not worried about the translation of Article 1 so long as the Emperor had no power related to the government, as provided in Article 4." Finally, he believed that Article 96, requiring two-thirds majority of both houses elected by the people for constitutional amendment, guaranteed that sovereignty would reside in the people (Kades, pers. comm., September 20, 1988).

After a great deal of serious discussion, the government formulated its position as follows, according to Satō. First, they would admit *shuken zaimin*—that the new Constitution placed sovereignty in those people who were the members of the Japanese nation. But the Emperor was also a member of the nation, therefore, he was one of the *kokumin*. Consequently, they would suggest that in some sense the Emperor was still a part of the sovereign. They were able to make the second statement in part because of the ambiguity inherent in the expression *shuken zaimin*. *Shuken zaimin* consists of *shu-ken* (principal power/right), ordinarily translated as "sovereignty" or "sovereign power," and *zai-min* (reside in people). But *min* is rarely used as an isolated word in contemporary Japanese. It usually appears as part of such expressions as *kokumin*, *shin-min* or *jin-min*. Thus, *zaimin* is also ambiguous. The government decided to take advantage of this ambiguity to say that *shuken zaimin* meant that sovereignty resides in the people, not in opposition to, but including, the Emperor. But the Emperor was also "the center of adoration" (*akogare*), or center of spirituality of the Japanese people. As such, the Emperor *qua* Emperor did not have a political function (*seiji-teki hataraki*) in the new democratic era. The government could use this fact to explain why the Preamble said that sovereign power resides with "the people" and not "the Emperor and the people." Second, the national polity (*kokutai*) was formed by the people united with the Emperor as the center of adoration (*akogare*) of the Japanese people. Third, there was no change in the national polity, because the Japanese political system would continue to have the Emperor as the symbolic head of state and the parliamentary system as in the past. The Constitution did not replace the Emperor with a president, or create a president in addition to the Emperor. It would therefore be proper to simply proceed with a constitutional revision according to the procedure established in the Meiji Constitution (Satō Tatsuo Kankei Bunsho 85).[31]

By means of this subtle reasoning, the government was able to take a middle-of-the-road position. While admitting that sovereignty now lay in the will of the people, the Emperor was part of the *kokumin*, so he was already part of the sovereign. Moreover, although the Emperor was only the symbolic head of the nation, he was the center of adoration, the spiritual unity of the people. In effect, by adoring the Emperor, the people would, by their will, leave the Emperor as sovereign. Thus the government could argue that nothing had really changed. This was a good practical solution to the government's problem, since

---

31. Although I have cited only one note, Satō Tatsuo Kankei Bunsho contains a number of memoranda related to this issue in files numbered 77 through 102.

they could count on the people to continue to exalt the Emperor. As we will see below, one member of the National Diet realized that the practical realities could not entirely obscure the legal change, a change that could become significant should popular attitudes toward the Emperor change substantially. But for the moment, the government was fortunate that Emperor Hirohito was so highly esteemed by the Japanese people. Since his reputation remained untainted by the nation's defeat, his personal prestige contributed to maintaining both the imperial institution and the illusion of continuity with the Meiji Constitution.

Two additional factors are noteworthy. The first is the psychological and emotional aspect of this issue for all Japanese participants, and particularly the government officials involved. The Japanese do not distinguish nearly as clearly as Americans do between their public life, or work, and private life. For many Americans, a job is like a suit of clothes that they put on in the morning and take off again at night. Time after work belongs to them to use as they please. Many Japanese, on the other hand, are far more committed to their jobs, and devote a much greater proportion of their emotional and psychological energy to their company or workplace than do Americans.[32] To put it another way, much more of their personal identity derives from their work group and the larger organization of which it is a part. Since a person's home life can affect his job performance, the Japanese consider it appropriate for the company or work group to be concerned about workers' private lives, and the workers themselves often accept or welcome such intervention. The Japanese work group resembles the *ie*, or extended household. Often, the head of a work group is not only the formal leader, but also a father figure to the group, as in a family, or household.[33] The relationship between the head and the people who work for him often involves close psychological ties in addition to the institutional or organizational relationship. That is why a section manager of a corporation does not hesitate to act as a go-between in the marriage of a subordinate, or to offer advice on personal matters whenever he sees fit.[34] Moreover, the head of the group, understood as "the father of a

---

32. These comments apply primarily to men. For the most part, young women stay in the work force only until they get married, and if they return, it is as temporary or part time help. They lack the same devotion to the company that male workers may have.

33. See chapter 6 for a more extended discussion of this point.

34. Ronald Dore (1985, p. 206) provides impressive evidence that the Japanese prefer this type of work environment: "In the so-called national character survey conducted by a government research institute every five years, a national sample of respondents is asked 'which would you prefer, a boss who abides strictly by the work rules and never asks for more, but doesn't take any interest in you as a person, or a boss who shows his concern for you and your personal problems but sometimes demands more than he is entitled to?' Every five years since the survey was started

family" and "the head of the household," is treated with deference not only on the job, but outside the workplace as well.

These comments also apply to the Emperor.[35] Emperor Hirohito was considered to be the head of the Japanese nation as a family.[36] Some government officials, as well as Diet members, had served him during the prewar period with a great deal of dedication. They knew the Emperor, and looked up to him as the nation's father. Government officials also consulted with him and sought his approval and cooperation several times throughout the deliberations on the Constitution, especially since they were following the imperial mandate in undertaking the task of constitutional revision. I think it is fair to say that, as individuals, they could not bear suddenly to admit that sovereignty no longer resided in the Emperor, and that he was being stripped of all authority. It would have been the same as telling their father that he no longer had his special place of honor in the family. Yet they knew that MacArthur and his staff wanted an unambiguous statement of popular sovereignty. The Americans had little understanding of the traditional Japanese concept of the nation as a family with the Emperor as its father, but so long as popular sovereignty was built into the legal structure created by the Constitution, they did not particularly care how the Japanese viewed their Emperor. He had, after all, only a symbolic status, and the

---

in 1948, 85 per cent of the sample, at all ages, have chosen the more intense relationship" (survey quoted from C. Hayashi et al., *Daiyon Nihonjin no Kokumin-sei*. Tokyo, 1981).

35. Shils and Young (1953, pp. 77–78) say that the British royal family is the idealized family of millions of British families and the nation as a whole. "The monarchy is idealized not so much for the virtue of the individual sovereign as for the virtue which he expresses in his family life." Thus, for better or for worse, the private lives of the members of the British royal family receive a great deal of attention in the press. Their reputed love affairs, marriages and other personal matters are reported in the newspapers because they are expected to exemplify the moral values of British society, and their conduct is therefore of great importance to the people. As discussed in chapter 2, at the beginning of the Meiji era, when the new Japanese government was attempting to reestablish the imperial institution, Emperor Meiji as an individual contributed to its effort by "direct imperial campaign." But once their efforts were successful, and the Emperor had become an object of adoration and loyalty, the Emperor ceased to make personal appearances, and withdrew from public life. Since then, the Emperor has become important mainly in his role as the center of the Japanese people's spiritual unity. Although after World War II the Japanese saw more of Emperor Hirohito and his family than before the war, the Emperor continues to be important as the spiritual head of the country, and not as an individual. Thus, the Japanese are less concerned with the private lives of members of the imperial family, and the Emperor and his family escape the kind of publicity that the British Queen and the royal family experience.

36. During the prolonged final illness of Emperor Hirohito, much of the nation was in the somber mood appropriate to a family with a seriously ill father. Not only did streams of people go to the registers that the Imperial Palace set up in Tokyo and a few other cities to sign their names to wish for his recovery, but many organizations and businesses voluntarily cancelled or postponed festivals and celebrations of all types throughout the country. This had a devastating effect on some businesses such as catering, which specialize in providing services at these occasions.

Constitution gave him no formal powers. Japanese government officials recognized that they could not challenge the Americans on this point, so they took refuge in ambiguity, hoping to persuade the Diet members that although the formal position of the Emperor had changed on paper, nothing had changed in substance.

The psychological point is reinforced by a linguistic feature. In reading Satō's notes on the Japanese government's position on the role of the emperor, it is not always clear whether the government officials were referring to the Emperor as a public institution, or as a private individual. This ambiguity is partly due to the orthographic conventions of the Japanese language. Unlike English, the Japanese writing system has no way of readily distinguishing "the Emperor" from "an emperor." The Emperor is simply referred to as *tennō*, written in Chinese characters. Some of the government officials might have had difficulty in making the distinction in their own minds.

### The Debate at the National Diet

The debate at the 90th Imperial Diet amply indicates that many of the Diet members shared the sentiments of the government, and knew exactly what was going on. Everyone seems to have recognized that the government was defending a constitution imposed on it. Thus, even though they had to acknowledge the inevitable change in Japan's political system, they conducted extensive discussions in both houses. The debates gave Diet members a chance to express their personal views. Some comments were unabashed expressions of preference for the Meiji Constitution; others reflected perplexity at the notion of popular sovereignty, wondering how the Emperor could no longer be sovereign, yet still be part of the sovereign people. Finally, some members took the opportunity to point out difficulties and contradictions in the government's position, causing Kanamori considerable embarrassment. The sharpest questions came from constitutional scholars in the House of Peers, though some interpellators in the House of Representatives also gave him some trouble.

A good example of the latter is the comment of Hara Fujirō, a member of the Progressive party, and long-time member of the House of Representatives. On June 26, 1946, the second day of the plenary session, Hara asked:

> Mr. Kanamori, you said that sovereignty resides in the people of Japan, including the Emperor. We are very pleased with that answer. But it is not clear where in the draft it says that the Emperor is included in the people. . . . Looking at

the draft as a whole, everyone agrees that sovereignty resides in *min*. If we are to maintain the principle that *kokumin* includes the Emperor, then I'm afraid there will be inconsistencies in various parts of this draft. I would like to hear your opinion. (Shūgi-in 1946a, 6:80, cols. 4–5)

An American would have no trouble with a similar question about the president. Sometimes the president acts in his institutional role, and at others, such as when he votes, he is just an ordinary citizen. As we have seen, that distinction does not come so easily to the Japanese, particularly with the head of any organization. Moreover, the Constitution states that the Emperor is the symbol of the state, so he is not just a member of the Japanese nation. Kanamori probably understood the problem, but he did not address the difficulty, instead using the occasion to emphasize the unity of the Emperor and the people:

> As I mentioned earlier, the word "sovereignty" (*shuken*) is interpreted differently by different people. If we are to interpret sovereignty as the source at which the will of the state originates, then, the correct answer in Japan will no doubt be that that place is the entire Japanese people, including the Emperor. You asked where in the Constitution such a statement is made. That is not explicitly stated in this Constitution. The reason is that Japan is a nation of *kummin ichinyo* (oneness of the ruler and the people; my translation). This nation is bound together through the spiritual ties of the people with the Emperor that are rooted in the depth of their hearts. There is no need to explain that that is the foundation of the existence of our nation (ibid., 82, cols. 1–2).

Two days later, Nosaka Sanzō, a leading member of the Communist party, took the floor, and expressed a very un-Japanese minority opinion about the Emperor. He pointed out the difficulties in the language of the Constitution and its interpretation by the government, and tried to get Kanamori to admit that sovereignty was really in the hands of the people under the new Constitution:

> Next, about the issue of sovereignty, which has been discussed repeatedly. If it is the case that the Emperor is a *kokumin*, how does it relate to Article 13 (current 14) which says, "All of the people are equal under the law, and there will be no discrimination in political, economic or social relations because of race, creed, sex, social status or family origin?" If [the Emperor] is a *kokumin*, he will be equal with

everyone else, and he will not be privileged in any way.
However, in the beginning of the Constitution, he is clearly
distinguished. I would like to hear how you would explain
this. If the Emperor is a *kokumin*, he has to have the right to
vote, and he can be elected [to a public office]. If the people
want him to be the head of state, why would we not elect
him? In the answers of the government representatives, it
has been said that the position of the Emperor is rooted in
the feelings (*kanjō*) of the people. Where in the world is
there a monarchy that is based on the feelings of the people?
That is a fiction. That can be regarded as a new mythical
theory, a new theory of divine right. Today, there is no
one who believes in the old theory of divine right, but
here we see a different version of it about to be born. I think
that is very dangerous. . . . The feelings of people change
rapidly. . . .

After some disruptions from the floor, he continued,

We want the government to state unambiguously, without
hocus-pocus, what its position is, whether sovereignty is in
the hands of the people or the Emperor. We can't understand
why you make this issue so vague. (Shūgi-in 1946a, 8:121,
col. 5–122, col. 2)

When Nosaka finally ended his barrage of questions and condemna-
tions, which was interrupted several times by other members, Kanamori
tried his best to defend the fiction that Nosaka was attacking:

Regarding the issue of sovereignty, . . . you asked why we
would not establish a system whereby we would elect the
Emperor, since he is one of the *kokumin* who are all equal,
and therefore he should be granted the right to vote and be
elected [to public offices]. As I said earlier, the Emperor is
the symbol of the state, and as such, he is in a position of
complete neutrality. Therefore, there is no need to give him
the right to vote and be elected [to public offices] . . . . As
for the feelings of the people being the basis of the imperial
institution . . . , I never said feelings (*kanjō*). I have said the
people's *kokoro* "heart," but, at any rate, how can you conceive of the unity of the people, or the foundation of a nation without the hearts of the people? (ibid., 125, cols.
2–3).

During the subsequent debate in the special committee of the House
of Representatives, the members repeatedly brought up the issue of sovereignty in connection with the meaning of *kokumin*. Some arguments

were well articulated and to the point, while others were rambling and unclear. One example of a specific and pointed question was raised on July 3, by Hozumi Shichirō of the Progressive party. He first called Kanamori's attention to the use of *kokumin* in the following four instances (my translations).

> We, the Japanese people, . . . do proclaim that will of the *kokumin* is supreme. . . . (Preamble)

> Government is sacred trust of the people, the authority for which is derived from the *kokumin*. . . . (Preamble)

> ARTICLE 1. The Emperor is the symbol of the State and the unity of the *kokumin*, and this position is founded on the supreme will of the *kokumin*.

> ARTICLE 92 (second clause of current Article 96). The Emperor will immediately promulgate amendments so ratified in the name of the *kokumin*, as an integral part of this Constitution.

Hozumi then pointed out the difficulty in imposing a uniform interpretation that the Emperor was a *kokumin*:

> As for the first two instances in the Preamble, if you have drafted this document so that everyone would understand it easily, then, in the ordinary people's common sense use of the word, *kokumin* would mean "subjects" in the traditional sense. But if you have used it in the way you just stated, putting aside the problem of terminology, I can understand what you mean. But . . . it will be extremely difficult to interpret *kokumin* in Articles 1 and 92 as including the Emperor. Since "the Emperor" and "the *kokumin*" are both in the same clause, if that is the case, do you mean to say that the Emperor's position is founded on his own will too? I would like to ask you once again. Do you mean to say that the Emperor's position is not founded on the will of the people, excluding the Emperor, but is founded on the will of the people, including that of the Emperor? Is the Emperor included in the *kokumin* in whose name he is to promulgate amendments? These are the instances where the Japanese people will have grave doubts [about your interpretation]. The instances of *kokumin* in the Preamble do not appear along with [the word] "Emperor," so it might be possible to explain it in a way that will convince people. But in ordinary Japanese usage, it will be hard to accept [the explanation] that the *kokumin* in Articles 1 and 92 include the Emperor. What do you think? (Shūgi-in 1946b, 4:45, cols. 3–4)

Kanamori ignored Hozumi's specific arguments, insisting that the word
*kokumin* included the Emperor, and that he was fundamentally opposed
to an ideology separating the Emperor from the people (ibid., col. 4).

On July 8, Mori Mikiji, of the Socialist party, having repeatedly
asked Kanamori to clarify the idea that sovereignty resided in the
people, finally, pointedly said to him that the Constitution should unambiguously state that sovereignty resides in the people, including the
Emperor, if that was what the government meant:

> Article 1 says "The Emperor is the symbol of the State and
> the unity of the People, and this position is founded on the
> supreme will of the People." I do not want to repeat the same
> question over and over again, but how about stating clearly
> that sovereignty resides in all of the people, including the
> Emperor? This Constitution is a document that we will read
> by morning and by night as the great holy book (*dai-kyōten*)
> of the people. I believe that the way to make this document
> survive for the next one hundred years is by avoiding confu-
> sion and making it easy for people to understand. For that
> reason, it will be very good if you clearly state in Article 1
> that sovereignty in the Japanese state resides in all *kokumin*
> including the Emperor. Then the people will understand the
> locus of sovereignty in this Constitution very clearly. I would
> like to request Mr. Kanamori's response. (Shūgi-in 1946b,
> 8:126, col. 1)

Kanamori replied by defending the ambiguity of the document, stating
that it was only a temporary confusion:

> As you point out, *kokumin* in Article 1 is ambiguous. In this
> period of changing thought, it poses the problem, which re-
> quires careful explanation, as to whether or not the Emperor
> is included. However, if we think about it carefully, this is
> an issue that the Japanese should have understood com-
> pletely in the past, but did not because they gave in to the
> drift of the time. I believe that future generations of the Japa-
> nese people will interpret the meaning of this word correctly.
> In this transitional period, there may be usages that are con-
> fusing to people, but since this Constitution is for the future
> generations to understand well and obey, it is better not to
> leave the remnants of this transitional period. . . . It is bet-
> ter to eliminate the idea that the Emperor and the people
> must be represented by two different words, and foster the
> feeling among people that when we use the term *kokumin* it
> always includes the Emperor—we are a nation of *kummin
> ichinyo* (unity of the Emperor and the people). We felt that

it was not appropriate to leave the remnants of the transi-
tional period in the language of the Articles (ibid., cols.
1–2).

Thus, while saying that the traditional interpretation of the term
kokumin included the Emperor, Kanamori insisted that there was no
need to make it explicit.

The debate over sovereignty continued at the House of Peers from
late August to the beginning of September. The character of this debate, however, was much different from that in the House of Representatives. Some Peers stated emphatically that there was no need for a
fundamental change in Japan's political system. Yet, they realized that
they could not prevent the new Constitution from bringing about such
a change, and were well aware of the government's serious dilemma.
Thus, they simply pointed out that the change was unavoidable, and
that it was futile for the government to insist both that the Emperor
was a kokumin and that the national polity would not change. On the
first day of the plenary session, Sawada Ushimaro declared that there
was no need for a new constitution. He began by saying,

> The constitutional revision is the most serious task since
> the beginning of the House of Peers, and I think it will
> most likely be its most serious final task. (Kizoku-in 1946a,
> 23:233, col. 3)

He went on to reprimand the government for suddenly discarding the
Meiji Constitution, and for presenting a drastically different, hastily
prepared constitution to the people. The problem, in his view, was not
with the old Constitution; it was rather a failure to criticize and restrain
the military:

> The Japanese people have honored the present Constitution
> until today. I think it is such fickleness for the Japanese to
> suddenly turn around and say that the present Constitution
> is very bad, and because of this Constitution Japan has been
> destroyed. I think one of the biggest faults of the Japanese is
> our tendency to follow blindly without much thought as if
> we are hanging lanterns at the eaves of our houses. . . .

> It goes without saying that a monarch reigns in a monarchy.
> Who else would it be? That's taken for granted. But in prac-
> tice, the prerogative of supreme command (tōsui-ken) has
> often been regarded as inviolable. For too long, we have held
> a broad view that criticizing the actions of the general staff
> office and the military headquarters was the same as infring-
> ing on the prerogative of supreme command. That was the
> cause of the misfortune. . . .

As I said earlier, in other countries one might see the phe-
nomenon of a missing pivot of unity, which is said to be the
weakness of the idea of separation of the three powers. But,
in Japan, in Article 4 of the present Constitution, the Emperor holds sovereign power. In other words, the Emperor is
the pivot of the three separate branches of the government.
I think the present Constitution is an excellent and ideal
constitution. If it had not been for defeat and the people's
miserable condition, how many Japanese out of a hundred
would have said that this Constitution was inappropriate and
therefore had to be immediately discarded? I am confident
that most of them would have said that it was excellent and
should be honored for several hundred years to come (ibid.,
234, cols. 2–4).

Kanamori and the government, of course, were more than sympa-
thetic with the sentiments Sawada expressed, and probably hoped that
the other Peers would restrict their remarks to similar sorts of comments. Some of the Peers, particularly the constitutional scholars, however, used the occasion to torment Kanamori by trying to force him to
admit the logical consequences of popular sovereignty. They pointed
out that the government's reliance on ambiguity could cause problems
in the future. Miyazawa Toshiyoshi, who spoke after Sawada, said that
he believed Japan accepted the ideology of popular sovereignty when it
accepted the Potsdam Proclamation, so that the assertion of popular
sovereignty in the constitutional revision was the inevitable consequence. He also pointed out the difference between the Emperor as a
public person and private individual, precisely the distinction the government hoped to avoid. He said,

As Minister Kanamori just said, the government has maintained that sovereignty resides in the *kokumin*, and the Emperor is included in the *kokumin*. But what is the meaning
of and the basis for the explanation that the Emperor is
included in the *kokumin* when the Emperor's position is
founded on the will of the people in whom sovereign power
resides? It goes without saying that the one who is in the
position of Emperor is, as an individual, a member of the
Japanese race (*minzoku*). Therefore, he is Japanese (*Nihonjin*), and he is included among the Japanese people (*Nihon
kokumin*). There is no need to make that point. The issue is
the Emperor within the constitutional system. The Emperor,
as an institution, clearly is founded on the will of all of the
people. [The notion] that the people have sovereignty is different from [the notion] that the state has sovereignty. It

means that, within the state, it is neither the king nor the
aristocracy that holds sovereignty. I understand very well
that you cannot bear the thought of declaring that we now
have simple popular sovereignty. Nonetheless, for you to
claim that the Emperor is included in the kokumin after you
have accepted popular sovereignty obscures the fundamental
principle that the position of Emperor is founded on the will
of the people. Moreover, it will also unnecessarily invite the
misunderstanding that the government is proclaiming popular sovereignty outwardly, but is covertly trying to reinstitute
the age-old imperial institution. I think it will incur ground-
less suspicion. I feel that your explanation is, theoretically
and practically, not appropriate (ibid., 242, cols. 2–3).

Thus, Miyazawa cautioned the government that its ambiguous position
on the Emperor would raise the possibility of future misuse or misunderstanding. But his logical resolution of the problem was precisely
what the government could not accept. Kanamori clearly did not appreciate Miyazawa's argument, and he did his best to be ambiguous and
noncommittal:

You believe that the explanation that the Emperor is included in the people who are sovereign is theoretically and
practically inappropriate, and you asked what I thought. I
unfortunately could not understand the intent of your question very well. Perhaps our explanation that the Emperor is
included in the kokumin was not adequate, and has caused
some misunderstanding. If we think about the Emperor in
his public role, he is certainly not included in the kokumin.
But the Emperor has a public position, and at the same time,
he has a private position. Now, the individuals who compose
the Japanese state are the Japanese people (Nihon kokumin)
. . . whether or not kokumin is the appropriate word, broadly
interpreted, we cannot say that [he] is not a constituent
member of the Japanese state. We cannot say that this [per-
son] is not a member of the kokumin in whom the nation's
sovereignty resides (ibid., 244, cols. 1–2)

Two days later, Asai Kiyoshi pointed out the problem in the government's position from another angle:

The third question that I would like to raise is the issue of
sovereignty. According to the history of theories of sovereignty, shuken zai-kun (sovereignty resides in the ruler)
means that sovereignty is not in the people, and shuken zai-
min (sovereignty resides in the people) means that it does
not reside in the ruler. To say that shuken zai-min includes

the ruler is just as contradictory as saying that *shuken zai-kun* includes the people. Such a claim cannot be universally acceptable as either a theory of *shuken zai-kun* or *shuken zai-min*. It rejects both of these two theories. . . .

Now, to examine the government's position through the record of the hearings at the special committee of the House of Representatives, the government is using the term *kokumin* in a completely different way from the way it is ordinarily used in theories of popular sovereignty, that is, "sovereignty resides in the people." In response to Representative Takahashi's interpellation on July 2, you stated as follows: "While we were preparing this draft constitution, we looked for a word which covers all of the Japanese people. Unfortunately, we could not find a term which refers to the people including the Emperor among past usages. So we chose *kokumin*." In other words, the government chose *kokumin* to refer to all the people who compose the nation and not the people in relation to the ruler. [It] was not an ordinary popular-rights theory. This is quite obvious when we think about Minister Kanamori's response to Representative Yoshida's interpellation at the same meeting. You said that you thought *shuken zai-min* should be explained as referring to both the Emperor and the people. The idea that *shuken zai-min* includes the Emperor and *shuken zai-kun* includes the people, in fact, denies both *shuken zai-kun* and *shuken zai-min*. In other words, the government's claim that sovereignty resides in the *kokumin* is merely following the current fad of *shuken zai-min*. I think it does not imply that [the government] has adopted the theory of popular sovereignty derived from Western democracy, but rather, this is nothing more than a reiteration of the idea of the nation as a corporate body, using a different language. So, when Representative Takahashi asked if it is correct to understand that sovereignty resides in the state (*shuken zai-koku*) at the July 2 meeting of the House of Representatives, Minister Kanamori, you accepted that. When Mr. Takahashi asked you again if he was correct in understanding that sovereignty is held by the state, you reassured him that that was correct. If that is the case, that is a legitimate position, so, why don't you say so clearly? If you think sovereignty resides in the *kokumin*, you should clearly call it *shuken zai-min* and avoid expressions that would secretly nullify it. To say that the ruler is included in *shuken zai-min* would not be universally accepted as a theory of popular sovereignty. If you say that this is a uniquely Japanese theory of sovereignty, I must point out how the idea that our nation is different has misled our nation. (Kizoku-in 1946a, 25:282, cols. 3–5)

To this Kanamori responded,

> It goes without saying that the Emperor that I spoke of at the House of Representatives, who is included in the *kokumin*, is a living person, an individual. That's what I meant, and I thought everyone understood. . . . From the point of view of the Emperor in a public role, he has special functions. But I think that that is not where general sovereignty (*ippan shuken*) resides, just as we cannot say that sovereignty resides in the Prime Minister or the members of the National Diet. We would like you to understand that we think that sovereignty of the state resides in all of the people who compose the nation. . . . To say that the state has sovereignty is not what we are looking for. What we are seeking is the locus of the will of the nation—going further back into the origin of the deep spiritual locus where the motivating forces for the nation's activities comes from (ibid., 286, cols. 2–4).

In this vague response, it appears that Kanamori was trying to assure the Diet members that the spiritual locus of the nation was in the Emperor and the people, and that the fundamental nature of the national polity had not changed.

Finally, Nambara Shigeru, President of Tokyo Imperial University, asked whether the government was prepared to stand by its present interpretation in the future:

> It is useless for us to argue about Japan's sovereignty or national polity any further. Forgive me for saying so, but looking at the process of debate at the House of Representatives and the House of Peers, the core of the problem is quite clear. . . .
>
> The most important issue is that the Emperor is included in the *kokumin*, be it *kokumin shuken* or *shuken zai-kokumin*. Therefore, the fundamental character of Japan, or the national polity in one sense, has not changed. We have repeatedly heard this as Minister Kanamori's explanation, but we understand it as the opinion of the entire government. The problem that I would like to address is the opinion of the government and that of the National Diet which gives its consent. When the new Constitution is publicized inside and outside the nation, how much support will the [government's] interpretation obtain, and how should the government respond? The Meiji Constitution has Marquis Itō's constitutional commentaries. Even if the government pre-

pared similar commentaries, how much authority will it
have? In the new age of freedom of speech and academic
studies, even if the government says that the national polity
and sovereignty should be interpreted thus and so, and tries
to promote [this interpretation], there is no guarantee that it
will be accepted. The truth will gain the final victory. I will
speak as a member of the academic community. Educated
people will not accept your interpretation that, unlike [the
idea of] popular sovereignty universally accepted in the world,
the Japanese idea of sovereignty has not changed, and that
it resides in the people including the Emperor. . . .

What will happen when the truth is finally spread, and an
interpretation much different from that of the present government wins? How will the government deal with it? . . .
Unlike the past, one cannot restrict speech. One will not be
able to place constraints on constitutional theories. What
will the government do? I think this is a serious issue. It's
one thing to tell the people that national polity and sovereignty have now been changed, and instruct them to brace
themselves for the consequences. You must have some coun-
termeasures in mind to say that things have not changed in
the face of such fundamental revisions. I'd like to have Minister Kanamori respond. (Kizoku-in 1946a, 24:259, cols.
1–4)

Kanamori simply said that he too believed that the final victor would
be the truth, and he did not intend to oppose it (ibid., col. 5).

To summarize, the Americans, strongly interested in establishing
their own version of popular sovereignty, but also acknowledging the
need to retain the Emperor, expressed two ideas in the Constitution
that the Japanese could not easily reconcile—that the Emperor was the
symbol of the state and the unity of the people, but that his position
derived from the sovereign will of the people. From a practical point of
view, the Japanese Emperor had not been sovereign in a political sense
for centuries, since ultimate power lay in the hands of whatever group
controlled the government. But from a formal point of view, the Emperor had always been sovereign. The MacArthur Constitution threatened this formal aspect of sovereignty, since it suggested the theoretical
possibility that the people could displace the Emperor. The Japanese
government officials, together with most Japanese, did not want such a
drastic change in the formal nature of their political system. They re-
vered the Emperor, and regarded him as the head of the nation, as a
family. Moreover, the leading party and the government found itself in

the awkward position of having said publicly that sovereignty resided in the Emperor, and then, two months later, presenting the nation a democratic constitution founded on the American idea of popular sovereignty. To rescue itself from this dilemma, the government formulated the argument that in the new Constitution, sovereignty resided in the will of the Japanese people (*kokumin*), including the Emperor. But the Emperor was also the center of adoration, or spiritual unity, of the Japanese people, and as such did not have a political function in the democratic era. Thus he could still retain some vestige of sovereignty without threatening the operation of popular sovereignty. The members of the National Diet were gravely concerned about the role of the Emperor in the new Constitution, for, despite their ostensible enthusiasm for democracy, many of them were conservative and did not want fundamental change. So all through the hot summer of 1946, Diet members repeatedly asked Kanamori, the government spokesman, the meaning of "popular sovereignty" and its relation to the word *kokumin*. The government steadfastly tried to preserve as much of the imperial institution as possible, taking refuge in the ambiguity of the Emperor's role as a member of the *kokumin*.

## Popular Sovereignty

ARTICLE 1. The Emperor is the symbol of the State and the unity of the People, and this position is founded on the People in whom sovereignty resides.

### The Negotiations Between the Americans and the Japanese

The United States has had some form of popular sovereignty from the beginning of its history. Nonetheless, in the minds of the Founding Fathers, "the people" did not even include all white men, let alone women, native Americans, or black slaves. Moreover, the meaning of "popular sovereignty" is hardly transparent. As Daniel T. Rodgers has shown, Americans have consistently disagreed about the role of the people in political life. For the most part, though, they believed that the people should excercise their power indirectly through their representatives (Rodgers 1987, pp. 80–111).

The Americans in 1946 were determined to establish popular sovereignty in Japan. Apart from creating a representative form of government, however, they did not pay much attention to the proper role of the people under the Constitution. Perhaps this is why they did not pay much attention to the Japanese interpretation of the Japanese word meaning "the people." But they were determined to strip the Emperor

chief, Courtney Whitney, cautioning him about the significance of the difference in the English and Japanese texts. It read, in part,

> 2. The repeated interpellations in the Diet and wide dis-
> cussions in the press as to the source and distribution of the
> sovereign powers under the new Constitution are indications
> that the Japanese text is unclear on this point and differs,
> therefore, from the official English version. Article 1 clearly
> states in English that the Emperor derives "his position from
> the sovereign will of the people." The Japanese version has
> changed the word "sovereign" to "supreme," using for the
> expression as a whole characters which convey no concep-
> tion of sovereignty in the juristic sense of the word. In the
> Preamble where the English version states "do proclaim the
> sovereignty of the people's will" again the word "supremacy"
> has been substituted for sovereignty. *Thus sovereignty is not
> located in the people as the basis of the state or nation, but has
> been shifted to the nation comprising the people, the Emperor and
> the government* [emphasis added].
> 3. This shift paves the way for the distribution of the ex-
> ercise of the powers of sovereignty among four, instead of
> three, organs of government. These organs are the Emperor,
> the Cabinet, the Diet and the Judiciary. . . .
> 4. This distribution of sovereign powers among these three
> organs should have been complete, and is so in the English
> version. The Chapter on the Emperor nowhere states or im-
> plies that he should possess or exercise a part of the sovereign
> power; on the contrary, he is to exist as the symbol of the
> state and exercise only ceremonial functions.[39]

Peake and the two advisors rightly cautioned Whitney about the Japanese choice of word *shikō* to stand for "sovereign," but they incorrectly
concluded that this implied that in the Japanese text sovereignty resided in the people, the Emperor, and the government. They appear to
have ignored the extensive discussions of whether the Emperor was a
*kokumin*, and mentioned nothing about the meaning of that word, even
though the Japanese were grappling with the same issue in their debates
on the proper interpretation of *kokumin*.

Whitney sent a copy of the memorandum to MacArthur on July 17,
along with a memorandum of his own, in which he expressed the need

---

39. For the complete text of this memorandum see GHQ/SCAP Records (RG 331), Microfiche sheet no. GS (B) 642, National Diet Library, Modern Political History Materials Room.
It is also in the National Archives of the United States, Box no. 2088, Folder title/number: Publicity (6).

to scrutinize the Japanese translation of English words and phrases, though he also stated that he considered the Japanese to be acting in good faith. Whitney's memorandum is worth quoting at length.

1. In view of repeated statement by Minister of State Kanamori in replying to interpellations on the proposed new Constitution for Japan by members of the Diet to the effect that the new Constitution will mean no change in the "national polity" (kokutai) of Japan, and the discrepancies between the Japanese and English versions of the Constitution in certain key words (for example, the use of the Japanese word for "supreme" instead of "sovereign" in speaking of the people's sovereignty), I am encouraging the closest scrutiny by members of the Government Section staff of the Constitution in the Japanese text and the commentaries explaining it in the Diet. I have decided to treat these matters as technical discrepancies resulting from the best of faith on the part of the Japanese which can be ironed out on a technical working level.

2. I fully realize your desire to refrain from any open interference in matters relating to the Constitution and your view that much weasel-worded explanation is offered to persuade the two-thirds majority required by the Government for its adoption and I have passed these views on to the members of my staff. It is my firm conviction, however, that we cannot fail to maintain the closest surveillance of the Government's draft in order to detect subtle changes which fundamentally alter the connotation and meaning of the words in the English translation and which can in all probability be corrected on an informal technical level of discussion.

3. In view of the possibility that the hand of Matsumoto is still contriving to shape the Constitution to his views, I believe it desirable to call these matters to your attention. Kanamori's explanations are consistent with Matsumoto's views as explained in written memoranda submitted to this Section when the Matsumoto draft was presented to you by Yoshida and which was wholly unacceptable to you. Kanamori's statement that the new Constitution means no change in "national polity" is laying the foundation for the undermining of the democratic spirit of the new Constitution and is paving the way for the return to the old system of authoritarian government. The term was usually surrounded with an aura of mysticism but in reality "national polity" summarizes briefly and completely the chauvinistic and militaristic political philosophy of the old regime in Japan. It is generally

understood to mean a state centering around the Emperor; a people obedient to and subservient to the authority of the executive agencies charged by the Emperor with the responsibility of governing the country; the "uniqueness" and, therefore, superiority of the Japanese as a race because they are the only ones to possess this "national polity"; the negation of the principles of domestic democracy and international cooperation toward which the Japanese are supposed to be striving.[40]

Thus, the American participants were highly suspicious that Japanese government officials were trying to retain as much of their existing political system as possible. Of course, the Japanese were attempting to do just that.

On July 16, Kanamori submitted six principles to GHQ, explicating in English the Japanese government's position on sovereignty:

1. Under the new constitution Japan's basic government structure with the Emperor as the center is radically modified. There are those who think that the basic government with the Emperor as the center constitutes Japan's national character. But that, I believe, is the form of government, and not the character of nationhood.

2. Under the present constitution the will of the people is concretely expressed through the Emperor. But that is not the case with the new constitution, according to which the people's will finds concrete expression largely through the Diet.

3. Under the new constitution the Emperor remains simply as a symbol. By saying that the Emperor is the symbol of the state and of national unity, it is meant essentially that in the person of the Emperor we may see the picture of Japan. It does not mean that he personifies the will of the state or of the people.

4. Under the present constitution the Emperor has the power to do practically everything. The new constitution clearly specifies his functions, beyond which he is not empowered to do anything. (It is absolutely impossible to extend or increase his functions by legislation.)

5. It has been generally considered that the position of the

---

40. Memorandum from the Government Section, dated July 17, 1946. National Diet Library, Modern Political History Materials Room, GHQ/SCAP Records (RG 331), Microfiche sheet no. GS (B) 642. Also in the National Archives of the United States no. 2088, Folder title/number: Publicity (6).

Emperor under the present constitution is based upon the will of the Emperor, or the hereditary will of the Imperial family. Under the new constitution the Emperor's position is derived solely from the will of the people.

6. *But in the moral and spiritual sphere, apart from the question of government structure, the Emperor remains throughout both before and after the constitutional reform the center of the nation's devotion. The statement that Japan's national character does not change has reference to this point.* (Satō Tatsuo Kankei Bunsho 183; emphasis added)

The Japanese thus refused to yield to the Americans.

But the Americans did not back down. When Kades met with Kanamori on July 23, he told Kanamori that the members of the Far Eastern Commission, and the American public, were extremely sensitive about this issue. If the Japanese government insisted on using *shikō*, MacArthur, who had earlier announced that "sovereignty is squarely in the hands of the people," would be regarded as either having misrepresented the Japanese Constitution to the world, or being stupid enough not to have recognized the discrepancy between the English and Japanese expressions. The world might even say that the Japanese government double-crossed them. Kanamori asked Kades what he would suggest. Kades replied that if changing the expression in the Preamble would make Kanamori's position too awkward, he would not insist, but the idea of popular sovereignty (*shuken zaimin*) had to be stated clearly at some point. He specifically suggested that the final portion of Article 1 be expanded to include the phrase "with whom sovereignty rests."[41] Kanamori replied that such a change would be difficult. Kades then suggested another possibility, adding the same language to the end of the phrase, "the authority for which is derived from the people," in the middle of the Preamble. Kanamori was apparently getting exasperated, as he protested that there was no reason for him to be accused of "double-crossing" the Americans. Kades asked Kanamori not to misunderstand him, and said that GHQ was trying to avoid the danger that those Allies antagonistic to Japan would reach such an interpretation (Satō Tatsuo Kankei Bunsho 184). In subsequent meetings on the 26th and 29th, Kades continued to press the Japanese officials to state clearly that sovereignty resided in the people. He said that he "was simply a mouthpiece for the Allies" (ibid., 185).

---

41. Kades's suggestions is somewhat ambiguous, but it appears that Article 1 would then read "The Emperor is the symbol of the State and the unity of the people, and this position is founded on the supreme (*shikō*) will of the people with whom sovereignty rests" (my translation).

### The Japanese Adoption of Kokumin-no Shuken

The Japanese finally discarded the word *shikō* and adopted *shuken* at the subcommittee meetings of the House of Representatives. Thus, the original Japanese version of Article 1 that read,

> The Emperor is the symbol of the State and the unity of the People, and this position is founded on *the supreme will of the People*

was changed to,

> The Emperor is the Symbol of the State and the unity of the People, and this position is founded on the will of the People, *in whom sovereignty resides.*[42] (My translations)

Likewise, the phrase in the Preamble that read,

> We, the Japanese people, . . . do proclaim that *the will of the people is supreme* . . .

was rewritten as,

> We, the Japanese people, . . . do proclaim that *sovereignty resides in the people. . . .*[43] (My translations)

Interestingly, however, by using the inherent ambiguity in a related Sino-Japanese expression *shuken zai-min* (sovereignty resides in the people), the committee members reaffirmed that they were not giving up the idea that sovereignty resides in all of the people, including the Emperor.

The discussions among the subcommittee members that took place between July 25 and August 2, when the changes were finally made, provide an interesting and valuable illustration of the Japanese mode of slowly building a consensus among participants with no overt confrontation or discussion of the various positions. Much of the work was obviously done behind the scenes.

On July 25, 1946, at the first meeting of the subcommittee, immediately after it began a substantive discussion, Etō Natsuo, a member of the Liberal party, took the floor to explain the revisions proposed by his party, and requested that the expression *kokumin-no sōi-ga shikō-na*

---

42. The final clause of *Tennō-wa, Nihonkoku-no shōchō-de ari Nihon kokumin tōgō-no shōchō-de atte, kono chii-wa, Nihon kokumin-no shikō-no sōi-ni motozuku*, was changed to *kono chii-wa, shuken-no son-suru Nihon kokumin-no sōi-ni motozuku* (Shimizu 1962–63, 4:456).

43. *Nihon kokumin-wa, . . . koko-ni kokumin-no sōi-ga shikō-na mono-de aru koto-o sengen-shi* was changed to *Nihon kokumin-wa, . . . shuken-ga kokumin-ni son-suru koto-o sengen-shi* (ibid.).

*mono-de aru* (the will of the people is supreme) be changed to *shuken-ga kokumin-ni son-suru* (sovereignty resides in the people). He said,

> There are several omissions and revisions in the Premable. Please correct the following in the Preamble. Please change *kokumin-no sōi-ga shikō-na mono-de aru-koto-o sengen shi* (proclaim that the will of the people is supreme), to *shuken-ga kokumin-ni son-suru koto-o sengen shi* (proclaim that sovereignty resides in the people). (Mori 1983, p. 6)

Immediately after Etō, Kita Reikichi of the same party said that he wanted to explain the revisions on the Preamble that both the Liberal and Progressive parties had agreed upon, and went on to discuss various other issues. In the middle of his lengthy statement, in which he compared various phrases in English and Japanese, he made the following comment on the translation of "sovereignty," indicating that he had not given up the idea that sovereignty was to be shared by the Emperor and the people:

> At the plenary session, the members of the Socialist and Communist parties strongly argued that the Japanese version of "sovereignty of the people" is not clear. I agree with them. The expression *kokumin-no sōi* (the will of all the people) has the danger of being interpreted as "the resolution of *the majority* of the people," so it would be better for us to say clearly that sovereignty (*shuken*) resides in *the people* (*kokumin*). We have the support of the Socialist and Communist parties on this. We should have the support of all of the Japanese people on such an issue. The reason we avoided the expression *jinmin shuken* is because the word *jinmin*, that the Communists use, refers not to the ordinary people in relation to the Emperor, but to the ruled in relation to the ruler. We think it is better to say that *shuken* resides in the people (*kokumin*) including the Emperor. The government recognizes the sovereignty of the people (*kokumin-no shuken*), so in reality, there is not much difference between sovereignty of the state and sovereignty of the people (ibid., p. 9).

The chair and other members made no comment, and moved on to other topics.

The following day, Suzuki Yoshio, of the Socialist party, complained that there were reports in the morning newspapers that the Liberal and Progressive parties had jointly determined that the translation of "the supreme will of the people" in the Preamble should be changed to *shuken-ga kokumin-ni son-suru* (sovereignty resides in the people), and that other parties were expected to join in.

The subcommittee was formed as a result of the judgment that this is an issue on which the parties should reach as much of a consensus as possible, and then make a joint proposal to the committee. Therefore, it is not desirable for one party to present a proposal without making prior efforts to unify the opinions of all parties. . . . You might say that this is a simple correction of a phrase, but this is a grave issue that determines the character of the Constitution. It is not desirable for various parties to take independent courses of action. Our party was in great disarray this morning over lack of cooperation by the Liberal and Progressive parties despite our insistence [on party cooperation]. . . . It was only yesterday that we agreed to cooperate, overcoming the feelings of members of the different parties. (ibid., pp. 21–22).

Chairman Ashida explained that the newspaper accounts did not report accurately what had happened. He said that the reporters asked him if the Socialist party agreed with the proposed amendments, so he replied that there might be some differences; there was nothing beyond that (p. 22). But Kita conceded that the credit for the proposal should have been given to the Socialist party:

What you say is legitimate. It is regrettable that this situation has developed. The Socialist party has argued for the idea of sovereignty residing in the people much more strongly than the Liberal party and the Progressive party. Despite this, the reports made it appear as if the Liberal and Progressive parties have taken your argument away from you and presented it as our own (ibid.).

The confusion was apparently resolved when the Chairman, representing the Liberal party, and Yoshida Yasushi, of the Progressive party, explained and apologized, respectively, for causing the inaccurate reports in newspapers.

Upon receiving this apology, the committee proceeded to discuss the precise meaning of a related Sino-Japanese expression, *shuken zai-min* (sovereignty resides in the people). This discussion is interesting, because it gave the members another opportunity to confirm that, although they were yielding to the American pressure and adopting the new term, *shuken*, they did not entirely accept the idea that sovereignty resides in the people as the Americans understood it. The members debated whether or not the expression, *min*, in *shuken zai-min* stood for *kokumin* or *jinmin*, and assured themselves that it stood for *kokumin*, so the meaning of *shuken zai-min* was, "sovereignty resides in the people, including the Emperor."

First, Yoshida Yasushi explained the Progressive party's proposed revisions.[44] He began,

> As Mr. Suzuki mentioned yesterday, the most important part in the Preamble is [the idea of] *shuken zai-min*. In order to clarify this part—

Immediately, Hatsukade Hiroshi, of the Liberal party, butted in to say,

> I have been repeatedly telling the newspaper reporters not to use the expression *shuken zai-min* under any circumstances. I think we should use the phrase *shuken zai-kokumin* (sovereignty resides in the *kokumin*), although it may be a rather unfamiliar expression.

The Chairman, Ashida Hitoshi, responded,

> I agree with Mr. Hatsukade. In reference to European political philosophy and various constitutions, we have been using the term *min* to refer to the people in opposition to the ruler. According to the government's official interpretation presented by Minister Kanamori, *min* in our contenxt includes the Emperor. There is, however, a possibility that the people will interpret *min* in opposition to the ruler. So Mr. Hatsukade is proposing the expression *zai-kokumin* (resides in the *kokumin*) to avoid giving the people a wrong impression. Is that right?
>
> HATSUKADE: That is correct, Chairman.

Kita spoke up again:

> What you just said has an important consequence. . . . If we use the term *shuken zai-min*, instead of *shuken zai-kokumin*, it might give the impression that *shuken* [merely] belongs to individual members. . . . According to the traditional interpretation, *jinmin* refers to the people in opposition to the Emperor, the ruled in opposition to the ruler, government and the ruling class in general in opposition to the ruled. *Shuken zai-min*, I think, might give the wrong impression that sovereignty resides in the *jinmin*. So I think in the amendment proposal of the subcommittee, we should use *shuken zai-kokumin*.
>
> YOSHIDA: I agree with the position of the representative of my party to use *shuken zai-kokumin* and not *shuken zai-min*. But putting this issue aside, let me explain the proposed amendments of our party.

44. The following extracts are from Mori 1983, pp. 24–25.

Kita tried to interrupt, but Suzuki Yoshio of the Socialist party opposed
Yoshida's proposal, saying that *shuken zai-min* was such a familiar expression that there was no reason for them to not use it. He also added
a vague comment suggesting that the Socialist party interpreted the *min*
of *zai-min* as referring to *jinmin*, and not *kokumin*.[45]

> We are using the expression *shuken zai-min* without much
> thought because it is familiar to us. It will be very strange
> not to use it. This situation requires careful attention, but I
> think we will not be criticized if we explain that *jinmin*
> means thus and so.

Thus, the committee appears to have reached a tentative consensus on
the use of the new expression in the Constitution by way of a discussion
on the meaning of a related Sino-Japanese expression, *shuken zaimin*.
The members agreed that the *min* of *shuken zai-min* derived from *kokumin*, and not *jinmin*, so *shuken zaimin* meant "sovereignty residing in
the people, including the Emperor."

At this point, the committee temporarily dropped the topic, and
moved on to discuss other parts of the Preamble. Shortly before a lunch
break, Suzuki once again suggested that the committee discuss the matter. Ashida brought in a draft of the report of the morning session which
said, "As for the revision of the phrase in the Preamble to, 'do proclaim
that sovereignty (*shuken*) resides in the people (*kokumin*),' all parties
have agreed jointly that the subcommittee will conduct further discussions" (Mori 1983, p. 33). Hayashi Heima, of the Cooperative Democratic party immediately objected that no such decision had been
reached. To this, Kita said, "I want to say that the subcommittee has a
consensus on the wording 'sovereignty (*shuken*) resides in *kokumin*.'"
Hayashi replied,

> We haven't reached a consensus yet. Our party is struggling
> with that part. . . . I don't think we need to state clearly
> "sovereignty resides in the people" (ibid., pp. 33–34).

Ashida asked the transcribers to stop taking notes. Kita said to Hayashi:

> Mr. Hayashi, if this (the committee's being hesitant to admit
> popular sovereignty) becomes known, it will have an unde-
> sirable consequence. From the perspective of international
> climate, it will be inappropriate for us not to express clearly
> that sovereignty resides in the people. Would you please re-
> port to your party that there is a consensus among all other

45. The draft constitution of the Socialist party, however, uses *kokumin*, and not *jinmin* (Satō
1962–64, 2:779–82).

parties; and try to get an agreement among your party members?

HAYASHI: It will be difficult, although not impossible. I will try (p. 34).

Here the subcommittee dropped the issue of popular sovereignty from their debate for the second time.

At the fourth meeting, on July 29, as the subcommittee was moving on to discuss Chapter 3, Suzuki Yoshio suddenly announced that he wanted to introduce a Socialist party amendment. He proposed that a separate article expressing popular sovereignty alone be created as Article 1.[46] He also proposed that, since the Preamble included the clause "the will of the people is supreme," Article 1 (to be renumbered 2) should read: "The Emperor is the symbol of the Japanese State and the unity of the Japanese people, and this position is founded on the will of the Japanese people in whom sovereignty resides" (Mori 1983, pp. 130–31; my translation). Once again, however, the discussion was immediately tabled.

On August 2, 1946, at the eighth meeting of the subcommittee, the Japanese participants were finally ready to change the wording in the Constitution. It had been exactly one week since the issue was first called to the committee's attention. In his opening statement, Ashida announced that the committee would take up Article 1, the most important article. After Ashida and Suzuki made some introductory comments, the members turned to the substance of the article. The ensuing discussion demonstrates that the Japanese had built a consensus resolving this most important issue.[47] First, Ashida reiterated the Socialist party's proposal to create a new Article 1, "Sovereignty resides in the people." He also restated the joint proposal by the Liberal and Progressive parties to change the final clause of Article 1, "this position is founded on *the supreme will of the people*," to "this position is founded on *the will of the people in whom sovereignty resides*." Suzuki emphatically stated that popular sovereignty should be expressed by itself in a separate article, rather than in an article whose purpose is to define the role of the Emperor. He said,

> The original purpose of Article 1 was to specify the role of the Emperor, and not the locus of sovereignty. I think that was the purpose of the drafters of the initial version. It is not

46. The article reads in Japanese, *Shuken-wa kokumin-ni son-suru.* However, the Socialist party's proposed amendments, included in the appendix of Mori 1983 (p. 421) gives the following Article 1: "The power of the state arises from the people (*Kokken-wa, kokumin-kara hassuru*)."
47. See Mori 1983, pp. 335–37.

good to use Article 1 to specify the locus of sovereignty. I ask
you to support our proposal.

Ashida said that he believed that the issue of sovereignty could not be
separated from the Emperor. It is therefore expressed in the article
specifying his position. He concluded that under the circumstances it
was not desirable to insist on a precise legal argument, and requested
the members to compromise and reach an agreement. The floor was
then turned over to Kasai Shigeharu, of the Club of Nonaffiliated
Members:

> [The Constitution] is rather vague about *shuken* (sovereign
> right/sovereignty) and *kokken* (state right). The best way to
> clarify this is to state, at the end of Article 1, that sover-
> eignty resides in the people. Or else, it could be placed in
> the beginning of the article. But because such an amend-
> ment might become the center of a great deal of controversy,
> I think it is sufficient to adopt the Chairman's suggestion and
> amend [the end of the current Article 1], to "[this position]
> is founded on the will of the Japanese people in whom sov-
> ereignty resides."

Thus, Kasai stated that the Club of Nonaffiliated Members preferred to
go along with the Liberal and Progressive parties' proposal, which did
not express popular sovereignty in a separate article. Ashida now turned
to two other party representatives:

> ASHIDA: What is the opinion of the Cooperative Liberal
> Democratic party?
> HAYASHI: Considering the domestic and international cli-
> mate, we go along with the Chairman's proposal.
> ASHIDA: What is your opinion, Mr. Ōshima [of the New Poli-
> tics Club]?
> ŌSHIMA: I go along with the Cooperative Liberal Democratic
> party.

Ashida said to Suzuki,

> Would you agree, Mr. Suzuki?
> SUZUKI: If that is the majority opinion, I have no choice but
> to follow. But to agree with you . . .
> ASHIDA: Even if you cannot give us active support, I would
> like you not to oppose.
> SUZUKI: For instance, if there is a possibility of bringing it up
> again at the meeting of the entire committee, I will avoid an
> unnecessary debate for now. But if it is the case that once I
> express our support there will be no more debate, then, we
> will have to withhold our commitment.

ASHIDA: I think it is all right for you to reserve [your commitment].

SUZUKI: If that is the case, there is no more [to be discussed] on this issue.

This series of exchanges may appear inconclusive, but the members of the subcommittee clearly understood that a consensus had been reached. As for the revision of the clause in the Preamble, it appears that this, too, was revised at the same time. I could not, however, find a separate discussion or a vote on the change from "We, the Japanese people, . . . do proclaim that the will of the people is supreme" to "do proclaim that sovereignty resides in the people."

Thus, the subcommittee of the House of Representatives ultimately accepted the straightforward expression that the Americans wanted, though in a circuitous and inconclusive manner. No one gave a clear reason for the change, and there was no systematic discussion of the issues. Even at the final session on August 2, there was no clear exchange of differing views among the party members representing their respective party platforms. Yet I believe that the repeated "discussions" were important in enabling the members to ponder the questions, individually and collectively, and come to terms with the inevitable result. When the members of subcommittee finally agreed to give up the expression "supreme" (*shikō*) and adopt "sovereignty" (*shuken*), it was partly a result of the discussion of the related Sino-Japanese expression *shuken zaimin*. They argued that just as *kokumin* could include the Emperor, the *min* of *zaimin* could include the Emperor. Thus, the Japanese did not give up the idea that the Emperor was a *kokumin* who shared sovereignty with all the other people of Japan.

## Summary

The position of the Emperor of Japan was the most important issue for both the Allied powers and the Japanese. Although some Americans initially regarded the Emperor as an obstacle to Japan's democratization, in the end, MacArthur decided to keep the Emperor both because he thought the Emperor was important to the political stability of Japan under his command, and because he was impressed by Emperor Hirohito as an individual. But the Americans wanted to make the Emperor merely a symbol of the state. Sovereignty in the new, democratic Japan had to belong to the people. To most Japanese in 1946, however, the role of the Emperor as sovereign was crucial to the continuation of Japan as a sovereign nation.

The sharp difference in views on the role of the Emperor in the new Constitution created serious disagreements between the American and

Japanese officials, and among the members of the 90th Imperial Diet themselves. The central issues were: (1) the Emperor's relationship to the Cabinet, specified in Article 3; (2) the Emperor's relationship to the Japanese people in connection with the meaning of the word *kokumin*; and finally, (3) the appropriate translation of the word "sovereign." The Americans wanted precise legal limits on the Emperor's power, while the Japanese were trying to preserve as much of the Emperor's symbolic status as possible.

The Americans insisted that Article 3 provide that in matters of state, the Emperor act with the "advice and consent" of the cabinet, for they believed that the Emperor's power had to be checked by the cabinet. The Japanese did not appreciate the American concern. They thought that the Emperor's power had always been checked by the members of the Cabinet and other high officials, so the Japanese term, *hohitsu*, meaning "assistance," would suffice. But they yielded to American pressure and eventually adopted the phrase *jogen-to shōnin* to stand for "advice and consent/agreement."

The Americans were also extremely interested in making sure that the Japanese expressed the idea of popular sovereignty in the new constitution. Yet, while the Americans insisted on a precise translation of "sovereignty," they did not pay much attention to the translation of "people." The Japanese, on the other hand, were gravely concerned about the proper interpretation of the "people" and insisted that the Emperor was a *kokumin*. The Japanese did not want to accept the fact that sovereignty in the new Constitution would reside solely in the Japanese people. By arguing that the Emperor was a *kokumin*, they were able to claim that sovereignty resided both in the Emperor and the people. This enabled them to maintain that the fundamental character of the national polity remained, because the Emperor was the center of adoration, even though he would have no political power. The Japanese yielded to American pressure and reluctantly adopted *shuken* to stand for "sovereign" and "sovereignty," but they insisted that "popular" and "people" in Japanese stood for *kokumin*. Thus, in an important sense, the Japanese managed to maintain the sense of tradition in the role of the Emperor as the spiritual center of the Japanese people under the new Constitution. But some Diet members also realized that the Constitution introduced a dramatic and unmistakable change in the locus of sovereignty that would, in effect, weaken the role of the Emperor to being, at best, the center of adoration. They could only hope that the Japanese people would retain and preserve this truly ceremonial role for the Emperor.

# Six

# INDIVIDUAL DIGNITY AND

# EQUALITY OF THE SEXES IN

# MARRIAGE

ARTICLE 24. Marriage has to be based only on the mutual consent of both sexes and it has to be maintained through mutual cooperation with the equal rights of husband and wife as a basis.

　　With regard to choice of spouse, property rights, inheritance, choice of domicile, divorce and other matters pertaining to marriage and the family, laws have to be enacted from the standpoint of individual dignity and the essential equality of the sexes. (My translation)

Of the thirty-one articles included in Chapter 3 of the new Constitution, "The Rights and Duties of the People," Article 24 was the most controversial at the constitutional hearings of the National Diet. The Americans were determined to transform not only the political system, but also some aspects of Japanese society, so that the rights and liberties of individuals would be respected. Article 24 was an important part of this effort, but it confronted the Japanese with the danger of losing their tradition of familism, codified and strengthened in the Meiji Civil Code, in exchange for the American ideology of individualism. In this chapter, I will discuss the Japanese adoption of this article, focusing on two key phrases: "individual dignity" and "equality of the sexes in marriage." I will begin with a short discussion of how individualism has shaped American social relations and the sense of self. I will then discuss the Japanese family in social relations. The comparison shows that, while Americans regard themselves as autonomous individuals whose social relations are secondary to their identity, the Japanese sense of self and dignity arises primarily out of their social relations. The debates at the National Diet show that, while the Japanese recognized the need for democratizing their traditional household system, they were also afraid that the new Constitution would destroy it. While they clearly understood the legal consequences of equality of the sexes in marriage, most Diet members did not appear to understand the idea of individual dignity, or its relation to the idea of equality of the sexes. They were

unable to grasp the link between abolishing the traditional family system and the idea of individual dignity and equality of the sexes in marriage that the Americans intended. However, government spokesmen,
and some Diet members, ultimately interpreted the meaning of individual dignity in a way that was compatible with their own social values, but which was subtly and significantly different from what the
Americans had intended. This, then, became the accepted interpretation of the idea of individual dignity expressed in the new Constitution.
Had this interpretation been thoroughly understood, it might have
made it easier for the Japanese to accept the government's argument
that, while the legal aspect of the family system would be abolished,
the social customs that supported it would continue.

### Individual Dignity and Equality of the Sexes in American Society

Individual dignity is connected with but not identical to the idea of
self-worth or self-esteem. As used here, self-worth refers to a person's
subjective evaluation of himself, and is linked to achievements, wealth,
social status, and a host of other considerations. This sense of self-
worth, or self-esteem, will be found in all societies, including Japan.
But in the United States, individual dignity, which incorporates this
sense of self-esteem, also includes the idea that each person has intrinsic value solely as an individual human being, quite apart from one's
personal characteristics or social position. The Declaration of Independence expresses this concept in the phrase that all men are created
equal. For Americans, individual dignity is also closely linked to freedom—the ability to organize and live one's life as one sees fit, free from
the interference of others. To preserve this area of autonomous action,
Americans grant individuals basic rights which other people, and the
government in particular, are required to respect, and not interfere
with. Some of these rights are incorporated in the American political
system through the Constitution, and particularly the Bill of Rights.
Individual dignity is thus associated with rights in the United States.
Those who have been systematically denied or deprived of their legal
rights know full well that, without them, it is difficult or impossible to
claim full dignity as an individual in American society.

But individual dignity involves far more than a legal principle. The
ideas of equal rights and individual dignity are reinforced by social practices and strongly held moral views that reflect a deeper assumption
regarding the relationship of the individual to society. This is the view
that individuals are, in a fundamental way, autonomous, with a basic
"core," or "essence," belonging to each person as an individual, and

having no necessary connection with or relationship to his social relations—the people he works with, those he associates with, the groups he belongs to, or the community he lives in. In *Habits of the Heart*, Robert Bellah and his co-authors (1985, p. 142) summarize the American idea of individual dignity as follows.

> We believe in the dignity, indeed the sacredness of the individual. Anything that would violate our right to think for ourselves, judge for ourselves, make our own decisions, live our own lives as we see fit, is not only morally wrong, it is sacrilegious. Our highest and noblest aspirations, not only for ourselves, but for those we care about, for our society and for the world, are closely linked to our individualism.

The sources of this conception of the individual lie far back in the Western intellectual tradition, but the idea became widely accepted as an operative social philosophy only in the nineteenth century, and then particularly in the United States.

One reason Americans found this philosophy so congenial is that in important ways it reflected the nature of American society. It has often been pointed out that, in contrast to Europe, the United States lacks a feudal tradition, with the associated notions of inherited status and the division of society into well-marked classes.[1] This meant, among other things, that there were no organized groups or classes claiming special privileges to oppose the establishment of democratic institutions based on equal rights. Instead, the new political system, and the political theory associated with it, were accepted by virtually everyone. Alexis de Tocqueville was one of the first to appreciate the extent to which American political institutions grew out of, and reflected a democratic social order, a set of social practices and mores centered around the idea of equality.

Tocqueville believed that Europe would ultimately and inevitably evolve in the same general direction as the United States, so he studied American society to discern both the dangers and the potential in this new form of social order. One of the most distinct manifestations he discovered was a loosening of social bonds, which he contrasted with the more fixed and stable aristocratic social order he knew in Europe.

> Aristocracy had made a chain of all the members of the community, from the peasant to the king; democracy breaks that chain and severs every link of it.

---

1. Alexis de Tocqueville was the first to make this point. In recent years, the idea has been developed by Louis Hartz (1955; 1967, pp. 59–77).

As social conditions become more equal, the number of persons increases who, although they are neither rich nor powerful enough to exercise any great influence over their fellows, have nevertheless acquired or retained sufficient education and fortune to satisfy their own wants. They owe nothing to any man, they expect nothing from any man; they acquire the habit of always considering themselves as standing alone, and they are apt to imagine that their whole destiny is in their own hands.

Thus not only does democracy make every man forget his ancestors, but it hides his descendants and separates his contemporaries from him; it throws him back forever upon himself alone and threatens in the end to confine him entirely within the solitude of his own heart. (Tocqueville [1835] 1945, 2:105–6)

Tocqueville chose the term "individualism" to describe this development. As a description of social relations, this idea of individualism is distinct from the political theory based on equal rights, with the related idea of the autonomous individual. But the loosening of social bonds Tocqueville described has made these individualistic ideas seem so natural to Americans that they find it difficult to conceive of political and social relations in any other terms.

The nature of the transformation from an aristocratic to a democratic, egalitarian social order is nicely illustrated by a linguistic change. As the networks of status and roles characteristic of European society prior to the rise of industrialization began to break down, the concept of individual dignity slowly replaced the aristocratic idea of honor. Peter Berger and his co-authors describe the shift in the following terms:

> The concept of honor implies that identity is essentially, or at least importantly, linked to institutional roles. The modern concept of dignity, by contrast, implies that identity is essentially independent of institutional roles. . . . In a world of honor, the individual discovers his true identity in his roles, and to turn away from himself—in "false consciousness," one is tempted to add. In a world of dignity, the individual can only discover his true identity by emancipating himself from his socially imposed roles—the latter are only masks, entangling him in illusion, "alienation" and "bad faith." It follows that the two worlds have a different relation to history. It is through the performance of institutional roles that the individual participates in history, not only the history of the particular institution

but that of his society as a whole. It is precisely for this reason that modern consciousness, in its conception of the self,
tends toward a curious ahistoricity. In a world of honor, identity is firmly linked to the past through the reiterated performance of prototypical acts. In a world of dignity, history is
the succession of mystifications from which the individual
must free himself to attain "authenticity." (Berger et al.
1973, pp. 90–91)

The shift in usage thus reflects a transformation of the concept of identity. In aristocratic society, people saw themselves as integral parts of
on-going social relationships, and drew their sense of identity, their
sense of who they were, from this social context. They did not have a
sense of self distinct from these relationships.

As Tocqueville noted, however, Americans see themselves as autonomous beings. The self comes before society, and individuals have
dignity and value quite apart from their social relations. In fact, many
Americans have a tendency to think of society as a voluntary association, arising out of consent or contract between autonomous individuals. The individual comes first, and social relations are secondary. The
American legal system, buttressed by widely held moral views, reinforces the notion of the autonomous individual by vigorously protecting
the individual from unwanted invasions of privacy and property.

Voluntary associations are an important source of social and political
action in the United States. Tocqueville noted the American tendency
to form such groups, and saw them as an important counterweight to
the individualistic tendencies he feared. As the label indicates, however, these groups arise out of the voluntary actions of individual citizens, and they are only as strong as the commitment of the individual
members. People can leave the group as easily as they join it, and they
are likely to remain enthusiastic only as long as they see the group as
promoting interests that coincide with or are close to their own. It is
rare for individuals to identify so closely with the association that they
subordinate their own interests to those of the group, or more accurately, define their own interests in terms of the association's interests.

In some respects, the structure of the American family also illustrates
these individualistic characteristics. Ideally, the family unit grows out
of a marriage of love between a man and a woman. Together with their
children, they form a nuclear family. As the children grow up, leave
home, and get married, they begin the process all over again in their
own right. Each couple thus creates a new family, and few think of the
family as having an existence over a period of generations, independent

of and prior to the particular individuals who compose it at any given moment. When the children leave, they form new families, and the old one dies with the parents.[2]

American child-rearing practices reflect and reinforce this idea of the family. In the American middle class family, a child is given a separate bed in a separate room from birth, and learns from an early age that separation from parents is the norm. Parents encourage children to make their own choices in food, clothing, and other matters, and as children grow older they are gradually allowed more and more freedom and responsibility. Indeed, the focus of childhood in America is learning to be independent and self-reliant in preparation for the all-important event of leaving home and setting up one's own life and family. While the link with one's parents is not broken, there is no expectation that this connection, and the connection with more remote ancestors, will incorporate or take precedence over the newly established family. A new social unit, which is not an extension of the older unit, comes into being.

Another idea associated with the nuclear family in the United States is equality of the sexes: men and women are free to choose their own mates and, in theory at least, a marriage is an equal relationship. There was, of course, a gap between rhetoric and reality in 1946, a gap that many have sought to narrow or eliminate in recent years. But there was no widespread women's liberation movement at the end of World War II, and most people may have believed that women in the United States had achieved legal and social equality. It was perhaps not surprising that when the Americans discovered the subordinate position of Japanese women, they sought to eliminate it. Thus, the American drafters included a clause granting Japanese women equal rights twenty-five years before a similar amendment to the U.S. Constitution was proposed. Not foreseeing the controversy that would develop over women's liberation and the ERA in this country, the Americans left it to the Japanese to puzzle out the meaning of equality of the sexes.

2. Although Americans are increasingly interested in tracing their roots, discovering one's ancestors does not mean one necessarily incorporates them into the family. In discussing who is to count as a relative for Americans, David Schneider (1980, p. 67) says, "One of the first things that anyone who works with American genealogies notices is that the system is quite clear as long as one takes Ego as the point of reference and does not venture far from there. As one goes out from Ego—in any direction—things get more and more fuzzy." In a sense, the individual chooses who his relatives will be. If one discovers a disreputable cousin or ancestor, that person can be safely ignored. He does not automatically have the status of a family relation by reason of a socially prescribed definition.

## Self and Society in Japan

The Japanese sense of self in society is distinctly different from that of Americans. Japanese social structure resembles Tocqueville's aristocratic world far more than the individualistic society of the United States, at least with regard to the individual's place in society. The Japanese do not think in terms of autonomous individuals, standing apart from society. Their sense of self is essentially linked to the hierarchical social relations in the groups to which they belong, particularly the family. They do not look upon themselves as autonomous beings with freedom to withdraw from membership in the family whenever they choose. Thus, whereas Americans regard stripping a child of the freedom to go out as a severe form of discipline, the Japanese consider shutting a child out of the house as a very serious punishment. The severest traditional form was *kandō*, the disowning of a family member.

During the Tokugawa era, the organization of Japanese families varied considerably from class to class, and region to region. Nonetheless, the basic family unit was the *ie*, literally meaning "house," which is translated in current anthropological literature either as "household" (Nakane 1970), or "stem family" (Befu 1971). The *ie* was a corporate residential group that included the head and his wife, the oldest son and his wife and children, and often unmarried siblings of the head, especially females. In farm and merchant families, the *ie* frequently included employees who were unrelated to the family either by blood or marriage. The *ie* was continued from generation to generation by succession to the headship, usually by the oldest son, who alone inherited the family property.[3]

In addition to the main household, the traditional Japanese family had an extended kinship structure composed of several subhouseholds, established by the head of the main household for his younger male siblings, and even occasionally for a female sibling whose husband had been adopted into the household, or a widow with children (Fukuo 1972, p. 204). The members of the main and branch households all carried the same surname. In farm and merchant families, long-term employees were often allowed to establish households of their own,

---

3. This succession was so important that families with no sons would commonly adopt the husband of one of the daughters to maintain the generational continuity. In some cases, a couple would adopt one of their grandsons to carry on the family name. My mother's marriage illustrates the importance of this practice. She had a brother living in America, but she was the only member of her family living in Japan. She had to go to court to receive special permission to marry my father, and let her family line become extinct in Japan.

with a share of the capital or the farmland given to them, and thus
became branches of the main household.

The traditional Japanese family maintained a hierarchical order
among the members of the household according to four basic criteria:
age, generation, sex, and the manner of recruitment—that is, whether
or not one was born into the family, or joined through marriage or
adoption. Members of the older generation commanded respect from
those of the younger, those who were older in age from those who were
younger, and men from women. The central idea holding the system
together was *on*, the sense of indebtedness toward one's parents, and
the duty to repay it by *kō*, filial piety. The husband-father who was the
head of the household commanded considerable authority and respect,
but he also carried a great deal of responsibility, including a strong
moral obligation to look after the members of the household, who depended on him economically, socially, and emotionally.

It is important to remember that the Japanese household not only
encompassed more than one family, but also extended over time
through generations of ancestors. This extension of the household was,
in fact, the basic meaning of *ie*. The present household was only a
temporary form it had taken (Pelzel 1970, p. 229). The househead was
a caretaker, responsible for looking after the family property not only
for his own generation, but also for his ancestors and the generations
to come. Nakane (1967a, p. 17) characterizes that sense of obligation
as follows: "If he should happen to lose the property by his mismanage-
ment, he would say, 'I don't know what excuse to make to our ancestors
(predecessors).'" Unlike the head of a Western family, the Japanese
househead acted, not as an individual, but as the member of the household community who happened to be designated to fulfill the role of
the headship.[4]

The Meiji family law of 1898, which the government finally adopted
after a great deal of controversy among legal scholars, incorporated the
traditional family system of the bushi class. Because the customs of the
bushi families were in many ways more conservative than those of other
classes, this family law strengthened the feudal family system of the
Tokugawa era (Fukuo 1972, pp. 202–23). One distinct difference from

---

4. One important duty of the househead in this respect was caring for the family grave and
conducting festivities memorializing the ancestors and the recently deceased members. As I mentioned in chapter 2, during the Tokugawa era most Japanese families were assigned to Buddhist
temples, where they maintained family graves. It was the househead's responsibility to maintain
the grave in good order, keep the family altar with the memorial tablets of ancestors and the
recently deceased, and hold memorial services at times designated by Buddhist tradition. See also
n. 25 (p. 249), for a discussion of the problems faced by contemporary Japanese families.

the feudal system, however, was the use of the language of rights. The Meiji family law codified many of the traditional powers, privileges, and responsibilities of the househead, and expressed many of his powers and privileges as rights (Noda 1976, pp. 200–202). Thus, the Meiji Civil Code introduced a subtle but significant change into Japanese social tradition. Nakane Chie (1967a, p. 17 n. 1) says,

> The absolute right of the head, as an individual, over the household property and the household members was introduced by the old Civil Code under the term *koshu-ken* (the right of househead). This modern law contradicted the traditional ideology of the Japanese *ie* institution.[5] In spite of this law, the traditional concept of household property continued, though there were some who abused this legal right.

The traditional social order had begun to change as Japan industrialized. At the beginning of the twentieth century, villagers began to move to the rapidly growing urban centers to work in offices and factories. Many were young unmarried people; those who were married had small nuclear families. They were far from the influence of the *ie*, and various other support groups in their native villages. But this did not mean that they became more individualistic, in Tocqueville's sense of the word. Instead, their places of work became a new source of security and identity. Having no other model of social relations to apply to their new situation, they began to think of their company section, usually a group of fewer than ten people, as if it were their substitute *ie*, with the section chief as head. Members of the section were ranked according to age, generation, seniority, and sex, just as the members of the *ie* were ranked. The same held true of the company as a whole in relation to other companies. This trend has continued, and in modern Japan, small groups in workplaces have become important sources of identity for many people. This is one reason why a Japanese businessman, when introduced, will first mention the company he works for, rather than the specific job he does. The company, not the job, is important to his sense of identity.

Small groups in Japanese workplaces operate quite differently in practice than the formal hierarchy might suggest. Ideally, the members de-

---

5. Nakane does not say how the modern law *contradicted* the traditional ideology, and thus we do not know what she had in mind. However, I believe that one way in which it deviated from the traditional ideology was its defining in specific terms the rights and obligations of the househead. Previously, these were undefined, or "nonspecific" rights and obligations whose precise content would depend on circumstances. See the discussion of the Japanese understanding of the concept of rights in chapter 2.

velop a strong sense of group spirit, and they cooperate with each other freely, irrespective of their official ranking, for the benefit of the group as a whole. In *Japanese Society*, Nakane (1970, p. 81) describes this important feature as follows:

> The distinguishing characteristic of the operation of the group is seen to be the absence of clearly differentiated roles for each according to his position. The formal organization of the group assigns to each member a certain prescribed role which he is to perform. However in practice the informal organization of the group takes precedence, and such formally prescribed roles are not always performed according to expectation. The actual role of an individual does not always or necessarily correspond to his rank or status. Rank functions to maintain the legitimate order in inter-personal relations, particularly when it is operating externally, but does not bind the member within the limits of an ascribed role. On the contrary, when the group is in action the roles of individual members are readily adjustable to changing situations.

Nakane uses the phrase "undifferentiated role" as the English equivalent of the Japanese expression, *ningen byōdō shugi* (human equality-ism),[6] noting that it is one of the most important aspects of the ethos of the Japanese society. She explains that the Japanese people have a deep-rooted belief that all human beings are born with essentially the same ability (*nōryoku*) to cope with life (Nakane 1967b, pp. 97–100). This belief in equality of ability is the essential justification for undifferentiated role playing in group activity.

Nakane's use of the term *byōdō*, which is usually translated as "equality," will be puzzling to Westerners, for what she describes is not usually labeled equality in the West.[7] The essence of *byōdō shugi* can best be understood by Americans if they look at the dynamics of a closely knit American family. Even in the most traditional of American families, where the husband has the primary responsibility for earning the family income, while his wife raises the children, describing these culturally prescribed roles is only the beginning of analysis. The roles themselves do not describe or explain how the members of a family with

6. The term *byōdō* comes from Buddhist terminology. The Japanese learned it when they imported Buddhism in the sixth century. The original term is *sama* in Sanskrit, which was translated into Chinese as *píngděng*. When the Japanese adopted it, they translated it as *byōdō* (Mochizuki 1958–63, 5:4358–59). I thank the anonymous reader for giving me the Chinese translation.

7. It is somewhat misleading to Japanese readers as well, because the term *byōdō* is also the term used in the phrase "equality of the sexes" (*ryōsei-no byōdō*) in Article 24 of the Constitution, which refers to the political equality of modern society.

a strong sense of cohesion actually interact with each other. The bonds that ideally hold such a family together include a strong sense of mutual dependency, trust, and love. Ideally, the members cooperate with one another out of love and out of commitment to the interest of the family as a whole, acting as if guided by the principle of "from each according to his ability, to each according to his needs." The sense of community among members of a closely knit American family can be called a sense of equality, although it is unlike the standard meaning of political equality—equality of rights and duties. Each family member has particular duties and responsibilities, as well as privileges, which will differ according to one's position and abilities. But ideally, their love and commitment to one another creates a sense that they are all equal in the life of the family as a whole. This is the sense of equality that Nakane calls *byōdō shugi* (equality-ism). This sense of equality is closer to equality of responsibility than rights. In America, it is shared only by the members of the family, and some very special family-like groups, such as religious orders, and it is not generally recognized as a valid and valuable social ideal.

The Japanese, on the other hand, extend this sense of equality beyond the family, and cultivate it within small groups in workplaces throughout society. The members of these groups socialize with each other after work and on holidays, talk about their personal problems among themselves and help each other to deal with them much more openly than American workers do.[8] For many people in contemporary

8. It took me a long time to see how American society is stratified: horizontally, not vertically. A clear example is found in my husband's former law firm, which held its office Christmas party at a fancy restaurant every year. One year, the secretaries, who had to drag their husbands out to the party, requested a special bonus in place of a Christmas dinner at an expensive restaurant to which they would ordinarily not go. In Japan, office parties do not involve spouses. This spares Japanese workers some of the problems that Americans have in their couple-oriented society. However, what is more important is that it would be unthinkable for Japanese to hold an office party excluding its low-ranking members. Such an act would definitely be regarded as "undemocratic."

Ronald Dore (1985, p. 210) discusses this issue in terms of the intra-class vs. inter-class authority relations in British and Japanese societies. In Britain, intra-class authority relations—those between seniors and juniors on the same career track—is similar to those existing in Japan. The senior and junior members are "equal" in a broader sense of belonging to the same group, though not equal in seniority. However, the British have a much harder time with inter-class authority relations. People in different career tracks are not considered equal, whereas in Japan, they are.

Dore also quotes a national character survey conducted by a Japanese government research institute in which respondents are asked whether they prefer a boss who abides strictly by the work rules and never asks for more, but doesn't take any interest in them as people, or a boss who shows his concern for them and their personal problems but sometimes demands more than he is entitled to. In every survey since it was started in 1948, 85 per cent of the sample, in all age levels, have chosen the more intense relationship (1985, p. 206; see p. 192 n. 34 for the quotation). Dore then says, "It is a long way from the contractualist assumptions which inform British employment relations and authority structures—assumptions which reflect a basic *egalitarianism* which is miss-

Japan, co-workers at the company are their best friends.[9] The strong
emotional ties that are established among members of the group, reinforced by traditional Japanese views about the basic equality of ability
of all human beings, make it possible for them to create a genuine sense
of common identity and equality, while at the same time maintaining
the formal ranking system. This sense of equality, in turn, allows each
member to play whatever work role may be necessary for the best and
most efficient operation of the group as a whole, helping to develop and
reinforce a strong sense of group spirit and cohesion.

The other side of this group spirit is a sense of exclusiveness against
the rest of society. The boundary between the group and the remainder
of society is often very sharp in Japan. Nakane (1978, pp. 38–39) draws
an interesting parallel between small groups in contemporary Japanese
society and individuals in the United States. She points out that small
groups in Japan regard themselves as essentially autonomous and independent of the larger groups within which they belong. In this sense
they are like individuals in the United States and Western society in
general. Thus, a group will resolve the problems of the group and its
members among themselves, and will not allow outsiders to interfere.
It will often actively resist pressures from the outside, either from the
more inclusive organization or neighboring groups, asserting its own
rights in response.

It is important to remember, however, that unlike American associations discussed earlier, the Japanese do not have a strong sense of identity apart from the group. While the group may assert its own rights
against outside pressures, the members will not see the group as the
collection, or sum of a number of individuals with the same or similar
interests. It is something quite different from a voluntary association of
individuals in the United States. The group comes first, and helps to
define the interests of its members. Thus, the members will strive to
achieve a strong consensus, and try to persuade disssenters to accept it.
Individuals are always expected to think of their own interests in refer-

---

ing in Japan. The admired section chief would, in Britain, be considered paternalistic, and no
manager likes to lay himself open to such a charge, for paternalism impugns the treasured sense of
self-reliant independence of his subordinates" (emphasis added).

Dore's use of the term "egalitarianism" is misleading, at least in Japanese terms. What is clearly
missing in Japan is the "contractualist assumptions," and not "egalitarianism," as Japanese would
understand it. Furthermore, for the Japanese, "paternalism" and "egalitarianism" are not mutually
exclusive, as they are for the British.

9. However, such friendships often weaken and eventually disappear over the years once the
person leaves the group. The Americans and Japanese have different views about friendship.
Americans make a much clearer distinction between friends and co-workers than do the Japanese,
and are far more likely to have friends who are not in their work group.

ence to those of the collective. The Japanese do not see this as an infringement of rights, or encroachment on the autonomy of the individual. Rather, the group helps create and define the individual's sense of identity.

The extension of Japanese family relationships into the workplace is reflected in an important feature of the language. Japanese has a system of "honorifics," whose sole function is to mark deference. The system has three types of expressions, polite, honoring, and humbling. When one speaks to or about someone higher than oneself, one uses honoring expressions. Polite forms are used when one speaks politely and formally, regardless of one's relationship to the addressee. These rules, which are anchored to the speaker, are extended to the members of one's family and work group. For example, in talking to one's own mother, a person would use the vocative form *o-kā-san*, which consists of the respectful prefix *o*, followed by *kā*, and an honoring suffix *-san*. The same form can be used when talking about someone else's mother. But when talking about one's own mother to someone outside the family, one would use the humbling form, *haha*. Similarly, when the members of a section address their section chief, they would use the job title *kachō*, with *-san*, *kachō-san*. But when speaking to someone outside the company, they would refer to him as *kachō*, without *-san*. In the latter situation, the section chief is treated as one would treat a member of one's own family.

The Japanese sense of group identity in adulthood is cultivated in their family life. Children are not taught to become independent and self-reliant in the way American children are. They sleep in the same room with parents, and they bathe with them throughout most of their childhood. Parents and children are greatly dependent on each other, and this dependency is encouraged. Even today, young men and women are expected to live at home until marriage. The American idea of "leaving home" is foreign to the Japanese, and their language reflects this. Japanese has a Sino-Japanese expression, *shukke* (leave-home), which means to enter monastic life, abandoning all ties of secular life. There also is an indigenous counterpart, *ie-de* (home-leave), the old meaning of which is the same as that of *shukke*. The contemporary sense of this word is "missing from home," and it is used in expressions such as *iede-nin* (missing person[s]), and *iede shōnen* (missing boy[s]). There is no word in the Japanese vocabulary that exactly stands for "leaving home" as Americans understand it.[10]

10. In 1959, when I was getting ready to go back to Japan after three years of college in this country, my American friends asked me where I would live in Japan. The question astounded me.

Finally, the Japanese concept of marriage, and the relationship between husband and wife, and between men and women in general, is
an integral part of the Japanese practice of maintaining hierarchical
ranks in form, but achieving equality in substance. Even today, when
nearly 40 percent of the nation's labor force is female, most Japanese
women do not aspire to compete with men to gain equal status in business and professional life. They continue to see themselves primarily as
wives and mothers.[11] Forty-five years ago, at the end of the war, these
views were even more predominant. The husband, as head of the
household, was clearly higher in status than his wife, particularly when
dealing with people outside the family. But the wife had a separate set
of duties and responsibilities in the household that were just as important as those of the husband, and women regarded themselves very
much as equal partners in the actual management of household affairs.
The wife normally made all the decisions about household expenditures
and education of children; the husband turned over his salary to her.
She then gave him an appropriate sum for his own expenses outside
the home.[12]

To summarize, the ethos of Japanese society is distinctly different
from that of American society. Most Americans think of themselves as
individualists, and believe that their basic identity is something inherent within them. They believe in the dignity of the individual, which
incorporates the right to think for themselves, judge for themselves,

---

I was returning to my family. The idea of finding my own apartment in Tokyo, or any other city
in Japan, had never occurred to me or anyone in my family. It made such a strong impression on
me that, several years later, I wrote a short essay on the incident, which appeared in the readers'
column of a Japanese newspaper, Asahi Shimbun. The few responses that I received from readers
made me feel that they did not understand what I was trying to say. Although I was coming to the
United States for an extended stay, it did not mean "leaving home" in the American sense. I was
simply absenting myself from home for a few years. In today's urban Japan, there are many more
young people who live apart from their families than in my younger days. Nevertheless, their idea
of "independence" is much different from that of their American contemporaries.

11. There are some signs of change. See chapter 4 of Frank K. Upham, Law and Social Change
in Postwar Japan (1987), for an interesting discussion of civil rights litigation by Japanese professional women, with its social and political effects.

12. When I first came to the United States in 1956, I believed that women in this country
were equal with men, and had a great deal more power than Japanese women. Thus, it was quite
a surprise for me to see my uncle always paying for all the groceries out of his own wallet when the
family went shopping. My aunt kept asking him for money to pay for various things she had to get
while he was out. It struck me as rather odd that women in America, who were supposedly equal
with men, did not hold the family purse strings. Back in Japan, my great-aunt, who raised my
mother, not only paid all the bills for the household, but made necessary investments to provide
for the financial security of the family all her married life. My mother has done the same for many
years. To be sure, there is variation among families in this division of labor between husband and
wife, but every Japanese knows that the wife has a great deal of actual power at home; her views
cannot be taken lightly.

and live their own lives as they see fit. They value autonomy and self-reliance, and see their membership in social groups as a secondary aspect of their sense of self. The Japanese, on the other hand, draw their sense of self from membership in the family and work groups, and have great difficulty in thinking of themselves apart from these social relationships. They derive their sense of self-worth from performing the duties and accepting the responsibilities appropriate to their assigned roles. The Japanese also believe that men and women are equal in their ability to cope with life. This sense of equality is much closer to equality of responsibility than of rights. Individual dignity and equality of the sexes grow naturally out of the American concept of the self, but do not fit well with the Japanese sense of self.

## The American Vision of the New Japanese Family

The members of the Committee on Civil Rights at GHQ who drafted the original version of Chapter 3 fervently believed that they had "the responsibility to effect a social revolution in Japan" (Takayanagi et al. 1972, 1:206). Their strongly negative view of traditional Japanese society, particularly the role of women, is illustrated by the summary of the comments by Pieter K. Roest at the committee's meeting with the Steering Committee on February 8, 1946:

> Colonel Roest stated that inclusion of social welfare provisions was accepted practice in modern European constitutions. It is peculiarly necessary to include them here since state responsibility for the welfare of its people is a new concept in Japan and demands constitutional approval to encourage its widespread acceptance. At present women are chattels here, bastards take precedence over legitimate sons on the mere whim of a father, and any peasant can sell his daughter if the rice crop is bad (ibid., 1:204, 206).

The members of the Steering Committee cautioned that it was not possible to "impose a new mode of social thought upon a country by law" (ibid., 1:206). Nonetheless, they, too, believed that Japan in 1946 was still a feudal society in need of a radical change.[13] Thus, they included Article XXIII, proposing the elimination of Japan's centuries-old family system:

> The family is the basis of human society and its traditions for good or evil permeate the nation. Marriage shall rest upon the indisputable legal and social equality of both sexes,

---

13. In Article XII of their draft they declared, "The feudal system of Japan shall cease."

founded upon mutual consent instead of parental coercion;
and maintained through cooperation instead of male domination. Laws contrary to these principles shall be abolished,
and replaced by others viewing choice of spouse, property
rights, inheritance, choice of domicile, divorce and other
matters pertaining to marriage and the family from the
standpoint of individual dignity and the essential equality of
the sexes.

Although I have found no record of the reactions of the Japanese
officials to this particular article, it must have come as a shock. When
Matsumoto and Satō brought the Japanese government's version modeled after the MacArthur draft to GHQ on the morning of March 4,
1946, this article had been rewritten to read simply as follows:

> ARTICLE 37. Marriage has to be based only on mutual con-
> sent of a man and a woman, and maintained through mutual
> cooperation of the spouses with the equal rights of husband
> and wife as a basis.[14] (My translation)

At the Americans' insistence, the two sides used the original American
version as the basis for discussion during the subsequent 30-hour marathon negotiation. Satō finally managed to get some of the clauses eliminated; the new and renumbered article, published on March 6, read as
follows:

> ARTICLE 22. Marriage should be based only on the mutual
> consent of both sexes, and maintained through mutual co-
> operation with the equal rights of husband and wife as a
> basis.
>     With regard to the choice of spouse, property rights, in-
> heritance, choice of domicile, divorce and other matters per-
> taining to marriage and family matters, [one] should enact
> laws from the standpoint of individual dignity and the essen-
> tial equality of the sexes.[15] (My translation)

In April, the Japanese government finally prepared a full version in
colloquial Japanese for the Cabinet's debate. In that version, the second

14. *Dai-sanjū-shichi-jō. Kon'in-wa danjo sōgo-no gōi-ni motozukite-nomi seiritsu-shi, katsu fūfu-ga
dōtō-no kenri-o yū suru koto-o kihon-to shi sōgo-no kyōryoku-ni yori iji seraru-beki mono-to su* (Shimizu
1962–63, 4:343).

15. *Dai-nijū-ni-jō. Kon'in-wa ryōsei sōhō-no gōi-ni motozukite-nomi seiritsu-shi katsu fūfu-ga dōtō-
no kenri-o yū suru koto-o kihon-to shi sōgo-no kyōryoku-ni yori iji seraru-beki koto.*

*Haigū-no sentaku, zaisan-ken, sōzoku, jūtaku-no sentei, rikon narabi-ni kon'in oyobi kazoku-ni kan
suru sono-ta-no jikō-ni kan-shi kojin-no ken'i oyobi ryōsei-no honshitsu-teki byōdō-ni rikkyaku suru
hōritsu-o sentei su-beki koto* (ibid., p. 354).

paragraph was rewritten in the passive voice, following the style of the American draft.

> Article 22. Marriage has to be based only on the mutual consent of both sexes and maintained through mutual cooperation with the equal rights of husband and wife as a basis.
>
> With regard to choice of spouse, property rights, inheritance, choice of domicile, divorce and other matters pertaining to marriage and family, laws have to be enacted from the standpoint of individual dignity (*ken'i*) and the essential equality of the sexes.[16] (My translation)

Unlike other articles mentioned earlier, Japanese officials did not attempt to negotiate any further changes in this one with the Americans.[17]

I should also add that among all the privately conceived constitutions, the Socialist party's proposal was the only one that specifically mentioned equality of the sexes in marriage. It stated: "The family life of the people will be protected. The basis of marriage will be that the men and the women have/will have equal rights (my translation)."[18] Two others implied that husbands and wives would have equal rights. The one suggested by the Constitutional Research Group stated that men and women would enjoy completely equal rights both in public and in private.[19] Takano Iwasaburō's version stated that there should be no discrimination between men and women in their enjoyment of education and other cultural activities.[20] Thus it appears that, in 1946, the Japanese people had little interest in abolishing their traditional family system. It is interesting, though, that the government officials did not worry about this article nearly as much as they did about the articles relating to the Emperor, and did not formulate any strategy for dealing

16. *Dai-nijū-ni jō. Kon'in-wa, ryōsei-no gōi-ni motozuite-nomi seiritsu-shi, fūfu-ga dōtō-no kenri-o yū-suru koto-o kihon-to shi, sōgo-no kyōryoku-ni yori, iji sare-nakereba naranai.*

*Haigūsha-no sentaku, zaisan-ken, sōzoku, jūkyo-no sentei, rikon narabi-ni kon'in oyobi kazoku-ni kan-suru sono-ta-no jikō-ni kan-shite-wa, hōritsu-wa, kojin-no ken'i-to ryōsei-no honshitsu-teki byōdō-ni rikkyaku shite seitei sare-nakereba naranai* (ibid., p. 366).

17. It is interesting that this article, as well as Article 14, has been hailed, both by the Americans and Japanese, as a landmark for the promotion of Japanese women's rights (Pharr 1987, pp. 224–31). This praise, however, seems to be premature, as the article has never been used effectively to claim a right. See Upham 1987, chapter 4.

18. *Kokumin-no katei seikatsu-wa hogo seraru. Kon'in-wa danjo-no dōtō-no kenri-o yū-suru koto-o kihon-to su* (Satō 1962–64, 2:781).

19. *Danjo-wa kōteki narabi shi-teki-ni kanzen-ni byōdō-no kenri-o yūsu* (Satō 1962–64, 2:785).

20. *Subete kyōiku sono-ta bunka-no kyōju-wa danjo-no aida-ni sai-o mōku bekarazu* (*Shiryō Nihonkoku Kempō*, vol. 1 (1945–1949), 1986, p. 52).

with the Diet members' potential opposition. Among Satō's private papers were several files containing a large number of notes and memoranda on the Emperor. In stark contrast, I found only two files containing a few memoranda directly related to this article—an indication that there was not much debate among the government officials. In one set of memos on Chapter 3, Satō listed a series of legal and social problems related to the change (Satō Tatsuo Kankei Bunsho 101). At the end of his notes he wrote, "At least superficially, the *ie* will be discarded" (my translation). Another document, dated March 24, 1946, lists the problematic issues identified by different ministries, and here there is one line that says "There is a problem in the issue of the order of succession. Would [the new article] not require abolishing of the system of househead and inheritance?" (ibid., 50; my translation).

## The Debate at the National Diet

The members of both Houses displayed a tremendous amount of resistance to Article 22 (current 24).[21] Even though it did not explicitly state that the rights of the househead would be abolished, many were aware that the emphasis on the equality of the sexes would effectively eliminate these rights. In both Houses, the government's spokesmen tried to reassure the members that the article was simply designed to eradicate the remnants of feudal society, and would have no effect on traditional Japanese family relationships. But their efforts were unpersuasive, and when pressed, they ultimately admitted that the househead would lose many legal rights. They retreated to the only defensible position, admitting that the legal rights of family members would change, but arguing that social values and customs would persist, so that the family would not really change that much.

As for the meaning of the phrase "individual dignity," the Diet members spent far less time on it than on the practical issues of family. Most of the discussion occurred in the House of Peers. The debate was extremely significant, however, because it resulted in an interpretation that was fully consistent with traditional Japanese culture.

We begin with the House of Representatives. On the second day of its plenary session, June 26, 1946, Hara Fujirō of the Progressive party

---

21. According to Shimizu's data, Article 22 (current 24) was by far the most frequently discussed article in Chapter 3. There were 65 pages of the transcript in which this article was discussed. The number of interpellators was 19; only Article 26, on universal education, was discussed by a larger number (20) (Shimizu 1962–63, vol. 4 appendix, pp. 90, 93). See chap. 5, p. 184 n. 23, for a full explanation of Shimizu's lists.

asked the government to explain how the article would affect the family:

> The Japanese family system and the imperial system have traditionally been closely linked. . . . The Japanese family system has contributed greatly to the development of Japanese culture and family education. The idea of the union of the Emperor and the people, and other key political issues, are also closely linked to the family system. I am not referring to all the stipulations in Article 22. I am only referring to the traditional right of succession and the rights of the househead. I would like to ask the Prime Minister about his views on the Japanese family system. (Shūgi-in 1946a, 6:79, cols. 4–5)

Prime Minister Yoshida's response was not really an answer:

> The second paragraph of Article 22 specifies property rights, succession, and other matters related to the family. This [clause] establishes them with the idea of individual dignity and equality of the sexes. Its ultimate aim is to eliminate the feudalistic elements [of the current system]. Thus it does not eliminate the rights of the househead, family, succession, and others. . . . The Japanese institution of the family and the right of succession are good ways, and beautiful customs that are uniquely Japanese (ibid., 81, col. 5).

His assurances did not convince the members of the Diet. In a lengthy interpellation on the same day, a second member, Kitaura Keitarō, of the Liberal party, expressed the anxiety traditionalists felt about the family:

> This draft constitution completely destroys familism centered around the rights of the househead, and replaces it with individualism centered around the husband and wife. . . . In his administrative policy speech the other day, the Prime Minister promised to promote education [of the young] in society and at home in order to strengthen social morality. But how can the government promote education in families while eliminating the rights of the househead and parents? It has been the unique feature of Japanese tradition that [the people] learned the reasons for respecting the family and parents through the government's recognition of the rights of househead and parents, and that, based on those rights, the nation maintained its peace and harmony by promoting the sense of indebtedness toward parents, friendship among siblings, love between the husband and wife, and cooperation

among the members of the family. As you said, Mr. Kanamori, the constitution of every nation reflects its unique
strengths and merits. . . . But this draft has demolished the
idea of loyalty toward the Emperor, which was a unique feature of the Imperial Constitution. That cannot be helped.
But to destroy filial piety which has been the basic moral
foundation of government—[this] requires serious thinking.
We have no objection to giving women the same rights as
men. But in this draft constitution, the existing family law
and the right of succession will be changed according to the
concept of individual rights, and therefore, unless you are
very careful, this law will invite a situation in which children
will marry, change residences, use the family wealth and divorce good wives against the wishes of their parents. I think
this constitutional draft recognizes all that. Can we [con-
tinue with] education in the family? What do the ladies
among the Representatives think about [all these changes]?
I would like to hear the opinions of the Prime Minister
(ibid., 85, cols. 2–3).

Kanamori took the floor and tried to convince the members of the
House of Representatives that radical changes in the family system were
not anticipated.

We can expect that there will be considerable changes in the
institutions of the family and succession, but, as the Prime
Minister has already explained, we do not assume that the
rights of the household or parents will immediately disappear. We will consult with various experts, draft appropriate
laws and eventually bring about a legal order that will be
most suitable for Japan. So we think that you need not worry
about such matters at this time (ibid., 87, col. 2).

Such evasions would not make the issue go away, however.

At the special committee hearing on July 5, Miura Toranosuke of the
Liberal party pressed Kanamori for further clarification:

I cannot help having considerable doubts about whether
the traditional family system can be maintained under this
draft. . . . I think this issue will be extensively debated from
the perspective of building a democratic social structure that
will be free of the feudal remnants of the Japanese family
system. . . . But I would like to ask whether we can maintain the family system, particularly the system of the househead and the right of succession. . . .

It goes without saying that the husband and wife should be
equal in marriage. Men and women are equal and have equal

rights, but I believe that they have different responsibilities (*shokubun*) [22] within a home. The woman has responsibilities as a housewife within her home, and the man has his responsibilities as a man. So I believe that in maintaining a home, each one should respect one's own role. I do not think that this would prevent equality between husband and wife. I don't know if my metaphor is appropriate, but if we compare [marriage] with a tree, the wife is the roots that hold the tree from below the ground, and the husband is the branches above ground. . . . I believe we can maintain the Japanese family system and equality of the sexes quite well along this line [of thinking]. It goes without saying that we must eliminate laws that permit only men to succeed as househead, and place women in the disadvantageous position of legal incompetency. I would like to hear Minister Kanamori's views on the family system. (Shūgi-in 1946b, 6:79, cols. 1–2)

Kanamori replied that he had no objection to the idea that men and women had different responsibilities, but he did not want to leave the impression that the existing distribution of duties and roles was appropriate. He said that Article 22 attempted to eradicate the remnants of feudal society and bring about equality between men and women and respect for individuals as human beings (ibid., cols. 2–3). But he did not identify these feudal remnants, or say what the proper distribution of roles and responsibilities might be.

The following day, when the minister of justice, Kimura Tokutarō, responded to Katō Shizue, the leading female member of the Socialist party, the tenor of the government's stand began to change. Instead of an evasive insistence that the Japanese family system would continue, its spokesman began to separate the legal issue from its social and moral aspects, admitting that the former would change under the new article. Katō actually suggested this change in her question:

At the plenary session the other day, a Representative said that this article specifies equal rights for men and women, and asked the Prime Minister whether [the new article] would not destroy the beautiful customs of the traditional Japanese family. I recall Prime Minister Yoshida saying that those customs have to be respected and maintained. Did the Prime Minister mean by beautiful customs the traditional

22. It is noteworthy that Miura uses the term *shokubun*, the same term used by the Meji intellectual leaders, Tsuda Mamichi (who used a variant, *bun*), Fukuzawa Yukichi, and Ueki Emori, in their discussions of the rights and responsibilities of the nation and the people in the late nineteenth century. See my discussion in chapter 2, pp. 56–63.

ethical virtues of the Japanese family system, such as members of the family protecting their family honor, cultivating harmony, manners, industrious habits, and the like? That was my understanding, but did he mean to say that the legal aspect of family life represented in the current Civil Code on family relations and succession as head of a household are also beautiful customs and must be preserved? I would like a clarification on this matter. (Shūgi-in 1946b, 7:101, cols. 1–2)

She then went on to express her own view of the Japanese family:

The life of a family must be where a man and woman engage in lawful and orderly sexual life, serving, at the same time, the function of maintaining and regulating the population of the race. It must also be the place where the members can rest and replenish their energy in body and heart. It must serve the function of protecting children until they mature, and fostering their moral and emotional growth. Home must be the place where all the members can live happily and freely, develop their respective unique personalities and develop maturity of character. I believe family life must be understood properly and protected amply so that it will serve those functions.

I understand Article 22 of the draft as a welcome basis for dramatically democratizing our family life. But I see that the current Civil Code . . . which has been the legal basis of the family life so far, is in extreme contradiction with the clauses in Article 22. The current family system not only does not recognize husband and wife as legally equal, but it also considers the wife legally incompetent. Furthermore, there are many legal actions of family members that require the permission of the househead. I think those violate the rights of the individual family members to grow as free individuals, and pursue happiness. I take Article 22 of the draft to be proposing the legal standard according to which the feudal family system must be changed into a new and democratic one. I would like Minister Kanamori's response (ibid., cols. 4–5).

Katō referred to some specific clauses in the Civil Code in reference to husband and wife, and asked whether the government intended to pursue further revisions in the spirit of the "beautiful customs of the traditional Japanese family system" (ibid., 102, cols. 1–3). Kimura replied that the beautiful customs were a matter of ethics and not law:

I believe that the beautiful customs are a matter of ethics and not the [legal] system. The Japanese regard home as a place where parents and siblings gather together and help each other, honor their family name and their ancestors. These are good customs that we must preserve as best as we can. But they are a matter of ethics, and not law. As far as the [legal] system is concerned, we hope to eliminate those aspects that are feudalistic, and [to] revise the Civil Code by paying close attention to Article 22 and others in the new Constitution (cols. 4–5).

Katō continued by raising a number of issues relating to women, children, and the family. She requested that the government strengthen social welfare programs to provide assistance to women and children, particularly widows and orphans created by the war, whom their relatives, themselves struggling, could not care for within the framework of the traditional family system (ibid., col. 5–108, col. 4).

On July 17, three members of the House of Representatives further debated some practical problems related to Article 22.[23] Amano Hisashi of the Progressive party inquired specifically about property rights and choice of domicile. He first asked,

About property rights, suppose the husband and wife each had property when they were married. Am I correct in understanding that when the property is to be inherited, [the combined property] is to be divided equally also?

Kimura replied,

No, [the new clause] does not mean that the property of husband and wife are to be combined to constitute joint property to be inherited. The respective properties of husband and wife are recognized as such.

Amano then asked,

As for the choice of domicile, according to this law the two sexes have equal rights. What happens when the husband and wife disagree on the choice of domicile?

Kimura answered,

According to the present Civil Code, the househead has the right to determine the domiciles of its members. So one cannot freely choose one's domicile against the will of the

23. Shūgi-in 1946b, 15:271, col. 5–275, col. 4.

househead. If one chooses it without permission, one can be reprimanded by the household. Under the new Constitution, such an act is not allowed. With regard to the husband and wife choosing to live separately, it is expected that the husband and wife, wishing to create a home, would live together. If there is marital discord, and the husband and wife live apart, we do not intend, by law, to force the wife to move in with the husband. The law is based on the premise that the husband and wife live together harmoniously.

Amano closed his interpellation with the following comment, which again gave voice to the fear that the new Constitution would undermine traditional Japanese society:

Finally, most of the Japanese people are farmers, poor farmers who have toiled in poverty, and served as the pillars of the nation. It is because of the family system that these farmers go out into the field early in the morning while the stars are still out and carry home their tired bodies in the shadow of the moon for thirty, fifty years. What they look forward to is the succession of the household, in other words, to have the household continued by their children and grandchildren. They look forward to being taken care of by their children, and the children by their children, so that the household is carried on. This is the consolation of the poor farmers in the countryside. If the new Constitution brings a breakdown of the family system, I am afraid there will be great ideological and economic confusion. I request that [the government] pay the utmost attention and take some measures to avoid such a crisis so that people will be able to continue to work for the nation without worry.

Next, a female member, Takeda Kiyo of the Liberal party, took the floor. Following the lead of Katō Shizue, Takeda Kiyo pressed for governmental protection of motherhood and the welfare of mothers and children. She first asked Kimura the meaning of marriage only by mutual consent, using a linguistically rather insignificant question about the position of the word "only" in the sentence:

In reference to the sentence, [Kekkon-wa] ryōsei-no gōi-nomi-ni motozui-te seiritsu-shi ([Marriage] has to be based only on the consent of both sexes), this expression nomi (only) is a very strong word. In the earlier government draft, the phrase read ryōsei-no gōi-ni motozui-te-nomi (only based on the mutual consent of both sexes). I wonder if the change in the position of nomi changes the meaning of the sentence? I also looked at the English version, and it seems that "only" is used casually there. I would like to ask your reason for changing the phrase to *gōi-nomi-ni motozui-te*.

KIMURA: As you know, the current Civil Code places a severe restriction on [marriage of] persons under age, requiring the consent of the household or a relative. The intent [of this clause] is to eliminate such a strict restriction and allow marriage based only on the mutual consent of both sexes.

TAKEDA: Does that mean that marriage will take effect merely by the mutual consent of a man and a woman? Don't other circumstances matter?

KIMURA: This refers to the general rule. A matter such as [marriage] registration is a separate issue. We are not so progressive as to think that marriage will take effect merely by two individuals consenting to it.

Thus, despite the plain language of the article, Kimura did not commit the government to the idea of marriage based solely on the mutual consent of the individuals concerned, as the Americans had intended. Takeda then objected that the use of the Japanese expression *nakere-ba nara-nai* in the article sounded too much like a command.

I know that a marriage must be validated by law, but it will be clearer if you add "as a rule." [The text] says "Marriage has to be maintained through mutual cooperation." I have noticed that the expression *nakere-ba nara-nai* (has to) is used in various places in other chapters as well. *Nakere-ba nara-nai* can be rephrased as *nani-nani su-beshi* (should do such and such). Marriage, however, is a matter of ethics—it is determined largely by the morality of the individuals. So there are many cases where [marriage] will not materialize, even if you command it. Of course, that is the reason why it says "through mutual cooperation," but "has to be maintained" sounds too strong, too much like a command. In the English text, it says "shall be." That is not the same as "must."

Takeda apparently did not understand the meaning of "shall" in English. Kimura eagerly embraced her incomplete understanding of the English expression:

This emphasizes the idea that it is good for the two individuals to cooperate in maintaining a marriage. I can guess what you are saying, but the government would like to keep the original wording.

Takeda pressed once again,

If it is not a strong command, then it will be better to use a phrase that will not be interpreted as a command. It will be more appropriate to say something that is more instructive, like *iji saru-beki mono-de aru* (is supposed to be maintained). What do you think?

KIMURA: I will accept your proposal as an opinion.

Thus, Takeda and Kimura agreed that the language of the article did not mean what it said.

Finally, Takeda asked Kimura whether the new clause about the equality of the sexes in marriage would guarantee equal rights to both mother and father in family matters:

You said earlier that [the government] is preparing a revision of the Civil Code in reference to the rights of the househead and the rights of the parents, so I will not request a clear statement . . . If we are to recognize the rights of the father and the mother equally, there might be situations in which the mother's opinion would conflict with the father's opinion. To take an example, when parents consider giving up a child for adoption because of poverty, the mother might think that she would want to raise the child by sacrificing her own share of food, but the father might think that he could no longer bear the burden. There often are cases when the opinions of the father and mother clash on the child's education. Until now, the father's right was absolute, so the mother followed the father, swallowing her own despair. If the father's and mother's parental rights are to be equal, whose opinion will come first? I would like to ask your opinion.

Kimura could not answer. He said,

Equality means essential equality; it does not mean superficial equality. As you know, nondiscrimination does not necessarily mean equality; there is equality in discrimination. I would like you to think about this. There are physical differences between the husband and the wife. . . . It is not possible to make everything equal. . . . We would like to think about the issues of the rights of the father and parents in the constitutional draft very carefully.

Takeda concluded her interpellation with the following remark, requesting that the government pay due respect to women as mothers:

I think it is important for the government to respect motherhood and raise [girls] to become fine mothers. . . . I request the government to respect mothers, rather than [simply] protect them, and deal with them with appropriate measures.

Finally, an exchange between Ii Seiichi, of the Socialist party, and Kimura, shows Kimura once again trying to combine the traditional values of the Japanese family with the new democratic idea of individual dignity and equality of the sexes:

> II: If [you] emphasize individual dignity and equality of the sexes strongly, I imagine [you] will not be able to recognize the househead [at the same time]. . . . I am afraid [you] will ultimately have to abolish the headship. And if [you] do, this will affect the whole system of the right of succession [as househead], and the entire system of the Japanese family. . . . When someone asked about this point, you said, Mr. Kimura, that the Special Investigative Committee on Legislation or the Committee on Judicial and Legislative Systems is studying [the issue], but your answer was not clear. . . . At any rate, I think our debate will not progress unless we hear [the government's] stand as to whether or not Article 22 will interfere with our family system, or whether it will impose a certain amount of constraint on it. I would like to hear your answer.
>
> KIMURA: The basic principles of this draft constitution are individual dignity, fundamental rights, and equality of the sexes—we intend to promote the family system according to such guidelines. As for the problem of the rights of the househead, I cannot definitely say whether or not the word *koshu-ken* (the rights of the househead) will be used. But I think there has to be a center to the household. I think that the basis of the traditional Japanese family is in family lineage and respect toward ancestors. What we are struggling with is to find ways to combine the positive aspects of the Japanese family system and individual dignity and equality of the sexes. We are studying the issues in various investigative committees. So, in this committee, too, I hope you will continue to investigate this issue along the lines of maintaining the family system.

In his reply, Kimura virtually admits that this article will create serious difficulties for the legal aspect of the traditional Japanese value system, but that the government will strive to maintain the moral values of the family system.

At the end of July, the discussion moved to the subcommittee hearings of the House of Representatives. Out of the fourteen meetings spent on the entire document, the members took the good part of two days to debate some of the serious practical effects of the new article on the Japanese family. Also, for the first time, they discussed the Japanese translation of the word "dignity," and eventually changed it from the original *ken'i* to *songen*.

The members clearly saw the problems the constitutional changes could create. At the fourth meeting on July 29, Suzuki Yoshio of the Socialist party once again expressed concern about farmers, who would be forced to divide their farmland equally among their children. He said,

> Until now the oldest son had the sole right of inheritance. From now on, the right of inheritance will be shared equally among all siblings. In the case of a farmer, however, this new idea is not necessarily practical. Therefore, in farming communities, the old law that places priority on the benefit of the family as a whole should be retained in some way. . . . It will be desirable to add some protective measures in the Constitution for the benefit of the family as a whole. It is desirable to consider measures to legally adjust the relationships of parents and children, and the male and female children, from the perspective of their interest as members of a community called "family," and not just from the point of view of the difference in sexes. (Mori 1983, p. 143)

Suzuki went on to say that this Constitution made it appear as if the essential equality of the sexes would be the foundation of the Japanese family life, and that, in his mind, the protection of the family superseded the equality of the sexes (ibid., pp. 144–45). A second member, Hara Fujirō of the Progressive party, asked Satō Tatsuo of the Cabinet Bureau of Legislation what policies the government had in mind regarding the rights of the househead and the right of succession to headship of a household. Satō replied,

> Our concern in drafting this article was [that marriage and the family] have to be based on the idea of individual dignity and equality of the sexes. However, as for the right of succession and the special position of the househead, no decisions were made whether to ignore them or not. I believe that there is room for further study (ibid., p. 145).

Hara was not satisfied. He asked Satō, "What do you mean by 'further study'? We would like to hear what you thought when you drafted this article" (ibid., pp. 145–46). Like the other government spokesmen, Satō could neither say that the Americans were imposing this article upon the Japanese, nor admit that he was fully aware of its true ramifications. His response expressed the serious dilemmas that the Japanese were facing:

> One of the important points was the individual dignity of the members of the family. If we are to recognize individual dignity (*ken'i*) of family members, we also have to recognize their rights in communal life. For instance, under the present family system, a member who wishes to leave the family is considerably constrained. So we have to readjust the present family system to eliminate a number of such restrictions. But whether or not the present family system should be totally ignored—this was a question that could not be readily resolved. Article 22 does not necessarily lead to such a consequence. It occurred to us that, although we have to recognize the family as a special communal unit, it should be left up to each person to decide whether or not to remain a family member. If the family is to be recognized as a special small community living together, then there will be a need for rules, for instance, for appointing the keeper of the family grave. [24] Then special funds will be necessary to take care of the family grave. It seemed to us that such household property would be passed on to the successors (continuing line of househeads) of the household in the same way it has been done in the past. Thus we could not determine whether or not the position of the househead and the right of succession within the present family system should be completely ignored by Article 22. I recall that the recent meeting of the special committee made no decision. Frankly, we have not made any decisions on this matter (ibid., p. 146). [25]

A third member, Kita Reikichi of the Liberal party, further elaborated on the grave impact on farming in Japan.

> As pointed out by Mr. Hara, the individual dignity expressed in this article means abolishing the family system and adopt-

24. Satō's statement is ambiguous. I have given my own interpretation based on the context of his entire statement.

25. In Japan today, most families still observe the tradition of maintaining the family grave, keeping the family altar, and holding memorial services at times designated in Buddhist tradition. However, without the househead, who had both the responsibility and the financial means to take charge of these matters, many families have serious disputes as to who should be responsible and in what way these traditional activities should be carried on. In many cases, the family expects the oldest son to take charge and he feels a moral obligation to do so, but other siblings are not willing to provide him with the financial means which will enable him to carry on the tradition adequately. In other cases, the oldest son completely disavows such responsibility and leaves the rest of the family in a quandary.

ing individualism. Individualism does not discriminate between men and women, and that is the basis of the essential
equality of the sexes. The idea that each person has dignity
as an individual derives from the essential equality of the
sexes. Laws have to be made from this point of view. That is
the principle behind Article 22, but there is a problem. . . .
One consequence of the literal interpretation of this article
that I am concerned about is related to the Agricultural Land
Act. From the viewpoint of farm reform, the right to own
farmland should be restricted as much as possible; one who
farms should be given three *chō* (one *chō* is equivalent to
2.45 acres) and absentee farmers should be given one *chō*.
Suppose there is a family with three or five children, and all
of them have the right to inherit the land specified in the
Constitution. The land reform, the purpose of which is to
create as many small landed farmers as possible, will surely
fail.[26] . . . We cannot agree on the Agricultural Land Act
until the legal application of these clauses is settled. . . . We
are not satisfied with the explanation given by the Cabinet
Bureau of Legislation because the issues related to this article
are at the core of the life of the people (ibid., p. 147).

On the following day, at the fifth subcommittee meeting, the members once again debated the practical problem of succession to headship
of a household.[27] The chairman said,

Let me add a word. If the [new] right of succession goes into
effect, and the system of equal inheritance is established,
would a farmer with only one *chō* have to divide it equally
among all his children, and would a middle-size factory
owner have to divide the factory equally among his children
also? . . . There are a lot of criticisms over the serious effect
on the farming policies of this country. We would like you to
consider [these consequences].

Kanamori replied,

Article 22 has been included as an attempt to eliminate two
so-called remnants of feudalism, namely lack of respect for
individual dignity and irrational discrimination in the treatment of men and women. We should interpret the article

26. Kita does not say how he thinks the farm reform will fail. He probably means that failure
will result from dividing farmland into uneconomically small pieces. Another problem might occur
if nonfarming siblings own the same amount of land as farming siblings. They could sell their own
shares and force a division of the land.
27. For the discussion that follows, see Mori 1983, pp. 207–14.

with that original intent in mind. As for inheritance, the clause "law has to be enacted from the standpoint of individual dignity and the essential equality of the sexes" does not negate the right of succession as househead; rather, laws have to be implemented so that they will be in line with the conditions listed [in the new Constitution]. That is the important point.

At this point, Hara Fujirō of the Progressive party asked,

Suppose there is an *ie* (household), and the person who takes care of it is the househead. But succession to the position of the househead [by this person] is possible only if he is recognized [legally] as the head. Can we assume that the rights of the househead will be recognized [under the new Constitution]?

Kanamori did his best to remain ambiguous. He replied,

If the continuation of the *ie* is recognized, then the rights of the househead should be recognized. But the current rights of the househead are incompatible in a number of ways with the idea of individual dignity . . . . If the rights of the househead are recognized, then whether or not to do so (to recognize the right of succession) needs to be determined on the basis of the new civil code, and other laws which will be established.

Hara continued,

About the right of succession, what will happen to the order of succession?
KANAMORI: [The officials] under the Minister of Justice are studying what kind of system to establish, so I can only answer abstractly. As for the foundation of the future legal system, [we] have to decide whether or not it is appropriate to recognize the *ie*. If we decide that it is appropriate to do so, then we will be faced with the problem of succession and then with that of the order of succession. On what basis should we decide? The foundation of the Constitution is the equal rights of men and women and their essential equality. But when we determine the order of succession, we will be faced with the problem of whether or not we should decide [this] from the standpoint of essential equality, or from a different standpoint recognizing a certain amount of inequality. These questions are now being studied by the Ministry of Justice, so it will not be appropriate for me to give clear answers. But in the current stage of investigation of the pro-

tection of the *ie*, work is under way to create a series of laws,
considering such factors as social circumstances in which the
difference between men and women will be secondary and
the cases in which it will be desirable to have a male succes-
sor rather than a female one.[28]
HARA: The [interpretation] of the word *ie* has been a problem, so I'd like to ask you a couple of questions. The word *ie*
refers to the home (*katei*) where members of the family (*kazoku*) live, and it consists of those who are registered as
members of the family who do not live there, as well as those
who do. What do you mean by saying that there are a lot of
problems related to the *ie*? I think "succession" (*sōzoku*) includes inheritance of property. In cases where there is no
property, there is no problem. But if there is, what will happen to its management?

Kanamori shifted his focus to acknowledge the distinction, made earlier
by the Minister of Justice, between the Meiji legal system of the household and the social customs of ancestor worship. He said that traditional social customs were important and that the new laws should
respect them:

There are many things about the *ie* that do not fit the current
situation in Japan. . . . There are a lot of problems that we
must consider. If we have the *ie*, we need a head (*koshu*).
There are various rights given to the head that [he] no longer
exercises. So we need to reexamine them. We need to reexamine the whole issue, taking into consideration such a
question. Another question is why we should recognize the
*ie*. We are studying the issue of succession [to the headship]
of the *ie*. When we think about the *ie* as an object of succession which has been maintained for generations, we have to
be aware that it involves our fundamental acceptance of [the
customs of] holding services to remember our ancestors and
maintaining lineage and pure blood. As long as such a tradition continues to exist, it is natural for us to approve of
the system [of succession to the headship of a household]. If
we maintain such a system, then it will not be enough simply
to divide the property—we need [the system of] succession
of the household and an order of succession.

As for inheritance of property, I think we need not think
about it too seriously. I do not wish to state [my position] too
clearly, but it will be good for you to decide [this issue], tak-

28. Kanamori's last statement does not make very good sense to me, but this is the best translation I can give.

ing into consideration the clause expressing the equality of
the sexes. Succession to the headship of the household involves descendants. Unless some fundamental changes occur, we will continue to have the situation where male
succession will be preferred. If a woman succeeds, [the
household] has to adopt [the person to be both her husband
and household]. Things will not move smoothly under the
current situation. We must take into consideration such matters when making laws.

But Kanamori could not ease the minds of the committee members.
The chairman said once again,

Most of the members think that the rights of the household
and the right of succession as household will all be thrown
to the winds if this article is accepted as it is. We are worried
that the rights of the household and the right of succession
will clash squarely with Article 22. We are inclined to think
that these laws are going too far, so we would like to recon-
firm [our understanding]. We understand the intent of your
replies, but I would like to ask you once again whether or
not the laws concerning the *ie* will conflict with Article 22.

Kanamori finally said,

I do not think Article 22 will immediately lead to such a
result. I hear there are people who are against recognizing
the *ie*, but I have not heard that that means termination of
lineage (their opposition means they support termination of
lineage). Aren't you talking about some superstitions? Even
if the *ie* disappears, the ancestral graves, ceremonial objects,
and the responsibility to carry on the ceremonies will remain
socially. When such social customs remain, there is no obstacle to protecting them by law. I did not realize that the
second clause of Article 22 could be viewed as placing a constraint on such a matter. . . .

To change our perspective, I think that the idea of the
essential equality of the sexes has no connection with the
idea of dividing the inherited farmland. The Constitution
does not require such a thing (in cases of inheritance of farmland). If it so happens that such is necessary to fulfill the
basic economic need of the country, I think such a provision
will be recognized.

Ashida was not convinced. He pointed out that if the new clause in the
Constitution did not apply to cases such as the inheritance of farmland,
there would be no point in having it in the Constitution. Ashida said,

I am somewhat relieved. However, looking at the second clause in Article 22, "With regard to property rights, inheritance . . . laws have to be enacted from the standpoint of individual dignity and the essential equality of the sexes," we are not sure if we can be so optimistic. If there is no problem [with inheritance of farmland], it seems to be meaningless to have rules about property rights and inheritance.

Finally, Yoshida Yasushi of the Progressive party pointedly criticized Kanamori for repeatedly giving ambiguous answers. He said,

As I see it, Minister Kanamori's replies concerning this clause are not entirely clear. For instance, I think when the Civil Code is revised, the issue of order of succession will become a point of dispute, but Minister Kanamori's opinion on this issue has been very vague. Minister Kanamori has used vague expressions such as "the rights of the household will probably be revised soon," and "when there comes a time when we will determine them by law." Frankly, Minister Kanamori, am I to understand that you think we have no alternative but to resolve these problems entirely by law?

But Kanamori refused to commit himself, saying,

I do not know how you took my explanations, but I meant to say the following. There is no intention in the Constitution itself to negate the right of succession [to the headship]. Moreover, when there is special need to establish laws that would treat men and women differently, as in the case of the right of succession, [the Constitution] does not include the right that both sexes be treated absolutely equally. That's the first part of my explanation. Whether or not we should recognize the right of succession in the future, and whether we should give priority to men—those issues will be in the laws established under the Constitution. Those require careful analysis and an appropriate measure. I cannot give any definite answer at this time.

Kanamori thus distinguished law from social custom. He tried to convince the committee members that the social customs pertaining to the Japanese family would continue, and that the Constitution did not absolutely require that the household system be abolished. Kanamori did not succeed in convincing the committee members, but this shift was probably an important element in the final Japanese acceptance of the loss of the legal rights of the household. In response to Morito Tatsuo, of the Socialist party, who said that he was worried that the new article overemphasized individuals and did not stress the importance of the family as a community, Kanamori said,

> The main purpose of creating this revision is to eliminate some extreme deficiencies in the contemporary Japanese social order. We are not thinking about changing the unique principles of cooperative life that have been respected in our society. [This Constitution] has been drafted principally to eliminate undesirable aspects.

Later, Kanamori added,

> I don't have definite opinions as to how to utilize Article 22. . . . We hope to abolish the system which gives unfairly strong power to the household that enables him to impose various restrictions on the members of the household against their will.

And the chairman said, rephrasing Kanamori's reply, "Article 22 is not intended to eliminate the unique features of Japan's traditional family system such as the right of succession to the headship and the rights of the household."

The members of the subcommittee of the House of Representatives also briefly considered the interpretation of individual dignity and its relationship to equality of the sexes. Shortly after Kita's statement about farming in the fourth meeting, the chairman, Ashida Hitoshi, abruptly changed the subject by asking the members whether or not the Japanese word *ken'i*, used to stand for "dignity," ought to be changed to *songen*. This discussion clearly shows that the Japanese did not know exactly what "individual dignity" meant, or how important it was to the Americans. To them "individual dignity" was a mere phrase that had no commonly shared meaning, or direct relevance to the issues of the Japanese family system with which they were faced. So they very briefly compared various words, and eventually settled on one of them, apparently without discussing or investigating the implications of their choice. Ashida said,

> I don't think it is included in the amendments proposed by the Liberal party, but since the English word is "[individual] dignity," it might be appropriate to change *kojin-no ken'i* to *kojin-no songen*. (Mori 1983, p. 148)

Shortly thereafter, he raised the point again:

> Should [*ken'i* of] *kojin-no ken'i* be changed to *hin'i* or *songen*? (ibid).

All three expressions, which consist of two components, are usually given in dictionaries as translations of the English word "dignity," but their meanings and usages differ in subtle but significant ways. In contemporary usage, the first expression, *ken'i*, refers more often to something like "authority," or "prestige," than "dignity." For instance, it may refer to a particular area of scholarly specialization, such as "someone is an authority on earthquakes." *Hin'i* was also an interesting suggestion. It is used infrequently in contemporary colloquial Japanese, but it usually refers to the dignified character of a person. Finally, the word *songen* means "solemn and dignified," or "noble and dignified." This expression, too, is not widely used.

Hayashi Heima of the Cooperative Democratic party said,

> I think *hin'i* is more widely used.

To this, Ashida replied,

> I think we ordinarily use *songen*, but *hin'i* would not be wrong.

Hayashi responded,

> I think *hin'i* and *songen* have nearly the same meaning. So if other people approve of *songen*, I think that will do."

Kita added the following comment, the only one that gave any reason for choosing a particular word as the proper translation:

> The word "dignity" can be translated either as *songen* or *hin'i*, but here it is appropriate to choose *songen*. I think that is more suitable because it conveys the sense that an individual should be respected whether or not the person is a second or a third son (ibid., pp. 148–49).

There is a suggestion here that individual dignity is in some way independent of social position, but Kita does not develop the idea. Nobody else gave a reason why one choice might be better than the others, and the discussion came to an end. The subcommittee approved the change from *ken'i* to *songen* without a full discussion, or a clear consensus.

The members of the subcommittee were also somewhat uncertain about the meaning of the phrase "the essential equality of the sexes," and particularly the word "essential" (*honshitsu-teki*). Some members said that men and women were, biologically, essentially different, and thus thought that the Japanese expression *honshitsu-teki* was not quite appropriate. But Hatsukade Hiroshi of the Liberal party said that if they interpreted the Buddhist notion of *byōdō* that refers to equality based

on differences, this concept would be more easily understood (ibid.,
pp. 152–53).

One other exchange provides a nice illustration of the problems the
Japanese had in linking individual dignity and equality of the sexes.
They were not certain whether individual dignity was prior to the essential equality of the sexes, or vice versa. Commenting on the phrase
"laws have to be enacted from the standpoint of individual dignity and
the essential equality of the sexes," Hayashi Heima of the Cooperative
Democratic party said,

> This sentence can be interpreted as consisting of two parts:
> in the former part, the emphasis is on men and women being
> respected regardless of their sexual identity, and in the latter,
> the emphasis is on men and women respecting each other on
> the basis of their essential equality (byōdō) (ibid., p. 149).

He seems to be saying that individual dignity means that men and
women should be equally respected because they are essentially equal.
To this, Kita Reikichi, of the Liberal party, stated that men and women
were equal in respect to individual dignity, implying that they might
not be equal in other ways. He concluded with a rather murky statement that Article 22 emphasized both familism and individualism. He
said (ibid.),

> Article 22 states that marriage has to be based only on the
> mutual consent of both sexes and has to be maintained
> through mutual cooperation based on the equal rights of hus-
> band and wife. In the second paragraph, we find a similar
> clause. It says that the feudalistic system of the househead
> has to be abolished not only in marriage, but in all other
> family relations—all members of the family, regardless of
> sex, have to be respected as individuals. There are, of course,
> differences of opinion as to whether men and women are
> essentially equal. . . . The point of these clauses is that, as
> far as individual dignity is concerned, men and women must
> be treated equally. In other words, it places special emphasis
> on both familism and individualism of this kind. I cannot
> help but interpret this clause in this way.

It is difficult to decide what Kita meant by this, and he may simply have
been confused. In an earlier comment, Kita first said that equality of
the sexes was based on individual dignity, and then in rephrasing it, he
reversed the order;

> Individual dignity expressed in this article implies abolishing
> the family system and adopting individualism. Individualism

does not discriminate between men and women, and that is
the basis of the essential equality of the sexes. The idea that
each person has dignity as an individual derives from the
essential equality of the sexes (ibid., p. 147).

The idea that individual dignity follows from equality of the sexes
would strike an American as peculiar, to say the least. In the United
States, the movement for women's rights starts from the idea of individual dignity, which means that an individual is worthy of respect because of his or her intrinsic value as a human being. It follows that
women are entitled to the same basic rights as men. Americans start
from individual dignity and arrive at egalitarian conclusions because
they think of the individual as prior to society. Furthermore, individual
dignity involves exercising one's right to make free choices as an autonomous individual. As Bellah and his co-authors noted, individual
dignity means "to think for ourselves, judge for ourselves, make our
own decisions, live our own lives as we see fit" (Bellah et al. 1985,
p. 142).

The Japanese, on the other hand, start from the implicit premise that
society is prior to the individual. They do not believe in the "right" to
think and act for themselves, apart from society. Rather, they gain their
sense of self through participantion in hierarchical social relations. In
the Japanese mind, particularly prior to 1945, self-esteem derived primarily from the sense of satisfaction in fulfilling one's social role. A
man's social role as husband-father was necessarily different from that of
a woman as wife-mother. The self-respect of each sex remained intact
as long as individuals adequately performed their respective duties and
responsibilities. As we have seen, the Japanese believe that individuals
are fundamentally equal in ability. Men and women are necessarily
equal in that fundamental sense as long as they perform their respective
duties adequately. Thus, if individual dignity is taken to mean self-
respect, Japanese style, it does not logically imply social equality,
American style; quite the opposite. The confusion or lack of clarity in
the comments of Hayashi and Kita probably stem from this very different social experience and understanding.

At the end of August, the debate moved to the House of Peers. The
Peers were also concerned about the position of the househead, and
asked the same type of questions as did the members of the House of
Representatives. The government spokesmen did not clarify their position much. But some of the Peers' questions on individual dignity and
equality of the sexes are more revealing, showing how the Japanese
interpreted these ideas in a manner meaningful to them.

At the special committee hearings on September 18 and 19, the Peers repeatedly asked the government spokesmen to clarify whether or not the rights of the househead and the right of succession would be maintained under the new Constitution. One example was Shimoyama Seiichi, who pressed Kanamori in essentially the same way that Kita of the House of Representatives had earlier, asking whether giving the househead rights to govern his household would violate the idea of individual dignity.[29] He began by saying that since the Meiji Restoration, Japanese society had been experiencing a conflict between the traditional familism and the foreign idea of individualism, and that the new article, renumbered Article 24, would have grave consequences. He said,

> The rights of the househead specified in the Civil Code are fairly large in number. The househead has the right to determine the domiciles of the members and give approval on various matters. Members of the household cannot establish a branch house without the seal of the househead, etc. . . . I would like to hear the government's position on whether or not keeping the current rights of the househead would violate individual dignity.

Kanamori responded vaguely,

> Since we have used a general expression *kojin-no songen,* it is difficult to make a definitive statement. We feel that there is no alternative but to examine each of the rights of the househead and determine, case by case, whether it violates individual dignity. We have not examined each of the rights, but we think that there are probably many that would not be harmonious with the idea of individual dignity.

Shimoyama pressed further:

> According to your explanation, you think that there are many rights of the househead that are not compatible with individual dignity. I agree with you completely. But if so, in other words, if one takes the position that the rights of househead are not compatible with individual dignity, then it will follow that the system of househead will not be compatible with individual dignity. You say that that issue is not settled, but if you conclude that the rights of the househead will not be recognized, then that will lead to accepting the abolition of the household.

29. For the discussion that follows, see Kizoku-in 1946b, 16:20, col. 5–21, col. 3.

Kanamori once again avoided agreeing with Shimoyama's suggestion that the idea of individual dignity would conflict with the rights of the househead. Instead, he said that the government was trying to find a new way of defining the family that would foster the continuation of healthy family units, even if the formal rights of househead eventually would have to be discarded:

> I have repeatedly responded on this issue. We do not have a clear statement to make at this stage. This is only my personal idea, but if we recognize the family as a legal unit, there is a question as to whether it is necessary to appoint a head. There may be a way to retain the family system in some way even if [the idea of] househead is bad. Laws can easily create the reality. So we have to be very careful so that the law will not lead the way and abolish [the rights of househead] when the people do not feel that it is necessary to go that far. Even if we abolish the rights of househead, we may be able to find ways to maintain the healthy family that has developed until now. That is the direction we are headed toward.

Thus Kanamori was forced to defend this article in the same manner he adopted in the House of Representatives.

The heated debate on the Japanese family system at the special committee of the House of Peers was more fruitful, however, because the Japanese arrived at an interpretation of the idea of individual dignity that was both meaningful to them and consistent with their own cultural tradition. On September 18, Viscount Ōkōchi Kikō asked for clarification of the expression *kojin-no songen*:

> I would like to ask Minister Kanamori about [the phrase] *kojin-no songen*. To explain concretely, . . . does it mean abolishing the right of succession of the househead and retaining only the right of inheritance? It's not clear, but does it mean that men and women, and older and younger [siblings] inherit [the property] equally? (Kizoku-in 1946b, 16:17, cols. 4–5)

Kanamori continued to give vague responses. He said that Article 24 did not clearly state whether or not the traditional family system was unacceptable. Ōkōchi pointedly asked, "What effect does 'individual dignity' have practically and legally [on the family system]?" Kanamori evaded Ōkōchi's question, although he admitted that the idea of individual dignity would affect the rights of househead. Interestingly, however, Kanamori also provided some meaning to "individual dignity" by linking the word *kojin* (individual) with *jinkaku* (character). He said,

*Kojin-no songen* means it is not good not to recognize *jinkaku* (character) in an ordinary sense without reason. . . . As for the specific rights of househead, there are quite a few that go too far and are too feudalistic. These will contradict *kojin-no songen*, so we will have to study them (ibid., 18, col. 1).

Similarly, the next day, Kimura Tokutarō, the Minister of Justice, said that the new Constitution placed a great deal of emphasis on *kojin-no jinken* and *jinkaku-no sonchō*:

As you know, this draft Constitution places a great deal of emphasis on the fundamental rights of individuals (*kojin-no jinken*). If you look at the articles in reference to the duties of the citizens—it is clear that [the Constitution] places a great deal of stress on *kojin-no jinken* and *jinkaku-no sonchō* (respect for character). Needless to say, Japanese society has made an unnecessary distinction between men and women. There were some very unreasonable rules, such as individuals being required to obtain the househead's permission to marry. This clause was prepared to express the individual dignity and equality of husband and wife, as well as men and women [in general]. But we think the significance of the family system is separate from Article 24. (Kizoku-in 1946b, 17:3, cols. 2–3)

The first expression, *kojin-no jinken* consists of *kojin-no* (individual's) and *jinken, jin* (person) and *ken* (right). So it means, "individual's right(s) as a person." *Jinkaku-no sonchō* means "respect for individual character." Later, when Matsumura Shin'ichirō asked Kimura what would happen to children's respect for their parents under the new Constitution, Kimura repeated that the basic principle behind the Constitution was *kojin-no jinkaku-no songen*, that is, respect for the character of the individual, but stated that this idea was not related to respect for parents.

MATSUMURA: This Constitution gives the impression that [the family] is made up of only the husband and wife and their children. The family will look after the children, but there is no concept of children looking up to the parents. I think this will be a natural consequence of abolishing the househead. What do you think will happen to the parents? (ibid., 4, col. 2).

Kimura replied,

I don't think it is necessary to talk about parents. As I said before, the fundamental principle of this Constitution is *kojin-no jinkaku-no songen*. This principle reflects the idea of

equality of the sexes. But this is separate from the idea of
[respect for] parents. The significance of parents is a universal matter that does not need to be specifically expressed
(ibid., cols. 2–3).

The key to understanding precisely what the two government spokesmen meant in rephrasing "individual dignity," is the word *jinkaku*. *Jinkaku* consists of *jin*, meaning "person," and *kaku*, meaning "rule, status,
rank." The literal meaning of this expression is thus "person's status/
rank." In contemporary Japanese usage, *jinkaku* is defined as "character," in the sense of ethical or moral character, and is not equivalent to
personality in the contemporary psychological sense, for which the
term *seikaku* is used. *Jinkaku* is used in expressions such as *jinkaku-sha*
(a person of high moral/ethical character), and *jinkaku-o takameru* (to
elevate or improve one's ethical/moral character).

For the Japanese, ethical character is formed by training in society's
ethical and moral values. The Japanese greatly emphasize such training,
partly because, influenced by Buddhist philosophy, they look upon life
as full of miseries and anxieties caused by conflicting desires. Rather
than attempt to eliminate these desires, the Japanese try to control
them, to put them in their proper place. Examples of activities used to
achieve this control are climbing mountains, standing under ice-cold
waterfalls, and various other strenuous and challenging physical activities.[30] They believe that such exercises strengthen one's character and
enable one to become an individual worthy of respect. Therefore, it
makes very good sense to the Japanese to respect the ethical character
of individuals in matters related to marriage and family.

There is one other noteworthy meaning associated with the word
*jinkaku*. Contemporary Japanese often use the expression *jinkaku-o kizu
tsukeru*, which literally means "to put a scar on character," in opposition to *jinkaku-o sonchō suru* (to respect character). *Jinkaku-o kizu tsukeru* means "to insult." The Japanese also consider this expression to be
very similar in meaning to *meiyo-o kizu tsukeru*, "to put a scar on
honor," or "to injure one's honor." In fact, the most comprehensive
Japanese-English dictionary, *Kenkyusha's New Japanese-English Dictionary* (4th edition, 1974, p. 1077), gives "defamation of character" as the
first translation for the phrase *meiyo kison* (honor-damage). Thus, the
term *jinkaku* is closely associated with the concept of honor in the Japa-

---

30. Kishimoto Hideo (1967, pp. 110–21) gives an excellent, concise discussion of this Japanese attitude.

nese mind. Such an interpretation is quite different from the American concept of individual dignity.[31]

By defining *kojin-no songen* (individual dignity) in terms of *jinkaku-no sonchō* (respect for ethical character), Kanamori and Kimura made the initial English phrase proposed by the Americans and its direct translation meaningful to the members of the National Diet. Since ethical character is linked to honor, and thus to proper performance of one's social role, they also made it possible for the members to reason that the values that contribute to forming ethical character would indeed be the values of the traditional family system. Although the following statement made by Socialist-party-member Ii Seiichi in the House of Representatives came early, at the special meeting on July 17, it beautifully illustrates one Japanese understanding of individual dignity:

> I think that the principle governing the entire draft of the Constitution is respect for the *jinkaku* of individuals. . . . To look at Article 22 from this point of view, the equality of the husband and wife in marriage has to come from *jinkaku sonchō* (respect for character). Marriage has to be maintained through the cooperation of husband and wife on that basis. I think, from this viewpoint, it goes without saying that one has the moral duty to maintain [marriage] by cooperation. To imagine the family in the future of our country, first, there will be a husband and wife who would respect each other's *jinkaku*, and who would maintain a family. Then, a child is born, thus creating a vertical relation of parents and child. There will be the child's respect and trust toward parents from the standpoint of respect for *jinkaku*. Likewise, there will be the parents' respect and affection toward the child. That will be the natural development. Moreover, where there are several siblings, they will respect each other's *jinkaku*. Thus I have no doubt that the principle of respect for *jinkaku* will make the Japanese families in the future the

31. In their article, "On the Obsolescence of the Concept of Honor," Peter Berger and his co-authors say that honor in an aristocratic society is linked to insult. Insult is "an assault on honor," which is more than an attack on the person insulted. It is also a threat to the values of the institutional role that he fulfills, and thus is an attack on the social order as well. As such, it is far more than a simple insult, today, because it strikes at the very roots of that person's identity—his sense of self. In America, however, an insult is more superficial, and does not pose such a threat. Berger and his co-authors point out that in American law, "insult in itself is not actionable, is not recognized as a real injury. The insulted party must be able to prove material injury. There are cases, indeed, where psychic harm may be the basis for a legal claim, but that, too, is a far cry from a notion of offense against honor" (Berger et al. 1973, p. 84).

families of truly moral democracy. . . . (Shūgi-in 1946b,
15:274, cols. 4–5)

This was the interpretation of individual dignity most compatible with
Japanese culture.

This interpretation did not emerge from an understanding of the
American concept and its relevance to Japanese society, but rather
arose spontaneously in the government spokesmen's attempt to clarify
this foreign idea to the Diet members. Since then it has become the
accepted Japanese interpretation of this important American concept.
In the preface of the booklet published by the Society for Popularization
of the Constitution (Kempō Fukyū-kai 1947), Ashida Hitoshi, its president, states that the first of the three most important principles set forth
by the new Constitution is for the Japanese people to respect each other's *jinkaku*. In his commentary on the Constitution, Miyazawa Toshiyoshi, a member of the House of Peers who assisted Matsumoto, also
says that the idea of individual dignity expressed in Articles 13 and 24
represents the fundamental principle of individualism. Then he explains that it means respecting all human beings equally as autonomous
*jinkaku* (Miyazawa 1978, pp. 197, 266). These comments indicate that
the Japanese understanding of individualism and individual dignity are
much different from that of the Americans.

## Summary

The Americans went to Japan determined to transform not only the
Japanese political system but also its feudalistic society, aiming at a
more individualistic society where individual rights and liberties would
be protected, and men and women would be equal. They expressed
their vision in Article XXIII, stating that marriage and family shall be
built on the concept of individual dignity and equality of the sexes.
Japanese officials appear not to have resisted the inclusion of this idea
in Article 24, which implicitly undermined the Japanese family system
and the rights of the household codified in the Meiji Civil Code. The
members of the National Diet, however, were keenly aware that this
article would destroy both the legal status of the household and the
right of succession to that position. In heated debates, government
spokesmen were forced to admit that these legal changes could result in
drastic changes in the normal pattern of Japanese family relations.
Kanamori and Kimura eventually argued that, although the legal system
of Japanese family would have to change, the traditional values and
social customs would persist, and that the traditional *ie* might persist as

a social institution. We do not know whether the Diet was persuaded by this view, but it was probably the best the government could do.

There was less discussion of the ideas of individual dignity and equality of the sexes. The Japanese understood that equality of the sexes in marriage would lead to abolition of the legal rights of the househead. But they did not understand the American idea of individual dignity, nor did they understand the logical link between the idea of individual dignity and equality of the sexes. The discussion in the House of Peers gave rise to the interesting idea that the term "individual" in "individual dignity" referred to the ethical character of the individual, and that "dignity" meant respect. This interpretation is much different from the usual American view that individual dignity refers to the right of autonmous individuals to think for themselves, make their own decisions, and live their own lives as they see fit. The Japanese interpretation is closer to a sense of duty or responsibility than to right. Therefore, it was quite compatible with their view of equality (*byōdō*), that is, equal ability to cope with the problems of life. It did not necessarily lead to the egalitarian relation between husband and wife that the Americans had intended. Moreover, it was fully consistent with Japanese social customs and values, and might not pose a threat to the continuation of the *ie* "household." This view, which emerged spontaneously in the responses of the government spokesmen, has become the accepted interpretation of the concept of individual dignity among the Japanese.

# CONCLUSION

One of the primary goals of the American occupation was to liberate the Japanese people from their despotic wartime government by introducing democratic reforms into Japanese society and politics. The Americans, and MacArthur in particular, believed that American democracy had universal appeal, so it is not surprising that when they drafted a constitution it reflected American constitutional principles and democratic practices. They had little knowledge of Japanese history and culture and did not speak Japanese. Consequently they were unaware of the vast cultural and linguistic gap that divided the two sides.

The Japanese participants, on the other hand, had all studied English and had some ability to use the language. Some had a great deal of competence, as well as knowledge of the legal and political traditions of the United States and other Western nations. Nevertheless, no one had a deep understanding of the principles underlying the U.S. Constitution or their pervasive influence on American thought and action. When the Japanese accepted the Potsdam Proclamation, they realized that the Meiji Constitution had to be amended, but they were shocked to learn how extensive a change they were expected to make. It was with a great deal of anguish and perturbation that government officials eventually faced up to creating a new Japanese constitution based on the American draft.

The Japanese often did not understand the democratic ideas on which the Americans insisted. Partly because they had little choice but to accept the democratic principles that the Americans insisted on, and partly because neither the Americans nor the Japanese realized how great the cultural differences were, the two sides rarely were able to correct each other's misunderstandings. In fact, the negotiations between the two sides were often conducted in the ambiguities of cross-cultural and cross-linguistic communication. In the end, the negotiators created and approved two versions of the Constitution, one in English and the other in Japanese, which were congenial to their respective cultural and political traditions. But neither side realized the differences in meaning between the two versions.

The discrepancies were of two different kinds. The most linguistically significant discrepancy between the two texts, the difference in the illocutionary force, came about entirely without debate. The English text, to a considerable extent, speaks to its audience in the same language as the U.S. Constitution: it commits the people to creating and maintaining a democratic political system, and commands the government not to infringe the rights and liberties of the people. In contrast, the Japanese text speaks to its audience in a language much like that of the Meiji Constitution. In that Constitution, the Japanese government, in the name of the Emperor, asserted its authority and responsibility to create a modern governmental system. In the new Constitution, the people and the government jointly take the responsibility for creating a democratic government, and jointly commit themselves to securing the fundamental rights and liberties of the people. The people and the government are to work together to implement and maintain the new political and social order. Thus, the Japanese version does not suggest, as the English version does, that the people are in some sense prior to the government. In fact, it reflects the reality of its origin better than the English text. This important difference in the language of the two versions of the Constitution came about when the Japanese officials carefully translated the initial English version into modern colloquial Japanese, without any intent to diverge from it. No one on either side noticed the change in the illocutionary force. I believe that this change contributed to the Japanese participants' acceptance of the democratic Constitution at that time, and to its survival during the past forty years.

The other type of difference concerns words and phrases representing some key democratic ideas of American democracy that were not well understood by the Japanese. The Japanese apparently did not appreciate the significance of religious freedom for the Americans. Freedom of conscience, separation of church and state, and prohibition of religious education in public schools are fundamental principles of American democracy, and the Americans believed that these rights and liberties had to be secured for the Japanese people. They did not realize that, because the Japanese religious tradition is so vastly different from their own Christian tradition, the Japanese might not understand the point behind guaranteeing such freedoms in the Constitution. The one issue that was important to the Japanese was the constitutional prohibition against state-sponsored religious education. They believed that the lives of religious leaders of the world could be used as examples to teach and strengthen the moral and ethical character of the young, so that they would become caring members of their community. Hence they sought to assure themselves that such educational material was not constitutionally proscribed. Although the distinction between religious education and education about religions does not fit well with the Japanese religious tradition, the Japanese participants convinced themselves that "religious education" did not mean "education about religions," and that the latter might be encouraged by the government to combat the postwar moral decay. Had the Americans understood what education about religions entailed, they might not have been so happy with the distinction that the Japanese had made.

The debate on the idea of individual dignity and the essential equality of the sexes in marriage in Article 24 revealed another type of misunderstanding. The Japanese did not understand American individualism, but they could not avoid talking about individual dignity and equality of the sexes. Eventually, they interpreted the expression "individual dignity" in a way congenial to their own traditional values of honor. The American concept of individual dignity refers to a person's value as a human being, apart from any social relations, and incorporates the right of a person to think and act for himself—to lead one's life as one sees fit. The Japanese interpreted it as respect for moral and ethical character. The Japanese derive their sense of self-worth largely from social relations and the part they play in society; they do not believe, as Americans do, that individuals exist apart from, and prior to their society. Thus, they understood individual dignity to mean their responsibility to respect each other as social beings, whatever roles individuals might play. This idea was consistent with their idea of equality—that all people are essentially equal in ability to cope with life. This sense of equality did not necessarily imply social equality. Rather, it meant that each person had the ability to fulfill the duties and responsibilities of his or her social position. These ideas were quite compatible with social inequality. The Japanese thus interpreted the expression "equality of the sexes" to mean men and women were essentially equal in their ability to fulfill their respective roles in the family. This, of course, was much different from what the Americans had intended—that women have, or should have, equal rights.

The negotiations between the Americans and the Japanese were not always conducted in a context of misunderstanding. The Japanese were acutely aware that the democratic principles that the Americans were imposing on them would have some serious consequences for their political and social life. Article 24 posed the most serious threat to the fabric of traditional Japanese society. By eliminating the legal rights and responsibilities of the househead, particularly the right of succession, it had the effect of abolishing the household system. The Japanese realized that the legal consequences of this change would be profound. All that the government could do was express the hope that, although the househead would be stripped of his legal rights, the customs of caring for the family ancestors would somehow be continued. The government's attempt to separate the legal effects from the social customs of the household was not very successful in convincing the Diet members that the Japanese family would remain the same in the years to come, but it was probably the only approach they could take. The Americans, of course, wanted to change the structure of the family, but they probably did not appreciate how significant the changes might be.

Finally, the Japanese were most fearful about the change in the status of the Emperor. The Japanese did understand that the status of the Emperor had to change, but there were still misunderstandings between the Americans and the Japanese. The Americans believed that the Emperor had considerably greater political power than he actually did. They thus insisted that the Constitution include clauses stating that his powers would be checked by the "advice and consent" of the Cabinet, and that sovereignty resided in the people. The Japanese knew that the Emperor had virtually no substantive political power, so they did not see the need for a clause explicitly stating that the Emperor could not act without the consent of the Cabinet. But the Emperor did have a great deal of formal authority as the symbolic head of state, and the father of the national family. For the Japanese, it was extremely important to have the appearance of sovereignty with the Emperor, and they did not want to suddenly reduce the status of the Emperor to being the mere symbol of the nation. The Americans, however, insisted that the Japanese include the explicit statement "*sovereignty* resides in the people." The Japanese government's chief spokesman resisted adopting the comparable Japanese term as best he could, but the Japanese finally had to yield to the Americans. The government, however, insisted to the end that the Emperor was a member of the *people* of Japan, and therefore retained some vestiges of sovereignty. Some Diet members did not hesitate to point out the obvious weakness in the government's argument. But the Americans did not pay much attention to this debate, largely because that was a debate over the semantics of a Japanese word. In the end, the 90th Imperial Diet passed the new Constitution with an overwhelming majority vote in its favor, and MacArthur approved it.

In retrospect, the acceptance of the new Japanese Constitution by both the Americans and the Japanese depended heavily on the ambiguities of cross-linguistic and cross-cultural communication between both parties. Had the Japanese really understood the democratic ideas that the Americans had intended, it would have been far more difficult and painful for them to accept them. Likewise, had MacArthur and his staff understood precisely how the Japanese were interpreting American democratic principles, they might have been more reluctant to approve the final version of the Constitution. The cultural and linguistic barriers in communication between the Americans and the Japanese were without doubt a hindrance to mutual understanding. But, ironically, the same difficulties made it possible for the two sides to agree on a document without agreeing on its fundamental meaning.

*Appendix One*

# THE CONSTITUTION OF JAPAN

## (*Nihonkoku Kempō*)

Source: The English version was prepared by the Ministry of Justice, Tokyo, 1958; it is taken from Itoh and Beer (1978).

　日本国民は、正当に選挙された国会における代表者を通じて行動し、われらとわれらの子孫のために、諸国民との協和による成果と、わが国全土にわたつて自由のもたらす恵沢を確保し、政府の行為によつて再び戦争の惨禍が起ることのないやうにすることを決意し、ここに主権が国民に存することを宣言し、この憲法を確定する。そもそも国政は、国民の厳粛な信託によるものであつて、その権威は国民に由来し、その権力は国民の代表者がこれを行使し、その福利は国民がこれを享受する。これは人類普遍の原理であり、この憲法は、かかる原理に基くものである。われらは、これに反する一切の憲法、法令及び詔勅を排除する。

　日本国民は、恒久の平和を念願し、人間相互の関係を支配する崇高な理想を深く自覚するのであつて、平和を愛する諸国民の公正と信義に信頼して、われらの安全と生存を保持しようと決意した。われらは、平和を維持し、専制と隷従、圧迫と偏狭を地上から永遠に除去しようと努めてゐる国際社会において、名誉ある地位を占めたいと思ふ。われらは、全世界の国民が、ひとしく恐怖と欠乏から免かれ、平和のうちに生存する権利を有することを確認する。

　われらは、いづれの国家も、自国のことのみに専念して他国を無視してはならないのであつて、政治道徳の法則は、普遍的なものであり、この法則に従ふことは、自国の主権を維持し、他国と対等関係に立たうとする各国の責務であると信ずる。

　日本国民は、国家の名誉にかけ、全力をあげてこの崇高な理想と目的を達成することを誓ふ。

## 第1章　天　　皇

第1条　天皇は、日本国の象徴であり日本国民統合の象徴であつて、この地位は、主権の存する日本国民の総意に基く。

第2条　皇位は、世襲のものであつて、国会の議決した皇室典範の定めるところにより、これを継承する。

第3条　天皇の国事に関するすべての行為には、内閣の助言と承認を必要とし、内閣が、その責任を負ふ。

第4条　天皇は、この憲法の定める国事に関する行為のみを行ひ、国政に関する権能を有しない。

We, the Japanese people, acting through our duly elected representatives in the National Diet, determined that we shall secure for ourselves and our posterity the fruits of peaceful cooperation with all nations and the blessings of liberty throughout this land, and resolved that never again shall we be visited with the horrors of war through the action of government, do proclaim that sovereign power resides with the people and do firmly establish this Constitution. Government is a sacred trust of the people, the authority for which is derived from the people, the powers of which are exercised by the representatives of the people, and the benefits of which are enjoyed by the people. This is a universal principle of mankind upon which this Constitution is founded. We reject and revoke all constitutions, laws, ordinances, and rescripts in conflict herewith.

We, the Japanese people, desire peace for all time and are deeply conscious of the high ideals controlling human relationship, and we have determined to preserve our security and existence, trusting in the justice and faith of the peace-loving peoples of the world. We desire to occupy an honored place in an international society striving for the preservation of peace, and the banishment of tyranny and slavery, oppression and intolerance for all time from the earth. We recognize that all peoples of the world have the right to live in peace, free from fear and want.

We believe that no nation is responsible to itself alone, but that laws of political morality are universal; and that obedience to such laws is incumbent upon all nations who would sustain their own sovereignty and justify their sovereign relationship with other nations.

We, the Japanese people, pledge our national honor to accomplish these high ideals and purposes with all our resources.

## Chapter I. *The Emperor*

Article 1. The Emperor shall be the symbol of the State and of the unity of the people, deriving his position from the will of the people with whom resides sovereign power.

Article 2. The Imperial Throne shall be dynastic and succeeded to in accordance with the Imperial House Law passed by the Diet.

Article 3. The advice and approval of the Cabinet shall be required for all acts of the Emperor in matters of state, and the Cabinet shall be responsible therefor.

Article 4. The Emperor shall perform only such acts in matters of state as are provided for in this Constitution and he shall not have powers related to government.

　　天皇は、法律の定めるところにより、その国事に関する行為を委任することができる。

第5条　皇室典範の定めるところにより摂政を置くときは、摂政は、天皇の名でその国事に関する行為を行ふ。この場合には、前条第1項の規定を準用する。

第6条　天皇は、国会の指名に基いて、内閣総理大臣を任命する。

　　天皇は、内閣の指名に基いて、最高裁判所の長たる裁判官を任命する。

第7条　天皇は、内閣の助言と承認により、国民のために、左の国事に関する行為を行ふ。

　　1　憲法改正、法律、政令及び条約を公布すること。

　　2　国会を召集すること。

　　3　衆議院を解散すること。

　　4　国会議員の総選挙の施行を公示すること。

　　5　国務大臣及び法律の定めるその他の官吏の任免並びに全権委任状及び大使及び公使の信任状を認証すること。

　　6　大赦、特赦、減刑、刑の執行の免除及び復権を認証すること。

　　7　栄典を授与すること。

　　8　批准書及び法律の定めるその他の外交文書を認証すること。

　　9　外国の大使及び公使を接受すること。

　　10　儀式を行ふこと。

第8条　皇室に財産を譲り渡し、又は皇室が、財産を譲り受け、若しくは賜与することは、国会の議決に基かなければならない。

## 第2章　戦争の放棄

第9条　日本国民は、正義と秩序を基調とする国際平和を誠実に希求し、国権の発動たる戦争と、武力による威嚇又は武力の行使は、国際紛争を解決する手段としては、永久にこれを放棄する。

　　前項の目的を達するため、陸海空軍その他の戦力は、これを保持しない。国の交戦権は、これを認めない。

2. The Emperor may delegate the performance of his acts in matters of state as may be provided by law.

ARTICLE 5. When, in accordance with the Imperial House Law, a Regency is established, the Regent shall perform his acts in matters of state in the Emperor's name. In this case, paragraph one of the preceding article will be applicable.

ARTICLE 6. The Emperor shall appoint the Prime Minister as designated by the Diet.

2. The Emperor shall appoint the Chief Judge of the Supreme Court as designated by the Cabinet.

ARTICLE 7. The Emperor, with the advice and approval of the Cabinet, shall perform the following acts in matters of state on behalf of the people:

(1) Promulgation of amendments of the constitution, laws, cabinet orders and treaties;

(2) Convocation of the Diet;

(3) Dissolution of the House of Representatives;

(4) Proclamation of general election of members of the Diet;

(5) Attestation of the appointment and dismissal of Ministers of State and other officials as provided for by law, and of full powers and credentials of Ambassadors and Ministers;

(6) Attestation of general and special amnesty, commutation of punishment, reprieve, and restoration of rights;

(7) Awarding of honors;

(8) Attestation of instruments of ratification and other diplomatic documents as provided for by law;

(9) Receiving foreign ambassadors and ministers;

(10) Performance of ceremonial functions.

ARTICLE 8. No property can be given to, or received by, the Imperial House, nor can any gifts be made therefrom, without the authorization of the Diet.

## CHAPTER II. *Renunciation of War*

ARTICLE 9. Aspiring sincerely to an international peace based on justice and order, the Japanese people forever renounce war as a sovereign right of the nation and the threat or use of force as means of settling international disputes.

2. In order to accomplish the aim of the preceding paragraph, land, sea, and air forces, as well as other war potential, will never be maintained. The right of belligerency of the state will not be recognized.

## 第3章　国民の権利及び義務

第10条　日本国民たる要件は、法律でこれを定める。

第11条　国民は、すべての基本的人権の享有を妨げられない。この憲法が国民に保障する基本的人権は、侵すことのできない永久の権利として、現在及び将来の国民に与へられる。

第12条　この憲法が国民に保障する自由及び権利は、国民の不断の努力によつて、これを保持しなければならない。又、国民はこれを濫用してはならないのであつて、常に公共の福祉のためにこれを利用する責任を負ふ。

第13条　すべて国民は、個人として尊重される。生命、自由及び幸福追求に対する国民の権利については、公共の福祉に反しない限り、立法その他の国政の上で、最大の尊重を必要とする。

第14条　すべて国民は、法の下に平等であつて、人種、信条、性別、社会的身分又は門地により、政治的、経済的又は社会的関係において、差別されない。

　　華族その他の貴族の制度は、これを認めない。

　　栄誉、勲章その他の栄典の授与は、いかなる特権も伴はない。栄典の授与は、現にこれを有し、又は将来これを受ける者の一代に限り、その効力を有する。

第15条　公務員を選定し、及びこれを罷免することは、国民固有の権利である。

　　すべて公務員は、全体の奉仕者であつて、一部の奉仕者ではない。

　　公務員の選挙については、成年者による普通選挙を保障する。

　　すべて選挙における投票の秘密は、これを侵してはならない。選挙人は、その選択に関し公的にも私的にも責任を問はれない。

第16条　何人も、損害の救済、公務員の罷免、法律、命令又は規則の制定、廃止又は改正その他の事項に関し、平穏に請願する権利を有し、何人も、かかる請願をしたためにいかなる差別待遇も受けない。

第17条　何人も、公務員の不法行為により、損害を受けたときは、法律の定めるところにより、国又は公共団体に、その賠償を求めることができる。

第18条　何人も、いかなる奴隷的拘束も受けない。又、犯罪に因る処罰の場合を除いては、その意に反する苦役に服させられない。

## CHAPTER III. *Rights and Duties of the People*

ARTICLE 10. The conditions necessary for being a Japanese national shall be determined by law.

ARTICLE 11. The people shall not be prevented from enjoying any of the fundamental human rights. These fundamental human rights guaranteed to the people by this Constitution shall be conferred upon the people of this and future generations as eternal and inviolate rights.

ARTICLE 12. The freedoms and rights guaranteed to the people by this Constitution shall be maintained by the constant endeavor of the people, who shall refrain from any abuse of these freedoms and rights and shall always be responsible for utilizing them for the public welfare.

ARTICLE 13. All of the people shall be respected as individuals. Their right to life, liberty, and the pursuit of happiness shall, to the extent that it does not interfere with the public welfare, be the supreme consideration in legislation and in other governmental affairs.

ARTICLE 14. All of the people are equal under the law and there shall be no discrimination in political, economic or social relations because of race, creed, sex, social status or family origin.

2. Peers and peerage shall not be recognized.

3. No privilege shall accompany any award of honor, decoration or any distinction, nor shall any such award be valid beyond the lifetime of the individual who now holds or hereafter may receive it.

ARTICLE 15. The people have the inalienable right to choose their public officials and to dismiss them.

2. All public officials are servants of the whole community and not of any group thereof.

3. Universal adult suffrage is guaranteed with regard to the election of public officials.

4. In all elections, secrecy of the ballot shall not be violated. A voter shall not be answerable, publicly or privately, for the choice he has made.

ARTICLE 16. Every person shall have the right of peaceful petition for the redress of damage, for the removal of public officials, for the enactment, repeal or amendment of laws, ordinances or regulations and for other matters, nor shall any person be in any way discriminated against for sponsoring such a petition.

ARTICLE 17. Every person may sue for redress as provided by law from the State or a public entity, in case he has suffered damage through illegal act of any public official.

ARTICLE 18. No person shall be held in bondage of any kind. Involuntary servitude, except as punishment for crime, is prohibited.

第19条　思想及び良心の自由は、これを侵してはならない。

第20条　信教の自由は、何人に対してもこれを保障する。いかなる宗教団体も、国から特権を受け、又は政治上の権力を行使してはならない。

　　何人も、宗教上の行為、祝典、儀式又は行事に参加することを強制されない。

　　国及びその機関は、宗教教育その他いかなる宗教的活動もしてはならない。

第21条　集会、結社及び言論、出版その他一切の表現の自由は、これを保障する。

　　検閲は、これをしてはならない。通信の秘密は、これを侵してはならない。

第22条　何人も、公共の福祉に反しない限り、居住、移転及び職業選択の自由を有する。

　　何人も、外国に移住し、又は国籍を離脱する自由を侵されない。

第23条　学問の自由は、これを保障する。

第24条　婚姻は、両性の合意のみに基いて成立し、夫婦が同等の権利を有することを基本として、相互の協力により、維持されなければならない。

　　配偶者の選択、財産権、相続、住居の選定、離婚並びに婚姻及び家族に関するその他の事項に関しては、法律は、個人の尊厳と両性の本質的平等に立脚して、制定されなければならない。

第25条　すべて国民は、健康で文化的な最低限度の生活を営む権利を有する。

　　国は、すべての生活部面について、社会福祉、社会保障及び公衆衛生の向上及び増進に努めなければならない。

第26条　すべて国民は、法律の定めるところにより、その能力に応じて、ひとしく教育を受ける権利を有する。

　　すべて国民は、法律の定めるところにより、その保護する子女に普通教育を受けさせる義務を負ふ。義務教育は、これを無償とする。

第27条　すべて国民は、勤労の権利を有し、義務を負ふ。

　　賃金、就業時間、休息その他の勤労条件に関する基準は、法律でこれを定める。

　　児童は、これを酷使してはならない。

ARTICLE 19. Freedom of thought and conscience shall not be violated.

ARTICLE 20. Freedom of religion is guaranteed to all. No religious organization shall receive any privileges from the State nor exercise any political authority.

2. No person shall be compelled to take part in any religious act, celebration, rite or practice.

3. The State and its organs shall refrain from religious education or any other religious activity.

ARTICLE 21. Freedom of assembly and association as well as speech, press and all other forms of expression are guaranteed.

2. No censorship shall be maintained, nor shall the secrecy of any means of communication be violated.

ARTICLE 22. Every person shall have freedom to choose and change his residence and to choose his occupation to the extent that it does not interfere with the public welfare.

2. Freedom of all persons to move to a foreign country and to divest themselves of their nationality shall be inviolate.

ARTICLE 23. Academic freedom is guaranteed.

ARTICLE 24. Marriage shall be based only on the mutual consent of both sexes and it shall be maintained through mutual cooperation with the equal rights of husband and wife as a basis.

2. With regard to choice of spouse, property rights, inheritance, choice of domicile, divorce and other matters pertaining to marriage and the family, laws shall be enacted from the standpoint of individual dignity and the essential equality of the sexes.

ARTICLE 25. All people shall have the right to maintain the minimum standards of wholesome and cultured living.

2. In all spheres of life, the State shall use its endeavors for the promotion and extension of social welfare and security, and of public health.

ARTICLE 26. All people shall have the right to receive an equal education correspondent to their ability, as provided by law.

2. All people shall be obligated to have all boys and girls under their protection receive ordinary education as provided for by law. Such compulsory education shall be free.

ARTICLE 27. All people shall have the right and the obligation to work.

2. Standards for wages, hours, rest and other working conditions shall be fixed by law.

3. Children shall not be exploited.

第28条　勤労者の団結する権利及び団体交渉その他の団体行動をする権利は、これを保障する。

第29条　財産権は、これを侵してはならない。

　財産権の内容は、公共の福祉に適合するやうに、法律でこれを定める。

　私有財産は、正当な補償の下に、これを公共のために用ひることができる。

第30条　国民は、法律の定めるところにより、納税の義務を負ふ。

第31条　何人も、法律の定める手続によらなければ、その生命若しくは自由を奪はれ、又はその他の刑罰を科せられない。

第32条　何人も、裁判所において裁判を受ける権利を奪はれない。

第33条　何人も、現行犯として逮捕される場合を除いては、権限を有する司法官憲が発し、且つ理由となつてゐる犯罪を明示する令状によらなければ、逮捕されない。

第34条　何人も、理由を直ちに告げられ、且つ、直ちに弁護人に依頼する権利を与へられなければ、抑留又は拘禁されない。又、何人も、正当な理由がなければ、拘禁されず、要求があれば、その理由は、直ちに本人及びその弁護人の出席する公開の法廷で示されなければならない。

第35条　何人も、その住居、書類及び所持品について、侵入、捜索及び押収を受けることのない権利は、第33条の場合を除いては、正当な理由に基いて発せられ、且つ捜索する場所及び押収する物を明示する令状がなければ、侵されない。

　捜索又は押収は、権限を有する司法官憲が発する各別の令状により、これを行ふ。

第36条　公務員による拷問及び残虐な刑罰は、絶対にこれを禁ずる。

第37条　すべて刑事事件においては、被告人は、公平な裁判所の迅速な公開裁判を受ける権利を有する。

　刑事被告人は、すべての証人に対して審問する機会を充分に与へられ、又、公費で自己のために強制的手続により証人を求める権利を有する。

　刑事被告人は、いかなる場合にも、資格を有する弁護人を依頼することができる。被告人が自らこれを依頼することができないときは、国でこれを附する。

第38条　何人も、自己に不利益な供述を強要されない。

ARTICLE 28. The right of workers to organize and to bargain and act collectively is guaranteed.

ARTICLE 29. The right to own or to hold property is inviolable.

2. Property rights shall be defined by law, in conformity with the public welfare.

3. Private property may be taken for public use upon just compensation therefor.

ARTICLE 30. The people shall be liable to taxation as provided by law.

ARTICLE 31. No person shall be deprived of life or liberty, nor shall any other criminal penalty be imposed, except according to procedure established by law.

ARTICLE 32. No person shall be denied the right of access to the courts.

ARTICLE 33. No person shall be apprehended except upon warrant issued by a competent judicial officer which specifies the offense with which the person is charged, unless he is apprehended, the offense being committed.

ARTICLE 34. No person shall be arrested or detained without being at once informed of the charges against him or without the immediate privilege of counsel; nor shall he be detained without adequate cause; and upon demand of any person such cause must be immediately shown in open court in his presence and the presence of his counsel.

ARTICLE 35. The right of all persons to be secure in their homes, papers and effects against entries, searches and seizures shall not be impaired except upon warrant issued for adequate cause and particularly describing the place to be searched and things to be seized, or except as provided by Article 33.

2. Each search or seizure shall be made upon separate warrant issued by a competent judicial officer.

ARTICLE 36. The infliction of torture by any public officer and cruel punishments are absolutely forbidden.

ARTICLE 37. In all criminal cases the accused shall enjoy the right to a speedy and public trial by an impartial tribunal.

2. He shall be permitted full opportunity to examine all witnesses, and he shall have the right of compulsory process for obtaining witnesses on his behalf at public expense.

3. At all times the accused shall have the assistance of competent counsel who shall, if the accused is unable to secure the same by his own efforts, be assigned to his use by the State.

ARTICLE 38. No person shall be compelled to testify against himself.

　強制、拷問若しくは脅迫による自白又は不当に長く抑留若しくは拘禁された後の自白は、これを証拠とすることができない。

　何人も、自己に不利益な唯一の証拠が本人の自白である場合には、有罪とされ、又は刑罰を科せられない。

第39条　何人も、実行の時に適法であつた行為又は既に無罪とされた行為については、刑事上の責任を問はれない。又、同一の犯罪について、重ねて刑事上の責任を問はれない。

第40条　何人も、抑留又は拘禁された後、無罪の裁判を受けたときは、法律の定めるところにより、国にその補償を求めることができる。

## 第4章　国　　会

第41条　国会は、国権の最高機関であつて、国の唯一の立法機関である。

第42条　国会は、衆議院及び参議院の両議院でこれを構成する。

第43条　両議院は、全国民を代表する選挙された議員でこれを組織する。

　両議院の議員の定数は、法律でこれを定める。

第44条　両議員の議員及びその選挙人の資格は、法律でこれを定める。但し、人種、信条、性別、社会的身分、門地、教育、財産又は収入によつて差別してはならない。

第45条　衆議院議員の任期は、4年とする。但し、衆議院解散の場合には、その期間満了前に終了する。

第46条　参議院議員の任期は、6年とし、3年ごとに議員の半数を改選する。

第47条　選挙区、投票の方法その他両議院の議員の選挙に関する事項は、法律でこれを定める。

第48条　何人も、同時に両議院の議員たることはできない。

第49条　両議院の議員は、法律の定めるところにより、国庫から相当額の歳費を受ける。

第50条　両議院の議員は、法律の定める場合を除いては、国会の会期中逮捕されず、会期前に逮捕された議員は、その議院の要求があれば、会期中これを釈放しなければならない。

第51条　両議院の議員は、議院で行つた演説、討論又は表決について、院外で責任を問はれない。

2. Confession made under compulsion, torture or threat, or after prolonged arrest or detention shall not be admitted in evidence.

3. No person shall be convicted or punished in cases where the only proof against him is his own confession.

ARTICLE 39. No person shall be held criminally liable for an act which was lawful at the time it was committed, or of which he has been acquitted, nor shall he be placed in double jeopardy.

ARTICLE 40. Any person, in case he is acquitted after he has been arrested or detained, may sue the State for redress as provided by law.

## CHAPTER IV. *The Diet*

ARTICLE 41. The Diet shall be the highest organ of state power, and shall be the sole law-making organ of the State.

ARTICLE 42. The Diet shall consist of two Houses, namely the House of Representatives and the House of Councillors.

ARTICLE 43. Both Houses shall consist of elected members, representative of all the people.

2. The number of the members of each House shall be fixed by law.

ARTICLE 44. The qualifications of members of both Houses and their electors shall be fixed by law. However, there shall be no discrimination because of race, creed, sex, social status, family origin, education, property or income.

ARTICLE 45. The term of office of members of the House of Representatives shall be four years. However, the term shall be terminated before the full term is up in case the House of Representatives is dissolved.

ARTICLE 46. The term of office of members of the House of Councillors shall be six years, and election for half the members shall take place every three years.

ARTICLE 47. Electoral districts, method of voting and other matters pertaining to the method of election of members of both Houses shall be fixed by law.

ARTICLE 48. No person shall be permitted to be a member of both Houses simultaneously.

ARTICLE 49. Members of both Houses shall receive appropriate annual payment from the national treasury in accordance with law.

ARTICLE 50. Except in cases provided by law, members of both Houses shall be exempt from apprehension while the Diet is in session, and any members apprehended before the opening of the session shall be freed during the term of the session upon demand of the House.

ARTICLE 51. Members of both Houses shall not be held liable outside the House for speeches, debates or votes cast inside the House.

第52条　国会の常会は、毎年１回これを召集する。

第53条　内閣は、国会の臨時会の召集を決定することができる。いづれかの議院の総議員の４分の１以上の要求があれば、内閣は、その召集を決定しなければならない。

第54条　衆議院が解散されたときは、解散の日から40日以内に、衆議院議員の総選挙を行ひ、その選挙の日から30日以内に、国会を召集しなければならない。

　衆議院が解散されたときは、参議院は、同時に閉会となる。但し、内閣は、国に緊急の必要があるときは、参議院の緊急集会を求めることができる。

　前項但書の緊急集会において採られた措置は、臨時のものであつて、次の国会開会の後10日以内に、衆議院の同意がない場合には、その効力を失ふ。

第55条　両議院は、各々その議員の資格に関する争訟を裁判する。但し、議員の議席を失はせるには、出席議員の３分の２以上の多数による議決を必要とする。

第56条　両議院は、各々その総議員の３分の１以上の出席がなければ、議事を開き議決することができない。

　両議院の議事は、この憲法に特別の定のある場合を除いては、出席議員の過半数でこれを決し、可否同数のときは、議長の決するところによる。

第57条　両議院の会議は、公開とする。但し、出席議員の３分の２以上の多数で議決したときは、秘密会を開くことができる。

　両議院は、各々その会議の記録を保存し、秘密会の記録の中で特に秘密を要すると認められるもの以外は、これを公表し、且つ一般に頒布しなければならない。

　出席議員の５分の１以上の要求があれば、各議員の表決は、これを会議録に記載しなければならない。

第58条　両議院は、各々その議長その他の役員を選任する。

　両議院は、各々その会議その他の手続及び内部の規律に関する規則を定め、又、院内の秩序をみだした議員を懲罰することができる。但し、議員を除名するには、出席議員の３分の２以上の多数による議決を必要とする。

THE CONSTITUTION OF JAPAN

ARTICLE 52. An ordinary session of the Diet shall be convoked once per year.

ARTICLE 53. The Cabinet may determine to convoke extraordinary sessions of the Diet. When a quarter or more of the total members of either House makes the demand, the Cabinet must determine on such convocation.

ARTICLE 54. When the House of Representatives is dissolved, there must be a general election of members of the House of Representatives within forty (40) days from the date of dissolution, and the Diet must be convoked within thirty (30) days from the date of the election.

2. When the House of Representatives is dissolved, the House of Councillors is closed at the same time. However, the Cabinet may in time of national emergency convoke the House of Councillors in emergency session.

3. Measures taken at such session as mentioned in the proviso of the preceding paragraph shall be provisional and shall become null and void unless agreed to by the House of Representatives within a period of ten (10) days after the opening of the next session of the Diet.

ARTICLE 55. Each House shall judge disputes related to qualifications of its members. However, in order to deny a seat to any member, it is necessary to pass a resolution by a majority of two-thirds or more of the members present.

ARTICLE 56. Business cannot be transacted in either House unless one-third or more of total membership is present.

2. All matters shall be decided, in each House, by a majority of those present, except as elsewhere provided in the Constitution, and in case of a tie, the presiding officer shall decide the issue.

ARTICLE 57. Deliberation in each House shall be public. However, a secret meeting may be held where a majority of two-thirds or more of those members present passes a resolution therefor.

2. Each House shall keep a record of proceedings. This record shall be published and given general circulation, excepting such parts of proceedings of secret session as may be deemed to require secrecy.

3. Upon demand of one-fifth or more of the members present, votes of the members on any matter shall be recorded in the minutes.

ARTICLE 58. Each House shall select its own president and other officials.

2. Each House shall establish its rules pertaining to meetings, proceedings and internal discipline, and may punish members for disorderly conduct. However, in order to expel a member, a majority of two-thirds or more of those members present must pass a resolution thereon.

第59条　法律案は、この憲法に特別の定のある場合を除いては、両議院で可決したとき法律となる。

　　衆議院で可決し、参議院でこれと異なつた議決をした法律案は、衆議院で出席議員の3分の2以上の多数で再び可決したときは、法律となる。

　　前項の規定は、法律の定めるところにより、衆議院が、両議院の協議会を開くことを求めることを妨げない。

　　参議院が、衆議院の可決した法律案を受け取つた後、国会休会中の期間を除いて60日以内に、議決しないときは、衆議院は、参議院がその法律案を否決したものとみなすことができる。

第60条　予算は、さきに衆議院に提出しなければならない。

　　予算について、参議院で衆議院と異なつた議決をした場合に、法律の定めるところにより、両議院の協議会を開いても意見が一致しないとき、又は参議院が、衆議院の可決した予算を受け取つた後、国会休会中の期間を除いて30日以内に、議決しないときは、衆議院の議決を国会の議決とする。

第61条　条約の締結に必要な国会の承認については、前条第2項の規定を準用する。

第62条　両議院は、各々国政に関する調査を行ひ、これに関して、証人の出頭及び証言並びに記録の提出を要求することができる。

第63条　内閣総理大臣その他の国務大臣は、両議院の一に議席を有すると有しないとにかかはらず、何時でも議案について発言するため議院に出席することができる。又、答弁又は説明のため出席を求められたときは、出席しなければならない。

第64条　国会は、罷免の訴追を受けた裁判官を裁判するため、両議院の議員で組織する弾劾裁判所を設ける。

　　弾劾に関する事項は、法律でこれを定める。

ARTICLE 59. A bill becomes a law on passage by both Houses, except as otherwise provided by the Constitution.

2. A bill which is passed by the House of Representatives, and upon which the House of Councillors makes a decision different from that of the House of Representatives, becomes a law when passed a second time by the House of Representatives by a majority of two-thirds or more of the members present.

3. The provision of the preceding paragraph does not preclude the House of Representatives from calling for the meeting of a joint committee of both Houses, provided for by law.

4. Failure by the House of Councillors to take final action within sixty (60) days after receipt of a bill passed by the House of Representatives, time in recess excepted, may be determined by the House of Representatives to constitute a rejection of the said bill by the House of Councillors.

ARTICLE 60. The budget must first be submitted to the House of Representatives.

2. Upon consideration of the budget, when the House of Councillors makes a decision different from that of the House of Representatives, and when no agreement can be reached even through a joint committee of both Houses, provided for by law, or in the case of failure by the House of Councillors to take final action within thirty (30) days, the period of recess excluded, after the receipt of the budget passed by the House of Representatives, the decision of the House of Representatives shall be the decision of the Diet.

ARTICLE 61. The second paragraph of the preceding article applies also to the Diet approval required for the conclusion of treaties.

ARTICLE 62. Each House may conduct investigations in relation to government, and may demand the presence and testimony of witnesses, and the production of records.

ARTICLE 63. The Prime Minister and other Ministers of State may, at any time, appear in either House for the purpose of speaking on bills, regardless of whether they are members of the House or not. They must appear when their presence is required in order to give answers or explanations.

ARTICLE 64. The Diet shall set up an impeachment court from among the members of both Houses for the purpose of trying those judges against whom removal proceedings have been instituted.

2. Matters relating to impeachment shall be provided by law.

## 第5章　内　　閣

第65条　行政権は、内閣に属する。

第66条　内閣は、法律の定めるところにより、その首長たる内閣総理大臣及びその他の国務大臣でこれを組織する。

　　内閣総理大臣その他の国務大臣は、文民でなければならない。

　　内閣は、行政権の行使について、国会に対し連帯して責任を負ふ。

第67条　内閣総理大臣は、国会議員の中から国会の議決で、これを指名する。この指名は、他のすべての案件に先だつて、これを行ふ。

　　衆議院と参議院とが異なつた指名の議決をした場合に、法律の定めるところにより、両議院の協議会を開いても意見が一致しないとき、又は衆議院が指名の議決をした後、国会休会中の期間を除いて10日以内に、参議院が、指名の議決をしないときは、衆議院の議決を国会の議決とする。

第68条　内閣総理大臣は、国務大臣を任命する。但し、その過半数は、国会議員の中から選ばれなければならない。

　　内閣総理大臣は、任意に国務大臣を罷免することができる。

第69条　内閣は、衆議院で不信任の決議案を可決し、又は信任の決議案を否決したときは、10日以内に衆議院が解散されない限り、総辞職をしなければならない。

第70条　内閣総理大臣が欠けたとき、又は衆議院議員総選挙の後に初めて国会の召集があつたときは、内閣は、総辞職をしなければならない。

第71条　前2条の場合には、内閣は、あらたに内閣総理大臣が任命されるまで引き続きその職務を行ふ。

第72条　内閣総理大臣は、内閣を代表して議案を国会に提出し、一般国務及び外交関係について国会に報告し、並びに行政各部を指揮監督する。

第73条　内閣は、他の一般行政事務の外、左の事務を行ふ。

## CHAPTER V. *The Cabinet*

ARTICLE 65. Executive power shall be vested in the Cabinet.

ARTICLE 66. The Cabinet shall consist of the Prime Minister, who shall be its head, and other Ministers of State, as provided for by law.

2. The Prime Minister and other Ministers of State must be civilians.

3. The Cabinet, in the exercise of executive power, shall be collectively responsible to the Diet.

ARTICLE 67. The Prime Minister shall be designated from among the members of the Diet by a resolution of the Diet. This designation shall precede all other business.

2. If the House of Representatives and the House of Councillors disagree and if no agreement can be reached even through a joint committee of both Houses, provided for by law, or the House of Councillors fails to make designation within ten (10) days, exclusive of the period of recess, after the House of Representatives has made designation, the decision of the House of Representatives shall be the decision of the Diet.

ARTICLE 68. The Prime Minister shall appoint the Ministers of State. However, a majority of their number must be chosen from among the members of the Diet.

2. The Prime Minister may remove the Ministers of State as he chooses.

ARTICLE 69. If the House of Representatives passes a nonconfidence resolution, or rejects a confidence resolution, the Cabinet shall resign en masse, unless the House of Representatives is dissolved within ten (10) days.

ARTICLE 70. When there is a vacancy in the post of Prime Minister, or upon the first convocation of the Diet after a general election of members of the House of Representatives, the Cabinet shall resign en masse.

ARTICLE 71. In the cases mentioned in the two preceding Articles, the Cabinet shall continue its functions until the time when a new Prime Minister is appointed.

ARTICLE 72. The Prime Minister, representing the Cabinet, submits bills, reports on general national affairs and foreign relations to the Diet and exercises control and supervision over various administrative branches.

ARTICLE 73. The Cabinet, in addition to other general administrative functions, shall perform the following functions:

　1　法律を誠実に執行し、国務を総理すること。

　2　外交関係を処理すること。

　3　条約を締結すること。但し、事前に、時宜によつては事後に、国会
　　の承認を経ることを必要とする。

　4　法律の定める基準に従ひ、官吏に関する事務を掌理すること。

　5　予算を作成して国会に提出すること。

　6　この憲法及び法律の規定を実施するために、政令を制定すること。
　　但し、政令には、特にその法律の委任がある場合を除いては、罰則を
　　設けることができない。

　7　大赦、特赦、減刑、刑の執行の免除及び復権を決定すること。

第74条　法律及び政令には、すべて主任の国務大臣が署名し、内閣総理大臣
が連署することを必要とする。

第75条　国務大臣は、その在任中、内閣総理大臣の同意がなければ、訴追さ
れない。但し、これがため、訴追の権利は、害されない。


## 第6章　司　　法

第76条　すべて司法権は、最高裁判所及び法律の定めるところにより設置す
る下級裁判所に属する。

　　特別裁判所は、これを設置することができない。行政機関は、終審として
裁判を行ふことができない。

　　すべて裁判官は、その良心に従ひ独立してその職権を行ひ、この憲法及び
法律にのみ拘束される。

第77条　最高裁判所は、訴訟に関する手続、弁護士、裁判所の内部規律及び
司法事務処理に関する事項について、規則を定める権限を有する。

　　検察官は、最高裁判所の定める規則に従はなければならない。

　　最高裁判所は、下級裁判所に関する規則を定める権限を、下級裁判所に委
任することができる。

第78条　裁判官は、裁判により、心身の故障のために職務を執ることができ
ないと決定された場合を除いては、公の弾劾によらなければ罷免されない。
裁判官の懲戒処分は、行政機関がこれを行ふことはできない。

第79条　最高裁判所は、その長たる裁判官及び法律の定める員数のその他の
裁判官でこれを構成し、その長たる裁判官以外の裁判官は、内閣でこれを任
命する。

(1) Administer the law faithfully; conduct affairs of state;

(2) Manage foreign affairs;

(3) Conclude treaties. However, it shall obtain prior or, depending on circumstances, subsequent approval of the Diet;

(4) Administer the civil service, in accordance with standards established by law;

(5) Prepare the budget, and present it to the Diet;

(6) Enact cabinet orders in order to execute the provisions of this Constitution and of the law. However, it cannot include penal provisions in such cabinet orders unless authorized by such law.

(7) Decide on general amnesty, special amnesty, commutation of punishment, reprieve, and restorations of rights.

ARTICLE 74. All laws and cabinet orders shall be signed by the competent Minister of State and countersigned by the Prime Minister.

ARTICLE 75. The Ministers of State, during their tenure of office, shall not be subject to legal action without the consent of the Prime Minister. However, the right to take that action is not impaired hereby.

## CHAPTER VI. *Judiciary*

ARTICLE 76. The whole judicial power is vested in a Supreme Court and in such inferior courts as are established by law.

2. No extraordinary tribunal shall be established, nor shall any organ or agency of the Executive be given final judicial power.

3. All judges shall be independent in the exercise of their conscience and shall be bound only by this Constitution and the laws.

ARTICLE 77. The Supreme Court is vested with the rule-making power under which it determines the rules of procedure and of practice, and of matters relating to attorneys, the internal discipline of the courts and the administration of judicial affairs.

2. Public procurators shall be subject to the rule-making power of the Supreme Court.

3. The Supreme Court may delegate the power to make rules for inferior courts to such courts.

ARTICLE 78. Judges shall not be removed except by public impeachment unless judicially declared mentally or physically incompetent to perform official duties. No disciplinary action against judges shall be administered by any executive organ or agency.

ARTICLE 79. The Supreme Court shall consist of a Chief Judge and such number of judges as may be determined by law; all such judges excepting the Chief Judge shall be appointed by the Cabinet.

　最高裁判所の裁判官の任命は、その任命後初めて行はれる衆議院議員総選挙の際国民の審査に付し、その後10年を経過した後初めて行はれる衆議院議員総選挙の際更に審査に付し、その後も同様とする。

　前項の場合において、投票者の多数が裁判官の罷免を可とするときは、その裁判官は、罷免される。

　審査に関する事項は、法律でこれを定める。

　最高裁判所の裁判官は、法律の定める年齢に達した時に退官する。

　最高裁判所の裁判官は、すべて定期に相当額の報酬を受ける。この報酬は、在任中、これを減額することができない。

第80条　下級裁判所の裁判官は、最高裁判所の指名した者の名簿によつて、内閣でこれを任命する。その裁判官は、任期を10年とし、再任されることができる。但し、法律の定める年齢に達した時には退官する。

　下級裁判所の裁判官は、すべて定期に相当額の報酬を受ける。この報酬は、在任中、これを減額することができない。

第81条　最高裁判所は、一切の法律、命令、規則又は処分が憲法に適合するかしないかを決定する権限を有する終審裁判所である。

第82条　裁判の対審及び判決は、公開法廷でこれを行ふ。

　裁判所が、裁判官の全員一致で、公の秩序又は善良の風俗を害する虞があると決した場合には、対審は、公開しないでこれを行ふことができる。但し、政治犯罪、出版に関する犯罪又はこの憲法第3章で保障する国民の権利が問題となつてゐる事件の対審は、常にこれを公開しなければならない。

## 第7章　財　　政

第83条　国の財政を処理する権限は、国会の議決に基いて、これを行使しなければならない。

第84条　あらたに租税を課し、又は現行の租税を変更するには、法律又は法律の定める条件によることを必要とする。

第85条　国費を支出し、又は国が債務を負担するには、国会の議決に基くことを必要とする。

第86条　内閣は、毎会計年度の予算を作成し、国会に提出して、その審議を受け議決を経なければならない。

第87条　予見し難い予算の不足に充てるため、国会の議決に基いて予備費を設け、内閣の責任でこれを支出することができる。

2. The appointment of the judges of the Supreme Court shall be reviewed by the people at the first general election of members of the House of Representatives following their appointment, and shall be reviewed again at the first general election of members of the House of Representatives after a lapse of ten (10) years, and in the same manner thereafter.

3. In cases mentioned in the foregoing paragraph, when the majority of the voters favors the dismissal of a judge, he shall be dismissed.

4. Matters pertaining to review shall be prescribed by law.

5. The judges of the Supreme Court shall be retired upon the attainment of the age as fixed by law.

6. All such judges shall receive, at regular stated intervals, adequate compensation which shall not be decreased during their terms of office.

ARTICLE 80. The judges of the inferior courts shall be appointed by the Cabinet from a list of persons nominated by the Supreme Court. All such judges shall hold office for a term of ten (10) years with privilege of reappointment, provided that they shall be retired upon the attainment of the age as fixed by law.

The judges of the inferior courts shall receive, at regular stated intervals, adequate compensation which shall not be decreased during their terms of office.

ARTICLE 81. The Supreme Court is the court of last resort with power to determine the constitutionality of any law, order, regulation or official act.

ARTICLE 82. Trials shall be conducted and judgment declared publicly. Where a court unanimously determines publicity to be dangerous to public order or morals, a trial may be conducted privately, but trials of political offenses, offenses involving the press or cases wherein the rights of people as guaranteed in Chapter III of this Constitution are in question shall always be conducted publicly.

## CHAPTER VII. *Finance*

ARTICLE 83. The power to administer national finances shall be exercised as the Diet shall determine.

ARTICLE 84. No new taxes shall be imposed or existing ones modified except by law or under such conditions as law may prescribe.

ARTICLE 85. No money shall be expended, nor shall the State obligate itself, except as authorized by the Diet.

ARTICLE 86. The Cabinet shall prepare and submit to the Diet for its consideration and decision a budget for each fiscal year.

ARTICLE 87. In order to provide for unforeseen deficiencies in the

　すべて予備費の支出については、内閣は、事後に国会の承諾を得なければ
ならない。

第88条　すべて皇室財産は、国に属する。すべての皇室の費用は、予算に計
上して国会の議決を経なければならない。

第89条　公金その他の公の財産は、宗教上の組織若しくは団体の使用、便益
若しくは維持のため、又は公の支配に属しない慈善、教育若しくは博愛の事
業に対し、これを支出し、又はその利用に供してはならない。

第90条　国の収入支出の決算は、すべて毎年会計検査院がこれを検査し、内
閣は、次の年度に、その検査報告とともに、これを国会に提出しなければな
らない。

　会計検査院の組織及び権限は、法律でこれを定める。

第91条　内閣は、国会及び国民に対し、定期に、少くとも毎年1回、国の財
政状況について報告しなければならない。


# 第8章　地方自治

第92条　地方公共団体の組織及び運営に関する事項は、地方自治の本旨に基
いて、法律でこれを定める。

第93条　地方公共団体には、法律の定めるところにより、その議事機関とし
て議会を設置する。

　地方公共団体の長、その議会の議員及び法律の定めるその他の吏員は、そ
の地方公共団体の住民が、直接これを選挙する。

第94条　地方公共団体は、その財産を管理し、事務を処理し、及び行政を執
行する権能を有し、法律の範囲内で条例を制定することができる。

第95条　一の地方公共団体のみに適用される特別法は、法律の定めるところ
により、その地方公共団体の住民の投票においてその過半数の同意を得なけ
れば、国会は、これを制定することができない。


# 第9章　改　　正

第96条　この憲法の改正は、各議院の総議員の3分の2以上の賛成で、国会
が、これを発議し、国民に提案してその承認を経なければならない。この承

budget, a reserve fund may be authorized by the Diet to be expended upon the responsibility of the Cabinet.

2. The Cabinet must get subsequent approval of the Diet for all payments from the reserve fund.

ARTICLE 88. All property of the Imperial Household shall belong to the State. All expenses of the Imperial Household shall be appropriated by the Diet in the budget.

ARTICLE 89. No public money or other property shall be expended or appropriated for the use, benefit or maintenance of any religious institution or association, or for any charitable, educational or benevolent enterprises not under the control of public authority.

ARTICLE 90. Final accounts of the expenditures and revenues of the State shall be audited annually by a Board of Audit and submitted by the Cabinet to the Diet, together with the statement of audit, during the fiscal year immediately following the period covered.

2. The organization and competency of the Board of Audit shall be determined by law.

ARTICLE 91. At regular intervals and at least annually the Cabinet shall report to the Diet and the people on the state of national finances.

## CHAPTER VIII. *Local Self-Government*

ARTICLE 92. Regulations concerning organization and operations of local public entities shall be fixed by law in accordance with the principle of local autonomy.

ARTICLE 93. The local public entities shall establish assemblies as their deliberative organs, in accordance with law.

2. The chief executive officers of all local public entities, the members of their assemblies, and such other local officials as may be determined by law shall be elected by direct popular vote within their several communities.

ARTICLE 94. Local public entities shall have the right to manage their property, affairs and administration and to enact their own regulations within law.

ARTICLE 95. A special law, applicable only to one local public entity, cannot be enacted by the Diet without the consent of the majority of the voters of the local public entity concerned, obtained in accordance with law.

## CHAPTER IX. *Amendments*

ARTICLE 96. Amendments to this Constitution shall be initiated by the Diet, through a concurring vote of two-thirds or more of all the

認には、特別の国民投票又は国会の定める選挙の際行はれる投票において、その過半数の賛成を必要とする。

　憲法改正について前項の承認を経たときは、天皇は、国民の名で、この憲法と一体を成すものとして、直ちにこれを公布する。

## 第10章　最高法規

第97条　この憲法が日本国民に保障する基本的人権は、人類の多年にわたる自由獲得の努力の成果であつて、これらの権利は、過去幾多の試錬に堪へ、現在及び将来の国民に対し、侵すことのできない永久の権利として信託されたものである。

第98条　この憲法は、国の最高法規であつて、その条規に反する法律、命令、詔勅及び国務に関するその他の行為の全部又は一部は、その効力を有しない。

　日本国が締結した条約及び確立された国際法規は、これを誠実に遵守することを必要とする。

第99条　天皇又は摂政及び国務大臣、国会議員、裁判官その他の公務員は、この憲法を尊重し擁護する義務を負ふ。

## 第11章　補　　則

第100条　この憲法は、公布の日から起草して6箇月を経過した日から、これを施行する。

　この憲法を施行するために必要な法律の制定、参議院議員の選挙及び国会召集の手続並びにこの憲法を施行するために必要な準備手続は、前項の期日よりも前に、これを行ふことができる。

第101条　この憲法施行の際、参議院がまだ成立してゐないときは、その成立するまでの間、衆議院は、国会としての権限を行ふ。

第102条　この憲法による第1期の参議院議員のうち、その半数の者の任期は、これを3年とする。その議員は、法律の定めるところにより、これを定める。

members of each House and shall thereupon be submitted to the people for ratification, which shall require the affirmative vote of a majority of all votes cast thereon, at a special referendum or at such election as the Diet shall specify.

2. Amendments when so ratified shall immediately be promulgated by the Emperor in the name of the people, as an integral part of this Constitution.

## CHAPTER X. *Supreme Law*

ARTICLE 97. The fundamental human rights by this Constitution guaranteed to the people of Japan are fruits of the age-old struggle of man to be free; they have survived the many exacting tests for durability and are conferred upon this and future generations in trust, to be held for all time inviolate.

ARTICLE 98. This Constitution shall be the supreme law of the nation and no law, ordinance, imperial rescript or other act of government, or part thereof, contrary to the provisions hereof, shall have legal force or validity.

2. The treaties concluded by Japan and established laws of nations shall be faithfully observed.

ARTICLE 99. The Emperor or the Regent as well as Ministers of State, members of the Diet, judges, and all other public officials have the obligation to respect and uphold this Constitution.

## CHAPTER XI. *Supplementary Provisions*

ARTICLE 100. This Constitution shall be enforced as from the day when the period of six months will have elapsed counting from the day of its promulgation.

2. The enactment of laws necessary for the enforcement of this Constitution, the election of members of the House of Councillors and the procedure for the convocation of the Diet and other preparatory procedures necessary for the enforcement of this Constitution may be executed before the day prescribed in the preceding paragraph.

ARTICLE 101. If the House of Councillors is not constituted before the effective date of this Constitution, the House of Representatives shall function as the Diet until such time as the House of Councillors shall be constitued.

ARTICLE 102. The term of office for half the members of the House of Councillors serving in the first term under this Constitution shall be three years. Members falling under this category shall be determined in accordance with law.

第103条　この憲法施行の際現に在職する国務大臣、衆議院議員及び裁判官竝びにその他の公務員で、その地位に相応する地位がこの憲法で認められてゐる者は、法律で特別の定をした場合を除いては、この憲法施行のため、当然にはその地位を失ふことはない。但し、この憲法によつて、後任者が選挙又は任命されたときは、当然その地位を失ふ。

ARTICLE 103. The Ministers of State, members of the House of Representatives and judges in office on the effective date of this Constitution, and all other public officials who occupy positions corresponding to such positions as are recognized by this Constitution shall not forfeit their positions automatically on account of the enforcement of this Constitution unless otherwise specified by law. When, however, successors are elected or appointed under the provisions of this Constitution, they shall forfeit their positions as a matter of course.

# THE AMERICAN DRAFT
# OF THE CONSTITUTION
## (The MacArthur Constitution)

Source: Miyazawa and Satō 1954, appendix.

## CONSTITUTION OF JAPAN

We, the Japanese People, acting through our duly elected representatives in the National Diet, determined that we shall secure for ourselves and our posterity the fruits of peaceful cooperation with all nations and the blessings of liberty throughout this land, and resolved that never again shall we be visited with the horrors of war through the action of government, do proclaim the sovereignty of the people's will and do ordain and establish this Constitution, founded upon the universal principle that government is a sacred trust the authority for which is derived from the people, the powers of which are exercised by the representatives of the people, and the benefits of which are enjoyed by the people; and we reject and revoke all constitutions, ordinances, laws and rescripts in conflict herewith.

Desiring peace for all time and fully conscious of the high ideals controlling human relationship now stirring mankind, we have determined to rely for our security and survival upon the justice and good faith of the peace-loving peoples of the world. We desire to occupy an honored place in an international society designed and dedicated to the preservation of peace, and the banishment of tyranny and slavery, oppression and intolerance, for all time from the earth. We recognize and acknowledge that all peoples have the right to live in peace, free from fear and want.

We hold that no people is responsible to itself alone, but that laws of political morality are universal; and that obedience to such laws is incumbent upon all peoples who would sustain their own sovereignty and justify their sovereign relationship with other peoples.

To these high principles and purposes we, the Japanese People, pledge our national honor, determined will and full resources.

### CHAPTER I. *The Emperor*

ARTICLE I. The Emperor shall be the symbol of the State and of the Unity of the People, deriving his position from the sovereign will of the People, and from no other source.

ARTICLE II. Succession to the Imperial Throne shall be dynastic and in accordance with such Imperial House Law as the Diet may enact.

ARTICLE III. The advice and consent of the Cabinet shall be required for all acts of the Emperor in matters of state, the Cabinet shall be responsible therefor.

The Emperor shall perform only such state functions as are provided for in this Constitution. He shall have no governmental powers, nor shall he assume nor be granted such powers.

The Emperor may delegate his functions in such manner as may be provided by law.

ARTICLE IV. When a regency is instituted in conformity with the provisions of such Imperial House Law as the Diet may enact, the duties of the Emperor shall be performed by the Regent in the name of the Emperor; and the limitations on the functions of the Emperor contained herein shall apply with equal force to the Regent.

ARTICLE V. The Emperor appoints as Prime Minister the person designated by the Diet.

ARTICLE VI. Acting only on the advice and with the consent of the Cabinet, the Emperor, on behalf of the people, shall perform the following state functions:

> Affix his official seal to and proclaim all laws enacted by the Diet, all Cabinet orders, all amendments to this Constitution, and all treaties and international conventions;
> Convoke sessions of the Diet;
> Dissolve the Diet;
> Proclaim general elections;
> Attest the appointment or commission and resignation or dismissal of Ministers of State, ambassadors and those other state officials whose appointment or commission and resignation or dismissal may by law be attested in this manner;
> Attest grants of amnesty, pardons, commutation of punishment, reprieves and rehabilitation;
> Award honors;
> Receive ambassadors and ministers of foreign States;
> and
> Perform appropriate ceremonial functions.

ARTICLE VII. No grants of money or other property shall be made to the Imperial Throne, and no expenditures shall be made by the Imperial Throne, unless authorized by the Diet.

## CHAPTER II. *Renunciation of War*

ARTICLE VIII. War as a sovereign right of the nation is abolished. The threat or use of force is forever renounced as a means for settling disputes with any other nation.

No army, navy, air force, or other war potential will ever be authorized and no rights of belligerency will ever be conferred upon the State.

## CHAPTER III. *Rights and Duties of the People*

ARTICLE IX. The people of Japan are entitled to the enjoyment without interference of all fundamental human rights.

ARTICLE X. The fundamental human rights by this Constitution guaranteed to the people of Japan result from the age-old struggle of man to be free. They have survived the exacting test for durability in the crucible of time and experience, and are conferred upon this and future generations in sacred trust, to be held for all time inviolate.

ARTICLE XI. The freedoms, rights and opportunities enunciated by this Constitution are maintained by the eternal vigilance of the people and involve an obligation on the part of the people to prevent their abuse and to employ them always for the common good.

ARTICLE XII. The feudal system of Japan shall cease. All Japanese by virtue of their humanity shall be respected as individuals. Their right to life, liberty and the pursuit of happiness within the limits of the general welfare shall be the supreme consideration of all law and of all governmental action.

ARTICLE XIII. All natural persons are equal before the law. No discrimination shall be authorized or tolerated in political, economic or social relations on account of race, creed, sex, social status, caste or national origin.

No patent of nobility shall from this time forth embody within itself any national or civic power of government.

No rights of peerage except those of the Imperial dynasty shall extend beyond the lives of those now in being. No special privilege shall accompany any award of honor, decoration or other distinction; nor shall any such award be valid beyond the lifetime of the individual who now holds or hereafter may receive it.

ARTICLE XIV. The people are the ultimate arbiters of their government and of the Imperial Throne. They have the inalienable right to choose their public officials and to dismiss them.

All public officials are servants of the whole community and not of any special groups.

In all elections, secrecy of the ballot shall be kept inviolate, nor shall any voter be answerable, publicly or privately, for the choice he has made.

ARTICLE XV. Every person has the right of peaceful petition for the redress of grievances for the removal of public officials and for the enactment, repeal or amendment of laws, ordinances or regulations; nor shall any person be in any way discriminated against for sponsoring such a petition.

ARTICLE XVI. Aliens shall be entitled to the equal protection of law.

ARTICLE XVII. No person shall be held in enslavement, serfdom or bondage of any kind. Involuntary servitude, except as a punishment for crime, is prohibited.

ARTICLE XVIII. Freedom of thought and conscience shall be held inviolable.

ARTICLE XIX. Freedom of religion is guaranteed to all. No religious organization shall receive special privileges from the State, nor exercise political authority.

No person shall be compelled to take part in any religious acts, celebrations, rites or practices.

The State and its organs shall refrain from religious education or any other religious activity.

ARTICLE XX. Freedom of assembly, speech and press and all other forms of expression are guaranteed. No censorship shall be maintained, nor shall the secrecy of any means of communication be violated.

ARTICLE XXI. Freedom of association, movement and choice of abode are guaranteed to every person to the extent they do not conflict with the general welfare.

All persons shall be free to emigrate and to change their nationality.

ARTICLE XXII. Academic freedom and choice of occupation are guaranteed.

ARTICLE XXIII. The family is the basis of human society and its traditions for good or evil permeate the nation. Marriage shall rest upon the indisputable legal and social equality of both sexes, founded upon mutual consent instead of parental coercion, and maintained through cooperation instead of male domination. Laws contrary to these principles shall be abolished, and replaced by others viewing choice of spouse, property rights, inheritance, choice of domicile, divorce and other matters pertaining to marriage and the family from the standpoint of individual dignity and the essential equality of the sexes.

ARTICLE XXIV. In all spheres of life, laws shall be designed for the promotion and extension of social welfare, and of freedom, justice and democracy.

Free, universal and compulsory education shall be established.

The exploitation of children shall be prohibited.

The public health shall be promoted.

Social security shall be provided.

Standards for working conditions, wages and hours shall be fixed.

ARTICLE XXV. All men have the right to work.

ARTICLE XXVI. The right of workers to organize and to bargain and act collectively is guaranteed.

ARTICLE XXVII. The right to own property is inviolable, but property rights shall be defined by law, in conformity with the public welfare.

ARTICLE XXVIII. The ultimate fee to the land and to all natural resources reposes in the State as the collective representative of the people. Land and other natural resources are subject to the right of the State to take them, upon just compensation therefor, for the purpose of securing and promoting the conservation, development, utilization and control thereof.

ARTICLE XXIX. Ownership of property imposes obligations. Its use shall be in the public good. Private property may be taken by the State for public use upon just compensation therefor.

ARTICLE XXX. No person shall be apprehended except upon warrant issued by a competent officer of a court of law specifying the offense upon which the person is charged, unless he is apprehended while committing a crime.

ARTICLE XXXI. No person shall be arrested or detained without being at once informed of the charges against him nor without the immediate privilege of counsel; he shall not be held incommunicado; he shall not be detained without adequate cause; and upon demand of any person such cause must be immediately shown in open court in his presence and the presence of his counsel.

ARTICLE XXXII. No person shall be deprived of life or liberty, nor shall any criminal penalty be imposed, except according to procedures established by the Diet, nor shall any person be denied the right of appeal to the courts.

ARTICLE XXXIII. The right of the people to be secure in their persons, homes, papers and effects against entries, searches and seizures shall not be impaired except upon judicial warrant issued only for probable cause, and particularly describing the place to be searched and the person or things to be seized.

Each search or seizure shall be made upon separate warrant issued for the purpose by a competent officer of a court of law.

ARTICLE XXXIV. The infliction of torture by any public officer is absolutely forbidden.

ARTICLE XXXV. Excessive bail shall not be required, nor cruel or unusual punishments inflicted.

ARTICLE XXXVI. In all criminal cases the accused shall enjoy the right to a speedy and public trial by an impartial tribunal.

He shall be permitted full opportunity to cross-examine all witnesses, and he shall have the right of compulsory process for obtaining witnesses on his behalf at public expense.

At all times the accused shall have the assistance of competent counsel who shall, if the accused be unable to secure the same by his own efforts, be assigned to his use by the government.

ARTICLE XXXVII. No person shall be declared guilty of a crime except by a court of competent jurisdiction.

No person shall be twice placed in jeopardy for the same offense.

ARTICLE XXXVIII. No person shall be compelled to testify against himself.

No confession shall be admitted in evidence if made under compulsion, torture or threat, or after prolonged arrest or detention.

No person shall be convicted or punished in cases where the only proof against him is his own confession.

ARTICLE XXXIX. No person shall be held criminally liable for an act lawful at the time it was committed.

## CHAPTER IV. *The Diet*

ARTICLE XL. The Diet shall be the highest organ of state power and shall be the sole lawmaking authority of the State.

ARTICLE XLI. The Diet shall consist of one House of elected representatives with a membership of not less than 300 nor more than 500.

ARTICLE XLII. The qualifications of electors and of candidates for election to the Diet shall be determined by law, and in determining such qualifications there shall be no discrimination because of sex, race, creed, color or social status.

ARTICLE XLIII. Members of the Diet shall receive adequate compensation from the national treasury as determined by law.

ARTICLE XLIV. Members of the Diet shall in all cases, except those specified by law, be free from arrest while attending the sessions of the Diet or while travelling to and from such sessions; and for any speech, debate, or vote in the Diet, they shall not be held legally liable elsewhere.

ARTICLE XLV. The term of the members shall be four years, but it may be terminated at an earlier date by dissolution of the Diet as provided herein.

ARTICLE XLVI. The method of election, apportionment, and voting shall be determined by law.

ARTICLE XLVII. The Diet shall convene at least once in every year.

ARTICLE XLVIII. The Cabinet may call special sessions and shall do so on petition of not less than twenty per cent of the members of the Diet.

ARTICLE XLVIX. The Diet shall be the sole judge of the elections and the qualifications of its members. The denial of a seat to anyone who is certified to have been elected and whose right to the seat has been questioned shall require the vote of a majority of the members present.

ARTICLE L. A quorum to transact business shall consist of not less than one-third of all the members. Except as otherwise provided herein all actions of the Diet shall be by majority vote of those present. In case of a tie the presiding officer shall cast the deciding vote.

ARTICLE LI. The Diet shall choose its presiding officer and other officials. It may determine the rules of its proceedings, punish members for disorderly behavior and expel them. On a motion for expulsion of a member a vote of not less than two-thirds of the members present shall be required to effect such expulsion.

ARTICLE LII. No law shall be passed except by bill.

ARTICLE LIII. The deliberations of the Diet shall be public, and no secret sessions shall be held. The Diet shall maintain and publish a record of its proceedings and this record shall be made available to the public. The individual votes of members on any question shall be recorded in the journal upon the demand of twenty per cent of those present.

ARTICLE LIV. The Diet shall have the power to conduct investigations, to compel the attendance and testimony of witnesses and the production of records, and to punish for refusal to comply.

ARTICLE LV. The Diet by a majority vote of those present shall designate the Prime Minister. The designation of a Prime Minister shall take precedence over all other business of the Diet.

The Diet shall establish the several Ministries of State.

ARTICLE LVI. The Prime Minister and the Ministers of State whether or not they hold seats in the Diet may at any time appear before that body for the purpose of presenting and arguing bills, and shall appear when required to answer interpellations.

ARTICLE LVII. Within ten days after the passage of a resolution of non-confidence or the failure to pass a resolution of confidence by a majority of the total membership of the Diet, the Cabinet shall resign or order the Diet to dissolve. When the Diet has been ordered dissolved a special election of a new Diet shall be held not less than thirty days nor more than forty days after the date of dissolution. The newly elected Diet shall be convoked within thirty days after the date of election.

ARTICLE LVIII. The Diet shall constitute from among its members a court of impeachment to try members of the judiciary against whom removal proceedings have been instituted.

ARTICLE LIX. The Diet shall enact all laws necessary and proper to carry into execution the provisions of this Constitution.

## CHAPTER V. *The Cabinet*

ARTICLE LX. The executive power is vested in a Cabinet.

ARTICLE LXI. The Cabinet consists of a Prime Minister, who is its head, and such other Ministers of State as may be authorized by the Diet.

In the exercise of the executive power, the Cabinet is collectively responsible to the Diet.

ARTICLE LXII. The Prime Minister shall with the advice and consent of the Diet appoint Ministers of State.

The Prime Minister may remove individual Ministers at will.

ARTICLE LXIII. Whenever a vacancy occurs in the office of Prime Minister or upon the convening of a new Diet, the Cabinet shall collectively resign and a new Prime Minister shall be designated.

Pending such designation, the Cabinet shall continue to perform its duties.

ARTICLE LXIV. The Prime Minister introduces bills on behalf of the Cabinet, reports to the Diet on general affairs of State and the status of foreign relations, and exercises control and supervision over the several executive departments and agencies.

ARTICLE LXV. In addition to other executive responsibilities, the Cabinet shall:

> Faithfully execute the laws and administer the affairs of State;
> Conduct foreign relations;
> Conclude such treaties, international conventions and agreements with the consent of the Diet by prior authorization or subsequent ratification as it deems in the public interest;
> Administer the civil service according to standards established by the Diet;
> Prepare and submit to the Diet an annual budget;
> Issue orders and regulations to carry out the provisions of this Constitution and the law, but no such order or regulation shall contain a penal provision; and
> Grant amnesty, pardon, commutation of punishment, reprieve and rehabilitation.

ARTICLE LXVI. The competent Minister of State shall sign and the Prime Minister shall countersign all acts of the Diet and executive orders.

ARTICLE LXVII. Cabinet Ministers shall not be subject to judicial process during their tenure of office without the consent of the Prime Minister, but no right of action shall be impaired by reason hereof.

## CHAPTER VI. *Judiciary*

ARTICLE LXVIII. A strong and independent judiciary being the bulwark of the people's rights, the whole judicial power is vested in a Supreme Court and in such inferior courts as the Diet shall from time to time establish.

No extraordinary tribunal shall be established, nor shall any organ or agency of the Executive be given final judicial power.

All judges shall be independent in the exercise of their conscience and shall be bound only by this Constitution and the laws enacted pursuant thereto.

ARTICLE LXIX. The Supreme Court is vested with the rule-making power under which it determines the rules of practice and of procedure, the admission of attorneys, the internal discipline of the courts, the administration of judicial affairs, and such other matters as may properly affect the free exercise of the judicial power.

Public procurators shall be officers of the court and subject to its rule-making power.

The Supreme Court may delegate the power to make rules for inferior courts to such courts.

ARTICLE LXX. Removals of judges shall be accomplished by public impeachment only and no disciplinary action shall be administered them by any executive organ or agency.

ARTICLE LXXI. The Supreme Court shall consist of a chief justice and such number of associate justices as may be determined by the Diet. All such justices shall be appointed by the Cabinet and shall hold office during good behavior but not after the attainment of the age of 70 years, provided however that all such appointments shall be reviewed at the first general election held following the appointment and thereafter at every general election held immediately following the expiration of ten calendar years from the next prior confirmation. Upon a majority vote of the electorate not to retain the incumbent the office shall become vacant.

All such justices shall receive, at regular, stated intervals, adequate compensation which shall not be decreased during their terms of office.

ARTICLE LXXII. The judges of the inferior courts shall be appointed by the Cabinet from a list which for each vacancy shall contain the names of at least two persons nominated by the Supreme Court. All such justices shall hold office for a term of ten years with privilege of reappointment and shall receive, at regular, stated intervals, adequate compensation which shall not be decreased during their terms of office. No judge shall hold office after attaining the age of 70 years.

ARTICLE LXXIII. The Supreme Court is the court of last resort. Where the determination of the constitutionality of any law, order, regulation or official act is in question, the judgment of the Supreme Court in all cases arising under or involving Chapter III of this Constitution is final; in all other cases where determination of the constitutionality of any law, ordinance, regulation or official act is in question, the judgment of the Court is subject to review by the Diet.

A judgment of the Supreme Court which is subject to review may be set aside only by the concurring vote of two-thirds of the whole number of representatives of the Diet. The Diet shall establish rules of procedure for reviewing decisions of the Supreme Court.

ARTICLE LXXIV. In all cases affecting ambassadors, ministers and consuls of foreign states, the Supreme Court has exclusive original jurisdiction.

ARTICLE LXXV. Trials shall be conducted and judgment declared publicly. Where, however, a court unanimously determines publicity to be dangerous to public order or morals, a trial may be conducted privately, but trials of political offenses, offenses of the press, and cases wherein the rights of citizens as reserved in Chapter III of this Constitution are in question, shall be conducted publicly without exception.

## CHAPTER VII. *Finance*

ARTICLE LXXVI. The power to levy taxes, borrow money, appropriate funds, issue and regulate the value of coins and currency shall be exercised through the Diet.

ARTICLE LXXVII. No new taxes shall be imposed or existing ones modified except by action of the Diet or under such conditions as the Diet may prescribe.

All taxes in effect at the time this Constitution is promulgated shall continue to be collected under existing regulations until changed or modified by the Diet.

ARTICLE LXXVIII. No contract shall be entered into in the absence of an appropriation therefor, nor shall the credit of the State be pledged except as authorized by the Diet.

ARTICLE LXXIX. The Cabinet shall prepare and submit to the Diet an annual budget setting forth the complete government fiscal program for the next ensuring fiscal year, including all proposed expenditures, anticipated revenues and borrowings.

ARTICLE LXXX. The Diet may disapprove, reduce, increase or reject any item in the budget or add new items.

The Diet shall appropriate no money for any fiscal year in excess of the anticipated income for that period, including the proceeds of any borrowings.

ARTICLE LXXXI. In order to provide for unforeseen deficiencies in the budget a reserve fund may be authorized to be expended under the direct supervision of the Cabinet.

The Cabinet shall be held accountable to the Diet for all payments from the reserve fund.

ARTICLE LXXXII. All property of the Imperial Household, other than the hereditary estates, shall belong to the nation. The income from all Imperial properties shall be paid into the national treasury, and allowances and expenses of the Imperial Household, as defined by law, shall be appropriated by the Diet in the annual budget.

ARTICLE LXXXIII. No public money or property shall be appropriated for the use, benefit or support of any system of religion, or religious institution or association, or for any charitable, educational or benevolent purposes not under the control of the State.

ARTICLE LXXXIV. A final audit of all expenditures and revenues of the State shall be made annually by a board of audit and submitted by the Cabinet to the Diet during the fiscal year immediately following the period covered.

The organization and competency of the board of audit shall be determined by the Diet.

ARTICLE LXXXV. At regular intervals and at least annually the Cabinet shall report to the Diet and the people on the state of public finances.

## CHAPTER VIII. *Local Government*

ARTICLE LXXXVI. The governors of prefectures, the mayors of cities and towns and the chief executive officers of all other subordinate bodies politic and corporate having taxing power, the members of prefectural and local legislative assemblies, and such other prefectural and local officials as the Diet may determine, shall be elected by direct popular vote within their several communities.

ARTICLE LXXXVII. The inhabitants of metropolitan areas, cities and towns shall be secure in their right to manage their property, affairs and government and to frame their own charters within such laws as the Diet may enact.

ARTICLE LXXXVIII. The Diet shall pass no local or special act applicable to a metropolitan area, city or town where a general act can be made applicable, unless it be made subject to the acceptance of a majority of the electorate of such community.

## CHAPTER IX. *Amendments*

ARTICLE LXXXIX. Amendments to this Constitution shall be initiated by the Diet, through a concurring vote of two-thirds of all its members, and shall thereupon be submitted to the people for ratification, which shall require the affirmative vote of a majority of all votes cast thereon at such election as the Diet shall specify.

Amendments when so ratified shall immediately be proclaimed by the Emperor, in the name of the People, as an integral part of this Constitution.

## CHAPTER X. *Supreme Law*

ARTICLE XC. This Constitution and the laws and Treaties made in pursuance hereof shall be the supreme law of the nation, and no public law or ordinance and no imperial rescript or other governmental act, or part thereof, contrary to provisions hereof shall have legal force or validity.

ARTICLE XCI. The Emperor, upon succeeding to the throne, and the Regent, Ministers of State, Members of the Diet, Members of the Judiciary and all other public officers upon assuming office, shall be bound to uphold and protect this Constitution.

All public officials duly holding office when this Constitution takes effect shall likewise be so bound and shall remain in office until their successors are elected or appointed.

## CHAPTER XI. *Ratification*

ARTICLE XCII. This Constitution shall be established when ratified by the Diet by roll-call vote of two-thirds of the members present.

Upon ratification by the Diet, the Emperor shall immediately proclaim, in the name of the People, that this Constitution has been established as the supreme law of the nation.

# THE RIGHTS AND DUTIES
# OF THE PEOPLE

## 第3章　国民の権利及び義務

第10条　日本国民たる要件は、法律でこれを定める!

第11条　国民は、すべての基本的人権の享有を妨げられない? この憲法が国民に保障する基本的人権は、侵すことのできない永久の権利として、現在及び将来の国民に与へられる?

第12条　この憲法が国民に保障する自由及び権利は、国民の不断の努力によつて、これを保持しなければならない? 又、国民はこれを濫用してはならない?のであつて、常に公共の福祉のためにこれを利用する責任を負ふ?

第13条　すべて国民は、個人として尊重される? 生命、自由及び幸福追求に対する国民の権利については、公共の福祉に反しない限り、立法その他の国政の上で、最大の尊重を必要とする?

第14条　すべて国民は、法の下に平等であつて? 人種、信条、性別、社会的身分又は門地により、政治的、経済的又は社会的関係において、差別されない?

　華族その他の貴族の制度は、これを認めない!

　栄誉、勲章その他の栄典の授与は、いかなる特権も伴はない? 栄典の授与は、現にこれを有し、又はこれを受ける者の一代に限り、その効力を有する?

第15条　公務員を選定し、及びこれを罷免することは、国民固有の権利である?

　すべて公務員は、全体の奉仕者であつて、一部の奉仕者ではない!

　公務員の選挙については、成年者による普通選挙を保障する?

　すべて選挙における投票の秘密は、これを侵してはならない? 選挙人は、その選択に関し公的にも私的にも責任を問はれない?

第16条　何人も、損害の救済、公務員の罷免、法律、命令又は規則の制定、廃止又は改正その他の事項に関し、平穏に請願する権利を有し? 何人も、かかる請願をしたためにいかなる差別待遇も受けない?

第17条　何人も、公務員の不法行為により、損害を受けたときは、法律の定めるところにより、国又は公共団体に、その賠償を求めることができる?

第18条　何人も、いかなる奴隷的拘束も受けない? 又、犯罪に因る処罰の場合を除いては、その意に反する苦役に服させられない?

## CHAPTER III. *Rights and Duties of the People*

ARTICLE 10. The conditions necessary for being a Japanese national shall[1] be determined by law.

ARTICLE 11. The people shall[2] not be prevented from enjoying any of the fundamental human rights. These fundamental human rights guaranteed to the people by this Constitution shall[3] be conferred upon the people of this and future generations as eternal and inviolate rights.

ARTICLE 12. The freedoms and rights guaranteed to the people by this Constitution shall[4] be maintained by the constant endeavor of the people, who shall[5] refrain from any abuse of these freedoms and rights and shall[6] always be responsible for utilizing them for the public welfare.

ARTICLE 13. All of the people shall[7] be respected as individuals. Their right to life, liberty, and the pursuit of happiness shall,[8] to the extent that it does not interfere with the public welfare, be the supreme consideration in legislation and in other governmental affairs.

ARTICLE 14. All of the people are[9] equal under the law and there shall[10] be no discrimination in political, economic or social relations because of race, creed, sex, social status or family origin.

Peers and peerage shall[11] not be recognized.

No privilege shall[12] accompany any award of honor, decoration or any distinction, nor shall[13] any such award be valid beyond the lifetime of the individual who now holds or hereafter may receive it.

ARTICLE 15. The people have[14] the inalienable right to choose their public officials and to dismiss them.

All public officials are[15] servants of the whole community and not of any group thereof.

Universal adult suffrage is[16] guaranteed with regard to the election of public officials.

In all elections, secrecy of the ballot shall[17] not be violated. A voter shall[18] not be answerable, publicly or privately, for the choice he has made.

ARTICLE 16. Every person shall[19] have the right of peaceful petition for the redress of damage, for the removal of public officials, for the enactment, repeal or amendment of laws, ordinances or regulations and for other matters, nor shall[20] any person be in any way discriminated against for sponsoring such a petition.

ARTICLE 17. Every person may[21] sue for redress as provided by law from the State or a public entity, in case he has suffered damage through illegal act of any public official.

ARTICLE 18. No person shall[22] be held in bondage of any kind. Involuntary servitude, except as punishment for crime, is[23] prohibited.

第19条　思想及び良心の自由は、これを侵してはならない[24]。

第20条　信教の自由は、何人に対してもこれを保障する[25]。いかなる宗教団体も、国から特権を受け、又は政治上の権力を行使してはならない[26]。

何人も、宗教上の行為、祝典、儀式又は行事に参加することを強制されない[27]。

国及びその機関は、宗教教育その他いかなる宗教的活動もしてはならない[28]。

第21条　集会、結社及び言論、出版その他一切の表現の自由は、これを保障する[29]。

検閲は、これをしてはならない[30]。通信の秘密は、これを侵してはならない[31]。

第22条　何人も、公共の福祉に反しない限り、居住、移転及び職業選択の自由を有する[32]。

何人も、外国に移住し、又は国籍を離脱する自由を侵されない[33]。

第23条　学問の自由は、これを保障する[34]。

第24条　婚姻は、両性の合意のみに基いて成立し[35]、夫婦が同等の権利を有することを基本として、相互の協力により、維持されなければならない[36]。

配偶者の選択、財産権、相続、住居の選定、離婚並びに婚姻及び家族に関するその他の事項に関しては、法律は、個人の尊厳と両性の本質的平等に立脚して、制定されなければならない[37]。

第25条　すべて国民は、健康で文化的な最低限度の生活を営む権利を有する[38]。

国は、すべての生活部面について、社会福祉、社会保障及び公衆衛生の向上及び増進に努めなければならない[39]。

第26条　すべて国民は、法律の定めるところにより、その能力に応じて、ひとしく教育を受ける権利を有する[40]。

すべて国民は、法律の定めるところにより、その保護する子女に普通教育を受けさせる義務を負ふ[41]。義務教育は、これを無償とする[42]。

第27条　すべて国民は、勤労の権利を有し[43a]義務を負ふ[43b]。

賃金、就業時間、休息その他の勤労条件に関する基準は、法律でこれを定める[44]。

児童は、これを酷使してはならない[45]。

ARTICLE 19. Freedom of thought and conscience shall[24] not be violated.

ARTICLE 20. Freedom of religion is[25] guaranteed to all. No religious organization shall[26] receive any privileges from the State nor exercise any political authority.

No person shall[27] be compelled to take part in any religious act, celebration, rite or practice.

The State and its organs shall[28] refrain from religious education or any other religious activity.

ARTICLE 21. Freedom of assembly and association as well as speech, press and all other forms of expression are[29] guaranteed.

No censorship shall[30] be maintained, nor shall[31] the secrecy of any means of communication be violated.

ARTICLE 22. Every person shall[32] have freedom to choose and change his residence and to choose his occupation to the extent that it does not interfere with the public welfare.

Freedom of all persons to move to a foreign country and to divest themselves of their nationality shall[33] be inviolate.

ARTICLE 23. Academic freedom is[34] guaranteed.

ARTICLE 24. Marriage shall[35] be based only on the mutual consent of both sexes and it shall[36] be maintained through mutual cooperation with the equal rights of husband and wife as a basis.

With regard to choice of spouse, property rights, inheritance, choice of domicile, divorce and other matters pertaining to marriage and the family, laws shall[37] be enacted from the standpoint of individual dignity and the essential equality of the sexes.

ARTICLE 25. All people shall[38] have the right to maintain the minimum standards of wholesome and cultured living.

In all spheres of life, the State shall[39] use its endeavors for the promotion and extension of social welfare and security, and of public health.

ARTICLE 26. All people shall[40] have the right to receive an equal education correspondent to their ability, as provided by law.

All people shall[41] be obligated to have all boys and girls under their protection receive ordinary education as provided for by law. Such compulsory education shall[42] be free.

ARTICLE 27. All people shall[43] have the right and the obligation to work.

Standards for wages, hours, rest and other working conditions shall[44] be fixed by law.

Children shall[45] not be exploited.

第28条　勤労者の団結する権利及び団体交渉その他の団体行動をする権利は、これを保障する。[46]

第29条　財産権は、これを侵してはならない。[47]

　財産権の内容は、公共の福祉に適合するやうに、法律でこれを定める。[48]

　私有財産は、正当な補償の下に、これを公共のために用ひることができる。[49]

第30条　国民は、法律の定めるところにより、納税の義務を負ふ。[50]

第31条　何人も、法律の定める手続によらなければ、その生命若しくは自由を奪はれ[51]又はその他の刑罰を科せられない。[52]

第32条　何人も、裁判所において裁判を受ける権利を奪はれない。[53]

第33条　何人も、現行犯として逮捕される場合を除いては、権限を有する司法官憲が発し、且つ理由となつてゐる犯罪を明示する令状によらなければ、逮捕されない。[54]

第34条　何人も、理由を直ちに告げられ、且つ、直ちに弁護人に依頼する権利を与へられなければ、抑留又は拘禁されない。[55]又、何人も、正当な理由がなければ、拘禁されず[56]要求があれば、その理由は、直ちに本人及びその弁護人の出席する公開の法廷で示されなければならない。[57]

第35条　何人も、その住居、書類及び所持品について、侵入、捜索及び押収を受けることのない権利は、第33条の場合を除いては、正当な理由に基いて発せられ、且つ捜索する場所及び押収する物を明示する令状がなければ、侵されない。[58]

　捜索又は押収は、権限を有する司法官憲が発する各別の令状により、これを行ふ。[59]

第36条　公務員による拷問及び残虐な刑罰は、絶対にこれを禁ずる。[60]

第37条　すべて刑事事件においては、被告人は、公平な裁判所の迅速な公開裁判を受ける権利を有する。[61]

　刑事被告人は、すべての証人に対して審問する機会を充分に与へられ[62]又、公費で自己のために強制的手続により証人を求める権利を有する。[63]

　刑事被告人は、いかなる場合にも、資格を有する弁護人を依頼することができる。[64]被告人が自らこれを依頼することができないときは、国でこれを附する。[65]

ARTICLE 28.  The right of workers to organize and to bargain and act collectively is[46] guaranteed.

ARTICLE 29.  The right to own or to hold property is[47] inviolable.

Property rights shall[48] be defined by law, in conformity with the public welfare.

Private property may[49] be taken for public use upon just compensation therefor.

ARTICLE 30.  The people shall[50] be liable to taxation as provided by law.

ARTICLE 31.  No person shall[51] be deprived of life or liberty, nor shall[52] any other criminal penalty be imposed, except according to procedure established by law.

ARTICLE 32.  No person shall[53] be denied the right of access to the courts.

ARTICLE 33.  No person shall[54] be apprehended except upon warrant issued by a competent judicial officer which specifies the offense with which the person is charged, unless he is apprehended, the offense being committed.

ARTICLE 34.  No person shall[55] be arrested or detained without being at once informed of the charges against him or without the immediate privilege of counsel; nor shall[56] he be detained without adequate cause; and upon demand of any person such cause must[57] be immediately shown in open court in his presence and the presence of his counsel.

ARTICLE 35.  The right of all persons to be secure in their homes, papers and effects against entries, searches and seizures shall[58] not be impaired except upon warrant issued for adequate cause and particularly describing the place to be searched and things to be seized, or except as provided by Article 33.

Each search or seizure shall[59] be made upon separate warrant issued by a competent judicial officer.

ARTICLE 36.  The infliction of torture by any public officer and cruel punishments are[60] absolutely forbidden.

ARTICLE 37.  In all criminal cases the accused shall[61] enjoy the right to a speedy and public trial by an impartial tribunal.

He shall[62] be permitted full opportunity to examine all witnesses, and he shall[63] have the right of compulsory process for obtaining witnesses on his behalf at public expense.

At all times the accused shall[64] have the assistance of competent counsel who shall,[65] if the accused is unable to secure the same by his own efforts, be assigned to his use by the State.

第38条　何人も、自己に不利益な供述を強要されない[66]

　強制、拷問若しくは脅迫による自白又は不当に長く抑留若しくは拘禁された後の自白は、これを証拠とすることができない[67]

　何人も、自己に不利益な唯一の証拠が本人の自白である場合には、有罪とされ、又は刑罰を科せられない[68]

第39条　何人も、実行の時に適法であつた行為又は既に無罪とされた行為については、刑事上の責任を問はれない[69]又、同一の犯罪について、重ねて刑事上の責任を問はれない[70]

第40条　何人も、抑留又は拘禁された後、無罪の裁判を受けたときは、法律の定めるところにより、国にその補償を求めることができる[71]

ARTICLE 38. No person shall[66] be compelled to testify against himself.

Confession made under compulsion, torture or threat, or after prolonged arrest or detention shall[67] not be admitted in evidence.

No person shall[68] be convicted or punished in cases where the only proof against him is his own confession.

ARTICLE 39. No person shall[69] be held criminally liable for an act which was lawful at the time it was committed, or of which he has been acquitted, nor shall[70] he be placed in double jeopardy.

ARTICLE 40. Any person, in case he is acquitted after he has been arrested or detained, may[71] sue the State for redress as provided by law.

# THE MEIJI CONSTITUTION

## (Dai-Nihon Teikoku Kempō)

Note: The imperial proclamation has been omitted, and old characters that are no longer in use have been replaced by those in contemporary use.

# 大日本帝國憲法

## 憲法發布勅語

朕國家ノ隆昌ト臣民ノ慶福トヲ以テ中心ノ欣榮トシ朕カ祖宗ニ承クルノ大權ニ依リ現在及將來ノ臣民ニ對シ此ノ不磨ノ大典ヲ宣布ス

惟フニ我カ祖我カ宗ハ我カ臣民祖先ノ協力輔翼ニ倚リ我カ帝國ヲ肇造シ以テ無窮ニ垂レタリ此レ我カ神聖ナル祖宗ノ威德ト竝ニ臣民ノ忠實勇武ニシテ國ヲ愛シ公ニ殉ヒ以テ此ノ光輝アル國史ノ成跡ヲ貽シタルナリ朕我カ臣民ハ卽チ祖宗ノ忠良ナル臣民ノ子孫ナルヲ回想シ其ノ朕カ意ヲ奉體シ朕カ事ヲ獎順シ相與ニ和衷協同シ益々我カ帝國ノ光榮ヲ中外ニ宣揚シ祖宗ノ遺業ヲ永久ニ鞏固ナラシムルノ希望ヲ同クシ此ノ負擔ヲ分ツニ堪フルコトヲ疑ハサルナリ

朕祖宗ノ遺烈ヲ承ケ萬世一系ノ帝位ヲ踐ミ朕カ親愛スル所ノ臣民ハ卽チ朕カ祖宗ノ惠撫慈養シタマヒシ所ノ臣民ナルヲ念ヒ其ノ康福ヲ增進シ其ノ懿德良能ヲ發達セシメムコトヲ願ヒ又其ノ翼贊ニ依リ與ニ俱ニ國家ノ進運ヲ扶持セムコトヲ望ミ乃チ明治十四年十月十二日ノ詔命ヲ履踐シ茲ニ大憲ヲ制定シ朕カ率由スル所ヲ示シ朕カ後嗣及臣民及臣民ノ子孫タル者ヲシテ永遠ニ循行スル所ヲ知ラシム

國家統治ノ大權ハ朕カ之ヲ祖宗ニ承ケテ之ヲ子孫ニ傳フル所ナリ朕及朕カ子孫ハ將來此ノ憲法ノ條章ニ循ヒ之ヲ行フコトヲ愆ラサルヘシ

朕ハ我カ臣民ノ權利及財産ノ安全ヲ貴重シ及之ヲ保護シ此ノ憲法及法律ノ範圍内ニ於テ其ノ享有ヲ完全ナラシムヘキコトヲ宣言ス

帝國議會ハ明治二十三年ヲ以テ之ヲ召集シ議會開會ノ時ヲ以テ此ノ憲法ヲシテ有效ナラシムルノ期トスヘシ

將來若此ノ憲法ノ或ル條章ヲ改定スルノ必要ナル時宜ヲ見ルニ至ラハ朕及朕カ繼統ノ子孫ハ發議ノ權ヲ執リ之ヲ議會ニ付シ議會ハ此ノ憲法ニ定メタル要件ニ依リ之ヲ議決スルノ外朕カ子孫及臣民ハ敢テ之カ紛更ヲ試ミルコトヲ得サルヘシ

朕カ在廷ノ大臣ハ朕カ爲ニ此ノ憲法ヲ施行スルノ責ニ任スヘク朕カ現在及將來ノ臣民ハ此ノ憲法ニ對シ永遠ニ從順ノ義務ヲ負フヘシ

　　御　名　御　璽
　　　明治二十二年二月十一日

## 第 1 章　天皇

第１條　大日本帝國ハ萬世一系ノ天皇之ヲ統治ス

第２條　皇位ハ皇室典範ノ定ムル所ニ依リ皇男子孫之ヲ繼承ス

第３條　天皇ハ神聖ニシテ侵スヘカラス

第４條　天皇ハ國ノ元首ニシテ統治權ヲ總攬シ此ノ憲法ノ條規ニ依リ之ヲ行フ

第５條　天皇ハ帝國議會ノ協贊ヲ以テ立法權ヲ行フ

第６條　天皇ハ法律ヲ裁可シ其ノ公布及執行ヲ命ス

第７條　天皇ハ帝國議會ヲ召集シ其ノ開會閉會停會及衆議院ノ解散ヲ命ス

第８條　天皇ハ公共ノ安全ヲ保持シ又ハ其ノ災厄ヲ避クル爲緊急ノ必要ニ由リ帝國議會閉會ノ場合ニ於テ法律ニ代ルヘキ勅令ヲ發ス

此ノ勅令ハ次ノ會期ニ於テ帝國議會ニ提出スヘシ若議會ニ於テ承諾セサルトキハ政府ハ將來ニ向テ其ノ效力ヲ失フコトヲ公布スヘシ

第９條　天皇ハ法律ヲ執行スル爲ニ又ハ公共ノ安寧秩序ヲ保持シ及臣民ノ幸福ヲ增進スル爲ニ必要ナル命令ヲ發シ又ハ發セシム但シ命令ヲ以テ法律ヲ變更スルコトヲ得ス

第10條　天皇ハ行政各部ノ官制及文武官ノ俸給ヲ定メ及文武官ヲ任免ス但シ此ノ憲法又ハ他ノ法律ニ特例ヲ揭ケタルモノハ各々其ノ條項ニ依ル

第11條　天皇ハ陸海軍ヲ統帥ス

第12條　天皇ハ陸海軍ノ編制及常備兵額ヲ定ム

第13條　天皇ハ戰ヲ宣シ和ヲ講シ及諸般ノ條約ヲ締結ス

第14條　天皇ハ戒嚴ヲ宣告ス

戒嚴ノ要件及效力ハ法律ヲ以テ之ヲ定ム

第15條　天皇ハ爵位勲章及其ノ他ノ榮典ヲ授與ス

第16條　天皇ハ大赦特赦減刑及復權ヲ命ス

第17條　攝政ヲ置クハ皇室典範ノ定ムル所ニ依ル

攝政ハ天皇ノ名ニ於テ大權ヲ行フ

## 第2章　臣民權利義務

第18條　日本臣民タルノ要件ハ法律ノ定ムル所ニ依ル

第19條　日本臣民ハ法律命令ノ定ムル所ノ資格ニ應シ均ク文武官ニ任セラレ及其ノ他ノ公務ニ就クコトヲ得

第20條　日本臣民ハ法律ノ定ムル所ニ從ヒ兵役ノ義務ヲ有ス

第21條　日本臣民ハ法律ノ定ムル所ニ從ヒ納税ノ義務ヲ有ス

第22條　日本臣民ハ法律ノ範圍内ニ於テ居住及移轉ノ自由ヲ有ス

第23條　日本臣民ハ法律ニ依ルニ非スシテ逮捕監禁審問處罰ヲ受クルコトナシ

第24條　日本臣民ハ法律ニ定メタル裁判官ノ裁判ヲ受クルノ權ヲ奪ハル、コトナシ

第25條　日本臣民ハ法律ニ定メタル場合ヲ除ク外其ノ許諾ナクシテ住所ニ侵入セラレ及捜索セラル、コトナシ

第26條　日本臣民ハ法律ニ定メタル場合ヲ除ク外信書ノ祕密ヲ侵サル、コトナシ

第27條　日本臣民ハ其ノ所有權ヲ侵サル、コトナシ

公益ノ爲必要ナル處分ハ法律ノ定ムル所ニ依ル

第28條　日本臣民ハ安寧秩序ヲ妨ケス及臣民タルノ義務ニ背カサル限ニ於テ信教ノ自由ヲ有ス

第29條　日本臣民ハ法律ノ範圍内ニ於テ言論著作印行集會及結社ノ自由ヲ有ス

第30條　日本臣民ハ相當ノ敬禮ヲ守リ別ニ定ムル所ノ規程ニ從ヒ請願ヲ爲スコトヲ得

第31條　本章ニ掲ケタル條規ハ戰時又ハ國家事變ノ場合ニ於テ天皇大權ノ施行ヲ妨クルコトナシ

第32條　本章ニ掲ケタル條規ハ陸海軍ノ法令又ハ紀律ニ牴觸セサルモノニ限リ軍人ニ準行ス

## 第3章　帝國議會

第33條　帝國議會ハ貴族院衆議院ノ兩院ヲ以テ成立ス

第34條　貴族院ハ貴族院令ノ定ムル所ニ依リ皇族華族及勅任セラレタル議員ヲ以テ組織ス

第35條　衆議院ハ選擧法ノ定ムル所ニ依リ公選セラレタル議員ヲ以テ組織ス

第36條　何人モ同時ニ兩議院ノ議員タルコトヲ得ス

第37條　凡テ法律ハ帝國議會ノ協贊ヲ經ルヲ要ス

第38條　兩議院ハ政府ノ提出スル法律案ヲ議決シ及各々法律案ヲ提出スルコトヲ得

第39條　兩議院ノ一ニ於テ否決シタル法律案ハ同會期中ニ於テ再ヒ提出スルコトヲ得ス

第40條　兩議院ハ法律又ハ其ノ他ノ事件ニ付各々其ノ意見ヲ政府ニ建議スルコトヲ得但シ其ノ採納ヲ得サルモノハ同會期中ニ於テ再ヒ建議スルコトヲ得ス

第41條　帝國議會ハ毎年之ヲ召集ス

第42條　帝國議會ハ三簡月ヲ以テ會期トス必要アル場合ニ於テハ勅命ヲ以テ之ヲ延長スルコトアルヘシ

第43條　臨時緊急ノ必要アル場合ニ於テ當會ノ外臨時會ヲ召集スヘシ
臨時會ノ會期ヲ定ムルハ勅命ニ依ル

第44條　帝國議會ノ開會閉會會期ノ延長及停會ハ兩院同時ニ之ヲ行フヘシ
衆議院解散ヲ命セラレタルトキハ貴族院ハ同時ニ停會セラルヘシ

第45條　衆議院解散ヲ命セラレタルトキハ勅命ヲ以テ新ニ議員ヲ選擧セシメ解散ノ日ヨリ五簡月以内ニ之ヲ召集スヘシ

第46條　兩議院ハ各々其ノ總議員三分ノ一以上出席スルニ非サレハ議事ヲ開キ議決ヲ爲スコトヲ得ス

第47條　兩議院ノ議事ハ過半數ヲ以テ決ス可否同數ナルトキハ議長ノ決スル所ニ依ル

第48條　兩議院ノ會議ハ公開ス但シ政府ノ要求又ハ其ノ院ノ決議ニ依リ祕密會ト爲スコトヲ得

第49條　兩議院ハ各々天皇ニ上奏スルコトヲ得

第50條　兩議院ハ臣民ヨリ呈出スル請願書ヲ受クルコトヲ得

第51條　兩議院ハ此ノ憲法及議院法ニ掲クルモノノ外内部ノ整理ニ必要ナル諸規則ヲ定ムルコトヲ得

第52條　兩議院ノ議員ハ議院ニ於テ發言シタル意見及表決ニ付院外ニ於テ責ヲ負フコトナシ但シ議員自ラ其ノ言論ヲ演説刊行筆記又ハ其ノ他ノ方法ヲ以テ公布シタルトキハ一般ノ法律ニ依リ處分セラルヘシ

第53條　兩議院ノ議員ハ現行犯罪又ハ内亂外患ニ關ル罪ヲ除ク外會期中其ノ院ノ許諾ナクシテ逮捕セラル、コトナシ

第54條　國務大臣及政府委員ハ何時タリトモ各議院ニ出席シ及發言スルコトヲ得

## 第4章　國務大臣及樞密顧問

第55條　國務各大臣ハ天皇ヲ輔弼シ其ノ責ニ任ス

凡テ法律勅令其ノ他國務ニ關ル詔勅ハ國務大臣ノ副署ヲ要ス

第56條　樞密顧問ハ樞密院官制ノ定ムル所ニ依リ天皇ノ諮詢ニ應ヘ重要ノ國務ヲ審議ス

## 第5章　司法

第57條　司法權ハ天皇ノ名ニ於テ法律ニ依リ裁判所之ヲ行フ

裁判所ノ構成ハ法律ヲ以テ之ヲ定ム

第58條　裁判官ハ法律ニ定メタル資格ヲ具フル者ヲ以テ之ニ任ス

裁判官ハ刑法ノ宣告又ハ懲戒ノ處分ニ由ルノ外其ノ職ヲ免セラル、コトナシ

懲戒ノ條規ハ法律ヲ以テ之ヲ定ム

第59條　裁判ノ對審判決ハ之ヲ公開ス但シ安寧秩序又ハ風俗ヲ害スルノ虞アルトキハ法律ニ依リ又ハ裁判所ノ決議ヲ以テ對審ノ公開ヲ停ムルコトヲ得

第60條　特別裁判所ノ管轄ニ屬スヘキモノハ別ニ法律ヲ以テ之ヲ定ム

第61條　行政官廳ノ違法處分ニ由リ權利ヲ傷害セラレタリトスルノ訴訟ニシテ別ニ法律ヲ以テ定メタル行政裁判所ノ裁判ニ屬スヘキモノハ司法裁判所ニ於テ受理スルノ限ニ在ラス

## 第6章　會計

第62條　新ニ租税ヲ課シ及税率ヲ變更スルハ法律ヲ以テ之ヲ定ムヘシ

但シ報償ニ屬スル行政上ノ手數料及其ノ他ノ收納金ハ前項ノ限ニ在ラス

國債ヲ起シ及豫算ニ定メタルモノヲ除ク外國庫ノ負擔トナルヘキ契約ヲ爲スハ帝國議會ノ協贊ヲ經ヘシ

第63條　現行ノ租税ハ更ニ法律ヲ以テ之ヲ改メサル限ハ舊ニ依リ之ヲ徵收ス

第64條　國家ノ歳出歳入ハ每年豫算ヲ以テ帝國議會ノ協贊ヲ經ヘシ

豫算ノ款項ニ超過シ又ハ豫算ノ外ニ生シタル支出アルトキハ後日帝國議會ノ承諾ヲ求ムルヲ要ス

第65條　豫算ハ前ニ衆議院ニ提出スヘシ

第66條　皇室經費ハ現在ノ定額ニ依リ每年國庫ヨリ之ヲ支出シ將來增額ヲ要スル場合ヲ除ク外帝國議會ノ協贊ヲ要セス

第67條　憲法上ノ大權ニ基ツケル既定ノ歳出及法律ノ結果ニ由リ又ハ法律上
政府ノ義務ニ屬スル歳出ハ政府ノ同意ナクシテ帝國議會之ヲ廢除シ又ハ削減
スルコトヲ得ス

第68條　特別ノ須要ニ因リ政府ハ豫メ年限ヲ定メ繼續費トシテ帝國議會ノ協
贊ヲ求ムルコトヲ得

第69條　避クヘカラサル豫算ノ不足ヲ補フ爲ニ又ハ豫算ノ外ニ生シタル必要
ノ費用ニ充ツル爲ニ豫備費ヲ設クヘシ

第70條　公共ノ安全ヲ保持スル爲緊急ノ需用アル場合ニ於テ内外ノ情形ニ因
リ政府ハ帝國議會ヲ召集スルコト能ハサルトキハ勅令ニ依リ財政上必要ノ處
分ヲ爲スコトヲ得

前項ノ場合ニ於テハ次ノ會期ニ於テ帝國議會ニ提出シ其ノ承諾ヲ求ムルヲ要
ス

第71條　帝國議會ニ於テ豫算ヲ議定セス又ハ豫算成立ニ至ラサルトキハ政府
ハ前年度ノ豫算ヲ施行スヘシ

第72條　國家ノ歳出歳入ノ決算ハ會計檢查院之ヲ檢查確定シ政府ハ其ノ檢查
報告ト俱ニ之ヲ帝國議會ニ提出スヘシ

會計檢查院ノ組織及職權ハ法律ヲ以テ之ヲ定ム

## 第7章　補則

第73條　將來此ノ憲法ノ條項ヲ改正スルノ必要アルトキハ勅命ヲ以テ議案ヲ
帝國議會ノ議ニ付スヘシ

此ノ場合ニ於テ兩議院ハ各々其ノ總員三分ノ二以上出席スルニ非サレハ議事
ヲ開クコトヲ得ス出席議員三分ノ二以上ノ多數ヲ得ルニ非サレハ改正ノ議決
ヲ爲スコトヲ得ス

第74條　皇室典範ノ改正ハ帝國議會ノ議ヲ經ルヲ要セス

皇室典範ヲ以テ此ノ憲法ノ條規ヲ變更スルコトヲ得ス

第75條　憲法及皇室典範ハ攝政ヲ置クノ間之ヲ變更スルコトヲ得ス

第76條　法律規則命令又ハ何等ノ名稱ヲ用キタルニ拘ラス此ノ憲法ニ矛盾セ
サル現行ノ法令ハ總テ遵由ノ効力ヲ有ス

歳出上政府ノ義務ニ係ル現在ノ契約又ハ命令ハ總テ第六十七條ノ例ニ依ル

*Appendix Five*

# UEKI EMORI, THE DRAFT CONSTITUTION OF THE GREAT JAPAN OF THE ORIENT

## (*Tōyō Dai-Nihonkoku Kokken-an*)

Source: Itō 1934. The table of contents has been omitted, and old characters that are no longer in use have been replaced by those in contemporary use.

## 東洋大日本國國憲按

### 第1編　國家ノ大則及權利

#### 第1章　國家ノ大則

第1條　日本國ハ日本國憲法ニ循テ之ヲ立テ之ヲ持ス。

第2條　日本國ニ一、立法院　一、行政府　一、司法廳ヲ置ク、憲法其規則ヲ設ク。

#### 第2章　國家ノ權限

第3條　日本ノ國家ハ國家政府ヲ達行センガ爲メニ必要ナル事物ヲ備フルヲ得。

第4條　日本國家ハ外國ニ對シテ交際ヲ爲シ條約ヲ結ブヲ得。

第5條　日本ノ國家ハ日本各人ノ自由權利ヲ殺減スル規則ヲ作リテ之ヲ行フヲ得ズ。

第6條　日本ノ國家ハ日本國民各自ノ私事ニ干渉スルコトヲ施スヲ得ズ。

### 第2編　聯邦ノ大則及權限並ニ各州ト相關スル法

#### 第1章　聯邦ノ大則

第7條　日本武藏州　山城州　大和州　和泉州　攝津州　伊賀州　伊勢州　志摩州　尾張州　三河州　遠江州　駿河州　甲斐州　伊豆州　相模州　安房州　上總州　下總州　常陸州　近江州　美濃州　飛驒州　信濃州　上野州　下野州　岩代州　磐城州　陸前州　陸中州　陸奧州　羽前州　羽後州　若狹州　越前州　加賀州　能登州　越後州　越中州　佐渡州　丹後州　但馬州　因幡州　伯耆州　出雲州　石見州　隱岐州　播磨州　美作州　備中州　安藝州　周防州　長門州　紀伊州　淡路州　阿波州　讚岐州　伊豫州　土佐州　筑前州　筑後州　豐前州　豐後州　肥前州　肥後州　日向州　大隅州　薩摩州　壹岐州　對馬州　琉球州ヲ聯合シテ日本聯邦トナス。

第8條　日本聯邦ニ大政府ヲ置キ聯邦ノ政ヲ統ブ。

第9條　日本聯邦ハ日本各州ニ對シ其州ノ自由獨立ヲ保護スルヲ主トスベシ。

第10條　日本國内ニ於テ未ダ獨立ノ州ヲ爲サザル者ハ聯邦之ヲ管理ス。

第11條　日本聯邦ハ日本各州ニ對シ外國ノ侵寇ヲ保禦スルノ責アリ。

#### 第2章　聯邦ノ權限並ニ各州ト相關スル法

第12條　日本聯邦ハ日本各州相互ノ間ニ關シテ規則ヲ立ツルコトヲ得。

第13條　日本聯邦ハ日本各州ニ對シテ其一州内各自ノ事件ニ干渉スルヲ得ズ。其州内郡邑等ノ定制ニ干渉スルヲ得ズ。

第14條　日本聯邦ハ日本各州ノ土地ヲ奪ウヲ得ズ。其州ノ肯テ諾スルニ非ザ
レバ一州ヲモ廢スルヲ得ズ。

第15條　憲法ニ非ザレバ日本諸州ヲ合割スルヲ得ズ。諸州ノ境界ヲ變ズルヲ
得ズ。

第16條　日本國内ニ於テ新タニ州ヲ爲スニ就テ日本聯邦ニ合セントスル者ア
ルトキハ聯邦ハ之ヲ妨グルヲ得ズ。

第17條　外國ト諸盟約ヲ結ブノ權、國家ノ體面ヲ以テ諸外國ト交際ヲ爲スノ
權ハ聯邦ニアリ。

第18條　聯邦中ニ用フル度量衡ヲ制定スルノ權ハ聯邦ニアリ。

第19條　通貨ヲ造ルノ權ハ聯邦ニアリ。

第20條　海關税ヲ定ムルノ權ハ聯邦ニアリ。

第21條　宣戰講和ノ權ハ聯邦ニアリ。

第22條　日本聯邦ハ聯邦ノ管スル處ニ燈船燈臺浮標ヲ設クルヲ得同種類ノ者
ハ順次揚グルヲ得。

第23條　日本聯邦ハ驛遞ヲ管理スルヲ得。

第24條　日本聯邦ハ特ニ聯邦ニ關スル事物ノ爲メニ諸法律規則ヲ定ムルヲ得。

第25條　日本聯邦ハ外國貨幣及尺度權衡ノ聯邦内ニ通用スルモノニ併位ヲ定
ムルヲ得。

第26條　日本聯邦ニ常備軍ヲ設置スルヲ得。

第27條　日本中一州ト一州ト相互ノ間ニ渉ル爭訟ハ聯邦之ヲ審判ス。

第28條　日本各州ト外國使節ト公務ノ往復アルトキハ聯邦行政府ヲ經由ス。

## 第3編　各州ノ權限並ニ聯邦ト相關スル法

第29條　日本各州ハ日本聯邦ノ大ニ牴觸スルモノヲ除クノ外、皆獨立シテ自
由ナルモノトス。何等ノ政體政治ヲ行フトモ聯邦之ニ干渉スルコトナシ。

第30條　日本各州ハ外國ニ向ヒ國家ノ權利體面ニ關シ國土ニ關スル條約ヲ結
ブコトヲ得ズ。

第31條　日本各州ハ各國ニ向ヒ聯邦並ニ他州ノ權利ニ關セザル事ニ限リ、經
濟上ノ件警察上ノ件ニ就キ互約ヲ爲スヲ得、又タ法則ヲ立ツルコトヲ得。

第32條　日本各州ハ既ニ寇賊ノ來襲ヲ受ケ危急ニ迫ルニアラザレバ戰ヲ爲ス
ヲ得ズ。

第33條　日本各州ハ互ヒニ戰鬪スルヲ得ズ。爭訟アレバ決ヲ聯邦政府ニ仰グ。

第34條　日本各州ハ現ニ强敵ヲ受ケ大亂ノ生ジタルガ如キ危急ノ時機ニ際シ

テハ、聯邦ニ報ジテ救援ヲ求ムルコトヲ得、又タ他州ニ向テ應援ヲ請フコト
ヲ得、各州右ノ次第ヲ以テ他州ヨリ應援ヲ請ハレシ時眞ニ其危急ニ迫ルヲ知
ルトキハ赴援スルヲ得、其費ハ聯邦ニ於テ之ヲ辨ズ。

第35條　日本各州ハ護郷兵ヲ設置スルヲ得。

第36條　日本各州ハ常備兵ヲ設置スルヲ得。

第37條　日本各州ハ聯邦ノ許允ヲ待タズシテ二州以上互ニ盟約ヲ結ブヲ得ズ。

第38條　日本各州ヲ二州以上協議ヲ以テ其境界ヲ變改スルヲ得、又タ其州ヲ
合スルヲ得此事アルトキハ必ズ聯邦ニ通ゼザルベカラズ。

第39條

## 第４編　日本國民及日本人民ノ自由權利

第40條　日本ノ政治社會ニアル者之ヲ日本國人民トナス。

第41條　日本ノ人民ハ自ラ必ンデ之ヲ脱スルカ及自ラ諾スルニ非ザレバ日本
人タルコトヲ削カルヽコトナシ。

第42條　日本ノ人民ハ法律上ニ於テ平等トナス。

第43條　日本ノ人民ハ法律ノ外ニ於テ自由權利ヲ犯サレザルベシ。

第44條　日本ノ人民ハ生命ヲ全フシ、四肢ヲ全フシ、形體ヲ全フシ、健康ヲ
保チ、面目ヲ保チ、地上ノ物件ヲ使用スルノ權ヲ有ス。

第45條　日本ノ人民ハ何等ノ罪アリト雖モ生命ヲ奪ハレザルベシ。

第46條　日本ノ人民ハ法律ノ外ニ於テ何等ノ刑罰ヲモ科セラレザルベシ。又
タ法律ノ外ニ於テ鞫治セラレ、逮捕セラレ、拘留セラレ、禁錮セラレ、喚問
セラルヽコトナシ。

第47條　日本人民ハ一罪ノ爲メニ身體汚辱ノ刑ヲ再ビセラルヽコトナシ。

第48條　日本人民ハ拷問ヲ加ヘラルヽコトナシ。

第49條　日本人民ハ思想ノ自由ヲ有ス。

第50條　日本人民ハ如何ナル宗敎ヲ信ズルモ自由ナリ。

第51條　日本人民ハ言語ヲ述ブルノ自由權ヲ有ス。

第52條　日本人民ハ議論ヲ演ブルノ自由權ヲ有ス。

第53條　日本人民ハ言語ヲ筆記シ版行シテ之ヲ世ニ公ケニスルノ權ヲ有ス。

第54條　日本人民ハ自由ニ集會スルノ權ヲ有ス。

第55條　日本人民ハ自由ニ結社スルノ權ヲ有ス。

第56條　日本人民ハ自由ニ歩行スルノ權ヲ有ス。

第57條　日本人民ハ住居ヲ犯サレザルノ權ヲ有ス。

第58條　日本人民ハ何クニ住居スルモ自由トス、又タ何クニ旅行スルモ自由
トス。

第59條　日本人民ハ何等ノ教授ヲナシ何等ノ學ヲナスモ自由トス。

第60條　日本人民ハ如何ナル產業ヲ營ムモ自由トス。

第61條　日本人民ハ法律ノ正序ニ據ラズシテ屋內ヲ探檢セラレ、器物ヲ開視
セラルヽコトナシ。

第62條　日本人民ハ信書ノ祕密ヲ犯サレザルベシ。

第63條　日本人民ハ日本國ヲ辭スルコト自由トナス。

第64條　日本人民ハ凡ソ無法ニ抵抗スルコトヲ得。

第65條　日本人民ハ諸財產ヲ自由ニスルノ權アリ。

第66條　日本人民ハ何等ノ罪アリト雖モ其私有ヲ沒收セラルヽコトナシ。

第67條　日本人民ハ正當ノ報償ナクシテ所有ヲ公用トセラルヽコトナシ。

第68條　日本人民ハ各其名ヲ以テ政府ニ上書スルコトヲ得、各其身ノ爲メニ
請願ヲナスノ權アリ。其公立會社ニ於テハ會社ノ名ヲ以テ其書ヲ呈スルコト
ヲ得。

第69條　日本人民ハ諸政官ニ任ゼラルヽノ權アリ。

第70條　政府國憲ニ違背スルトキハ日本人民ハ之ニ從ハザルコトヲ得。

第71條　政府官吏壓制ヲ爲ストキハ日本人民ハ之ヲ排斥スルヲ得。
政府威力ヲ以テ擅恣暴虐ヲ逞フスルトキハ日本人民ハ兵器ヲ以テ之ニ抗スル
コトヲ得。

第72條　政府恣ニ國憲ニ背キ、擅ニ人民ノ自由權利ヲ浸害シ、建國ノ旨趣ヲ
妨グルトキハ日本國民ハ之ヲ覆滅シテ新政府ヲ建設スルコトヲ得。

第73條　日本人民ハ兵士ノ宿泊ヲ拒絕スルヲ得。

第74條　日本人民ハ法廷ニ喚問セラルヽ時ニ當リ、詞訴ノ起ル原由ヲ聽クヲ
得。
己レヲ訴フル本人ト對決スルヲ得、己レヲ助クル證據人及表白スルノ人ヲ得
ルノ權利アリ。

## 第5編　皇帝及皇族攝政
### 第1章　皇帝ノ特權

第75條　皇帝ハ國政ノ爲メニ責ニ任ゼズ。

第76條　皇帝ハ刑ヲ加ヘラルヽコトナシ。

第77條　皇帝ハ身體ニ屬スル賦稅ヲ免カル。

## 第2章　皇帝ノ權限

第78條　皇帝ハ兵馬ノ大權ヲ握ル、宣戰講和ノ權ヲ統ブ、他國ノ獨立ヲ認ムルト認メザルトヲ決ス。

但シ和戰ヲ決シタルトキハ直チニ立法院ニ報告セザルベカラズ。

第79條　皇帝ハ平時ニ在リ立法院ノ議ヲ經ズシテ兵士ヲ徵募スルヲ得。

第80條　皇帝ハ外國事務ノ總裁タリ、諸外交官ヲ命ズルヲ得、外國交際ノ禮ヲナスヲ得。

但シ國權ニ關スル條約連盟ハ立法院ノ議ヲ經ルニ非ラザレバ決行スルヲ得ズ。

第81條　皇帝ハ人民ニ勳等賞牌ヲ與フルコトヲ得、位階ヲ與フルコトヲ得ズ。

第82條　皇帝ハ立法院ノ議ニ由ラザレバ通貨ヲ創造若クハ改造スルヲ得ズ。

第83條　皇帝ハ立法議會ノ承諾ヲ經テ聯邦ノ罪囚ヲ赦免シ及降減スルコトヲ得。

聯邦既定ノ裁判ヲ他ノ裁判所ニ移シテ復審セシムルコトヲ得。

法司ノ法權ヲ施スヲ阻格スルヲ得ズ。

聯邦執政ノ職務罪ニ係ル者ハ聯邦立法院ニ反シテ恩赦ヲ與ヘ降減ヲナスコトヲ得ズ。

第84條　皇帝ハ立法議會ヲ延引スルヲ得、立法議院ノ承諾ナクシテ三十日ヲ越ユルコトヲ得ズ。

第85條　皇帝ハ諸兵備ヲ爲スヲ得。

第86條　皇帝ハ國政ヲ施行スルガ爲メニ必要ナル命令ヲ發スルコトヲ得。

第87條　皇帝ハ人民ノ權利ニ係ルコト、國家ノ金錢ヲ費スベキコト、國家ノ土地ヲ變ズベキコトヲ專行スルヲ得ズ。必ズ聯邦立法院ノ議ヲ經ルヲ要ス、立法院ノ議ヲ經ザルモノハ實行スルノ效ナシ。

第88條　皇帝ハ聯邦行政政府ニ出頭シテ政ヲ乘ル。

第89條　皇帝ハ聯邦行政政府ノ長タリ、常ニ聯邦行政ノ權ヲ統ブ。

特別ニ定ムル者ノ外聯邦諸行政官吏ヲ命ズルコトヲ得。

第90條　皇帝ハ聯邦司法廳ノ長タリ、其名ヲ以テ法權ヲ行フ、又タ法官ヲ命ズ。

第91條　皇帝ハ現行ノ法律ヲ廢シ、已定ノ法律ヲ格置スルヲ得ズ。

第92條　皇帝ハ法ノ外ニ於テ租税ヲ收ムルヲ得ズ。

第93條　皇帝ハ法ノ外ニ於テ立法院ノ議ヲ拒ムヲ得ズ。

第94條　皇帝ハ立法議會ト意見ヲ異ニシテ和セザルニ當リ、一タビ其議會ヲ解散スルコトヲ得、之ヲ解散シタルトキハ必ズ三日内ヲ以テ其旨ヲ各選擧區

ニ達シ、且人民ヲシテ更ラニ議員ヲ選バシメ、必ズ六十日以内ヲ以テ議會ヲ
復開セザルベカラズ。一タビ解散シタル上ニテ復開シタル議會ハ同事件ニ就
テ再タビ解散スルコトヲ得ズ。

第95條　立法院ノ議決シタルコトニシテ皇帝之ヲ實施シ難シト爲ストキハ、
議會ヲナシテ之ヲ再議セシムルヲ得、此ノ如キトキハ皇帝ハ其由ヲ詳記陳辯
セザルベカラズ。

第3章　皇帝及帝位繼承

第96條　日本國皇帝ノ位ハ、今上天皇　睦仁陛下ニ屬ス。

第97條　今上皇帝陛下位ヲ去レバ陛下ノ正統子孫ニ傳フ。若シ子孫ナキトキ
ハ尊族ノ親近ナル者ニ讓ル、左ノ次序ニ循フ。

今上皇帝ノ位ハ第一　嫡皇子及其統ニ世傳ス。

第二　嫡皇子及其統ナキトキハ嫡庶子及其統ニ世傳ス。

第三　嫡庶子及其統ナキトキハ庶皇子及其統ニ世傳ス。

第四　以上統ナキトキハ嫡皇女及其統ニ世傳ス。

第五　以上統ナキトキハ庶皇女ニ世傳ス。

第六　若シモ以上ノ嫡皇子孫庶皇子孫及其統ナキトキハ皇帝兄弟姉妹及其統
ニ世傳ス。

第七　若シモ皇帝ノ嫡庶子孫兄弟姉妹伯叔父母及其統ナキトキハ立法院ノ議
ヲ以テ皇族中ヨリ選デ其嗣ヲ定ム。

第98條　帝位繼承ノ順序ハ男ハ女ニ先チ長ハ幼ニ先チ嫡ハ庶ニ先ツ。

第99條　非常特別ノコトアリ、帝位繼承ノ順序ヲ變ゼントスルコトアレバ、
皇帝ト立法院トノ協議ヲ經テ之ヲ行フベシ。

第4章　皇帝ノ卽位

第100條　皇帝ノ卽位ハ必ズ立法議員列席ノ前ニ於テス。

第5章　皇帝ノ婚姻

第101條　皇帝ノ婚姻ハ必ズ立法院ノ議ヲ經ルヲ要ス。

第102條　女帝ノ夫婿ハ王權ニ干渉スルヲ得ズ。

第6章　皇帝ノ歳俸

第103條　皇帝ハ年々國庫ヨリ　萬圓ノ俸ヲ受ク。

第7章　皇帝ノ年齢

第104條　皇帝ノ歳未ダ十八歳ニ至ラザル内ハ之ヲ未成年ト定ム。十八歳ニ及
ベバ之ヲ成年ト定ム。

## 第8章　攝政

第105條　皇帝未成年ノ間ハ攝政ヲ置ク。

第106條　皇帝長ク事故アリテ親カラ政ヲ秉ルコト能ハザルトキハ攝政職ヲ置ク。

第107條　皇帝事故アリテ攝政職ヲ置クノ時ニ際シ、皇太子成年ナルトキハ皇太子ヲ以テ攝政ニ當ツ。

第108條　攝政ハ皇帝ノ名ヲ以テ王權ヲ行フ。

第109條　攝政ノ職制章程ハ立法院ニ於テ之ヲ立定ス。

第110條　攝政官ハ皇帝又ハ主相之ヲ指名シ、立法院之ヲ定ム。

第111條　皇帝嗣未成年中ニ其位ヲ讓シトスルノ場合ニ於テハ、豫メ攝政官ヲ指名シテ立法院ノ議ニ附シ之ヲ定ムルコトヲ得。

## 第9章　皇族

第112條　皇太子ハ身體ニ關スル賦課ヲ免カル。

第113條　皇太子ハ年々國庫ヨリ支給ヲ受ク、法章之ヲ定ム。

# 第6編　立法權ニ關スル諸則

## 第1章　立法權ニ關スル大則

第114條　日本聯邦ニ關スル立法ノ權ハ日本聯邦人民全體ニ屬ス。

第115條　日本聯邦人民ハ皆聯邦ノ立法議政ノ權ニ與カルコトヲ得。

第116條　日本皇帝ハ日本聯邦立法權ニ與カルコトヲ得。

第117條　日本聯邦ノ法律制度ハ聯邦立法院ニ於テ立定ス。

第118條　聯邦立法院ハ全國ニ一ヲ置ク。

第119條　聯邦立法ノ權ハ限數人代議ノ制ヲ用ヒテ之ヲ行フ。

## 第2章　立法院權限

第120條　聯邦立法院ハ聯邦ニ關スル租税ヲ定ムルノ權ヲ有ス。

第121條　聯邦立法院ハ聯邦ノ軍律ヲ定ルコトヲ得。

第122條　聯邦立法院ハ聯邦裁判所ノ訴訟法ヲ定ルヲ得。

第123條　聯邦立法院ハ聯邦ニ關スル兵制ヲ議定スルコトヲ得。

第124條　聯邦立法院ハ聯邦ノ名ヲ以テ國債ヲ起シ金錢ヲ借リ及之ヲ償却スルノ法ヲ立ルコトヲ得。

第125條　聯邦立法院ハ通貨ニ關スル法律ヲ立ルコトヲ得、聯邦ニ對スル國事犯罪律ヲ定ルヲ得。

第126條　聯邦立法院ハ郵便ノ制ヲ立ルヲ得。

第127條　聯邦立法院ハ聯邦ノ通貨ヲ增減改造スルノ議ヲ定ルコトヲ得。

第128條　聯邦立法院ハ聯邦ノ共有物ヲ所置スルコトヲ得。

第129條　聯邦立法院ハ聯邦政府ノ保證ヲ爲ス銀行會社ノ規則ヲ立ルコトヲ得。

第130條　聯邦立法院ハ切要ナル調査ニ關シ聯邦ノ官吏ヲ議場ニ提喚スルノ權アリ、又聯邦人民ヲ召喚スルノ權アリ、又聯邦人民ヲ召喚シテ事情ヲ質スルコトヲ得。

第131條　聯邦立法院ハ憲法ノ許ス所ノ權利ヲ行フガ爲メニ諸規則ヲ立ルヲ得。

第132條　聯邦立法院ハ外國人並ニ國外ノ者ニ關スル規則ヲ立ツルコトヲ得。

第133條　聯邦立法院ハ聯邦行政府諸執行ノ職務ニ關セル罪科並ニ國事犯罪ヲ彈劾論告シ正的ノ法院ニ求刑スルノ權ヲ有ス。

第134條　聯邦立法院ハ本院議ノ權任ヲ監査スルノ權アリ。

第135條　聯邦立法院ハ議員ニシテ其職分ニ係スル命令規則ニ違背スル者ヲ處分スルヲ得。

第136條　聯邦立法院ハ既往ニ溯ルノ法律ヲ立ルヲ得ズ。

第137條　聯邦立法院ハ外國ト條約ヲ結ビ連盟ヲ爲スヲ決定スルノ權アリ。但シ國權ノ獨立ヲ失フノ契約ヲナスヲ得ズ。

第138條　聯邦立法院ハ行政部ニ對シ推問ノ權ヲ有ス。

### 第3章　立法議員ノ權力

第139條　聯邦立法議員ハ其職ヲ行フニ付キ發言シタル意見ニ就テ糾治檢索セラル、コトナシ。

第140條　聯邦立法議員ハ本院ノ許可ヲ經ズシテ開會ノ間並ニ其前後三十日間ハ要領ノ爲メニ拘引拘留セラル、コトナシ。刑事ノ爲メニ拿捕セラレ、糾治セラル、コトナシ。

但シ現行犯ハ此ノ限リニアラズ。

### 第4章　議員選擧及被選擧ノ法

第141條　聯邦議員ハ聯邦人民之ヲ直選ス。

第142條　聯邦議員ハ一州各七名ト定ム。

第143條　現ニ租税ヲ納メザル者、現ニ法律ノ罪ニ服シ居ル者、政府ノ官吏ハ議員ヲ選擧スルコトヲ得ズ。

第144條　現ニ法律ノ罪ニ服シ居ル者、政府官吏ハ議員ニ選擧セラル、コトヲ得ズ。

第145條　日本各州ハ何レノ州ノ人ヲ選擧シテ議員トナスモ自由トス。

## 第5章　議員ノ任期

第146條　聯邦ノ立法議員ハ三年ヲ一期トシ、三年毎ニ全員ヲ改選ス。

## 第6章　議員ノ償給旅費

第147條　聯邦ノ立法議員ハ年々國庫ヨリ三千圓ノ手當金ヲ受ク、又其會議ニ出ヅル毎ニ往復旅費ヲ受ク。

## 第7章　議員ノ制限

第148條　聯邦ノ立法議員ハ聯邦行政官ヲ兼ヌルヲ得ズ。

## 第8章　立法會議

第149條　聯邦ノ立法會議ハ毎年一回之ヲ爲ス、其ノ他事ナキニ於テハ十月第一ノ月曜日ニ之ヲ開ク。

第150條　議事ノ多少ニ依リ皇帝ハ時々期日ヲ伸縮スルヲ得、然レドモ議員過半數ノ同意アルトキハ皇帝ノ命アリト雖モ議會其伸縮ヲ定ム。

## 第9章　立法會議開閉集散

第151條　非常ノ事件アリテ會議ヲ要スルトキハ皇帝ハ臨時會ヲ開クコトヲ得。

第152條　聯邦會議ノ開閉ハ皇帝之ヲ司ル。

第153條　毎年ノ常會ハ皇帝ノ命ナシト雖モ聯邦議員ハ自ラ會シテ議事ヲ爲スコトヲ得。

第154條　皇帝死去ノ時ニ在リテハ聯邦議會ハ臨時會ヲ開ク。

第155條　現在議員ノ年期已ニ盡クルノ際、未ダ交代ス可キノ議員ノ選擧セラレザルノ間ニ於テ皇帝崩ズルコトアルトキハ、前期ノ議員集合シテ新議員ヲ生ズル迄會議ヲ爲スコトヲ得。

第156條　立法會議皇帝ノ爲メニ解散セラレ、皇帝國法ノ通リニ復立セザルトキハ解散セラレタル議會ハ自ラ復會スルヲ得。

## 第10章　會議規則

第157條　聯邦立法議案ハ立法院國王倶ニ之ヲ出スコトヲ得。

第158條　聯邦立法議會ノ議長ハ立法院ニ於テ議員ヨリ公選ス。

第159條　凡會議ハ議員全數ノ過半數ノ出席ナレバ之ヲ開クコトヲ得。但シ同一事件ニ付再度以上集會ヲ催シタルトキハ、過半數ノ出席ナシト雖モ議事ヲナスコトヲ得。

第160條　特別ニ定メタル規則ナキ事件ノ議事ハ綜テ出席員過半數ノ議ヲ以テ決定ス。兩議同數ナルコトアルトキハ議長ノ傾向スル所ニ決ス。

第161條　聯邦ノ立法會議ハ公ニ傍聽ヲ許ス。其特異ノ時機ニ際シテハ秘密ニスルヲ得。

### 第11章 立法院ノ決議ヲ國法トナスニ就テ皇帝ト相關スル規則

第162條 　聯邦立法院ニテ決定シタル成説ハ皇帝ニ呈シテ承認ヲ得ルヲ必トス。

第163條 　皇帝立法院ノ成議ヲ受取ラバ三日以内ニ必ズ其答ヲ爲サザルベカラズ。若シ其熟考セント要スルコトアラバ其趣ヲ申通シテ二十日以内ニ可否ヲ示ス。

第164條 　聯邦立法院ノ決定スル所ニシテ皇帝準許セザルコトアルトキハ立法院ヲシテ之ヲ再議セシム。

立法院之ヲ再議シタルトキハ議員總數過半以上ノ同意アルヲ見レバ更ラニ奏シテ必ズ之ヲ行フニ定ム。

## 第7編 　行政權ニ關スル諸則
### 第1章 　行政權ニ關スル大則

第165條 　日本聯邦行政權ハ日本皇帝ニ屬ス。

第166條 　日本聯邦ノ行政府ハ日本皇帝ニ於テ統轄ス。

第167條 　日本聯邦ノ行政權ハ聯邦行政府ニ於テ開施ス。

第168條 　皇帝ノ行政權ヲ行フニ就テハ、國家ニ一ノ主相ヲ置キ、又諸政ノ類ヲ分テ其ノ各省ヲ設ケ其各主務官ヲ命ズ。

第169條 　皇帝ヨリ出ス諸件ノ布告ハ主相ノ名ヲ署シ、當該ノ本任長官副署シテ之ヲ發ス。執政ノ副署ナキモノハ實行スルノ效ナシ。

第170條 　皇帝ヨリ發スル諸件ノ布告ニ就テハ、主相及當該ノ本任長官其責ニ任ズ。但シ執政ノ副署ナキモノハ執政ハ責ニ任ゼズ。

### 第2章 　行政官

第171條 　聯邦行政官ハ皇帝ノ命ニ從フテ其職務ヲ取ル。

第172條 　主相ハ皇帝ニ奏シテ諸省ノ長官ヲ任命スルヲ得。

第173條 　聯邦執政ハ議案ヲ草シテ立法議會ニ提出スルヲ得、又議會ニ參スルヲ得、決議ノ數ニ入ルコトヲ得ズ。

第174條 　聯邦行政官ハ聯邦立法議員ヲ兼ヌルヲ得ズ。

第175條 　聯邦行政官ハ其執行スル政務ニ就キ皇帝並ニ國民ニ對シテ責ニ任ズ。

其一執政ノ分テ爲セシコトハ當該ノ一執政乃チ其責ニ任ズ。其衆執政分テ爲セシコトハ衆執政連帶シテ其責ニ任ゼズ。

第176條　聯邦行政官タル者職務上ノ罪犯過失ニ就キ彈劾セラレ糺問セラル、間ハ、其職ヲ辭スルヲ得ズ。

## 第3章　行政府

第177條　聯邦行政府ハ毎歳國費ニ關スル議案ヲ草シ立法議會ニ出ス。

第178條　聯邦行政府ハ毎歳國費決算書ヲ製シ立法議院ニ報ズ。

## 第4章　統計局

第179條　國家歳出入ノ豫算表精算表ハ行政府統計局ニ於テ之ヲ調成ス。

第180條　統計局ノ長官ハ立法院之ヲ選任ス。

第181條　統計局ハ國家ノ出納會計ヲ檢査監察スルコトヲ得。

第182條　統計局ハ行政各部ヨリ會計ニ關スル一切ノ書類ヲ拾聚スルコトヲ得。

## 第8編　司法權ニ關スル諸規則
### 第1章　司法權ニ關スル大則

第183條　聯邦司法權ハ法律ニ定メタル法衙ニ於テ之ヲ實施ス。

第184條　特別ノ定メナキ民事刑事ノ裁判訴訟ハ司法權ノ管理ニ歸ス。

第185條　非常法衙ヲ設ケ非常法官ヲ選デ臨時ニ司法權ヲ行フコトヲ得ズ。

第186條　軍人ノ軍律ヲ犯スモノハ其軍ノ裁判所ニ於テ其軍ノ律ニ處ス。

### 第2章　法官

第187條　凡ソ聯邦法官ハ立法議院ニ於テ任免ス。

第188條　法官ハ俸給アル職任ヲ兼ヌルコトヲ得ズ、立法議員ヲ兼ヌルコトヲ得ズ。

### 第3章　法衙

第189條　聯邦法衙ハ憲法ニ遵フノ外不羈ニシテ他ノ管轄ヲ受ケズ。

### 第4章　裁判

第190條　凡ソ裁判ハ理由ヲ附シ所以ヲ明ニス。

第191條　民事裁判ハ代言ヲ許ス。

第192條　刑事裁判ハ陪審ヲ設ケ辯護人ヲ許ス。

第193條　裁判ハ衆人ノ傍聽ヲ許シテ公ケニ之ヲ行フ、風俗ヲ害スル事件ニ限リテ傍聽ヲ禁ズルコトヲ得。

### 第5章　高等法院

第194條　諸法衙ノ外日本全國ニ一ノ高等法院ヲ置ク。

第195條　高等法院ハ執政ノ職務ニ係ル事案ヲ審判ス。

第196條　高等法院ハ皇帝ニ對スル犯罪、聯邦ニ對スル犯罪ノ如キ通常罪犯ノ外ナル非常ノ大犯罪ヲ審明ス。

### 第9編　土地

第197條　國家土地ハ全國家ノ共有トス。

第198條　國家ノ土地ハ立法院ノ議ニ非ラザレバ一モ動カス事ヲ得ズ。

第199條　國家ノ土地ハ立法院ノ議ニ非ラザレバ之ヲ他國ニ賣リ、若クハ讓リ、若クハ交換シ、若クハ抵當ニ入ルヽコトヲ得ズ。

### 第10編　租税

第200條　聯邦ノ租税ハ各州ヨリ課ス。其額ハ法律之ヲ定ム。

第201條　聯邦ノ租税ハ聯邦立法ノ議ヲ經ルニ非ラザレバ一モ徵收スルヲ得ズ。

第202條　聯邦ノ租税ハ毎年一回立法院ニ於テ議定ス。

### 第11編　國金

第203條　聯邦ノ金錢ハ憲法ニ依ルニ非ラザレバ之ヲ使用シ之ヲ消費スルヲ得ズ。

### 第12編　財政

第204條　憲法ニ依ルニ非ラザレバ政府ハ國債ヲ起スヲ得ズ。

第205條　憲法ニ依ラザレバ政府ハ諸債ノ保障ニ立ツコトヲ得ズ。

### 第13編　會計

第206條　毎年一切ノ出納ハ豫算表並ニ精算表ニ掲ゲテ必ズ國家ニ公示ス。

### 第14編　軍兵

第207條　國家ノ兵權ハ皇帝ニ在リ。

第208條　國軍ノ大元帥ハ皇帝ト定ム。

第209條　國軍ノ將校ハ皇帝之ヲ選任ス。

第210條　常備兵ハ法則ニ從ヒ皇帝ヨリ民衆中ニ募リテ之ニ應ズルモノヲ用ユ。

第211條　常備軍ヲ監督スルハ皇帝ニ在リ。非常ノコトアルニ際シテハ皇帝ハ
常備軍ノ外ニ於テ軍兵ヲ募リ、志願ニ隨フテ之ヲ用フルヲ得。

第212條　他國ノ兵ハ立法院ノ議ヲ經ルニ非ラザレバ雇使スルヲ得ズ。

（本編初條ニ
置ク見込ミ）軍兵ハ國憲ヲ護衞スルモノトス。

## 第15編　外國人歸化

第213條　日本國ハ外國人ノ歸化ヲ許ス。

## 第16編　特法

第214條　内外戰亂アル時ニ限リ、其地ニ於テハ一時人身自由住居自由言論出
版自由集會結社自由等ノ權利ヲ行フ力ヲ制シ、取締ノ規則ヲ立ツルコトアル
ベシ。其ノ時機ヲ終ヘバ必ズ直チニ之ヲ廢セザルヲ得ズ。

第215條　戰亂ノ爲メニ已ムヲ得ザルコトアレバ相當ノ償ヲ爲シテ民人ノ私
有ヲ收用シ、若クハ之ヲ滅盡シ、若クハ之ヲ消費スルコトアルベシ。其最モ
急ニシテ豫メ本人ニ照會シ豫メ償ヲ爲スコト暇ナキトキハ、後ニテ其償ヲ爲
スヲ得。

第216條　戰亂アルノ場合ニハ、其時ニ限リ已ムヲ得ザルコトノミ法律ヲ置格
スルコトアルベシ。

## 第17編　鐵道電信陸路水利

第217條　新ニ鐵道ヲ造リ、電信ヲ架シ、陸路ヲ啓キ、水利ヲ通ズル等ノコト
ハ通常會議ニ於テ之ヲ議スルヲ得ズ。立法議員特別ノ會議ヲ以テ之ヲ定ムル
ヲ得。議員過半數ノ同意アルモノハ之ヲ行フコトヲ得。

## 第18編　憲法改正

第218條　日本國憲法ヲ添削改正スルトキハ必ズ立法會議ニ於テ之ヲ定ム。

第219條　憲法改正ノ議事ハ其日ノ出席議員數如何ニ關セズ議員總數ノ過半
數ノ同意ニアラザレバ決定スルヲ得ズ。

### 附則

第220條　日本國憲法施行ノ日ヨリ一切ノ法律條例布告等ノ國憲ニ牴觸スル
モノハ皆之ヲ廢ス。

# REFERENCES AND

# BIBLIOGRAPHY

Adams, Bert N. 1971. *The American Family: A Sociological Interpretation.* Chicago: Markham Publishing Company.

Akita, George. 1967. *Foundations of Constitutional Government in Modern Japan, 1868–1900.* Cambridge: Harvard University Press.

Amakawa Akira, and Takemae Eiji. 1977. *Nihon Senryō-hishi* (A Secret History of the Occupation).* 2 vols. Tokyo: Asahi Shimbunsha.

Arblaster, Anthony. 1984. *The Rise and Decline of Western Liberalism.* Oxford: Basil Blackwell.

Arieli, Yehoshua. 1964. *Individualism and Nationalism in American Ideology.* Baltimore: Penguin Books.

Arikura Ryōkichi, and Hasegawa Masayasu, eds. 1978. *Kempō Gakusetsu-shi* (A History of Constitutional Theories). 16 vols. Tokyo: Sanseidō.

Aruga Kizaemon. 1966–71. *Aruga Kizaemon Chosaku-shū* (Complete Works of Aruga Kizaemon). 11 vols. Tokyo: Miraisha.

———. 1967. "Senzo-to Uji-gami" (The Ancestors and the Uji-gami). *Minzoku-gaku Kenkyū* 32, no. 3, pp. 175–84.

Ashida Hitoshi. 1986. *Ashida Hitoshi Nikki* (The Diary of Ashida Hitoshi). 7 vols. Tokyo: Iwanami Shoten.

Ashida Hitoshi et al. 1952. "Kempō-wa Nishūkan-de Dekita-ka" (Was the Constitution Created in Two Weeks?). *Kaizō,* supplement to the April 1952 issue, pp. 13–25. A round table discussion by Ashida Hitoshi, Iwabuchi Tatsuo, Suzuki Yasuzō, Miyake Kiyoteru, and Abe Shinnosuke (moderator).

Asō Yoshiteru. 1942. *Kinsei Nihon Tetsugaku-shi* (A History of Modern Philosophy). Tokyo: Kondō Shoten.

Aston, W. G. 1972. *Nihongi: Chronicle of Japan from the Earliest Time to* A. D. *607,* translated from the original Chinese and Japanese by W. G. Aston. Tokyo: Charles E. Tuttle Co.

Austin, J. L. 1962. *How to Do Things With Words.* London: Oxford University Press.

---

* This and all other English titles of the books and articles in parentheses are my own translations, unless otherwise noted.

Baelz, Erwin. 1932. *Awakening Japan: The Diary of a German Doctor: Erwin Baelz*, edited by his son, Toku Baelz. New York: Viking Press. (Repr. Bloomington: Indiana University Press, 1974). Originally published as *Das Leben eines deutschen Arztes im erwachenden Japan.* Stuttgart: J. Engelhorns Nachf., 1931.

Bailyn, Bernard. 1960. *Education in the Forming of American Society: Needs and Opportunities for Study.* Chapel Hill: University of North Carolina Press.

———. 1967. *The Ideological Origins of the American Revolution.* Cambridge: Harvard University Press.

———. 1968. *The Origins of American Politics.* New York: Vintage Books.

Barraclough, Geoffrey. 1967. *An Introduction to Contemporary History.* Middlesex, England: Penguin Books Ltd.

Basso, Keith H., and Henry A. Selby, eds. 1976. *Meaning in Anthropology.* Albuquerque: University of New Mexico Press.

Beckmann, George M. 1957. *The Making of the Meiji Constitution: The Oligarchs and the Constitutional Development of Japan, 1868–1891.* Westport, Conn.: Greenwood Press.

Beer, Lawrence Ward. 1976. "Freedom of Expression in Japan with Comparative Reference to the United States." Pp. 99–126 in *Comparative Human Rights,* ed. Richard P. Claude. Baltimore: Johns Hopkins University Press.

Beer, Lawrence Ward, ed. 1979. *Constitutionalism in Asia: Asian Views of the American influence.* Berkeley: University of California Press.

Befu Harumi. 1971. *Japan: An Anthropological Introduction.* New York: Harper and Row.

Bellah, Robert N. 1985. *Tokugawa Religion: The Cultural Roots of Modern Japan.* New York: The Free Press. Originally published 1957.

Bellah, Robert N., Richard Madsen, William M. Sullivan, Ann Swidler, and Steven M. Tipton. 1985. *Habits of the Heart: Individualism and Commitment in American Life.* Berkeley: University of California Press.

Benedict, Ruth. 1946. *The Chrysanthemum and the Sword: Patterns of Japanese Culture.* New York: New American Library.

Benn, S. I., and R. S. Peters. 1959. *Principles of Political Thought.* New York: Collier Books.

Berger, Peter, Brigitte Berger, and Hansfried Kellner. 1973. *The Homeless Mind: Modernization and Consciousness.* New York: Vintage Books.

Bisson, Thomas A. 1983. *Nihon Senryō Kaisō-ki* (Recollections on the Occupation of Japan). Tokyo: Sanseidō. A translation by Nakamura Masanori and Miura Yōichi of the manuscript "Reform Years in Japan, 1945–47: An occupation memoir."

Blacker, Carmen. 1964. *The Japanese Enlightenment: A Study of the Writings of Fukuzawa Yukichi.* Cambridge: Cambridge University Press.

Boles, Janet K. 1979. *The Politics of the Equal Rights Amendment: Conflict and the Decision Process.* New York: Longman Inc.

Borton, Hugh. 1967. *American Presurrender Planning for Postwar Japan.* New York: East Asian Institute, Columbia University.

Brown, Roger W. 1980. *Rebellion and Democracy in Meiji Japan: A Study of Commoners in the Popular Rights Movement.* Berkeley: University of California Press.

Burke, Kenneth. 1973. *The Philosophy of Literary Form: Studies in Symbolic Action.* 3d ed. Berkeley: University of California Press.

Byrnes, James F. 1947. *Speaking Frankly.* New York: Harper and Brothers.

Christopher, Robert C. 1983. *The Japanese Mind: The Goliath Explained.* New York: Simon and Schuster.

Claude, Richard P., ed. 1976. *Comparative Human Rights.* Baltimore: Johns Hopkins University Press.

Commission on the Constitution. *See* Kempō Chōsa-kai

Curry, Thomas J. 1986. *The First Freedoms: Church and State in America to the Passage of the First Amendment.* New York: Oxford University Press.

DeFrancis, John. 1989. *Visible Speech: The Diverse Oneness of Writing Systems.* Honolulu: University of Hawaii Press.

Doi Takeo. 1971. *Amae-no Kōzō* (The Structure of Dependence). Tokyo: Kōbundō.

———. 1973. *The Anatomy of Dependence.* Trans. John Besler. Tokyo: Kodansha.

———. 1975. *Amae Zakkō* (Miscellaneous Essays on Dependence). Tokyo: Kōbundō.

———. 1985. *Omote-to Ura* (Outside and Inside). Tokyo: Kōbundō.

Dore, Ronald. 1985. "Authority and Benevolence: The Confucian Recipe for Industrial Success." An amended version of the McCallum Lecture, Pembroke College, Oxford, 3 November 1984. *Government and Opposition* 2, no. 2 (Spring 1985), pp. 196–217.

Earhart, H. Byron. 1982. *Japanese Religion: Unity and Diversity.* 3d ed. Belmont, Calif.: Wadsworth Publishing Company.

Emura Eiichi. 1984. *Jiyū Minken Kakumei-no Kenkyū* (A Study of the Popular Rights Revolution). Tokyo: Hōsei Daigaku Shuppan-kyoku.

Etō Jun. 1978. *Mō-hitotsu-no Sengo-shi* (Another History of the Postwar Japan). Tokyo: Kōdansha.

Fairbank, John King. 1982. *Chinabound: A Fifty-Year Memoir.* New York: Harper and Row.

The Federalist. 1961. *The Federalist,* by Alexander Hamilton, James Madison, and John Jay. Edited by Benjamin F. Wright. Cambridge: Belknap Press of Harvard University Press.

Fujii Shin'ichi. 1965. *The Constitution of Japan: A Historical Survey.* Tokyo: Kokushikan University.

Fukuo Takeichirō. 1972. *Nihon Kazoku Seido Gaisetsu* (A Survey of the Japanese Family System). Tokyo: Yoshikawa Kōbunkan.

Fukuzawa Yukichi. 1966. *The Autobiography of Yukichi Fukuzawa.* Rev. translation by Eiichi Kiyooka, with a foreword by Carmen Blacker. New York: Columbia University Press.

———. 1969. *An Encouragement of Learning.* Trans. David A. Dilworth, and Umeyo Hirano. Tokyo: Sophia University Press.

————. 1980–81. *Fukuzawa Yukichi Senshū* (Selected Works of Fukuzawa Yukichi). Ed. Tomita Masafumi. 14 vols. Tokyo: Iwanami Shoten.

Gaimu-shō (Ministry of Foreign Affairs), ed. 1952. *Shūsen Shiroku* (A Historical Record of the War's End). Tokyo: Shimbun Gekkansha.

Gayne, Mark. 1981. *Japan Diary*. Rutland, Vermont: Charles E. Tuttle Co.

Geertz, Clifford. 1973. *The Interpretation of Cultures: Selected Essays*. New York: Basic Books.

Gluck, Carol. 1985. *Japan's Modern Myths: Ideology in the Late Meiji Period*. Princeton, N.J.: Princeton University Press.

Greene, Jack P., ed. 1968. *The Reinterpretation of the American Revolution, 1763–1789*. New York: Harper and Row.

Grew, Joseph C. 1952. *Turbulent Era: A Diplomatic Record of Forty Years, 1904–1945*. 2 vols. Ed. Walter Johnson. Boston: Houghton Mifflin.

Habien, Yaeko Satō. 1984. *The History of the Japanese Written Language*. Tokyo: University of Tokyo Press.

Haley, John O. 1982. "Sheathing the Sword of Justice in Japan: An Essay on Law without Sanctions." *Journal of Japanese Studies* 8, no. 2, pp. 265–81.

Hall, John Whitney. 1961. "Foundations of the Modern Japanese Daimyo." *Journal of Asian Studies* 20, no. 3, pp. 317–29.

————. 1968. "A Monarch for Modern Japan." Pp. 11–64 in *Political Development in Modern Japan*, ed. Robert E. Ward. Princeton: Princeton University Press.

Handō Kazutoshi. 1985. *Seidan: Tennō-to Suzuki Kantarō* (The Sacred Decision: The Emperor and Suzuki Kantarō). Tokyo: Bungei Shunjūsha.

Hane Mikiso. 1986. *Modern Japan: A Historical Survey*. Boulder, Colo.: Westview Press.

Hardwig, John. 1984. "Should Women Think in Terms of Rights?" *Ethics* 94, no. 3, pp. 441–55.

Haring, Douglas G., ed. 1946. *Japan's Prospect*. Cambridge: Harvard University Press.

Harries, Meirion, and Susie Harries. 1987. *Sheathing the Sword: The Demilitarisation of Japan*. London: Hamish Hamilton.

Hartz, Louis. 1955. *The Liberal Tradition in America: An Interpretation of American Political Thought since the Revolution*. New York: Harcourt, Brace and Co.

————. 1967. "The Rise of the Democratic Idea." Pp. 59–77 in *Origins of American Political Thought*, ed. John P. Roche. New York: Harper and Row.

Hayashi Ōki. 1981. "Hōritsu-to Bumpō-ya" (Law and a Grammarian). Pp. 241–64 in *Hō-to Nihongo* (Law and the Japanese Language), ed. Hayashi Ōki, and Aomi Jun'ichi. Tokyo: Yūhikaku.

Hayashi Ōki, and Aomi Jun'ichi, eds. 1981. *Hō-to Nihon-go: Hōritsu Yōgo-wa Naze Muzukashii-ka* (Law and the Japanese Language: Why the Legal Terms are Difficult). Tokyo: Yūhikaku.

Henderson, Dan Fenno, ed. 1968. *The Constitution of Japan: Its First Twenty Years, 1947–67.* Seattle: University of Washington Press.

———. 1968. "Law and Political Modernization in Japan." Pp. 387–456 in *Political Development in Modern Japan,* ed. Robert E. Ward. Princeton, N.J.: Princeton University Press.

Hirai Atsuko. 1979. "Self-Realization and Common Good: T. H. Green in Meiji Ethical Thought." *Journal of Japanese Studies* 5, no. 1, pp. 107–36.

Hiramatsu Yoshirō. 1976. *Tokugawa Law.* Trans. Dan F. Henderson. Reprint from *Law in Japan* 14 (1981). 48 pp.

House of Peers. *See* Kizoku-in

House of Representatives. *See* Shūgi-in

Hussey, Alfred R., Jr. N.d. The Hussey Papers. Asia Library, University of Illinois at Urbana-Champaign. Microfilm reels 5 and 6 on the making of the Japanese Constitution.

Ienaga Saburō. 1955. *Kakumei-no Senkusha: Ueki Emori-no Hito-to Shisō* (A Pioneer in the Popular Rights Movement: The Ideas and Personality of Ueki Emori). Tokyo: Iwanami Shoten.

———. 1960. *Ueki Emori Kenkyū* (A Study of Ueki Emori). Tokyo: Iwanami Shoten.

Ike Nobutaka. 1950. *The Beginnings of Political Democracy in Japan.* Baltimore: Johns Hopkins Press.

———. 1978. *A Theory of Japanese Democracy.* Boulder, Colo.: Westview Press.

Inada Masatsugu. 1960–62. *Meiji Kempō Seiritsu-shi* (A History of the Making the Meiji Constitution). 2 vols. Tokyo: Yūhikaku.

———. 1979. *Meiji Kempō Seiritsu-shi-no Kenkyū* (A Study of the History of the Making of the Meiji Constitution). Tokyo: Yūhikaku.

Inoue Kiyoshi. 1967. *Tennō-sei* (The Imperial Institution). Tokyo: Tokyo Daigaku Shuppankai.

Inoue, Kyōko. 1979. "Japanese: A Story of Language and People." Pp. 241–300 in *Languages and Their Speakers,* ed. Timothy Shopen. Cambridge, Mass.: Winthrop Publishers, Inc. Reprinted in paperback by University of Pennsylvania Press, 1987.

———. 1982. "The Making of the Japanese Constitution: A Linguist's Perspective." *Language Problems and Language Planning* 6, no. 3, pp. 271–85.

———. 1986. "The Constitution of Japan and Its English Translation." Pp. 199–212 in *Languages in the International Perspective,* ed. Nancy Schweda-Nicholson. Norwood, N.J.: Ablex Publishing Corp.

———. 1987. "Democracy in the Ambiguities of Two Languages and Cultures: The Birth of a Japanese Constitution." *Linguistics* 25, no. 3, 595–606.

Irie Toshio. 1955. "Kempō Sōan Yoroku" (Some Unofficial Notes on the Constitutional Draft). *Hōsō,* no. 54, pp.1–3; no. 55, pp. 1–3; no. 56, pp. 7–10; no. 57, pp. 1–3; no. 58, pp. 7–9; no. 59, pp. 16–18.

———. 1976. *Kempō Seiritsu-no Keii-to Kempō-jō-no Sho-mondai* (The Process of Making the Constitution, and Some Constitutional Issues). Tokyo: Daiichi Hōki Shuppan.

Ishii Ryōsuke. 1981. *Ie-to Koseki-no Rekishi* (A History of the Household and the Family Register). Tokyo: Sōbunsha.

Isono Seiichi, and Isono Fujiko. 1958. *Kazoku Seido* (The Family System). Tokyo: Iwanami Shoten.

Itō Hirobumi, ed. 1934. Kempō Shiryō (Sources for the Constitution). 3 vols. Ed. Hiratsuka Kentarō and Kaneko Kentarō. Tokyo: Kempō Shiryō Kankō-kai.

Itoh, Hiroshi, and Lawrence Ward Beer, eds. 1978. *The Constitutional Case Law of Japan: Selected Supreme Court Decisions, 1961–70*. Seattle: University of Washington Press.

Iwabuchi Tatsuo. 1961. "Iwabuchi Tatsuo-shi-ni Kiku" (Listening to Mr. Iwabuchi Tatsuo). An informal discussion about the events and the participants involved in the making of the Japanese Constitution between Iwabuchi and the members of the Commission on the Constitution, recorded on April 7, 1961. Kempō Chōsa-kai Jimukyoku. Included in Satō Tatsuo Kankei Bunsho 542.

James, D. Clayton. 1985. *The Years of MacArthur*. 3 vols. Boston: Houghton Mifflin Company.

Kades, Charles L. 1987. Interview by Kyōko Inoue at Heath, Massachusetts, June 24–25, 1987. 7 tapes.

——. 1989. "The American Role in Revising Japan's Imperial Constitution." *Political Science Quarterly* 104, no. 2, pp. 215–47.

Kades, Charles C., and Eiji Takemae. 1986. "Kades Memoir on Occupation of Japan (An Interview)." Reprinted from *Journal of Tokyo Keizai University*, no. 148, pp. 243–327.

Kammen, Michael. 1988. *Sovereignty and Liberty: Constitutional Discourse in American Culture*. Madison: University of Wisconsin Press.

Kanamori Tokujirō. 1928. *Teikoku Kempō Yōkō* (An Outline of the Imperial Constitution). 13th edition. Tokyo: Genshōdō Shoten.

——. 1947. *Kempō Zuisō* (Essays on the Constitution). Tokyo: Miwa Shobō.

——. 1959. *Kempō Igen* (The Final Commentaries on the Constitution). This is a series of commentaries on various aspects of the Constitution, recorded in shorthand, during the period February 4–15, 1947. In November 1959, five months after Kanamori's death, Irie Toshio, Satō Tatsuo, and others who had worked with Kanamori during the process of making the Constitution published this book in his memory. Tokyo: Gakuyō Shobō.

——. 1962. *Kempō Ura Omote* (The Constitution, Unofficial and Official). Reminiscences on the making of the Constitution and comments on the principal ideas incorporated in the document. Tokyo: Gakuyō Shobō.

Kawashima Takeyoshi. 1951. "Giri" (Social Obligation). *Shisō*, no. 327, pp. 759–66.

———. 1967. *Nihonjin-no Hō-ishiki* (The Japanese Understanding of Law). Tokyo: Iwanami Shoten.

Kempō Chōsa-kai (The Commission on the Constitution).* 1959. *Teikoku Kempō Kaisei Shingi-roku* (A Record of the Debates Related to the Revision of the Imperial Constitution). 12 vols. Tokyo: Ministry of Finance Printing Office.

———., ed. 1964. *Kempō Chōsa-kai Hōkoku-sho* (Report of the Commission on the Constitution). Tokyo: Ministry of Finance Printing Office.

Kempō Chōsa-kai Shō-iinkai (Subcommittee of the Commission on the Constitution). 1961. *Nihonkoku Kempō Seitei-no Yurai—Kempō Chōsa-kai Shō-iinkai Hōkoku-sho* (The Origin of the Making of the Japanese Constitution—Report of the Subcommittee of the Commission on the Constitution). Tokyo: Jiji Tsūshinsha.

Kempō Fukyū-kai (Society for the Popularization of the Constitution), ed. 1947. *Atarashii Kempō: Akarui Seikatsu* (The New Constitution: The Bright Life). Tokyo: Kempō Fukyū-kai.

Kennan, George F. 1967. *Memoirs, 1925–1950*. Boston: Little, Brown and Co.

Kishimoto, Hideo. 1967. "Some Japanse Cultural Traits and Religions." Pp. 110–21 in *The Japanese Mind*, ed. Charles A. Moore. Honolulu: University of Hawaii Press.

Kizoku-in (The House of Peers). 1946a. *Dai-Kyūjukkai Teikoku Gikai. Kizoku-in Giji Sokki-roku* (The 90th Imperial Diet. Stenographic Record of the Proceedings of the House of Peers), nos. 23–27, 39, 40. Tokyo, National Diet Library, Modern Political History Materials Room.

———. 1946b. *Dai-Kyūjukkai Teikoku Gikai Kizoku-in. Kempō Kaisei-an Tokubetsu Iinkai Giji Sokki-roku* (The 90th Imperial Diet, the House of Peers. Stenographic Record of the Special Committee Debates on the Revision of the Imperial Constitution), nos. 1–24. Tokyo, National Diet Library, Modern Political History Materials Room.

Kobori Keiichirō. 1982. *Saishō Suzuki Kantarō* (Premier Suzuki Kantarō). Tokyo: Bungei Shunjūsha.

Kojima Noboru. 1972. *Shiroku Nihonkoku Kempō* (A Historical Record of the Making of the Japanese Constitution). Tokyo: Bungei Shunjūsha.

Koschmann, J. Victor. 1978. *Authority and the Individual in Japan: Citizen Protest in Historical Perspective*. Tokyo: University of Tokyo Press.

Koseki Shōichi. 1989. *Shin-Kempō-no Tanjō* (The Birth of the New Constitution). Tokyo: Chūō Kōronsha.

Kudō Kyōkichi. 1965. *Bakumatsu-no Shakai-shi* (A Social History of the End of the Tokugawa Era). Tokyo: Kinokuniya Shoten.

Kuno, Susumu. 1973. *The Structure of the Japanese Language*. Cambridge, Mass.: MIT Press.

* This translation is used in Maki 1980.

Kuroda, Shigeyuki. 1965. "Generative Grammatical Studies in the Japanese Language." Ph.D. diss., Massachusetts Institute of Technology.

Lebra, Takie Sugiyama. 1976. *Japanese Patterns of Behavior*. Honolulu: University of Hawaii Press.

Lebra, Takie Sugiyama, and William P. Lebra, eds. 1986. *Japanese Culture and Behavior: Selected Readings*. Rev. ed. Honolulu: University of Hawaii Press.

Levy, Leonard W. 1972. *Judgments: Essays on American Constitutional History*. Chicago: Quadrangle Books.

Locke, John. 1960. *Two Treatises of Government: A Critical Edition with an Introduction and Apparatus Criticus by Peter Laslett*. Rev. ed. New York: Cambridge University Press.

Lu, David John. 1974. *Sources of Japanese History*. 2 vols. New York: McGraw Hill Co.

Lukes, Steven. 1973. *Individualism: Key Concepts in the Social Sciences*. Oxford: Basil Blackwell.

MacArthur, Douglas. 1964. *Reminiscences*. New York: McGraw-Hill.

McCawley, James D. 1981. *Everything that Linguists have Always Wanted to Know about Logic, but were Ashamed to Ask*. Chicago: University of Chicago Press.

McDonald, Forrest. 1965. *The Formation of the American Republic, 1776–1790*. Baltimore: Penguin Books.

McNelly, Theodore H. 1987. "'Induced Revolution': The Policy and Process of Constitutional Reform in Occupied Japan." Pp. 76–106 in *Democratizing Japan*, eds. Robert E. Ward, and Yoshikazu Sakamoto. Honolulu: University of Hawaii Press.

Maeda Masaharu. 1975. "Kenri-to Kenri Kakusho" (Comments on Rights). *Hō-to Seiji* 25, nos. 3–4 (March 1975): 347–86. Kansei Gakuin University Association for the Study of Law and Politics.

Maeda Tamon. 1962. "Ningen Sengen-no Uchi Soto" (Episodes Related to the Emperor's Declaration of Humanness). *Bungei Shunjū*, March 1962, special issue, pp. 84–90.

———. 1963. *Maeda Tamon: Sono-bun Sono-hito* (Maeda Tamon: His Writings and Personality). Tokyo: Maeda Tamon Kankō-kai.

Maki, John M. 1969. "United States Initial Postsurrender Policy for Japan." Pp. 30–56 in *Essays on Modern Politics and History, Written in Honor of Harold M. Vinacke*, ed. Han-Kyo Kim. Athens, Ohio: Ohio Univesity Press.

———, ed. 1980. *Japan's Commission on the Constitution: The Final Report*. Trans. and ed. John M. Maki. Seattle: University of Washington Press.

Makino Eiichi. 1949. *Nihonkoku Kempō Kōwa* (Lectures on the Japanese Constitution). Tokyo: Keibunsha.

Marty, Martin E. 1987. *Religion and Republic: The American Circumstance*. Boston: Beacon Press.

Maruyama Masao. 1952. *Nihon Seiji Shisō-shi Kenkyū* (A Study of the History of Japanese Political Thought). Tokyo: Tokyo Daigaku Shuppankai.

————. 1974. *Studies in the Intellectual History of Tokugawa Japan*. Trans. Mikiso Hane. Tokyo: University of Tokyo Press; copublished by Princeton University Press. This is the English translation of Maruyama, 1952.

Matsumoto Jōji. 1958. "Nihonkoku Kempō-no Sōan-ni Tsuite—Matsumoto Jōji Kōjutsu" (About the Constitutional Revision—An Oral Statement). *Ken-shi Sō* (General Materials on the Constitution), no. 28, October 1958. Kempō Chōsa-kai Jimukyoku (Secretariat of the Commission on the Constitution). Tokyo, National Diet Library, Modern Political History Materials Room.

Meiji Bunka Kenkyū-kai (Association for the Study of Meiji Culture). 1967–74. *Meiji Bunka Zenshū* (A Complete Collection of the Writings of the Meiji Period). 32 vols. Tokyo: Nihon Hyōronsha.

Midgley, Mary. 1983. *Animals and Why They Matter: A Journey around the Species Barrier*. New York: Penguin Books.

Miller, John C. 1960. *The Federalist Era: 1789–1801*. New York: Harper and Row.

Miller, Roy Andrew. 1967. *The Japanese Language*. Chicago: University of Chicago Press.

Minamoto Ryōen. 1969. *Giri-to Ninjō* (Social Obligation and Empathy). Tokyo: Chūō Kōronsha.

————. 1973. *Tokugawa Shisō Shō-shi* (A Short History of Tokugawa Thought). Tokyo: Chūō Kōronsha.

Ministry of Foreign Affairs. *See* Gaimu-shō

Miyagawa Mitsuru. 1983. *Kazoku-no Rekishi-teki Kenkyū* (A Historical Study of the Family). Tokyo: Nihon Tosho Sentā.

Miyazawa Toshiyoshi. 1978. *Zentei Nihonkoku Kempō*—Ashibe Nobuyoshi Hotei (A Complete Annotated Text of the Constitution of Japan—Supplements by Ashibe Nobuyoshi). Tokyo: Nihon Hyōronsha.

Miyazawa Toshiyoshi, and Satō Isao. 1954. "Makkāsā Kempō Sōan Kaisetsu" (A Commentary on the MacArthur Constitution), with the MacArthur Constitution, translated by the Ministry of Foreign Affairs and distributed to the Cabinet on February 26, 1946. *Kokka Gakkai Zasshi* 68, nos. 1 and 2, pp. 1–6. This issue contains a reprint of the text of the MacArthur Constitution in a 37-page appendix.

Mizuno Kōgen. 1972. *Bukkyō Yōgo-no Kiso Chishiki* (Basic Information about Buddist Terminology). Tokyo: Shunjūsha.

Mochizuki Shinkō. 1958–63. *Mochizuki Bukkyō Dai-jiten* (Mochizuki's Unabridged Dictionary of Buddhism), zōtei-ban (expanded edition). 10 vols. Tokyo: Sekai Seiten Kankō Kyōkai.

Moore, Charles, ed. 1967. *The Japanese Mind: Essentials of Japanese Philosophy*. Honolulu: University Press of Hawaii.

Morgan, Edmund S. 1956. *The Birth of the Republic, 1763–1789*. Chicago: University of Chicago Press.

————. 1988. *Inventing the People: The Rise of Popular Sovereignty in England and America*. New York: W. W. Norton.

Mori Kiyoshi, ed. 1983. *Kempō Kaisei Shō-iinkai Himitsu Gijiroku: Beikoku*

358 References and Bibliography

*Kōbun-sho Kōkai Shiryō* (The Secret Record of the Subcommittee Meetings on the Constitutional Revision: Public Document of the United States). Tokyo: Daiichi Hōki.

Morison, Samuel Eliot. 1970–71. *Amerika-no Rekishi* (A History of the United States). Trans. and ed. Nishikawa Masami. 3 vols. Tokyo: Shūeisha. The original title: *The Oxford History of the American People* (1965).

Morison, Samuel Eliot, Henry Steele Commager, and William E. Leuchtenburg. 1980. *The Growth of the American Republic*. 7th ed., 2 vols. New York: Oxford University Press.

Morris, Colin. 1972. *The Discovery of the Individual: 1050–1200*. New York: Harper and Row.

Murakami Yōichirō. 1980. *Nihonjin-to Kindai Kagaku* (The Japanese and Modern Science). Tokyo: Shin'yōsha.

Murakawa Ichirō. 1986. *Teikoku Kempō Kaisei-an Gijiroku—Sūmitsu-in Teikoku Kempō Kaisei-an Shingi Iin-kai Gijiroku* (The Record of the Debates on the Revision of the Imperial Constitution—The Minutes of the Meetings of the Privy Council Committee on the Revision of the Imperial Constitution), edited and annotated by Murakawa Ichirō. Tokyo: Kokusho Kankōkai.

Nagai Ken'ichi, and Toshitani Nobuyoshi, eds. 1986. *Shiryō Nihonkoku Kempō* (Documents Related to the Constitution of Japan). 5 vols. Tokyo: Sanseidō.

Nagano Masaru. 1983. "Yamamoto Yūzō Hyōden Shin-shiryō 38—Kokumin-no Kokugo Undō-to Nihonkoku Kempō-no Kōgoka" (A Critical Biography of Yamamoto Yūzō—New Document 38: The People's National Language Movement and Adoption of the Colloquial Language in the Japanese Constitution). *Kokubungaku Kaishaku-to Kanshō*, vol. 48, no. 15, pp. 187–95.

Najita, Tetsuo. 1974. *Japan: The Intellectual Foundations of Modern Japanese Politics*. Chicago: University of Chicago Press.

Nakamura Kichiji. 1957. *Ie-no Rekishi* (A History of the Household). Tokyo: Kadokawa Shoten.

Nakane, Chie. 1967a. *Kinship and Economic Organization in Rural Japan*. London School of Economics Monographs on Social Anthropology No. 32. London: Athens Press.

———. 1967b. *Tate-shakai-no Ningen Kankei: Tan'itsu Shakai-no Riron* (Human Relations in a Vertical Society: A Theory of a Homogeneous Society). Tokyo: Kōdansha. This is the original Japanese version of *Japanese Society* (1970).

———. 1970. *Japanese Society*. Berkeley: University of California Press.

———. 1978. *Tate-shakai-no Rikigaku* (Power Relations in a Vertical Society). Tokyo: Kōdansha.

*Nihon-no Rekishi* (A History of Japan). 1959–61. 13 vols. Tokyo: Yomiuri Shimbunsha.

*Nihongo-no Rekishi* (A History of the Japanese Language). 1963–66. 7 vols. Tokyo: Heibonsha.

Nishi Osamu. 1986. *Dokyumento Nihonkoku Kempō* (The Making of the Japanese Constitution—A Document). Tokyo: Sanshūsha.

Noda Yoshiyuki. 1976. *Introduction to Japanese Law*. Trans. and ed. Anthony H. Angelo. Tokyo: University of Tokyo Press.

———. 1979. "Kenri-to-yū Kotoba-ni Tsuite" (On the Word "Right"). *Gakushūin Daigaku Hōgaku-bu Kenkyū Nempō*, no. 14, pp. 1–30.

Norman, E. H. 1975. *Origins of the Modern Japanese State: Selected Writings of E. H. Norman*. Ed. John W. Dower. New York: Pantheon Books.

Ōki Masao. 1983. *Nihonjin-no Hō-kannen: Seiyō-teki Hō-kannen to-no Hikaku* (The Japanese Concept of Law: A Comparison with the Western Concept of Law). Tokyo: Tokyo Daigaku Shuppankai.

Ōkubo Toshiaki. 1956. *Meiji Kempō-no Dekiru-made* (The Making of the Meiji Constitution). Tokyo: Shibundō.

Okuizumi Eizaburō. 1985. "Nihon-go Jiten Senji Beikokuban-to Sono Haikei" (An Account of the Emergence of the Wartime American Editions of Japanese Language Dictionaries). *Senryō-shi Kenkyū-kai Nyūsu*, August 1, 1985, pp. 4–6.

Ōmori Minoru. 1975–76. *Sengo Hishi* (A Secret History of the Postwar Japan). 10 vols. Tokyo: Kōdansha.

O'Neill, Onora. 1988. "Children's Rights and Children's Lives." *Ethics*, vol. 98, no. 3, pp. 445–63.

Oppler, Alfred C. 1976. *Legal Reform in Occupied Japan: A Participant Looks Back*. Princeton, N.J.: Princeton University Press.

Ōta Tomoyuki. 1964. "Kenri-to-yū Kotoba-no Imi-ni Tsuite" (About the Meaning of the Word "Right"). *Shisō* 5, no. 479, pp. 25–35.

Ōtake Hideo, and Maki Hidemasa, eds. 1975. *Nihon Hōsei-shi* (A History of the Japanese Legal System). Tokyo: Seirin Shoin Shinsha.

Ouchi, William G. 1981. *Theory Z: How American Business Can Meet the Japanese Challenge*. New York: Avon Books.

Palmer, F. R. 1986. *Mood and Modality*. Cambridge: Cambridge University Press.

Passin, Herbert. 1965. *Society and Education in Japan*. New York: Teachers College Press, Columbia University.

Pelzel, John C. 1970. "Japanese Kinship: A Comparison." Pp. 227–48 in *Family and Kinship in Chinese Society*, ed. Maurice Freedman. Stanford: Stanford University Press.

Pharr, Susan V. 1987. "The Politics of Women's Rights." Pp. 221–52 in *Democratizing Japan*, ed. Robert E. Ward and Yoshikazu Sukamoto. Honolulu: University of Hawaii Press.

Quigley, Harold S. and John E. Turner. 1956. *The New Japan: Government and Politics*. Minneapolis: University of Minnesota Press.

Reischauer, Edwin O. 1974. *Japan: The Story of a Nation*. Rev. ed. New York: Alfred A. Knopf.

———. 1981. *The Japanese*. Cambridge, Mass.: Harvard University Press.

———. 1986. *My Life between Japan and America*. New York: Harper and Row.

Reischauer, Haru Matsukata. 1986. *Samurai and Silk: A Japanese and American Heritage.* Cambridge, Mass.: Harvard University Press.

Reynolds, David K. 1980. *The Quiet Therapies: Japanese Pathways to Personal Growth.* Honolulu: University Press of Hawaii.

Richardson, Bradley M., and Scott C. Flanagan. 1984. *Politics in Japan: A Country Study.* Boston: Little, Brown and Co.

Roche, John P., ed. 1967. *Origins of American Political Thought: Selected Readings.* New York: Harper and Row.

Rodgers, Daniel T. 1987. *Contested Truths: Keywords in American Politics Since Independence.* New York: Basic Books.

Rossiter, Clinton. 1963. *The Political Thought of the American Revolution.* New York: Harcourt, Brace and World.

Rousseau, Jean Jacques. 1950. *The Social Contract and Discourse.* Trans. with an introduction, by G. D. H. Cole. New York: E. P. Dutton.

Rutland, Robert Allen. 1962. *The Birth of the Bill of Rights, 1776–1791.* New York: Collier Books.

Sakata Yoshio. 1984. *Tennō Shinsei: Meiji-ki-no Tennō-kan* (The Secred Rule of the Emperor: The Meiji view of the Emperor). Kyoto: Shibunkaku Shuppan.

Sakomizu Hisatsune. 1964. *Kikanjū-ka-no Shushō Kantei—Ni-ni-roku Jiken-kara Shūsen made* (The Prime Minister's Official Residence Under Machine Gun Fire—From the February 26, 1936 Incident to the End of the War). Tokyo: Kōbunsha.

Sakurai Masashi. 1971. *Meiji Shūkyō-shi Kenkyū* (A Study of Religious History of the Meiji Era). Tokyo: Shunjūsha.

Sakurai Shōtarō. 1949. *Nihon Hōken-shakai Ishiki-ron* (A Theory of Social Consciousness in Feudal Japan). Tokyo: Nikkō Shoin.

———. 1971. *Meiyo-to Chijoku* (Honor and Shame). Tokyo: Hōsei Daigaku Shuppankyoku.

Sansom, George B. 1958–63. *A History of Japan.* 3 vols. Stanford, Calif.: Stanford University Press.

———. 1970. *The Western World and Japan: A Study in the Interaction of European and Asiatic Cultures.* New York: Alfred A. Knopf.

Satō Tatsuo. 1955a. "Nihonkoku Kempō Tanjō-ki" (The Birth of the Japanese Constitution). 17 installments. *Toki-no Hōrei* 169–75, 177–80, 182–87 (May–November 1955).

———. 1955b. "'Makkāsā Kempō' Ura-banashi: Nankin Tetsuya-no Samba-yaku-ga Zenkokumin-ni Okuru Hiwa (A Behind-the-Scenes Account of the "MacArthur Constitution"). *Seikei Shishin* 2, no. 8, pp. 18–47.

———. 1955–58. "Nihonkoku Kempō Seiritsu-shi: 'Makkāsā Kempō' kara 'Nihonkoku Kempō' made" (A History of the Making of the Constitution of Japan: From "The MacArthur Constitution" to "The Constitution of Japan"). 57 installments. *Jurisuto* (May 3, 1955–February 15, 1958).

———. 1962–64. *Nihonkoku Kempō Seiritsu-shi* (A History of the Making of the Constitution of Japan). 2 vols. Tokyo: Yūhikaku.

————. n.d. Satō Tatsuo Kankei Bunsho (Satō Tatsuo Papers). 2328 files. Tokyo, National Diet Library, Modern Political History Materials Room.

SCAP. See Supreme Commander for the Allied Powers

Schneider, David M. 1976. "Notes toward a Theory of Culture." Pp. 197–220 in *Meaning in Anthropology*, eds. K. H. Basso, and H. A. Selby. Albuquerque: University of New Mexico Press.

————. 1980. *American Kinship: A Cultural Account*. 2d ed. Chicago: University of Chicago Press.

Schneider, David M., and Raymond T. Smith. 1973. *Class Differences and Sex Roles in American Kinship and Family Structure*. Englewood Cliffs, N.J.: Prentice-Hall.

Searle, John R. 1970. *Speech Acts*. Cambridge: Cambridge Univesity Press.

————. 1979. *Expressions and Meaning: Studies in the Theory of Speech Acts*. Cambridge: Cambridge University Press.

Sebald, William J. 1965. *With MacArthur in Japan: A Personal History of the Occupation*. With Russell Brines. New York: W. W. Norton.

Shidehara Heiwa Zaidan (Shidehara Peace Foundation). 1955. *Shidehara Kijūrō*. Tokyo: Shidehara Heiwa Zaidan.

Shigemitsu Mamoru. 1952. *Shōwa-no Dōran* (The Shōwa Disturbances). 2 vols. Tokyo: Chūō Kōronsha.

————. 1986. *Shigemitsu Mamoru Shuki* (Shigemitsu Mamoru Memoir). Ed. Itō Takashi, and Watanabe Yukio. Tokyo: Chūō Kōronsha.

————. 1986. "Sensō-o Ato-ni-shite" (Leaving the War Behind). *Chūō Kōron*, April 1986, special enlarged edition, pp. 220–46. This is a portion of Shigemitsu's memoranda from shortly before the termination of the war through the fall of 1945.

Shils, Edward and Michael Young. 1953. "The Meaning of the Coronation." Reprinted from *Sociological Review* 1, pp. 63–81. The Bobbs-Merrill reprint series in the social sciences.

Shimizu Shin, ed. 1962–63. *Chikujō Nihonkoku Kempō Shingi-roku* (A Record of the Article-by-Article Debate of the Constitution of Japan). Ed. Shimizu Shin. 4 vols. Tokyo: Yūhikaku.

————. 1971–74. *Meiji Kempō Seiteishi* (A History of the Making of the Meiji Constitution). 3 vols. Tokyo: Hara Shobō.

*Shiryō Nihonkoku Kempō* (Documents Related to the Constitution of Japan). 1966. Nagai Ken'ichi and Toshitani Nobuyoshi, general editors. 5 vols. Tokyo: Sanseidō.

Shisō-no Kagaku Kenkyū-kai (Research Group on the Science of Thought). 1973. *Nihon Senryōgun: Sono Hikari-to Kage* (The Occupation Army of Japan: Its Light and Shadow). 2 vols. Tokyo: Gendai-shi Shuppan-kai. There is a supplementary volume, published in 1978: *Nihon Senryō Kenkū Jiten* (A Dictionary of the Occupation of Japan).

Shūgi-in. 1946a. *Dai-kyūjukkai Teikoku Gikai. Shūgi-in Giji Sokki-roku* (The 90th Imperial Diet. The Stenographic Record of the Proceedings of the House of Representatives), nos. 5–8, 25, 35, 54. Tokyo, National Diet Library, Modern Political History Materials Room.

————. 1946b. *Dai-Kyūjukkai Teikoku Gikai Shūgi-in. Teikoku Kempō Kaisei-an Iinkai Giroku (sokki)* (The 90th Imperial Diet, the House of Representatives. The Record (stenographic) of the Special Committee Debates on the Revision of the Imperial Constitution), nos. 1–21. Tokyo, The National Diet Library, Modern Political History Materials Room.

Siemes, Johannes. 1968. *Herman Roesler and the Making of the Meiji State: An Examination of His Background and His Influence on the Founders of Modern Japan.* Tokyo: Sophia University, in cooperation with Charles E. Tuttle Co.

Sirjamaki, John. 1953. *The American Family in the Twentieth Century.* Cambridge: Harvard University Press.

Slater, Philip E. 1970. *The Pursuit of Loneliness: American Culture at the Breaking Point.* Boston: Beacon Press.

Smith, Robert J. 1974. *Ancestor Worship in Contemporary Japan.* Stanford, Calif.: Stanford University Press.

————. 1983. *Japanese Society: Tradition, Self, and the Social Order.* Cambridge: Cambridge University Press.

Smith, Thomas C. 1959. *The Agrarian Origins of Modern Japan.* Stanford, Calif.: Stanford University Press.

————. 1961. "Japan's Aristocratic Revolution." *Yale Review* 50, pp. 370–83.

Society for the Popularization of the Constitution. *See* Kempō Fukyū-kai

Sone Eki. 1978. "Senryō Seisaku-no Ichimen" (One Aspect of the Occupation Policies). Pp. 137–65 in *Mō-hitotsu-no Sengo-shi* (Another Postwar History), by Etō Jun. Tokyo: Kōdansha.

Subcommittee of the Commission on the Constitution. *See* Kempō Chōsa-kai Shō-iinkai

Suekawa Hiroshi. 1974. *Hō-to Jiyū* (Law and Freedom). Tokyo: Iwanami Shoten.

Supreme Commander for the Allied Powers, Government Section (SCAP). 1968. *Political Reorientation of Japan, September 1945 to September 1948.* 2 vols. Grosse Point, Mich.: Scholarly Press.

Suzuki Yasuzō. 1948. *Jiyū Minken* (Freedom and Popular Rights). Tokyo: Hakuyōsha.

Takagi, Yasaka. 1935. *A Survey of Japanese Studies in the Universities and Colleges of the United States.* Honolulu: Institute of Pacific Relations.

————. 1969. "Nihon-no Kempō Kaisei-ni Taishite Senkyūhyaku-yonjūgo-nen-ni Konoe-kō-ga Nashita Kiyo-ni Kan-suru Oboegaki" (Memorandum on Prince Konoe's Contribution in 1945 to Constitutional revision in Japan). The Japanese translation (by Negishi Tomojirō) of an informal talk to the faculty of the International Christian University on May 30, 1952. Secretariat of the Commission on the Constitution, *Ken-shi Sō* 36, June 1969. Included in Satō Tatsuo Kankei Bunsho 490 (Tokyo, National Diet Library, Modern Political History Materials Room).

Takayanagi Kenzō, Ōtomo Ichirō, and Tanaka Hideo, eds. 1972. *Nihonkoku Kempō Seitei-no Katei* (The Making of the Japanese Constitution). 2 vols. Tokyo: Yūhikaku.

Takeda Kiyoko. 1978. *Tennō-kan-no Sōkoku: Sen-kyūhyaku yonjūgo-nen Zen-go* (Conflicts in the Ideas of the Emperor: Around 1945). Tokyo: Iwanami Shoten.

Takemae Eiji. 1983. *GHQ*. Tokyo: Iwanami Shoten.

Takemae Eiji, and Amakawa Akira. 1977. *Nihon Senryō Hishi* (A Secret History of the Occupation of Japan). 2 vols. Tokyo: Asahi Shimbunsha.

Tamaru Noriyoshi, Muraoka Kū, and Miyata Noboru, eds. 1972–73. *Nihonjin-no Shūkyō* (The Religions of the Japanese People). 4 vols. Tokyo: Kōsei Shuppansha.

Tanaka Akira. 1979. *Kindai Tennō-sei-e-no Dōtei* (The Road to the Modern Imperial System). Tokyo: Yoshikawa Kōbunkan.

Tanaka Hideo. 1979. *Kempō Seitei Katei Oboegaki* (Notes on the Process of Making the Constitution). Tokyo: Yūhikaku.

————. n.d. "Nihonkoku Kempō Seiritsu-no Katei-ni Okeru Futatsu-no Hō-bunka-no Shōtotsu" (A Clash between Two Legal Cultures in the Making of the Japanese Constitution). Manuscript. The original Japanese text of Tanaka (1987).

————. 1987. "The Conflict between Two Legal Traditions in Making the Constitution." Pp. 104–32 in *Democratizing Japan*, ed. Robert E. Ward, and Yoshikazu Sakamoto. Honolulu: University of Hawaii Press.

Titus, David Anson. 1974. *Palace and Politics in Prewar Japan*. New York: Columbia University Press.

Tocqueville, Alexis de. [1835] 1945. *Democracy in America*. 2 vols. New York: Vintage Books.

Toland, John. 1970. *The Rising Sun: The Decline and Fall of the Japanese Empire, 1936–1945*. New York: Random House.

Totman, Conrad. 1981. *Japan before Perry: A Short History*. Berkeley: University of California Press.

Tōyama Shigeki. 1985. *Jiyū Minken-to Gendai* (Freedom and Popular Rights and the Modern Times). Tokyo: Tsukuma Shobō.

Truman, Harry S. 1955. *Memoirs*. 2 vols. Garden City, N.Y.: Doubleday.

Tsunoda Fusako. 1980. *Isshi Daizai-o Shasu: Rikugun Daijin Anami Korechika* (An Apology in Death for a Great Sin: The Minister of Army Anami Korechika). Tokyo: Shinchōsha.

Ueki Emori. 1974. *Ueki Emori Senshū* (Selected Works of Ueki Emori). Ed. Ienaga Saburō. Tokyo: Iwanami Shoten.

Uemura Sen'ichirō. 1982. *Kempō Minaoshi Sagyō Oboegaki—Zembun Kankei* (A Note on the Reexamination of the Constitution—On the Preamble). Tokyo: Daiichi Hōki.

Ujita Naoyoshi. 1958. *Shidehara Kijūrō*. Tokyo: Jiji Tsūshinsha.

Umeda Yoshihiko. 1971. *Nihon Shūkyō Seido-shi: Kindai-hen* (A History of the Japanese Religious System: Modern). Kaitei Zōho (Revised and Enlarged). Tokyo: Tōsen Shuppan.

Upham, Frank K. 1987. *Law and Social Change in Postwar Japan*. Cambridge, Mass.: Harvard University Press.

U.S. Army. 1966. *Reports of General MacArthur*. Vol. 1 supplement, *MacAr-*

thur in Japan: The Occupation: Military Phase, Prepared by His General Staff. Washington, D.C., Government Printing Office.

U.S. Department of State. 1947. *Activities of the Far Eastern Commission, February 26, 1946–July 10, 1947.* Report by the Secretary General. Department of State Publication 2888, Far Eastern Series 24. Washington, D.C.: Goverment Printing Office.

———. 1960. *Foreign Relations of the United States. Diplomatic Papers. The Conference of Berlin* [The Potsdam Conference] 1945, vol. 1. Washington, D.C.: Government Printing Office.

———. 1965. *Foreign Relations of the United States 1944.* Vol. 5: *The Near East, South Asia and Africa, the Far East.* Washington, D.C.: Government Printing Office.

———. 1971. *Foreign Relations of the United States 1946.* Vol. 8: *The Far East.* Washington, D.C.: Government Printing Office.

Varenne, Hervé. 1977. *Americans Together: Structural Diversity in a Midwestern Town.* New York: Teachers College Press.

Ward, Robert E. 1956. "The Origins of the Present Japanese Constitution." *American Political Science Review* 50, no. 4, pp. 980–1010.

———. 1967. *Japan's Political System.* Englewood Cliffs, N.J.: Prentice-Hall.

———. 1987. "Presurrender Planning: Treatment of the Emperor and Constitutional Changes." Pp. 1–41 in *Democratizing Japan,* ed. Robert E. Ward, and Yoshikazu Sakamoto. Honolulu: University of Hawaii Press.

Ward, Robert E., and Yoshikazu Sakamoto, eds. 1987. *Democratizing Japan: The Allied Occupation.* Honolulu: University of Hawaii Press.

Watanabe Manzō. 1930. *Genkō Hōritsugo-no Shiteki Kōsatsu* (A Historical Survey of Present Legal Language). Tokyo: Banrikaku Shobō.

Watkins, Frederick M. 1946. "Prospects of Constitutional Democracy." Pp. 305–331 in *Japan's Prospect,* ed. Douglas G. Haring. Cambridge, Mass.: Harvard University Press.

Whitney, Courtney. 1968. *MacArthur: His Rendezvous with History.* New York: Alfred A. Knopf.

Wildes, Harry Emerson. 1954. *Typhoon in Tokyo.* New York: Macmillan.

Williams, Justin, Sr. 1965. "Making the Japanese Constitution: A Further Look." *American Political Science Review* 59, no. 3, pp. 665–79.

———. 1979. *Japan's Political Revolution under MacArthur: A Participant's Account.* Athens, Ga.: University of Georgia Press.

———. 1982. "From Charlottesville to Tokyo: Military Government Training and Democratic Reforms in Occupied Japan." *Pacific Historical Review* 51, no. 4, pp. 407–22.

Wood, Gordon S. 1969. *The Creation of the American Republic, 1776–1787.* Chapel Hill: University of North Carolina Press.

Woodward, William P. 1972. *The Allied Occupation of Japan 1945–1952 and Japanese Religions.* Leiden: E. J. Brill.

Yamada Yoshio. 1908. *Nihon Bumpōron* (On Japanese Grammar). Tokyo: Hōbunsha.

Yokota Kisaburō. 1981. "Kempō-no Hiragana Kōgo" (The Colloquial Language in Hiragana of the Constitution). Pp. 265–72 in *Hō-to Nihongo* (Law and the Japanese Language), ed. Hayashi Ōki, and Aomi Jun'ichi. Tokyo: Yūhikaku.

Yoshida Shigeru. 1957. *Kaisō Jū-nen* (A Memoir of Ten Years). 4 vols. Tokyo: Shinchōsha.

―――. 1962. *The Yoshida Memoirs: The Story of Japan in Crisis*. Trans. Ken'ichi Yoshida. Boston: Houghton Mifflin.

# NAME INDEX

# SUBJECT INDEX

373

cans and Japanese on, 205–11. See
also *Shuken zaimin*
Potsdam Proclamation, 1, 6n, 7n, 11,
13, 32, 139, 186, 200, 266
Privy Council, 27, 31, 32, 35n, 50,
113, 116, 117n
Procedural rights, 77, 85
Purge, 182

"References (Sanshō)," 113, 115
Religion and state. *See* Separation of re-
ligion and state
Religions League of Japan, 145
Religious education, 147–55
Religious syncretism in Japan, 105–8
Rights, Japanese views, 51–55; linked
to nonspecific obligations, 51–52,
52n; translation as *kenri*, 56; Tsuda's
discussion, 56–59; Ueki's views,
63–66
Risshi-sha, 49

*Saikō*, 207
*Sandō*, 172
Satsuma, 46, 48n, 49
Satsuma Rebellion, 47
*Seiyō Jijō* (The Conditions of the West),
56, 56n
Sekigahara, 39n
Senate, U.S., 7, 59, 60, 161, 165–66
Separation of powers in U.S. Constitution, 167–68
Separation of religion and state, 3, 104,
267–68; American misunderstanding
of Japan, 126–28, 158; and education, 120–21, 123, 147–55; Diet debates, 136–58; Emperor's renunciation of divinity and, 126; GHQ directives, 122–23; in Constitution, 126–
27; Japanese government views on,
128, 130–31; in Meiji Constitution,
112–15; private Japanese views on,
129; Shrine Shinto (Jinja Shinto),
117–18, 128; Western views on,
118–20
"Shall," in U.S. Constitution, 72–73;
meanings of, 72; uses in American
draft of 1946 Japanese Constitution,
76–79
*Shikō*, translation of "supreme," 206–8,
211, 212, 212n, 213, 219
*Shinmin* (also *Shimmin*), 188, 189, 190.
See also, *Nihon shimmin*
*Shinsei*, 114–15, 128

Shinto, 3, 104–8, 120, 158; and Christianity compared, 114; control of land
by government, 111; Emperor's renunciation of divinity, 125; GHQ directives concerning, 122–26; Jinja
Shinto, 112–13, 113n, 117–18, 121,
131; Kyōha Shinto, 112–13, 112n,
113n; lack of institutionalized church
in, 104; role of Emperor in, 115;
separation from Buddhism, 110; sup-
port from *kokugaku-sha*, 43
Shintoism. *See* Shinto
*Shison*, 129
*Shuken*, 206–7, 212–16, 217n, 218–20
*Shuken zai-koku*, 202
*Shuken zai-kokumin*, 203, 215–16
*Shuken zai-kun*, 201–2
*Shuken zai-min*, 191, 201–2, 211–12,
214–16, 219
*Shūsen Shiroku*, 8, 8n
Society for the Popularization of the
Constitution, 264
*Songen*, translation of "dignity." See *Ko-
jin-no songen*
*Sonnō jōi*, 46
"Sovereignty." *See* "Popular sovereignty";
*Shuken*
State-War-Navy Coordinating Commit-
tee (SWNCC), 9, 15, 16n, 161–62
"Status of the Japanese Emperor," 160
Steering Committee of Government
Section (GHQ), 16, 17, 74n,
127–28, 235
Suffrage, women's, 182
Substantive rights, 77
Succession of househead, right of, 227,
227n, 238; Diet debate on, 239–55,
259, 260, 261, 264
Supreme Commander for the Allied
Powers (SCAP), 1, 1n, 6, 7, 13n, 26,
36n, 46

*Taisei Kokuhō-ron*, 56–59
*Tera-koya*, 42
*-Te-wa nara-nai*, 84
Tokugawa regime, 38–46; four-class
structure, 40; hostage system (*sankin
kōtai*), 40; ineffective rule, 44–45,
55; policy of seclusion, 43, 45; principles, 39; social structure changes, 43
Topic-comment construction, 95–102;
explanation of, 96–97
Tosa, 46, 48n